Not Even Past

Not Even Past

How the United States Ends Wars

Edited by
David Fitzgerald, David Ryan,
and John M. Thompson

berghahn
NEW YORK • OXFORD
www.berghahnbooks.com

First published in 2020 by
Berghahn Books
www.berghahnbooks.com

© 2020 David Fitzgerald, David Ryan, and John M. Thompson

All rights reserved. Except for the quotation of short passages for the purposes of criticism and review, no part of this book may be reproduced in any form or by any means, electronic or mechanical, including photocopying, recording, or any information storage and retrieval system now known or to be invented, without written permission of the publisher.

Library of Congress Cataloging-in-Publication Data

Names: Fitzgerald, David, 1984- editor. | Ryan, David, 1965- editor. | Thompson, John M., 1977- editor.

Title: Not even past / edited by David Fitzgerald, David Ryan, and John M. Thompson.

Description: First edition. | New York : Berghahn Books, 2020. | Includes bibliographical references and index.

Identifiers: LCCN 2019048669 (print) | LCCN 2019048670 (ebook) | ISBN 9781789202151 (hardback) | ISBN 9781789202250 (paperback) | ISBN 9781789202168 (ebook)

Subjects: LCSH: United States--History, Military--20th century. | United States--History, Military--21st century. | United States--Military policy--20th century | United States--Military policy--21st century | Vietnam War, 1961-1975--United States. | Iraq War, 2003-2011--United States. | War on Terrorism, 2001-2009--United States. | Militarism--United States.

Classification: LCC E840.4 .N68 2020 (print) | LCC E840.4 (ebook) | DDC 355.00973/0904--dc23

LC record available at https://lccn.loc.gov/2019048669

LC ebook record available at https://lccn.loc.gov/2019048670

British Library Cataloguing in Publication Data

A catalogue record for this book is available from the British Library

ISBN 978-1-78920-215-1 hardback
ISBN 978-1-78920-225-0 paperback
ISBN 978-1-78920-216-8 ebook

Marilyn B. Young. Photo credit: David Ryan.

Marilyn Young died peacefully at her Greenwich Village home on 19 February 2017, shortly after contributing an essay to this volume but before the book was completed. She was one of the keynote speakers in Dublin, Ireland, where some of the ideas in this book were first presented. For more than a decade she was a frequent visitor to Ireland and made enormous contributions to local conferences. She is pictured above in Kinsale, County Cork in 2007.

After studying at Vassar for her undergraduate degree, Marilyn earned her PhD in history from Harvard, working with Ernest May and John King Fairbanks. She taught at the University of Michigan until 1980 and then moved to New York to take a post at NYU. She retired at the end of 2016.

Marilyn was a brilliant teacher and scholar. She is perhaps best known for her many edited books on the Vietnam War and her prize-winning *The Vietnam Wars*. She was an ardent feminist and relished engagement with political issues; she was forthright and reveled in exchanges at conferences. Much of her life's work was dedicated to resisting militarism and the concept and reality of perpetual war, and she could hold her own in any argument over the use of force. Her erudition and sometimes acerbic humor were legendary. She was the recipient of many fellowships, including those with the Guggenheim Foundation and the National Endowment for the Humanities. She served as president of the Society for Historians of American Foreign Relations (SHAFR) in 2011.

Anyone who knew Marilyn experienced her endless generosity and her welcome gift of friendship. She was mentor to everyone who asked. Among those who benefited from her generosity and friendship were many of the contributors to this volume. We hope that she would have found what follows in these pages to be engaging.

We would like to dedicate this book to her.

David Fitzgerald
Robert K. Brigham
David Ryan

Contents

Acknowledgments — ix

Introduction — 1
David Ryan and David Fitzgerald

Part I. Vietnam — 17

Chapter 1
The Importance of Being Popular: Richard Nixon, Henry Kissinger, and Domestic Support for the Vietnam War — 21
Sarah Thelen

Chapter 2
The Things They Carry: Vietnam and the Legacies of the American War — 45
Edwin A. Martini

Chapter 3
"His Epitaph Is Also Ours": Robert McNamara, the Iraq and Afghanistan Wars, and the Vietnam War's Contested Usable Past — 69
David Kieran

Chapter 4
After the Fall of Saigon: Strategic Implications of America's Involvement in Vietnam — 88
Robert K. Brigham

Part II. Iraq and Afghanistan — 107

Chapter 5
The Ironies of Overwhelming "Victory": Exits and the Dislocation of the Gulf War — 111
David Ryan

Chapter 6
Failing to End: Obama and Iraq — 141
David Fitzgerald and David Ryan

Chapter 7
A "Responsible End" to the Afghan War: The Politics and Pitfalls of Crafting "Success" Narratives — 161
Jeffrey H. Michaels

Chapter 8
Flawed Afghanization: Underestimating and Misunderstanding the Taliban — 180
Antonio Giustozzi

Part III. The Cultural and Strategic Costs of War in the Early Twenty-First Century — 195

Chapter 9
Changing the Subject: How the United States Responds to Strategic Failure — 199
Andrew J. Bacevich

Chapter 10
How Wars Do Not End: The Challenges for Twenty-First Century US Foreign Policy and Intervention — 211
Scott Lucas

Chapter 11
Coming Home: Soldier Homecomings and the All-Volunteer Force in American Society and Culture — 230
David Fitzgerald

Chapter 12
How the United States Ends Wars — 252
Marilyn B. Young

Index — 269

Acknowledgments

The editors would like to thank the Clinton Institute for American Studies, University College Dublin, and the School of History, University College Cork, Ireland, for their dedication and coordination on this project. We would especially like to thank Professor Liam Kennedy and Catherine Carey from the Clinton Institute.

We would also like to thank the editorial team at Berghahn, particularly Chris Chappell and Soyolmaa Lkhagvadorj, for their efficiency and patience throughout the publication process.

Finally, we would like to thank our contributors for all of their efforts, from start to finish.

Introduction

David Ryan and David Fitzgerald

On 28 July 1945, the evening after the United Nations Charter passed the Senate after protracted debate, Assistant Secretary of State Breckinridge Long wrote in his diary, "The faith of Woodrow Wilson has been vindicated. The record of the United States of 1920 has been expunged. Civilization has a better chance to survive." Similarly, the State Department's Livingston Hartley wrote, "We threw away our first chance, and the cost has been very great. ... Now we have a second under much more difficult conditions." The vote took place as the victors of World War II met in Potsdam to discuss the postwar order in Europe and the ultimatum calling on Japan to surrender. Historian Robert Divine relates that President Harry Truman, already in Potsdam, had requested immediate notice so that he could inform Joseph Stalin and British prime minister Clement Attlee of the Senate's decision to advance world peace.

Truman's predecessor, Franklin D. Roosevelt, had been haunted by Woodrow Wilson's failure to construct a just peace in the wake of World War I and dreamed of "completing his mentor's final mission" even to his dying days. In March 1945, he told a crowd, "This time we are not making the mistake of waiting until the end of the war to set up the machinery of peace." Divine writes of this episode that the protagonists "were drawn irresistibly back to the past, reliving again and again the moment of tragedy when the Senate killed the League."[1] The wording echoes the final lines of F. Scott Fitzgerald's *The Great Gatsby*: "So we beat on, boats against the current, borne back ceaselessly into the past."[2]

The title of Divine's book tracing the rise of internationalism that culminated in the ratification of the United Nations Charter is *Second Chance*, and there is a huge irony in this "second chance" thesis. Even as the internationalism that the UN embodied triumphed, a certain mindset, the Cold War consensus coupled with a liberal international triumphalism, held by both Truman and later Lyndon B. Johnson would contribute to decisions to go to war in Korea and Vietnam, conditioned by the cultural and political paradigms of containment and dominoes falling. Historian Andrew Preston notes how a newly capacious American definition of "national security"—one that stressed the interconnectedness of global economics, security, and values—both informed visions of a postwar Pax Americana and stretched the notion of American vital interests so broadly that self-defense naturally encompassed Seoul and Saigon as much as it did San Francisco.[3] By the late 1940s the United States was an emerging hegemonic power and in the not too subtle words of Secretary of State Dean Acheson, they now had the chance to "grab hold of history and make it conform."[4]

This time, with the second chance, Washington could get it right. After the political and diplomatic failures of the conclusion to World War I, the United States could exercise what historian Charles Maier has called "consensual hegemony"[5] in the emerging West and advance solutions that would bring a cold but lasting peace to at least the Western portion of Europe (elsewhere the consent was not so obvious; nor was the peace). This time they would not repeat the mistakes of the Wilson era by punishing Germany, imposing a war guilt clause, and demanding reparations. Instead, Germany and Japan would be integrated into the United States-centered Western economy, the political tack would be one that bent in favor of relief, reconstruction, and reconciliation. It seemed a magnanimous gesture, ultimately solidified by postwar economic assistance to Western Europe as part of the Marshall Plan. Yet, of course, it made sense too as part of a larger reading of the American national interest. Succinctly put, the United States decided that by serving others, it simultaneously served its own interests.[6]

Such enlightenment did not follow the conclusion of the Vietnam Wars, the Gulf War, or indeed the unending wars in Iraq or Afghanistan. But for George H. W. Bush, the opportunity to advance a "new world order" echoed Woodrow Wilson's aspirations for a more peaceful world. So too, in 1991, did Bush seek to create an order, to make war in the future less likely.[7] While the concern in the wake of the Gulf War was regional order, the Bush administration's deliberations took place in the context of the seemingly endless possibilities afforded by the end of the Cold War. Yet, as the columnist William Safire infamously observed, Bush snatched defeat from the jaws of victory in the Gulf War.[8] The war continued throughout the 1990s, albeit at a much lower temperature, with no-fly zones, sanctions, and occasional air strikes doing the work of containing Saddam in the absence of a postwar settlement.

Bush was constrained by his adherence to the lessons of Vietnam distilled to the Weinberger principles, especially relating to the immediacy of defined objectives, avoiding urban warfare, potential quagmires in Baghdad, and most pointedly, the strictures on an exit strategy. Despite Bush's credentials as the ultimate foreign policy president, to which his track record and experience testified, he still failed to engage the longer term issues that strategic victory necessitated. Unlike in 1945, there was little hope for political accommodation or economic integration with Saddam still in power. The dual containment of Iraq and Iran coupled with the sanctions regime that was imposed ensured ongoing enmity and irresolution of local and regional issues.

From the second half of the twentieth century onward, the aftermath of American wars has looked more like 1991 than 1945, with the "forever war" in Iraq serving as a precursor for America's twenty-first-century conflicts. The current generation of Americans has grown up with their country constantly at war in Afghanistan and Iraq, with other more episodic interventions in Libya and Syria, and drone strikes in a multitude of other places. But there is simultaneously a growing disconnect, as these wars seem to gain attention in the media only occasionally and through an obscure lens. It was with good reason that a 2017 issue of *Foreign Affairs* was devoted to "America's Forgotten Wars."[9] Yet the country has also come to appreciate, even revere, US service personnel; the soldiers who fight these wars are treated as heroes, even if there is little consideration of or debate about the violent work that they do, or its civilian victims. There is still less thought for or concern with the Other: the Iraqis, the Afghans, or, earlier, the Vietnamese.[10] There is little concern with what these wars have wrought, with what the United States and others leave behind.

The question then is why the United States, so adroit at shaping the world order in 1945, was so inept at doing so in 1991? How is it that, for all the interventionism of the American century, it has been over seventy-five years since the United States, a hegemonic superpower, has been able to end a major war on its preferred terms? This collection aims to answer this question by examining the different ways in which the United States has sought to end its wars in the late twentieth and early twenty-first centuries. The contributors are concerned with how various American policymakers have approached the challenge of ending wars, how these endings have played out in American culture, and, crucially, what the United States has left behind in the countries with which it has been at war.

The chapters tackle a diverse range of topics, from the environmental damage wrought on Vietnam to the failure to understand the Taliban's continuing operational resilience to the ways in which soldiers have been welcomed home from American wars. Yet all coalesce around the point that, despite its immense power, the United States has been remarkably myopic in its approach to the ending of wars; it has failed to appreciate the broader understanding of the national interest. American policymakers have been unable to articulate a coherent strategy for exiting wars, the United States has shown little concern for or understanding of the consequences for other countries and peoples, and—despite the repeated attempts of elites to move on from these conflicts—there has been little closure in American culture either, as these wars continue to be discussed and debated. Yet that discourse is an insular one, narrow in scope, simultaneously promoting a form of forgetting.

The central claim of the book is that the United States has disengaged from a number of wars, but it has not managed to end them. It pulled out of Vietnam, yet that war, more so than others, lingers in US culture, collective memory, and consciousness. It pulled out of Iraq twice, only to be drawn back in. It has yet to extract itself from Afghanistan. President Ford declared that the Vietnam War was "finished as far as America is concerned,"[11] even though neither he nor any other president ever sought a declaration of war from Congress. President Obama simply sought to turn the page on Iraq, even as the ink on the US epilogue had yet to dry. These audacious narrative turns invite a cultural amnesia, a silencing and a distancing from an abandoned war that minimizes reflection, lessons learned, and the construction of a deeper historical knowledge.

The refusal to engage in historical thinking, that form of reflection deeply immersed in the US experience of war and intervention, means that this cultural amnesia is related to a strategic incoherence and, in these wars, the United States has failed in its strategic objectives because it did not define, precisely, what they were. If Vietnam was the tragedy, Iraq and Afghanistan were repeated failures. The objectives and the national interests were elusive beyond issues of credibility, identity, and revenge; the end point was undefined because it was not clear what the point was. What did the United States want from these wars? What did it want to leave behind?

American wars in three countries are at the center of our analysis. First, the ending of the American War in Vietnam—at the time the United States' longest war—provides us with some clues as to how such quagmires can recur. As Sarah Thelen demonstrates in her chapter on the domestic politics of Nixon's attempts to end the war, the administration was not even interested in making any positive case for US strategy.

Yet only a few years after the last helicopters lifted from the roofs of the Pittman building in Saigon, Ronald Reagan not only contributed to the rehabilitation of the Vietnam War by labeling it a "noble cause" but also popularized the term "Vietnam syndrome" to identify the inhibiting factor that restrained US presidents from going to war. Whether it was Congress or putative public opinion, most administrations, including his own, opted for stirring rhetoric instead of war. Instrumental lessons were crafted to inhibit the resort to war but also to ensure that should the military be deployed for purposes of warfare, it would do so under clear criteria.

These requirements were identified in 1984 by the US secretary of defense, Caspar Weinberger, and were later modified to become the Powell Doctrine. Intervention would involve, supposedly, clarity of purpose, overwhelming power, reliance on technology, and, crucially, an exit strategy, among other things. On the one hand, these stipulations represented some reflection on the Vietnam experience, counseling caution and restraint. On the other hand, the doctrine was, in the formulation of Secretary of State George Shultz, strategy via checklist, and — crucially — every item on that list referred to American will or American capabilities; an assessment of the capabilities or intent of the other side was still missing.

This doctrine, crafted in order to provide a blueprint for clean, victorious exits from wars, did not survive the American wars in Iraq. As Andrew Bacevich argues in his chapter on the US response to strategic failure, the doctrine promotes a civil-military relationship in which both sides of the divide are given an excuse to avoid hard questions about the use and misuse of military power. Even in the first Gulf War, the conflict in which the doctrine was put to use with most effect, the United States failed to achieve its strategic objectives because it had not thought seriously about the war's end and its aftermath. David Ryan's chapter shows that while the Bush administration sincerely believed and hoped longingly that Saddam would fall, there were no plans or contingencies put in place to ensure that outcome. The strategy was myopic — odd for an administration famed for its cautious realism. The new world order they sought was supposed to be more peaceful, as Bush argued in his address before a joint session of Congress at war's end.[12] Yet in Iraq, because Saddam remained in power, the United States instituted a punitive sanctions regime throughout the 1990s that had devastating consequences for life within the country.

As US officials surmised in 1991, an ongoing US presence would fuel radicalism and resentment in the region and beyond. And though President George H. W. Bush noted and celebrated US primacy after the

Gulf War, goading critics of US decline (famously Paul Kennedy's *Rise and Fall of Great Powers*) that they were looking the wrong way,[13] it was the administration of his son, George W. Bush, that wanted to transform US power and hoped to turn the "unipolar moment" into a unipolar era. But like Shakespeare's *Macbeth*, the vaulting ambition of the George W. Bush administration "o'erleaps itself, And falls on th'other." And thus, 2003 begat an even greater tragedy than 1991, and the lack of a coherent, plausible vision for a postwar order destabilized an entire region.

A similar script played out in Afghanistan, a place that few Americans were deeply conscious of in the 1970s. By the end of that decade the Soviets had invaded Afghanistan and the US National Security Advisor, Zbigniew Brzezinski, was quick to try to capitalize on the situation by turning it into a Soviet Vietnam.[14] The strategic impulse was to impose a cost, to drain the will, to bleed the country through protracted warfare, even in a political context in which the Soviets did not have to worry about public opinion to the extent that the United States did. To some extent, President Carter's and President Reagan's support for the Mujahedin fighting the Soviet invaders did create a quagmire from which Moscow found it difficult to extract itself. Yet after they departed, Washington paid scant attention to the country and the radical developments there during the 1990s.

Afghanistan eventually became host to al Qaeda and shortly after the attacks of 9/11, Washington began military operations there in October of that year. In 2018, despite the Obama administration's rhetoric about withdrawal, the US military are still there; there does not appear to be any clarity of thought or purpose in the Trump administration on what the US objectives are or on when the troops might leave. Antonio Giustozzi's essay in this volume documents a perpetual American tendency to underestimate the strength of the Taliban. This tendency was closely related to a desire to disengage from Afghanistan and to only highlight evidence that reinforced the dominant narrative in Washington, DC.

This track record, which stretches over fifty years of war, is one of extended failure. The puzzle is that, despite the frequency of second chances for the United States, more often than not, postwar opportunities were missed; the "vision thing," as Bush called it in another context, was absent. Historian Lawrence Freedman has argued that strategy should be understood in narrative terms, that good strategists are those who author "scripts" that can be understood by both participants and observers.[15] When looking to those Americans who tried to imagine postwar scenarios, we do indeed see a penchant for using narrative devices to understand the world. These devices can be useful in terms of imposing meaning on a chaotic world, but in an American context, they have often instead provided a means with which to avoid difficult questions rather than resolve them. Indeed, Jeffrey Michaels' chapter on the Obama administration's quest for a "responsible end" to the war in Afghanistan demonstrates that scripts and narratives had more of an influence on American thinking than events on the ground did.

This tendency has a long history, stretching from Cold War narratives of containment, to visions of dominoes falling, to fantasies of American soldiers being greeted as liberators in a newly democratic Iraq in 2003. In surveying this history of repeated inability to author scripts that take into account the agency or perspective of others, we are reminded of F. Scott Fitzgerald's assessment of Hollywood producers in his unfinished novel, *The Last Tycoon*, that the "tragedy of these men was that nothing in their lives had really bitten deep at all."[16]

How is it that despite the heavy costs of these wars, these failures continue to occur? How was it that nothing seemed to "bite deep" in certain policy making circles in Washington, and why do the scripts not change? Part of the answer might lie in the failure to think historically: after the US withdrawal from Vietnam, the deeper implications of that war were largely ignored and forgotten, even as the "collective memory" of the war remained a constant. In *How Modernity Forgets*, memory scholar Paul Connerton argues that accelerating time scales of information flow and media production induce a "cultural forgetting" on the part of society.[17]

The forgetting has been strategically useful to certain protagonists within the executive. Even as the United States had just left Vietnam, Henry Kissinger concluded that the war was relatively unique and that there were not that many lessons that could be usefully drawn from the situation; President George H. W. Bush argued that great nations could not be sundered by memories.[18] Yet there is another, deeper, lingering memory of the war that vitiates US policy making. Robert Brigham's chapter on the Vietnam syndrome shows that it has in some respect influenced the thinking of every presidential administration since 1975, while David Kieran notes that the war continues to resonate in US culture.

There is an unsustainable duality in US culture between memory and forgetting. When Ronald Reagan identified the "Vietnam syndrome," he did so to imply a cultural wariness, an illness of sorts, a reticence about going to war and deploying troops—it is frequently used as a negative term, something that the United States needs to get over, to heal itself from. Rather, it could be used in a positive frame, a reticence about going to war especially when the national interests are not apparent, when objectives are ill defined and when outcomes and exits are elusive. The repetition of US wars and failed outcomes since the 1960s reflects a broad strategic myopia and an inability within policy circles to engage with historical thinking apart from the "lessons" that might advance its tactical engagement.

All too often, the lessons literature is confined to the instrumental aspects of warfare and military intervention. The wider strategic costs, the consequences of war, the opportunity costs, and the fundamental lessons are elided.[19] By confining the "depth" of lessons to the instrumental, one can seemingly engage in historical thinking, albeit within narrow parameters. As such, the focus is on greater efficiency, fewer costs, reduced risks, and fatalities instead of engaging the wider question of whether war and intervention really serve the US national interests or whether they bring about a more stable and peaceful regional order. Would diplomacy and other forms of engagement address US objectives at even lower costs, less risk, no casualties? Political scientist David Hendrickson observes, "Obama was a far more moderate character than George W. Bush, and really did want to stay out of new wars; that a fellow pacifically inclined should use force as often as he did speaks volumes about the weight of the Washington consensus." His plea in *Republic in Peril* is for a turn to "liberal pluralism" and a new historically informed understanding of US internationalism.[20]

Gideon Rose has argued that these unending wars are in part a product of the failure of American strategic imagination. As the United States contemplates war, it usually addresses a number of phases in sequential order—from planning to D-Day to execution, termination, and aftermath—and Rose has suggested that Washington should reverse the order of the phases, to begin with the clear notion of what they want the aftermath of the conflict to look like before decisions for war are made.[21] Yet this has rarely been how Americans have approached war. The Cold War that John Lewis Gaddis famously termed the "long peace"[22] maintained forms of stability in Western Europe while other parts of the Third World were pacified or subject to intervention to contain or rollback forms of communism, socialism, nationalism, or other forms of resistance to the Western system.

The broad conception of "national security" present at the end of World War II remained, but the means by which this security would be pursued narrowed considerably. Brutal national security states and authoritarian governments were supported to maintain forms of violent order or stability. Thus, the Cold War was a condition to be lived with, rather than a campaign that could be sequenced out in a precise order with a defined end state.

We can see this most clearly in how the United States operated in the Third World, an imagined theater that was in many ways the center, rather than the periphery of Cold War (and other) conflicts and wars.[23]

In these regions, wars did not have to end when the United States could wage them with alternative instruments: the use of CIA and covert operations, the reliance on regional allies to maintain stability, the use of "proxy" or indigenous forces. The limited nature of these commitments conformed to the advice given to the Nixon administration by the British counterinsurgent Sir Robert Thompson in 1971.

Discussing how the United States might maintain a presence in South Vietnam despite domestic hopes for an end to the war, Thompson argued:

> If you have a long struggle one of the important things is to keep the temperature down. You do not want to fight a long struggle at a high temperature and at a high cost and at a high tension because that in itself will be damaging to the unity of your country.[24]

For Thompson, it was "therefore very important to fight a long war with determination but with a great deal of coolness." Thus, American strategic thinking on conflict termination, with its sequential series of steps, bore little relation to its actual practice during the Cold War, where wars were never designed to end in the first place. These conflicts, devastating in their consequences for those at their center, remained largely invisible in the United States, both in political and cultural terms.

Of course, it is certainly not the case that the United States has not suffered, even if American wars have become increasingly less visible to the public. The costs of war have had a profound impact; these have been written about extensively.[25] The wars in Iraq and Afghanistan coincided with the financial recession, compounding the costs and accelerating the relative decline of the United States.[26] David Hendrickson observes that the $5 trillion cost of the wars in Iraq and Afghanistan mean that the "capital that might have rebuilt America was fruitlessly extended on unachievable objects, in the most inhospitable environment imaginable, in pursuit of a phantom vision of American security, at great wastage of life."[27] Yet it is clear that despite these considerable costs the United States has been inhibited only to a certain degree. War and military intervention remained attractive, whether because of the primacy of presidential power within the US system—the so-called imperial presidency—or because, as Chris Hedges put it, war is "a force that gives us meaning."[28]

Whether it was a war of choice or necessity, whether it involved wars on poverty, on race, on AIDS, on drugs, and any number of other issues, historian Michael Sherry and others have emphasized the importance of war in shaping US culture.[29] More often than not, though, it has been imagined war, either metaphorical or symbolic, that has shaped the US polity. The specific ways in which war has shaped American cultures has meant that the costs of war, even those costs borne by Americans, have been difficult to perceive. Marilyn Young has argued, in this volume and elsewhere, that the aftermath of every American war was marked by attempts to erase the experiences of that war from popular memory. David Fitzgerald's chapter on soldier homecomings shows that even as the US public venerates soldiers coming home from war, it puts some distance between those who have gone to war and those who have not.

There is a geopolitical as well as a cultural context to these practices; thus, we need to be mindful not only of the politics of the erasure of war but also of the ways in which the absence of any existential external threats to the American homeland shaped the character of US engagement with the world, and thus its cultural interpretation of war. Indeed, historian Mary Dudziak has shown that the cultural erasure of war and the relative geographical isolation of the United States are interlinked. Even during World War II, a conflict in which millions of Americans participated, American civilians were largely spared the sensory experience of war itself. Unlike the "republic of suffering" experienced by Americans during the Civil War and by other nations throughout their histories, war was distant, understood largely through news reports and letters home.[30]

Andrew Preston has argued that the "free security" generated by this isolation, although no longer in existence by 1945, "was a unique condition in world history, one that indelibly shaped America's approach to the world, even long after the conditions of free security had vanished."[31] Indeed, Scott Lucas argues in his essay in this volume that the American inability to adjust to the end not only of this period of free security but of unipolar hegemony has meant that the United States has become increasingly inadept at understanding the agency of local actors and what the regional consequences of its actions are.

The objective of this collection is not just to critique this American carelessness, although our contributors surely do that, but to suggest that thinking historically about these issues includes not just a consideration of what lessons might be learned for "next time" but a full accounting of the costs and of what the United States has left behind. Philosopher Mark Evans suggests that in addition to the two traditional concepts of just war theory, *jus ad bellum* and *jus in bello*, which deal with issues before and during the war, a *jus post bellum* framing is needed to assess responsibilities during occupation or after the war. Evans relates that the theory at least has to address a wide variety of potential scenarios, including, first, what victors might do *to* their former enemies "with respect to punishment and reparations"; second, what they might do *for* them, "with respect to reconstruction"; and, third, what they might do more broadly, such as "contributing towards future peace and security" through initiatives, institutions, or mechanisms.[32]

Obviously, such thinking usually refers to wars that are clearly defined and conventional, wars that end in a *USS Missouri*-style capitulation—not the "new wars" of the 1990s and beyond. Nonetheless, Evans' theory condemns the postwar behavior of the United States. If we look to the Vietnam War we can see how, as Ed Martini's chapter shows, the overwhelming costs of war in lives, infrastructure, and environment, were borne by the Vietnamese, despite American promises in the Paris Peace Accords. When we look at Iraq, we see a neglect of *jus post bellum* in the spring of 1991, when the United States won the war but lost the peace as Saddam retained power and exacted revenge against the Shia and the Kurds after uprisings inspired by Washington, and in 2011, when the United States tried to move on from the damage it had caused during its occupation. The constraints of such considerations of *jus post bellum* are unlikely to exercise officials after they leave Afghanistan, despite the long-term blowback from the failure to provide aid after the Soviet withdrawal in 1989.

In his conclusion to his devastating book *The Deaths of Others*, political theorist John Tirman explores the "epistemology of war." He argues that the formula for calculating success in American wars includes "the costs in American blood and treasure to save Rhee or Diem, or to bring down Saddam, or prop up Karzai, but this state-centric calculus never includes the blood of those who lived there."[33] The United States-centered narratives have rarely advanced the broader conception of the national interest as it had done in Europe after WWII; that ultimately it was in the US interests to stabilize and to rebuild these areas, to mitigate radicalism or extremism, through the politics of prosperity that animated some thinking in the 1940s. There have rarely been deep questions or extended discussion about the impact of war in Vietnam, in Iraq and in Afghanistan, and US visions of the postwar did not take into account conditions in these countries or US obligations toward them. For even if the United States departed all of these three wars as the vanquished, the *comparative* damage and costs are very much one sided.

The countries have been devastated; reconciliation has been slow in the case of Vietnam; reconstruction, such as it was, was not through relief or integration. When Obama finally arranged the orderly withdrawal of US forces from Iraq, he talked simply about turning a page and new beginnings.[34] In Afghanistan, Washington lowered the threshold of its objectives to such a point that many in the United States will forget why they are there or no longer recall the purpose of the war. The primary objective nearly two decades after war commenced is to get out. Such a recursive, self-centered approach to these wars can only be the product of a polity that has lost the ability to imagine a world in which American wars *do* in fact end and in which the United States takes responsibility for the damage that it has caused abroad. In their different ways, the contributors to this volume argue for a more expansive epistemology of war, one that is not beholden to the myopic visions and assumptions of Washington.

David Ryan is professor of modern history at University College Cork, Ireland. He has published extensively on contemporary history and US foreign policy concentrating on interventions in the post-Vietnam era. His books include *Obama, US Foreign Policy and the Dilemmas of Intervention* coauthored with David Fitzgerald (Palgrave, 2014), *US Foreign Policy and the Other*, edited with Michael Cullinane (Berghahn, 2015), *Frustrated Empire: US Foreign Policy from 9/11 to Iraq* (Pluto and University of Michigan, 2007), *Vietnam in Iraq: Tactics, Lessons, Legacies and Ghosts*, edited with John Dumbrell (Routledge, 2007), *The United States and Europe in the Twentieth Century* (Longman, 2003), *US Foreign Policy in World History* (Routledge, 2000), and *US-Sandinista Diplomatic Relations: Voice of Intolerance* (MacMillan, 1995). He is also the author of numerous articles.

David Fitzgerald is lecturer in international politics in the School of History, University College Cork, Ireland. He has written numerous articles and books on military and foreign policy, especially counterinsurgency warfare and "small wars." His first book, *Learning to Forget: US Army Counterinsurgency Doctrine from Vietnam to Iraq* (Stanford, 2013), was a runner-up for the Society for Military History's Edward M. Coffman first manuscript prize. His current research focuses on consequences of the all-volunteer force for American society and the rise of a "warrior ethos" within the post-Vietnam US military. Together with David Ryan, he is the coauthor of *Obama, US Foreign Policy and the Dilemmas of Intervention* (Palgrave Macmillan, 2014).

Notes

1. Robert A. Divine, *Second Chance: The Triumph of Internationalism in America during World War II* (New York: Atheneum, 1967), 310–11.
2. F. Scott Fitzgerald, *The Great Gatsby* (Harmondsworth: Penguin, 1984 originally 1926), 172.
3. Andrew Preston, "Monsters Everywhere: A Genealogy of National Security," *Diplomatic History* 38, no. 3 (2014): 477–500, https://doi.org/10.1093/dh/dhu018.

4. Benjamin Schwarz, 'Why America Thinks It Has to Run the World,' The Atlantic (June 1996), https://www.theatlantic.com/magazine/archive/1996/06/why-america-thinks-it-has-to-run-the-world/376599/.
5. Charles S. Maier, "Hegemony and Autonomy within the Western Alliance," in *Origins of the Cold War: An International History*, ed. Melvyn P. Leffler and David S. Painter (London: Routledge, 1994), 154–74.
6. H. W. Brands, "The Idea of the National Interest," *Diplomatic History* 23, no. 2 (1999): 239–61.
7. Jeffrey A. Engel, *When the World Seemed New: George H. W. Bush and the End of the Cold War* (Boston: Houghton Mifflin Harcourt, 2017), 415–16.
8. William Safire, "The April Surprise," *New York Times*, 13 January 1992, https://www.nytimes.com/1992/01/13/opinion/essay-the-april-surprise.html.
9. Gideon Rose, "America's Forgotten Wars," *Foreign Affairs* 96, no. 6 (2017).
10. John Tirman, *The Deaths of Others: The Fate of Civilians in America's Wars* (Oxford: Oxford University Press, 2011), 337–67.
11. Gerald R. Ford, speech, Tulane University, New Orleans, 23 April 1975, Gerald R. Ford Presidential Library, https://www.fordlibrarymuseum.gov/library/document/0122/1252291.pdf.
12. George H. W. Bush, "Address Before a Joint Session of Congress on the End of the Gulf War" (The Miller Center, 6 March 1991).
13. George H. W. Bush, Address before a Joint Session of the Congress on the State of the Union, 29 January 1991, The American Presidency Project, http://www.presidency.ucsb.edu/ws/?pid=19325.
14. Zbigniew Brzezinski, "Reflections on Soviet Intervention in Afghanistan," memorandum, 26 December 1979, Jimmy Carter Presidential Library.
15. Lawrence Freedman, *Strategy: A History* (Oxford: New York: Oxford University Press, 2013), 599.
16. Wayne Baker, "Second Acts: Was Fitzgerald Decrying American Shortcuts?" *Our Values*, 6 December 2017, https://www.readthespirit.com/ourvalues/second-acts-was-fitzgerald-decrying-american-shortcuts/.
17. Paul Connerton, *How Modernity Forgets* (Cambridge: Cambridge University Press, 2009), 2, 40.
18. Henry A. Kissinger, "Lessons of Vietnam" (Presidential Country files for East Asia and the Pacific. Country File: Vietnam, Vietnam (23), box 20, Gerald R. Ford Presidential Library, 12 May 1975), Gerald R. Ford Presidential Library; George H. W. Bush, "Inaugural Address" (George H. W. Bush Presidential Library, 20 January 1989), https://bush41library.tamu.edu/archives/public-papers/1.
19. Earl C. Ravenal, *Never Again: Learning from America's Foreign Policy Failures* (Philadelphia: Temple University Press, 1978).
20. David C. Hendrickson, *Republic in Peril: American Empire and the Liberal Tradition* (New York: Oxford University Press, 2018), 54.
21. Gideon Rose, *How Wars End* (New York: Simon & Schuster, 2010).
22. John Lewis Gaddis, *The Long Peace: Inquiries into the History of the Cold War* (Oxford: Oxford University Press, 1987).
23. Odd Arne Westad, *The Global Cold War: Third World Interventions and the Making of Our Times* (Cambridge: Cambridge University Press, 2005).
24. David Fitzgerald, "Sir Robert Thompson, Strategic Patience and Nixon's War in Vietnam," *Journal of Strategic Studies* 37, nos. 6–7 (2014): 1011, https://doi.org/10.1080/01402390.2014.898582.
25. *Costs of War Project* (Watson Institute International and Public Affairs, Boston University, n.d.), http://watson.brown.edu/costsofwar/; William L. Nash and Mona Sutphen, *In the Wake of War: Improving US Post-Conflict Capabilities* (New York: Council

of Foreign Relations, 2005); Stephen Daggett, *Costs of Major US Wars* (Washington, DC: Congressional Research Service, 2010); Richard A. Falk, *The Costs of War: International Law, the UN, and the World Order after Iraq* (New York: Routledge, 2008).
26. Michael Cox, "Is the United States in Decline—Again?" *International Affairs* 83, no. 4 (2007): 643–53.
27. Hendrickson, *Republic in Peril*, 212–213.
28. Chris Hedges, *War Is a Force That Gives Us Meaning* (New York: Anchor Books, 2002).
29. Michael S. Sherry, *In the Shadow of War: The United States since the 1930s* (New Haven: Yale University Press, 1995); Andrew J. Bacevich, *The New American Militarism: How Americans Are Seduced by War* (New York: Oxford University Press, 2005); John W. Dower, *Cultures of War: Pearl Harbor, Hiroshima, 9-11, Iraq* (New York: W.W. Norton, 2010).
30. Mary L. Dudziak, "'You Didn't See Him Lying … beside the Gravel Road in France': Death, Distance, and American War Politics," *Diplomatic History*, accessed 11 December 2017, https://doi.org/10.1093/dh/dhx087.
31. Preston, "Monsters Everywhere," 482.
32. Mark Evans, "Balancing Peace, Justice and Sovereignty in Jus Post Bellum: The Case of 'Just Occupation,'" *Millennium* 36, no. 3 (2008): 533–54; Mark Evans, "Moral Responsibilities and the Conflicting Demands of Jus Post Bellum," *Ethics and International Affairs* 23, no. 2 (2009): 147–64; Larry May, *After Wars End: A Philosophical Perspective* (Cambridge: Cambridge University Press, 2012); Brian Orend, *The Morality of War* (Toronto: Broadview, 2013).
33. Tirman, *Deaths of Others*, 366.
34. David Fitzgerald and David Ryan, *Obama, US Foreign Policy and the Dilemmas of Intervention* (London: Palgrave, 2014), 35.

Select Bibliography

Bacevich, Andrew J., *The New American Militarism: How Americans Are Seduced by War* (New York: Oxford University Press, 2005).
Brands, H. W., "The Idea of the National Interest," *Diplomatic History* 23, no. 2 (1999).
Connerton, Paul, *How Modernity Forgets* (Cambridge: Cambridge University Press, 2009).
Cox, Michael, "Is the United States in Decline—Again?" *International Affairs* 83, no. 4 (2007).
Divine, Robert A., *Second Chance: The Triumph of Internationalism in America during World War II* (New York: Atheneum, 1967).
Dower, John W., *Cultures of War: Pearl Harbor, Hiroshima, 9-11, Iraq* (New York: W.W. Norton, 2010).
Dudziak, Mary L., "'You Didn't See Him Lying … beside the Gravel Road in France': Death, Distance, and American War Politics," *Diplomatic History*, accessed 11 December 2017, https://doi.org/10.1093/dh/dhx087.
Engel, Jeffrey A., *When the World Seemed New: George H. W. Bush and the End of the Cold War* (Boston, MA: Houghton Mifflin Harcourt, 2017).
Evans, Mark, "Balancing Peace, Justice and Sovereignty in Jus Post Bellum: The Case of 'Just Occupation,'" *Millennium* 36, no. 3 (2008).

_____, "Moral Responsibilities and the Conflicting Demands of *Jus Post Bellum*," *Ethics and International Affairs* 23, no. 2 (2009).

Falk, Richard A., *The Costs of War: International Law, the UN, and the World Order after Iraq* (New York: Routledge, 2008).

Fitzgerald, David, "Sir Robert Thompson, Strategic Patience and Nixon's War in Vietnam," *Journal of Strategic Studies* 37, nos. 6–7 (2014).

Fitzgerald, David and David Ryan, *Obama, US Foreign Policy and the Dilemmas of Intervention* (London: Palgrave, 2014).

Fitzgerald, F. Scott, *The Great Gatsby* (Harmondsworth: Penguin, 1984 originally 1926).

Freedman, Lawrence, *Strategy: A History* (Oxford: Oxford University Press, 2013).

Gaddis, John Lewis, *The Long Peace: Inquiries into the History of the Cold War* (Oxford: Oxford University Press, 1987).

Hedges, Chris, *War Is a Force That Gives Us Meaning* (New York: Anchor Books, 2002).

Hendrickson, David C., *Republic in Peril: American Empire and the Liberal Tradition* (New York: Oxford University Press, 2018).

Layne, Christopher and Benjamin Schwarz, "American Hegemony—without an Enemy," *Foreign Policy*, no. 92 (Fall 1993).

Maier, Charles S., "Hegemony and Autonomy within the Western Alliance," in Melvyn P. Leffler and David S. Painter (eds.), *Origins of the Cold War: An International History* (London: Routledge, 1994).

May, Larry, *After Wars End: A Philosophical Perspective* (Cambridge: Cambridge University Press, 2012).

McMahon, Robert J., *The Cold War: A Very Short Introduction* (Oxford: Oxford University Press, 2003).

Orend, Brian, *The Morality of War* (Toronto: Broadview, 2013).

Preston, Andrew, "Monsters Everywhere: A Genealogy of National Security," *Diplomatic History* 38, no. 3 (2014).

Ravenal, Earl C., *Never Again: Learning from America's Foreign Policy Failures* (Philadelphia: Temple University Press, 1978).

Rose, Gideon, "America's Forgotten Wars," *Foreign Affairs* 96, no. 6 (2017).

Sherry, Michael S., *In the Shadow of War: The United States since the 1930s* (New Haven: Yale University Press, 1995).

Tirman, John, *The Deaths of Others: The Fate of Civilians in America's Wars* (Oxford: Oxford University Press, 2011).

Westad, Odd Arne, *The Global Cold War: Third World Interventions and the Making of Our Times* (Cambridge: Cambridge University Press, 2005).

Part I

Vietnam

The historian George Herring famously described the American War in Vietnam as the "unending war." Certainly, its aftermath lingered long in the minds of policymakers and the broken bodies of those who fought the war alike; American and Vietnamese culture and the Indochinese landscape were marked by the experience. But if the war remained alive in the American imagination, it was not for lack of trying on the part of policymakers to turn the page.

As Robert K. Brigham notes in his chapter, the Ford administration declared the Vietnam War "finished, from an American perspective" even as the remnants of the Thieu regime attempted to hold off the final North Vietnamese advance into Saigon in April 1975. The Korean War—in which negotiations and trench warfare dragged on for two years after the war reached a stalemate in the summer of 1951—provided a harbinger of the American inability to come to terms with a result short of complete victory, but the extent to which policymakers were unable to coherently articulate their vision for an exit from Vietnam is striking.

As Sarah Thelen demonstrates in her chapter, the Nixon administration made no attempt to make a case to the American people for their policies, instead turning to appeals to nationalism to provide political cover for their actions. Nixon and his aides struggled to balance the demands for more troops and resources to strengthen the military situation, the need to project strength in the negotiations while ensuring that they continued, and to simultaneously quiet domestic dissent and rally support. Nixon's solution was not to make a substantive case to the American people for either "victory" or a comprehensive vision for a peace that would end the war, but rather to rally his own supporters around issues of identity and nationalism and reflexive support for the president regardless of policy.

The strategy was effective in the short term, but in the longer term it both failed to build an effective consensus for the eventual peace agreement and helped to create a toxic political environment, the consequences of which would be felt in the United States for decades to come. The strategy evinced a duality in US culture that is unsustainable in the medium to longer term. At one level the narrative is brought to closure, even as the culture, all too silently, struggles with its lingering effects. Thus, the United States does not get to deal with the strategic implications of defeat. The need to move on stunts any significant reflection or discourse on the strategic implications on decisions for war, especially wars of choice. Instead, the interactions between US culture and the US executive are muted conversations that occasionally blow up over questions on military intervention but are ultimately confined to how better to do it next time, rather than more serious strategic reflections on whether intervention and war are necessary or effective instruments of US foreign policy.

If Richard Nixon left behind a metaphorically toxic political atmosphere, then Ed Martini's chapter demonstrates the literally toxic consequences of the American war for Vietnam. In enumerating what was left behind by the United States, Martini shows us the long-term devastation of human and environmental health caused by contamination from Agent Orange and other herbicides. Not only that, but the Vietnamese were faced with the difficult tasks of political and economic reconstruction of a divided country and a massive humanitarian crisis. What is striking about this analysis is that in turning the page on the war and ignoring their obligations and promises of reconstruction aid that they agreed to in the Paris Peace Accords, the United States effectively continued the war by actively resisting Vietnamese sovereignty and independence.

Thus, the tragedy was that even as the United States turned inward and refused to reckon with the consequences of their exit from Vietnam and as policymakers attempted to turn the page on the conflict, that very act of turning the page prevented reconciliation and prolonged hostility, and it meant that Vietnam continued to suffer. The carelessness with which the United States ended its war in Vietnam speaks to the ways in which it was relatively insulated from the consequences of the war, even in defeat.

Despite the best efforts of policymakers, the Vietnam War's hold on the American imagination did not end when the last helicopters left the rooftop of the embassy compound in Saigon. As David Kieran demonstrates, the consequences of the war continued to reverberate in American culture. Focusing on the figure of Secretary Robert McNamara, one of the key architects of the war, Kieran examines the 2003 release of Errol Morris' documentary *The Fog of War* and coverage of McNamara's death in 2009. He uses those two moments to argue that they reveal how the contested, malleable legacy of the Vietnam War continues to shape political discourse in the United States. The chapter shows how wars do not simply end in American culture, as their meanings remain unstable and competing remembrances serve different contemporary agendas. As Kieran argues, the Vietnam War continues to provide "a language and a set of ideas for advancing competing—and often oppositional—ideas about US foreign policy."

Indeed, in his chapter on the strategic implications of America's involvement in Vietnam, Robert K. Brigham demonstrates that these ideas equally affected policymakers, even those who wished to move on from Vietnam. In his history of the Vietnam syndrome, Brigham argues that particular ways of remembering the war had a stark impact on US foreign policy formulation and shows that ghosts of Vietnam haunted various administrations, up to and including the Obama White House. The lessons of Vietnam were inescapable, and few policymakers would embrace open-ended military commitments without a clear exit strategy. And yet these exit strategies were never clearly defined in terms of US objectives or in terms of the outcomes they sought in the local and regional context. The exit was thought of more in culturally myopic ways that related to the ability to get out as opposed to leaving the situation behind. There have been few positive outcomes. Despite the official narratives of turning the page, the wars linger; they have devastated the countries.

In *Nothing Ever Dies*, his examination of the ways in which the American War in Vietnam has been remembered, Viet Thanh Nguyen calls for "an unbounded empathy that extends to all, including others."[1] As the authors of these chapters make clear, empathy was lacking in the American withdrawal from Vietnam, as it was denied to the Vietnamese and even, at times, fellow Americans. This unwillingness to understand the Other and fully reckon with the implications of American defeat in Vietnam had profound and negative consequences for US foreign policy in the war's aftermath.

Note

1. Viet Thanh Nguyen, *Nothing Ever Dies: Vietnam and the Memory of War* (Cambridge, MA: Harvard University Press, 2016), 272.

Chapter 1

The Importance of Being Popular
Richard Nixon, Henry Kissinger, and Domestic Support for the Vietnam War

Sarah Thelen

"Once on the tiger's back we cannot be sure of picking the place to dismount," warned George Ball in 1964. Although not his intended audience, President Richard M. Nixon and his national security advisor Henry Kissinger could certainly attest to the truth of Ball's warning by the time Nixon announced the Paris Peace Accords in January 1973. Their efforts to extricate the United States from the Vietnam War highlight a painful reality of ending wars, namely, that it is not enough to simply desire an end to a conflict; instead anyone wishing to do so must balance competing and often contradictory demands from military, diplomatic, and domestic audiences. This is particularly true in a participatory democracy such as the United States, in which presidents have tremendous latitude but do not make policy in a vacuum.

Seeking to end US involvement in Vietnam, Nixon and his aides struggled to balance demands for more troops and resources to strengthen the military situation, the need to project strength in the negotiations while ensuring that they continued, and the need to simultaneously quiet domestic dissent and rally support. Congress, a coequal branch of government with the power to fund or defund presidential priorities and more susceptible to domestic political pressures, further complicated the already delicate calculus—as did Nixon's determination to win reelection in 1972.

Although both Nixon and Kissinger publicly rejected the suggestion that domestic politics shaped their approach to the US war in Vietnam, their private discussions and memoirs underscore the ways that the three were interrelated. The rest of the country, too, recognized the connections between what one *New York Times* journalist described as the negotiations' three broad fronts: Nixon's need to counter North Vietnamese military and diplomatic initiatives, secure the cooperation of their South Vietnamese allies, and ease domestic pressure from both hawks and doves.[1] In presenting the final agreement to the American public, Nixon insisted it created "the right kind of peace" on all three fronts and thanked the American people for their support and refusal to "settle for a peace that would have betrayed our allies, that would have abandoned our prisoners of war, or that would have ended the war for us but would have continued the war for the 50 million people of Indochina."[2]

Of course, war did continue for the people of Vietnam and Cambodia for many years after US troops left, and even before January 1973 many in the antiwar movement worried that the Paris agreement would have just that effect. At the same time, Nixon's supporters were delighted and looked forward to putting the Vietnam War behind them. This contrast between optimism and pessimism reflected long-standing domestic divisions over US involvement in the Vietnam War. That these hardened as US troops returned home and that the US role in Vietnam declined reflects Nixon's decision to focus attention on the president's supporters, the so-called silent majority. In doing so, Nixon avoided having to make a substantive case for his Vietnam War policies but also lost the chance to ensure broad support for the eventual peace.

That Nixon would make this choice was almost inevitable given his own political background and lessons learned from the political travails of his predecessor, Lyndon Baines Johnson. Having benefited from Johnson's failed efforts to counter the antiwar movement, Nixon faced the same problem in 1969 that had stymied Johnson: the decisions most likely to result in a military or diplomatic victory in Vietnam were the ones least likely to result in a political victory at home. Faced with the diplomatic, political, and military challenges of the Vietnam War, Nixon opted to focus on a battle he thought he could win: the war for domestic public opinion. Rather than seek to unite the nation, Nixon and his aides adopted a divide and conquer approach to domestic public opinion. Not only did they work to isolate and undermine the antiwar movement—a story told ably elsewhere—but they sought to rally supporters to embrace the president's policies simply because they were the president's.[3]

This new group of active supporters would in turn serve as an important domestic counterpoint to the antiwar movement and would, White

House aides hoped, eventually neutralize the Vietnam War as a domestic political issue. Doing so was of vital importance for Nixon and Dr. Henry Kissinger, his national security advisor, as both men recognized that domestic opposition had the potential to constrain their policy choices for the Vietnam War.

Worse yet, the North Vietnamese were careful students of US politics and delighted in reminding Kissinger of domestic criticism during the meetings in Paris. In recollecting the negotiations and, more broadly, most of Nixon's first term, neither Nixon nor Kissinger could ignore public opinion in their calculations and policymaking. Even before taking office in January 1969, Nixon observed that although "a significant percentage of the public favored a military victory in Vietnam," his first task once in office would be to "prepare public opinion for the fact that total military victory was no longer possible."[4] In doing so, Nixon was not so much breaking with his predecessors—indeed, neither Johnson nor John F. Kennedy had been "willing to pay the cost in money and blood of actually conquering North Vietnam"—as aligning public rhetoric with previously secret expectations.[5]

This new definition of "victory" not only eschewed the word itself but privileged the political survival of South Vietnam over the defeat or destruction of North Vietnam. Furthermore, it stressed that the United States could not be expected to settle Vietnamese political arguments and so reframed US involvement as military support, thus laying the foundation for a 1973 agreement that glossed over the major political issues. That Nixon took this path would have pleased Townsend Hoopes, Johnson's undersecretary of the air force, who argued in March 1968 for just such a "redefinition" of US objectives because the current approach to the conflict was "tearing apart the social and political fabric of our own country."[6] These domestic tensions, of course, benefited candidate Nixon, but frustrated a President Nixon who saw domestic impatience and criticism as inimical to his own efforts to negotiate an end to US involvement.

Echoing Nixon, Kissinger also blamed domestic debates for North Vietnamese intransigence in Paris. Analyzing the failure to restart the secret talks in November 1971, Kissinger argued, "Many factors contributed to Hanoi's decision, including the monomania of a lifetime. But in my view the biggest single factor was the divisions within America."[7] That they were still a worry even after significant efforts to rally support speaks both to their depth and to the limited effectiveness of a public opinion strategy that ignores a large portion of the population. Even so, this approach minimized an irritating weakness in negotiations with the North Vietnamese. As Kissinger recalled in his memoir *White House*

Years, "No meeting with the North Vietnamese was complete without a recitation of the statements of our domestic opposition."[8] Kissinger repeatedly tried to prevent these embarrassing litanies without much success, and Le Duc Tho, the senior North Vietnamese figure at the secret talks, repeatedly quoted media coverage and congressional statements despite Kissinger's insistence that "domestic discussions are no concern of yours."[9]

As Nixon and Kissinger saw the situation, popular support was proof of US credibility and the role of public opinion in the Paris negotiations increased the importance of winning the domestic debate. Nixon and his aides therefore privileged visible demonstrations of support over actually changing minds at home. Having made this choice, they were disinclined to engage with their critics and instead focused their attention on organizing and mobilizing the president's supporters. Tellingly, they did not promise victory but insisted that "peace with honor" would preserve American credibility and prestige abroad just as countering the antiwar movement at home would similarly protect traditional values and patriotism.

Mobilizing the Silent Majority

The first significant test of this approach was Nixon's 3 November 1969 "silent majority speech." In it, the president attempted to reframe US involvement in the Vietnam War as a product of the nation's history and ideals. Rather than announcing a change in policy or approach, the speech sought to reframe domestic expectations—emphasizing Vietnamization and the likelihood of a negotiated peace—and to rally support for continued US involvement. In seeking to mobilize support, Nixon made clear his intended audience. Breaking with established practice, he ended the speech with an appeal not to the nation as a whole but to the "great silent majority" of Americans who, presumably, supported the war in contrast to the vocal critical "minority." This appeal came between two major antiwar demonstrations—the 15 October Moratorium and the 15 November Mobilization—which sought to convince undecided Americans that antiwar activists "weren't just crazy radicals."[10]

Success would have normalized opposition to the war and, more broadly, criticism of the president and official policy. This, in turn, would have severely limited Nixon's ability to wage war in Vietnam. Indeed, the success of the October Moratorium—with more than two million participants across the country—forced Nixon to rethink his approach to the Vietnam War, as he realized that domestic public opinion would not allow him to escalate the conflict as originally planned if the North Vietnamese missed a 1 November deadline to return to the negotiations. And even as the speech became a more general statement on the Vietnam War, Nixon and his aides saw it as an opportunity to launch a broader prowar movement that would counter the antiwar movement in the media, domestic debates, and Paris.

To this end, aides worked closely with outside supporters such as the Tell It to Hanoi Committee, a group of Nixon loyalists led by New York lawyer William J. Casey. The group had worked to counter the October protests, and its members "responded, to a man, even before they knew the details," when approached about the November effort.[11] Their enthusiastic participation would be vital, as the speech was to be the launching pad for a great patriotic movement promoting Nixon and his policies, "a grand rally by the great (heretofore silent) majority of Americans ... [and] a visible demonstration of American unity."[12]

Aides also reached out to a bipartisan group formed during the Johnson administration, the Citizens Committee for Peace with Freedom in Vietnam, as well as veterans' organizations, local business groups, and individual supporters across the country. Each would pursue its own projects, but the general message was set in the White House and aides took an active role in coordinating the resulting demonstrations and advertising, petition, and letter-writing campaigns.[13] These prowar efforts did not offer arguments for continued US involvement—nor did they address specific criticisms of US policy—but instead emphasized the importance of support for the president, patriotism, and national pride. As a result of these efforts and careful, yet covert, coordination between government officials, grassroots organizations, and outside administration allies, the White House mailroom was overwhelmed in the days and weeks following the president's speech with letters, telegrams, and petitions encouraging the president to "Keep believing in us—'The Silent Americans'—and we will continue to believe in you."[14]

This initial response was certainly gratifying, but Nixon and his aides needed more than an immediate outpouring of support for a speech to convince the North Vietnamese that the president had the political strength at home to continue to wage war in Vietnam. White House officials, therefore, worked to ensure that the initial enthusiasm became lasting, and active, support. Fortunately for them, administration efforts to promote and solidify the silent majority overlapped with a series of grassroots patriotic events and displays during National Unity Week— including both Veterans' Day on 11 November and an antiwar protest scheduled for 15 November.[15]

The bulk of these events was organized without White House prompting long before the president's speech but dovetailed nicely with administration plans. Large demonstrations on 11 and 15 November more than accomplished the administration's goal of showing "that *not all* of the crowd is anti-administration" with appeals to patriotism, national identity, and support for the president even as they did not address substantive concerns about US policy in Vietnam.[16] Despite antiwar protests across the country on 15 November, administration aides chose to focus their attention on participants in National Unity Week, who saw room for neither compromise nor a loyal opposition: particularly reports of "ubiquitous signs" saying, "AMERICA ... LOVE IT OR LEAVE IT" and the claim that "there are more of us patriotic Americans than those pro-Hanoicrats."[17]

Tellingly, neither Nixon nor his aides were disturbed by the national division in such statements, as their priority was ensuring that Nixon's supporters were visibly united. While meeting in Paris in February 1970, Kissinger pointed to this support and warned his North Vietnamese counterpart, Le Duc Tho, not to assume that what worked with Johnson would work with Nixon: "President Nixon can appeal to people whom President Johnson could not reach."[18] By this, of course, Kissinger meant the silent majority, many of whom had taken to the streets for the first time following Nixon's November speech. Tho and other North Vietnamese officials dismissed Kissinger's references to polling and pro-Nixon demonstrations as "'only' public opinion" even as Tho, in Kissinger's analysis, "revealed the importance Hanoi attached to our public opinion by giving it pride of place" in his opening remarks.[19] In doing so, the North Vietnamese forced US officials to face domestic considerations in Paris even as those same issues constrained their options in Vietnam and at home.

Countering Congress

In practically the same breath as he challenged White House claims of popular support, Tho reminded Kissinger and Nixon of more dangerous critics: those in Congress and among the political elite. Tho remarked, "I have seen many statements by the Senate Foreign Relations Committee, by the Democratic Party, by [former Johnson administration official] Mr. Clifford, which have demanded the total withdrawal of American forces."[20] Kissinger replied not by challenging Tho's reading of the domestic debate, but rather by insisting it was not an appropriate topic for the Paris talks. Kissinger recounts that in this case, "I replied sharply that I would listen to no further propositions from Hanoi regarding American public opinion. ... Painful as I found our domestic dissent, I did not think it compatible with our dignity to debate it with an adversary."[21] But even as Kissinger adamantly refused to debate US public opinion, both sides knew that he and Nixon could not ignore it entirely.

Congressional opposition and domestic dissent were inextricably tied to military and diplomatic decisions, complicating Kissinger's goal of keeping the negotiations focused exclusively on the situation in Vietnam. Kissinger ruefully remembered, "It took several meetings to get that point across and I never succeeded totally."[22] That Tho invoked both popular and congressional opinion demonstrates that the North Vietnamese were well aware of the domestic political pressures Nixon faced and were, in 1970, quite confident that these pressures would ultimately work to their advantage.

At the same time, just as public opinion limited the president's options, aides knew they could leverage popular support for the president to pressure his congressional opponents and so worked diligently to organize the nascent silent majority into a reliable support movement. They successfully used these supporters to dampen criticism of US and South Vietnamese incursions into Cambodia in the spring and summer of 1970 and hoped for a similar result in their efforts to counter senators George McGovern and Mark Hatfield's efforts to legislate limits on US involvement in Vietnam. Their 1970 amendment to a military procurement bill would have capped US military forces in Vietnam at 280,000 troops by April 1971 with a complete withdrawal by 31 December 1971.

While street protests were certainly problematic both at home and in Paris, legislation such as the McGovern-Hatfield amendment had the potential to concretely constrain the president's options in Vietnam. Both Nixon and Kissinger saw troop withdrawals as one of the few things they could offer the North Vietnamese without compromising their promises to South Vietnam, so such legislative limits directly, and explicitly, challenged Nixon's carefully cultivated executive branch monopoly over foreign policy. Reflecting Nixon's primary focus on presidential power rather than specific vote counts, special counsel to the president and White House domestic liaison Charles W. Colson's response to this threat emphasized fostering vocal public support for Nixon's policies—resulting in an active pro-Nixon, anti–McGovern-Hatfield group: Americans for Winning the Peace (AWP).

Colson and Gene Bradley, a businessman with an interest in foreign policy and the administration's "man from the outside," organized high-level Nixon backers to oppose the amendment and its supporters.[23] Working with both outside organizers and White House staffers, Colson and Bradley created AWP during the summer of 1970. Despite close ties to the Nixon White House, AWP presented itself as a bipartisan, nonpolitical group of private individuals working to support Nixon's foreign policies.[24] With Bradley as its public face, most White House involvement consisted of behind-the-scenes organizing and support.

Despite Colson's determination to maintain control over the organization, he recognized that "if it lost its autonomy it would be virtually useless to us."[25] White House statements of support were therefore balanced by careful denials of administration involvement. At the same time, AWP's criticisms of the amendment tracked closely with White House arguments against it: that legislation would impede, not promote, US withdrawal from Vietnam and might even "enliven" North Vietnamese officials "just as the Munich negotiations 'enlivened' Hitler"; that precipitate withdrawal would be "disastrous" and risked "destroy[ing] all we have fought for in that region"; and that Nixon's policies protected US security and that "a US retreat to isolation ... would be fatal."[26] These parallels led many observers to question the relationship between the White House and its outside allies, but AWP and administration officials were prepared. Internal guidance "for answering questions" included phrasing for denying suggestions that the group was "a front for the president" or "a Republican Party attempt to further advance the image of a partisan silent majority."[27]

Obscuring the links between AWP and the administration also helped recruitment, as many potential members, regardless of party affiliation, joined AWP "with the understanding that this activity is separate and distinct from the United States Government."[28] To bolster this nonpartisan image, AWP attempted to recruit nationally recognized Democrats such as Lyndon Johnson and George Meany, as well as Walter and Eugene Rostow, to serve on the national committee.[29] Bradley, Colson, and other organizers took advantage of AWP's bipartisan credentials and popular support for Nixon to organize local committees in over twenty-five cities by late August.[30]

These groups worked with other administration supporters—particularly Young Americans for Freedom and the Tell It to Hanoi Committee—to advance and defend administration positions as well as to discredit opponents. Tell it To Hanoi's attack campaign freed AWP to take the high road and reframe the debate in ways favorable to the administration.[31] Using administration-compiled and NSC-cleared fact sheets, AWP members labored throughout August to convince their fellow citizens to oppose the McGovern-Hatfield amendment. To this end, committee members wrote articles and letters to the editor criticizing the amendment, spoke publicly against it, and placed anti–McGovern-Hatfield advertisements in local papers.[32] Most of these committee-sponsored advertisements ran 29–30

August 1970 to best influence the 1 September Senate vote.[33] Describing the McGovern-Hatfield amendment as "tantamount to surrender" and claiming that it "cripples our chances to win a just peace," advertisements asked readers in Memphis, Dallas, and San Diego to "help our Nation win the Peace" and to "tell your senator to vote no on the McGovern-Hatfield amendment."[34]

Another directed New Yorkers to "phone, wire, or write your Senator to vote 'NO.'"[35] Ultimately, fifty-five senators did vote against the amendment, defeating it by sixteen votes. While the effectiveness of public opinion efforts is hard to measure, vocal local and regional groups helped Nixon and his supporters create the appearance of widespread opposition to the McGovern-Hatfield amendment. On a national scale, these voices countered the antiwar movement and likely would not have been so unified or so geographically diverse without White House coordination and support.

Looking back on the fight over the McGovern-Hatfield amendment, both Nixon and Kissinger emphasized the damage it could have done to the US negotiating position. This is unsurprising given the ways that domestic politics shaped military and diplomatic options in Vietnam. Highlighting the interrelatedness of domestic and international considerations, Kissinger explained in *White House Years* that "once a final withdrawal date had been established by the law, the already narrowing margin for negotiations would evaporate."[36]

As Kissinger and Nixon saw the situation, without North Vietnamese uncertainty about how long the United States would stay in Vietnam, the United States would, "lose the capacity to bargain even for our prisoners for we would have literally nothing left to offer except South Vietnam"—something both men publicly refused to consider despite growing frustrations with their erstwhile ally.[37] Reflecting on the damage domestic opposition did to the United States in the Paris negotiations, Kissinger argued, "To end the war honorably we needed to present our enemy with the very margin of uncertainty about our intentions that our domestic opponents bent every effort to remove."[38]

With congressional and public pressure combining to force Nixon to commit to significant troop withdrawals, the North Vietnamese were increasingly confident that they could outlast the US. Legislation such as McGovern-Hatfield was even more damaging, and Kissinger bemoaned the fact that the domestic debates consistently undermined his efforts to negotiate in Paris and, worse perhaps, "reduc[ed] the North's incentive for serious negotiation."[39] Defeating the McGovern-Hatfield amendment was an important step, but it was far from sufficient to convince the North Vietnamese that the United States would stay in Vietnam.

Building a Majority in 1972

A resounding victory in the 1972 presidential election, however, would be very convincing. And by early 1971, Nixon and his staff had pivoted to planning for the 1972 election. They did so confident that their earlier efforts had, as Colson observed in February, "succeeded over the past year in making the war pretty much a non-issue."[40] With this shift, aides attempted to retain key elements of the silent majority while minimizing the Vietnam War as a factor in domestic debates. In this way, officials hoped to unite the disparate groups—including "white ethnics," organized labor, wealthy businessmen, conservatives, veterans—seen as crucial to the president's reelection while avoiding potentially damaging debates over the Vietnam War. Even so, aides knew they could not ignore the conflict completely and so cast Nixon in the role of peacemaker. In this context, Nixon and his staff saw the lack of a final peace agreement as a strength, and Colson recommended that campaign workers tell voters that the president's accomplishments—including progress on the Vietnam War—were part of an "unfinished agenda" that would "be realized in the next four years."[41]

In this way, aides sought to transform the stalled and frustrating peace process into a reason to vote for Nixon in the hope he would negotiate a final peace in his second term. At the same time, both Nixon and his staff knew that they had to continue to appear to be actively pursuing peace to avoid a resurgence of antiwar sentiment that would spoil the peacemaker narrative even as attitudes toward their domestic opponents had not changed and, in fact, had hardened. As Nixon observed, "We can't pretend to want to unify everybody, we've got to build our majority."[42]

Even as Nixon and his political allies sought to "build their majority," the president and Kissinger continued their efforts to negotiate the long-promised "peace with honor." Well aware that the North Vietnamese followed US domestic politics closely, Nixon waged the 1972 campaign with both an international and a domestic audience in mind. Minimizing the war as a political issue eased domestic pressure for a rapid agreement and gave Nixon and Kissinger more latitude in the negotiations. Furthermore, it limited the ability of North Vietnamese negotiators to use domestic public opinion to pressure their US counterparts. Yet, there was a very real risk of leading citizens to believe that the war was effectively over. While an understandable conclusion given administration optimism about the negotiations and the ongoing troop withdrawals, these expectations put the Nixon administration in a similar position as Johnson's in 1968. The public believed the United States was on its way out of Vietnam and that the war would end soon, complicating efforts to use military force to pressure the North Vietnamese and reassure their allies in the south. Thus, when the North Vietnamese launched the Easter Offensive in March 1972, Nixon and his aides struggled to balance the international and domestic considerations.

US military and civilian officials had long expected the invasion and so were prepared to respond militarily, but the president and his political aides found it much harder to manage the domestic reaction to both the offensive and the military response. Unfortunately for them, earlier success in depoliticizing Vietnam — at least for supporters — made it quite difficult to mobilize them in response to a perceived escalation of the conflict. One White House aide observed that because so many citizens believed the war was almost over, US and South Vietnamese bombings were "perceived more as an escalation and ... it undermines the president's credibility much more."[43]

Nixon, however, believed that his silent majority would remain loyal and reminded Kissinger in late April that "unless we hit the Hanoi-Haiphong complex this weekend, we probably are not going to be able to hit it at all before the election."[44] Thus, the president announced on 8 May 1972 that the bombing of North Vietnam would continue and that the United States would mine its ports and increase attacks against rail and communications lines.[45] Nixon carefully framed this decision as the only responsible option, the only way to ensure that North Vietnam would return to negotiations after Nixon had already "offered the maximum of what any president of the United States could offer."[46] The president urged the American people to "stand together in purpose and resolve" and support his efforts to end the Vietnam War with "a genuine peace, not a peace that is merely a prelude to another war."[47]

Reflecting its domestic and international importance, White House planning for the 8 May speech was almost as involved as were efforts surrounding the 3 November 1969 speech. In a memorandum sent the day before the speech, Nixon insisted that his staff "do everything within our power to follow up — with an effort far exceeding the speech of November 3"[48] to ensure that their preferred lines and interpretation of the speech shaped public discussions. Specifically, Nixon wanted to justify the blockade, highlight "the courage of the president in going all out for peace," and "blame the two previous administrations for getting us into the war."[49] To this end, Nixon specifically requested that "all of the hawks, not only in the Congress but in the media and among the Governors, etc., be mobilized."[50] Not content with public support from outside surrogates — many of them politicians or local elites, Nixon reminded his aides that a successful response to his speech "requires stimulating mail and wire response to the speech to the White House so that we can use it as we did after November 3."[51]

At the same time, White House officials recognized the need to "avoid the crisis atmosphere now … we should radiate stability, we should radiate calmness."[52] When these White House efforts bore fruit, he pushed for even more aggressive efforts against the North Vietnamese, telling Kissinger, "I cannot emphasize too strongly that I have determined that we should go for broke. … Our greatest failure now would be to do too little too late. It is far more important to do too much at a time that we will have maximum public support for what we do."[53]

Subsequent polling and public responses validated Nixon's analysis—particularly the arrival of over 143,000 letters and telegrams to the White House, "the heaviest response to a presidential speech" since November 1969.[54] A sizable number of these letters and telegrams likely originated in the offices of the Committee to Reelect the President, but as aides obscured their origins and framed them as sincere, grassroots responses, the media tended to take them at face value.[55] Even as they publicly pointed to these responses as evidence of popular agreement with Nixon's policies, the president and his allies could not ignore the reality that the bombing campaigns faced significant domestic opposition that Nixon later described as "immediate and shrill."[56]

Anticipating such criticism, Nixon explicitly asked Americans for "the same strong support you have always given your president" and reminded his listeners of the importance of domestic public opinion on the international stage: "It is you most of all that the world will be watching."[57] Furthermore, while White House efforts sought to justify the blockade and bombings, the priority was to mobilize the president's supporters, as they would be crucial in both winning the election in November and improving the US negotiating position in Paris. And, for the most part, this approach worked, at least as far as the administration's short-term goals were concerned. Pro-Nixon and prowar voices did indeed counterbalance the president's critics, giving Kissinger much needed credibility in Paris. In his memoirs, Nixon recalled that throughout the spring and summer of 1972, "efforts to attack me on the war were to no avail" and by August, "public support of my conduct of the war had actually risen."[58]

Both Nixon and Kissinger expected this endorsement to improve their international position, and even years later, Nixon reveled in the fact that while Democrats and other domestic critics failed to realize that they were "out of touch with the majority of the American people," North Vietnamese officials "apparently got the message" and sought to restart the secret negotiations in Paris at the end of the month.[59]

Reaching an Agreement

Even more encouraging, Nixon recalled that August 1972 marked "the first time the Communists actually seemed to be interested in reaching a settlement."[60] Both he and Kissinger credited the North Vietnamese expectation of a Nixon victory in November for this shift, assuming that their opponents hoped to "get better terms from me before the election than after it."[61] Of course, Kissinger could have disabused them of this idea, as he knew that Nixon "would just as soon have put the whole negotiating process on ice until after the election."[62] While there was, of course, a very real risk that the North Vietnamese would be less willing to compromise after the election, Nixon was confident in his domestic support and expected that "Immediately after the election we will have an enormous mandate ... and the enemy then either has to settle or face the consequences of what we could do to them."[63]

Kissinger did not agree and worried that, after the election, the North Vietnamese would "revert to their earlier intransigence and let the war drag on at a reduced level in the hope that American public opinion would eventually force us to withdraw."[64] This worry, combined with a recognition that much of his personal credibility and prestige depended on a successful conclusion to the negotiations, led Kissinger to pursue an agreement perhaps more doggedly than Nixon would have preferred, but not without results.

On 12 October 1973, a jubilant Kissinger returned from Paris and reported to Nixon that the most recent North Vietnamese proposal "met almost all our major requirements."[65] Unsurprisingly, the October agreement did not address underlying political issues but did provide for a cease-fire, withdrawal of US troops, and an exchange of prisoners of war (POWs). These terms matched the scaled-back version of "victory" as presented by administration officials although they were a far cry from the conventional, much less military, definitions. Although not a final agreement—South Vietnamese president Thieu had yet to concur—both Nixon and Kissinger believed they were finally close to achieving one of their major foreign policy goals for Nixon's first term. A confident Kissinger returned to Paris on 17 October and after "tense and pressured"[66] meetings with the North Vietnamese, went on to Saigon with an agreement both he and Nixon believed "could now be considered complete."[67]

The plan was for Kissinger to meet with Thieu in Saigon and then travel to Hanoi, where the agreement would be finalized and signed on 31 October. Although informed that "we have no reasonable alternative but to accept this agreement," Thieu was "polite but noncommittal" in his meetings with Kissinger.⁶⁸ Ultimately, Thieu's hesitation and "obstructionism"⁶⁹ stopped the agreement in its tracks. Likely hoping to pressure the United States, the North Vietnamese publicized the general terms, forcing Kissinger to desperately attempt to reframe the delay in a 26 October press conference. Promising that "peace is at hand," Kissinger minimized the obstacles facing a final agreement. Nixon worried that this optimism would result in "premature hopes for an early settlement" and electoral consequences when those hopes were dashed but was pleased that Kissinger's statement "succeeded in completely undercutting the enemy's ploy."⁷⁰

While Nixon recalled that his own preference was for waiting until after the election to finalize an agreement, he claimed that the timing was less important than the quality of the agreement. In a speech on 2 November 1972, Nixon spoke to both the US public and the North Vietnamese:

> We are not going to allow an election deadline or any other kind of deadline to force us into an agreement that would be only a temporary truce and not a lasting peace. We are going to sign the agreement when the agreement is right, not one day before. And when the agreement is right, we are going to sign, without one day's delay.⁷¹

In saying this, Nixon sought to ease domestic pressure for—and, indeed, expectations of—a rapid settlement while making it clear to both North and South Vietnamese officials that the United States was determined to reach an agreement. To maintain the pressure on the North Vietnamese, particularly as the US election was only five days away, Nixon authorized increased bombing in North Vietnam that Nixon, unlike some historians, claimed "seemed to work almost immediately" in securing North Vietnamese agreement to a continuation of the talks on the US timetable.⁷²

After Nixon's impressive victory on 7 November—he won over 60 percent of the popular vote and every state except Massachusetts and the District of Columbia—Kissinger returned to Paris representing a much-strengthened president. Even so, Nixon's domestic triumph did not immediately translate to success in the negotiations. For while Kissinger no longer confronted taunts about domestic opposition; he now faced the very real challenge of reconciling Thieu's demands with North Vietnamese ambitions—all while the US public expected a speedy departure from Vietnam. When the United States, North Vietnam, and South Vietnam failed to reach an agreement in December, Kissinger urged Nixon to rally the nation behind taking a hard line in response to North Vietnamese intransigence. He argued that the North Vietnamese paid close attention to US public opinion and that public support would lend credibility to his threats as in November 1969 and May 1972. Nixon, however, felt that such an effort would be both "frantic and probably foredoomed" and that it would be much better, politically, to bomb first and explain after.[73]

He therefore did not announce the start of the Linebacker II bombings on 18 December, but rather had Kissinger explain the situation in a press conference. The devastating bombings continued, with only a short pause for Christmas, until 29 December, when the beleaguered North Vietnamese agreed to restart the Paris talks. On 30 December, Nixon announced that Kissinger and Le Duc Tho would meet in Paris on 8 January. This round of negotiations would prove to be the last with all sides eventually coming to an agreement in mid-January. As in October, South Vietnamese president Thieu was the main obstacle, but he eventually agreed to sign after Nixon secretly promised significant support after the US departure. Nixon announced the agreement on 23 January, and with its signing on 27 January 1973, official US involvement in Vietnam ended although Americans would remain in Vietnam until April 1975.

After the Peace

Even before Nixon announced the agreement, White House aides were preparing the groundwork for a favorable response as they had before for so many previous presidential statements. Unlike with previous public opinion campaigns, though, aides hoped to rally popular support behind the agreement itself, rather than the president. Without popular support for the final terms, Nixon knew that it would be impossible to enforce the agreement. He therefore reminded Haldeman that "our first objective should be to develop pride in the settlement—its soundness, etc., and to counteract the effort that will be made by the liberal opposition to kill our whole foreign policy program that is based on patriotism and national honor."[74]

Following the president's announcement, White House officials solicited statements from congressional allies, friendly journalists, and POW wives. Additionally, Colson's successor Bill Baroody reported that he and Colson had "reconstituted the Americans for Winning the Peace Committee ... and mobilized them to issue supporting statements and generate telegrams, letters of support, etc."[75] Reactivating this group marked a partial return to earlier efforts to organize the president's outside allies under the larger umbrella of the silent majority, but it was far less successful and public opinion on the settlement continued to be mixed.

By the end of January, Haldeman accepted that the White House would be unable to secure broad public support for the agreement and told White House aides to "stop worrying about defending the agreement. It either works or it doesn't and it doesn't make any difference one way or the other what we say."[76] At the same time, he stressed that public support for the agreement—and for the nation of South Vietnam more broadly—would be crucial if the United States was to honor the president's promise "to go back in to back up Vietnam. The president won't be able to just mobilize the country again."[77]

Crucially, this support would be needed at an unknown, future date, so White House officials began to focus their attentions on the larger narrative around the war and the agreement, rather than in securing immediate approval for the specific terms. Echoing earlier efforts to isolate the antiwar movement, Haldeman reminded staffers that "the other point to make is the difference between a peace with honor and a bug-out."[78] In promoting the settlement by denigrating their opponents, White House officials hoped to appeal to the same loyalty and pride that had mobilized the silent majority in November 1969. Furthermore, by framing the final agreement in such black-and-white terms, spokesmen continued earlier efforts to isolate and marginalize the antiwar movement even when the apparent success of the president's Vietnam policies had the potential to reunite the nation around the new peace in Vietnam. Still, "very few Americans felt like celebrating the peace accord itself," and administration officials blamed the lack of public celebration on the "shocking attitude of the press on the Vietnam settlement."[79]

Although coverage was not universally positive, the media was not the main cause of administration difficulties in rallying support for the agreement. Rather the Nixon White House faced countless obstacles in their efforts to sell the peace, of which some were inevitable and others were self-inflicted.

First, the US public was heartily sick of the conflict and had been for years and was in no mood to rally behind anything to do with it. In April 1971, an aide noted that "the great majority of Americans want Vietnam to go away as quickly and quietly as possible. The sooner the better,"[80] and so it is not entirely surprising that many Americans took Nixon's announcement as a sign to return to normality. Second, the end of the Vietnam War meant more attention on the Watergate investigation, distracting both the public and White House officials who would otherwise have managed the public opinion campaign around the settlement. Third, Nixon had a number of ambitious plans for his second term, none of which included Vietnam. With White House officials focused on these new priorities, including diplomatic initiatives and an ambitious effort to reorganize the executive branch, there were few resources for Vietnam projects. Lastly, the nature of the agreement itself challenged White House efforts to frame it as a successful conclusion to the long conflict.

Throughout the negotiations, Nixon and Kissinger had repeatedly promised that the United States "would not agree to any terms that required or amounted to our overthrow of President Thieu" and "which resolved the issues once and for all" as "we had no wish to repeat the experience of all previous agreements that had been armistices in an endless war."[81] At the same time, neither was inclined to address the root causes of the war—the political differences between North and South—in negotiating the US departure. Kissinger explicitly told the North Vietnamese that the United States "sought a practical, not a theoretical, end to the war" and had advocated exactly that approach in a 1968 *Foreign Affairs* article. In his memoirs, though, Kissinger insisted that the US decision "to separate the military and political issues, to settle the military issues (cease-fire, prisoners, withdrawal) first, and to leave the political issues for negotiation between the Vietnamese" was not abandoning an ally, but rather, would give the South Vietnamese "the opportunity to flourish by their own efforts."[82]

The North Vietnamese, in Kissinger's account, were less optimistic and criticized the decision to separate the military and political aspects of the conflict, as reaching a political settlement was "a process which might take forever."[83] While neither side was entirely accurate in their stated expectations for a post-settlement Vietnam, the Vietnamese were closer to the reality. The months following the last US withdrawals were not ones in which the South Vietnamese "flourished," nor, in the end, did the final resolution take "forever." Rather, on 10 March 1975, a North Vietnamese offensive quickly moved south. President Gerald R. Ford, in office since Nixon's resignation the previous August, struggled in vain to convince Congress to authorize military and financial support for the South Vietnamese.

Unimpressed by Nixon's 1973 promises, representatives and senators echoed their constituents and refused to permit the United States to return to Vietnam. Without US support, the South Vietnamese failed to halt the Northern advance, and by 30 April 1974, North Vietnamese troops controlled Saigon, and the Americans along with many—but not all—of their South Vietnamese allies were gone. Just under thirty years after Ho Chi Minh declared Vietnamese independence, the country was united under Vietnamese rule.

Conclusion

Ultimately, the January 1973 agreement resulted in neither peace for the Vietnamese nor honor for the Americans but did remove the United States from the conflict. And, for many Americans, that was enough. Neither Nixon nor Johnson explained US involvement in terms of Vietnamese concerns, so it is not surprising that the decision to reach a military settlement separate from a political one bothered few Americans. Furthermore, that Nixon and Kissinger were able to leverage the Paris agreement and years of negotiation to build reputations as peacemakers is a testament to their careful construction of both the peace agreement and their definition of US goals for the conflict.

By focusing on the US role in the negotiations, they avoided many of the thornier political issues in Paris and eventually found common ground with the North Vietnamese. A similar divide and conquer mentality shaped their approach to domestic public opinion. Recognizing the importance of domestic public opinion in North Vietnamese calculations, both Nixon and Kissinger were keen to rally the nation behind the president. Both men knew that Nixon's threats to remain in Vietnam until a satisfactory agreement depended on the president finding a way to quiet dissent and create domestic political space for his Vietnam War policies. The creation and mobilization of the silent majority effectively accomplished both domestic and international goals.

With the 3 November 1969 appeal to the "great, silent majority," Nixon and his aides succeeded in rallying supporters to counter the very visible antiwar movement. The vocal support of this group at the end of 1969 strengthened Kissinger's position in his February 1970 meeting with the North Vietnamese whereby he insisted that Nixon would not face the same domestic constraints as had Lyndon Johnson. While Le Duc Tho and other North Vietnamese officials were not immediately convinced, the September 1970 defeat of the McGovern-Hatfield amendment demonstrated that the Congress would not legislate an end to the war. Congress's failure proved to be Nixon's gain, as it strengthened Kissinger's position in Paris—as did Nixon's success in the 1972 presidential campaign. Even before his election in November, the North Vietnamese anticipated his victory and initiated the most productive period in the negotiations.

Yet even as both Kissinger and the North Vietnamese pushed for an agreement before the election, Nixon gambled that he would be in an even stronger position after and was disinclined to make additional concessions. Nixon's landslide victory in November combined with intensive bombing at the end of 1972 contributed to the final January agreement.

Although one would expect an administration responsible for the success of the silent majority, the failure of the McGovern-Hatfield amendment, and Nixon's 1972 landslide to be well positioned to promote a peace agreement, the administration struggled to mobilize support behind the Paris Peace Accords.

This failure was in part due to a misunderstanding about the nature of the silent majority's support. While appeals to patriotism, loyalty, and pride enabled Nixon to credibly threaten the North Vietnamese and even to escalate the war, these appeals were not designed to create lasting support for South Vietnam. Once US troops left and the POWs returned home, few Americans were inclined to give Vietnam their attention, much less sacrifice more American lives. Nixon's previous success in rallying his supporters had convinced him that he could do so at will, but he underestimated the ways that Watergate would damage both his own influence as well as the symbolic role of the presidency. Furthermore, a critical misunderstanding of the nature of his silent majority support led Nixon to believe that, if necessary, he could rally support for an escalation—or even a return of US troops to Vietnam.

Nixon failed to appreciate that their support was rooted in patriotism and national pride rather than in any loyalty to South Vietnam or even belief in the stated reasons for US involvement. Thus, it is unlikely that even Nixon would have been able to fulfill his promises to Thieu in April 1974, but the bitter legacy of Watergate and the domestic debates over Vietnam ensured that it was impossible for Ford. Therefore, instead of "peace with honor," the lasting memory of the end of US involvement in Vietnam was the image of helicopters evacuating US officials and collaborators as North Vietnamese troops marched into Saigon.

Sarah Thelen lectures in US history at University College Cork, Ireland and has published a number of articles on the silent majority and other aspects of the domestic debates over the war in Vietnam. She holds a PhD from American University in Washington, DC and is writing a monograph on White House efforts to rally support for the US war in Vietnam. Her research also explores the changing nature of patriotism, nationalism, and American identity in the twentieth century.

Notes

1. Max Frankel, "Nixon Is Forced to 'Negotiate' on Three Fronts," *New York Times*, 23 March 1969. See also Gregory A. Daddis, *Withdrawal: Reassessing America's Final Years in Vietnam* (New York: Oxford University Press, 2017).
2. Richard Nixon, "Address to the Nation Announcing Conclusion of an Agreement on Ending the War and Restoring Peace in Vietnam," 23 January 1973, online by Gerhard Peters and John T. Woolley, the American Presidency Project, https://www.presidency.ucsb.edu/documents/address-the-nation-announcing-conclusion-agreement-ending-the-war-and-restoring-peace, accessed 15 December 2018.
3. The literature on both the Vietnam War and the antiwar movement is vast, but for a good overview of the Vietnam War antiwar movement, see Charles DeBenedetti, *An American Ordeal: The Antiwar Movement of the Vietnam Era* (Syracuse: Syracuse University Press, 1990); Melvin Small, *Johnson, Nixon, and the Doves* (New Brunswick: Rutgers University Press, 1988); Tom Wells, *The War within: America's Battle over Vietnam* (Berkeley: University of California Press, 1994).
4. Richard M. Nixon, *RN: The Memoirs of Richard Nixon* (London: Sidgwick and Jackson, 1978), 347, 349.
5. Daddis, *Withdrawal*, 51.
6. Undersecretary of the Air Force Townsend Hoopes to Secretary of Defense McNamara (14 March 1968) as quoted in Daddis, *Withdrawal*, 24–25.
7. Henry Kissinger, *White House Years* (Boston: Little, Brown, 1979), 1041.
8. Ibid., 1041.
9. Ibid., 1170.
10. Wells, *War Within*, 330.
11. "Charles West to Alex Butterfield," 15 October 1969, Memoranda Received Oct thru Dec 1969; Box 8; WHSF: SMOF Butterfield, NPLM, College Park, MD.
12. "Game Plan for the President's November 3rd Speech on Vietnam, Master Copy," n.d., 13, Silent Majority; Box 1; WHCF: SMOF Butterfield, NPLM, College Park, MD.
13. Sarah Thelen, "Helping Them Along: Astroturf, Public Opinion, and Nixon's Vietnam War," *49th Parallel*, no. 37 (2015); Sarah Thelen, "Mobilizing a Majority: Nixon's 'Silent Majority' Speech and the Domestic Debate over Vietnam," *Journal of American Studies* 51, no. 3 (2017): 887–914, https://doi.org/10.1017/S0021875816001936.
14. "Larry Doyle to Richard Nixon," 4 November 1969, 2, Alex Butterfield (Nov 1969); Box 1; WHSF: SMOF Butterfield, NPLM, College Park, MD.
15. Sandra Scanlon, *The Pro-War Movement: Domestic Support for the Vietnam War and the Making of Modern American Conservatism* (Amherst: University of Massachusetts Press, 2013), 190–96.
16. "Game Plan for the President's November 3rd Speech on Vietnam, Master Copy," 10. Underlining in original.
17. "Love It or … Leave It," *Newsweek*, 24 November 1969, Silent Majority; Box 1; WHCF: SMOF Butterfield, NPLM, College Park, MD.
18. Kissinger quoted by Nixon in Nixon, *RN*, 446.
19. Kissinger, *White House Years*, 444.
20. Ibid.
21. Ibid.
22. Ibid.
23. "Charles Colson to H. R. Haldeman," 24 July 1970, HRH-July-August 1970—Staff Memos—Cole-D; Box 61; WHSF: SMOF Haldeman, NPLM, College Park, MD.
24. "Gene Bradley to Charles Colson," 11 August 1970, Americans for Winning the Peace [4 of 7]; Box 36; WHSF: SMOF Colson, NPLM, College Park, MD; "Prominent New Yorkers Take Full-Page Ad in *New York Times* in Support of President's Vietnam

Policies," 28 August 1970, Americans for Winning the Peace [1 of 7]; Box 36; WHSF: SMOF Colson, NPLM, College Park, MD.
25. "Charles Colson to H. R. Haldeman," 10 December 1970, Americans for Winning the Peace [2 of 7]; Box 36; WHSF: SMOF Colson, NPLM, College Park, MD.
26. "Questions RE Americans for Winning the Peace," n.d., Americans for Winning the Peace [3 of 7]; Box 36; WHSF: SMOF Colson, NPLM, College Park, MD.
27. "Fact Sheet—Americans for Winning the Peace," 31 July 1970, Vietnam—Various Groups [1]-Americans for Winning the Peace; Box 123; WHSF: SMOF Colson, NPLM, College Park, MD.
28. "Gene Bradley to Peter White," 18 August 1970, Americans for Winning the Peace [4 of 7]; Box 36; WHSF: SMOF Colson, NPLM, College Park, MD.
29. "Gene Bradley to Charles Colson," 11 August 1970; "Abbott Washburn to Gene Bradley," 31 August 1970, Americans for Winning the Peace [5 of 7]; Box 36; WHSF: SMOF Colson, NPLM, College Park, MD; "Comments by Walt Rostow," 3 August 1970, Americans for Winning the Peace [4 of 7]; Box 36; WHSF: SMOF Colson, NPLM, College Park, MD; "Gene Bradley to Tom Evans," 31 July 1970, Vietnam—Various Groups [1]-Americans for Winning the Peace; Box 123; WHSF: SMOF Colson, NPLM, College Park, MD; "Charles Colson to Dwight Chapin," 27 November 1970, Americans for Winning the Peace [3 of 7]; Box 36; WHSF: SMOF Colson, NPLM, College Park, MD; "Gene Bradley to Charles Colson [1]," 20 August 1970, Americans for Winning the Peace [4 of 7]; Box 36; WHSF: SMOF Colson, NPLM, College Park, MD.
30. "Gene Bradley to AWP Chairmen and Representatives," 10 August 1970, HRH-July-August 1970—Staff Memos—Cole-D; Box 61; WHSF: SMOF Haldeman, NPLM, College Park, MD.
31. "Charles Colson to H. R. Haldeman," 12 August 1970, HRH-July-August 1970—Staff Memos—Cole-D; Box 61; WHSF: SMOF Haldeman, NPLM, College Park, MD.
32. "Gene Bradley to Tom Evans"; "Gene Bradley to George Bell, Frank Barnett, Charles Colson, Senator Robert J. Dole, Roscoe Drummond, Morris Leibman, Mary P. Lord, John O. Marsh, Dan McMichael, and Abbot Washburn," 20 August 1970, HRH-July-August 1970—Staff Memos—Cole-D; Box 61; WHSF: SMOF Haldeman, NPLM, College Park, MD; "Telephone Call Recommendation from George Bell," 19 August 1970, Telephone Call Requests [2 of 2]; Box 116; WHSF: SMOF Colson, NPLM, College Park, MD; "Charles Colson to Larry Higby," 8 September 1970, Americans for Winning the Peace [5 of 7]; Box 36; WHSF: SMOF Colson, NPLM, College Park, MD; "Joseph Hall to Gene Bradley," 26 August 1970, Americans for Winning the Peace [5 of 7]; Box 36; WHSF: SMOF Colson, NPLM, College Park, MD.
33. Ft. Lauderdale, Broward Co. Committee of Americans for Winning the Peace, "Advertisement," *Fort Lauderdale News and Sentinel*, 30 August 1970, Americans for Winning the Peace [5 of 7]; Box 36; WHSF: SMOF Colson, NPLM, College Park, MD; "Prominent New Yorkers Take Full-Page Ad"; "Joseph Hall to Gene Bradley."
34. Ft. Lauderdale, Broward Co. Committee of Americans for Winning the Peace, "Advertisement"; "Gene Bradley to Charles Colson," 27 August 1970, Americans for Winning the Peace [5 of 7]; Box 36; WHSF: SMOF Colson, NPLM, College Park, MD.
35. "Prominent New Yorkers Take Full-Page."
36. Kissinger, *White House Years*, 970.
37. Ibid.
38. Ibid.
39. Ibid., 971.
40. "Charles Colson to H. R. Haldeman," 18 February 1971, 3, Lam Son / Laos; Box 77; WHSF: SMOF Colson, NPLM, College Park, MD.
41. "Charles Colson to H. R. Haldeman," 7 August 1972, 1, Political Strategy 1972; Box 99; WHSF: SMOF Colson, NPLM, College Park, MD.

42. William Safire, *Before the Fall: An Inside View of the Pre-Watergate White House* (Garden City: Doubleday, 2005), 341. Robert Mason provides a nuanced overview of administration efforts to appeal to the many constituencies that made up this pro-Nixon majority in Robert Mason, *Richard Nixon and the Quest for a New Majority* (Chapel Hill: University of North Carolina Press, 2004), 113–60.
43. "Doug Hallett to Charles Colson," 19 April 1972, 1, Presidential Meetings and Conversations [4/1/72–4/28/72]; Box 17; WHSF: SMOF Colson, NPLM, College Park, MD.
44. "Richard Nixon to Henry Kissinger," 30 April 1972, 1, P Memos 1972 II; Box 230; WHSF: SMOF Haldeman, NPLM, College Park, MD. For these negotiations, see Robert Dallek, *Nixon and Kissinger: Partners in Power* (London: Allen Lane, 2007), 373–80; Jeffrey P. Kimball, *Nixon's Vietnam War* (Lawrence: University Press of Kansas, 1998), 305–11; Henry Kissinger, *Ending the Vietnam War: A History of America's Involvement in and Extrication from the Vietnam War* (New York: Simon & Schuster, 2003), 256–68; Nixon, *RN*, 587–88, 591–92, 599–608.
45. Echoing Dallek's conclusions about the 1972 presidential election guiding Nixon and Kissinger's response to the North Vietnamese invasion, Jeffrey Kimball concludes that this escalation, "was aimed less at stopping the invasion and more at pleasing his constituents, frightening the North Vietnamese and Soviets, influencing the negotiations, and diminishing Hanoi's future war-fighting capability in the struggle that lay ahead for the South Vietnamese." Nixon and Kissinger, of course, insist that they had no alternative. Dallek, *Nixon and Kissinger*, 384–88; Kimball, *Nixon's Vietnam War*, 311–16; Kissinger, *Ending the Vietnam War*, 268–88; Nixon, *RN*, 604-8.
46. Richard Nixon, "Address to the Nation on the Situation in Southeast Asia," 8 May 1972, online by Gerhard Peters and John T. Woolley, The American Presidency Project. http://www.presidency.ucsb.edu/ws/?pid=3404.
47. Nixon, "Address to the Nation on the Situation in Southeast Asia."
48. "Richard Nixon to H.R. Haldeman," 7 May 1972, 2, P Memos 1972 II; Box 230; WHSF: SMOF Haldeman, NPLM, College Park, MD.
49. Ibid.
50. Ibid.
51. Ibid., 2–3.
52. "Larry Higby to Charles Colson," 9 May 1972, 3, Charles Colson May 1972; Box 96; WHSF: SMOF Haldeman, NPLM, College Park, MD. The Higby memorandum included a list of postspeech suggestions from Colson annotated by Haldeman including "Right" next to the quoted suggestion.
53. "Richard Nixon the Henry Kissinger," 9 May 1972, 3, P Memos 1972 II; Box 230; WHSF: SMOF Haldeman, NPLM, College Park, MD. Of the 5,827 telegrams recorded by the White House staff as of 5:00pm on 9 May 1972, 4,390 supported the President's actions while 1,390 opposed with 16,000 telegrams not yet processed. "Bruce Kehrli to Charles Colson," 9 May 1972, Vietnam Speech Western Union Situation [4 of 4]; Box 122; WHSF: SMOF Colson, NPLM, College Park, MD.
54. "ABC News Poll," n.d., Vietnam Speech 5/8/72 [3 of 4]; Box 122; WHSF: SMOF Colson, NPLM, College Park, MD; "Public Opinion Strongly Behind President Nixon on Vietnam," n.d., Vietnam Speech 8 May 1972 [3 of 4]; Box 122; WHSF: SMOF Colson, NPLM, College Park, MD; "Charles Colson, Conversation with Lou Harris," 11 May 1972, Presidential Meetings and Conversations [1 May 1972–31 May 1972]; Box 17; WHSF: SMOF Colson, NPLM, College Park, MD; "Roland Elliott to Charles Colson, John Ehrlichman, H.R. Haldeman, Herb Klein, Clark MacGregor, Richard Moore, Ray Price, Ron Ziegler," 1 June 1972, Presidential Meetings and Conversations [1 June 1972–10 June 1972]; Box 17; WHSF: SMOF Colson, NPLM, College Park, MD.
55. Small, *Johnson, Nixon, and the Doves*, 221–22.

56. Nixon, *RN*, 606.
57. Nixon, "Address to the Nation on the Situation in Southeast Asia."
58. Nixon, *RN*, 689.
59. Ibid.
60. Ibid.
61. Ibid.
62. Kissinger, *White House Years*, 1317.
63. Nixon, *RN*, 701.
64. Ibid.
65. Ibid., 692.
66. Ibid., 694.
67. Ibid., 695.
68. Ibid., 696.
69. Ibid., 705.
70. Ibid.
71. Richard M. Nixon, "Address to the Nation: 'Look to the Future.,'" Online by Gerhard Peters and John T. Woolley, The American Presidency Project., 2 November 1972, Online by Gerhard Peters and John T. Woolley, The American Presidency Project, https://www.presidency.ucsb.edu/documents/address-the-nation-look-the-future, accessed 15 December 2018.
72. Nixon, *RN*, 707. In contrast to Nixon's assessment, historians such as Jeffrey Kimball and Larry Berman argue that the bombings were unnecessary. See: Larry Berman, *No Peace, No Honor: Nixon, Kissinger, and Betrayal in Vietnam* (New York: Free Press, 2001); Kimball, *Nixon's Vietnam War*.
73. Nixon, *RN*, 726.
74. "Action Memo, H. R. Haldeman [3]," 19 January 1973, Action Memos 1/73; Box 179; WHSF: SMOF Haldeman, NPLM, College Park, MD.
75. "Bill Baroody to H. R. Haldeman," 26 January 1973, 1, Vietnam; Box 178; WHSF: SMOF Haldeman, NPLM, College Park, MD.
76. "PR Memorandum, H. R. Haldeman," 30 January 1973, 2, Action Memos 1/73; Box 179; WHSF: SMOF Haldeman, NPLM, College Park, MD.
77. Ibid., 3.
78. Ibid.
79. DeBenedetti, *An American Ordeal*, 349; "Action Memo, H. R. Haldeman," 30 January 1973, Action Memos 2/73; Box 179; WHSF: SMOF Haldeman, NPLM, College Park, MD.
80. "Andre LeTendre to Charles Colson," 13 April 1971, 3, Bell April 1971; Box 76; WHSF: SMOF Haldeman, NPLM, College Park, MD.
81. Nixon, *RN*, 348; Kissinger, *White House Years*, 443.
82. Kissinger, *White House Years*, 1328.
83. Ibid.

Select Bibliography

Berman, Larry, *No Peace, No Honor: Nixon, Kissinger, and Betrayal in Vietnam* (New York: Free Press, 2001).
Daddis, Gregory A., *Withdrawal: Reassessing America's Final Years in Vietnam* (New York: Oxford University Press, 2017).
Dallek, Robert, *Nixon and Kissinger: Partners in Power* (London: Allen Lane, 2007).

DeBenedetti, Charles, *An American Ordeal: The Antiwar Movement of the Vietnam Era* (Syracuse, NY: Syracuse University Press, 1990).

Kimball, Jeffrey P., *Nixon's Vietnam War* (Lawrence: University Press of Kansas, 1998).

Kissinger, Henry A., *Ending the Vietnam War: A History of America's Involvement in and Extrication from the Vietnam War* (New York: Simon & Schuster, 2003).

―――, *White House Years* (Boston, MA: Little, Brown, 1979).

Mason, Robert, *Richard Nixon and the Quest for a New Majority* (Chapel Hill: University of North Carolina Press, 2004).

Nixon, Richard M., *RN: The Memoirs of Richard Nixon* (London: Sidgwick and Jackson, 1978).

Safire, William, *Before the Fall: An Inside View of the Pre-Watergate White House* (Garden City, NY: Doubleday, 2005).

Scanlon, Sandra, *The Pro-War Movement: Domestic Support for the Vietnam War and the Making of Modern American Conservatism* (Amherst: University of Massachusetts Press, 2013).

Small, Melvin, *Johnson, Nixon, and the Doves* (New Brunswick: Rutgers University Press, 1988).

Thelen, Sarah, "Helping Them Along: Astroturf, Public Opinion, and Nixon's Vietnam War," *49th Parallel*, no. 37 (2015).

―――, "Mobilizing a Majority: Nixon's 'Silent Majority' Speech and the Domestic Debate over Vietnam," *Journal of American Studies* 51, no. 3 (2017).

Wells, Tom, *The War within: America's Battle over Vietnam* (Berkeley: University of California Press, 1994).

Chapter 2

The Things They Carry
Vietnam and the Legacies of the American War

Edwin A. Martini

In 1976, less than a year after the fall or liberation of Saigon that ended the Second Indochina War, a United Nations mission visited Vietnam and detailed firsthand the ruins in which much of the nation, and region, found itself, the result of what the report called "a savage war of destruction."[1] It detailed the utter devastation of Vietnam's industrial infrastructure, agricultural base, and transportation system; and it spoke of the large loss of life experienced by the Vietnamese and how that loss would affect the nation's ability to rebuild.

When this report was included in a staff report for the US Senate judiciary committee in 1976, Committee Chair Edward Kennedy noted how stark the situation was in Southeast Asia and how the United States was finally positioned to help, rather than harm, the people of that region: "Having contributed so heavily to the years of war, our country must not fail now to pursue policies and programs that will contribute to the peace."[2] But far from pursuing peace and reconciliation in the years immediately following the end of the US War in Vietnam, the US government began to pursue "war by other means," reclassifying the newly reunited nation of Vietnam as an "enemy" and pursuing openly hostile and unprecedented economic and diplomatic policies against the Vietnamese.

Although free from foreign occupation for the first time in over a century, Vietnam remained surrounded by hostile regimes and faced the difficult task of rebuilding a devastated nation that was deeply divided after thirty years of sustained warfare. The task of national reconstruction would have proven daunting enough under any circumstances; it would have been long and arduous even with the billions of dollars in US aid that had been promised as part of the 1973 peace accords; it would have been a financially imposing project even with the full and unfettered access to sources of international economic and humanitarian aid to which the Vietnamese were not only entitled but in dire need of as well. But as the Vietnamese were quickly learning in the years immediately following the US withdrawal, one of the few things worse than *fighting* a war against the United States is *winning* a war against the United States. In contrast to Germany and Japan, for example, which after World War II received billions in direct US support, Vietnam found itself quickly cut off from American-controlled sources of economic assistance, humanitarian aid, and development loans.

As this volume considers how the United States has ended wars, what is particularly striking about the case of the US War in Vietnam is the degree to which this war has not actually ended. Other chapters in this collection make clear that the battle over the war in US culture, focusing in particular on what the war did to US soldiers and US culture, continues decades after the war formally ended. As veteran and writer Tim O'Brien wrote in *The Things They Carried*, US veterans carried many things during and after the war. In addition to the burdens of violence, trauma, and memory, they carried "the land itself—Vietnam, the place, the soil—a powdery orange-red dust that covered their boots and fatigues and faces. They carried the sky. The whole atmosphere, they carried it, the humidity, the monsoons, the stink of fungus and decay, all of it, they carried gravity."[3] US veterans indeed carried a great deal during and after the war. But what about the land, the place, the soil, and the people they left behind after the war was over? What did they carry in the wake of US destruction, and what do they carry to this day?

This chapter focuses on what the US war left behind for the Vietnamese: a deeply divided country faced with a difficult economic and political reconstruction; a massive regional humanitarian refugee crisis exacerbated by yet another war; and, perhaps most infamously, the long-term devastation of human and environmental health caused by dioxin contamination from Agent Orange and other herbicides. Taking on any of these challenges would have proven difficult for a newly liberated nation, but in each case, the Vietnamese government and people faced the additional challenge that the United States did not simply leave them behind to carry these burdens. Instead, it continued to resist the Vietnamese movement toward sovereignty and independence, repeatedly thwarting efforts at reconciliation and cleaning up the myriad messes left behind by the United States and its allies.

Had the United States simply abandoned the nation altogether, rejecting calls for reparations, aid, and trade, the rebuilding of Vietnam may still have failed. The United States, however, instead maintained an aggressively hostile policy, under which the nation and people of Vietnam would continue to suffer. Before the guns had even gone silent in Saigon, policymakers in the United States had initiated a series of punitive policies against Vietnam that would define the course of relations between the two nations for the next two decades. As the Vietnamese war for national independence trudged on in the spring of 1975, a new phase of the US war against Vietnam began.

A Continuation of War by Other Means

15.35 million tons of bombs.
2.5 million occupying troops.
2 million hectares of forests defoliated or destroyed.
80 million liters of chemical agents deployed.
300,000 missing in action.
14 million wounded.
More than 3,000,000 dead.[4]

For many of the statistics of the US War in Vietnam listed above, a comparison or equivalency with the United States is not even possible. The Vietnamese did not, of course, occupy, bomb, defoliate, or wage chemical warfare on the United States at any time. Yet even for those for which a comparison is possible, the numbers clearly suggest who the victims in the war were and who the aggressors were. For example, the United States at the end of the war had only a few thousand servicemen unaccounted for, whereas Vietnam had 300,000 Vietnamese unaccounted for. The United States lost close to 60,000 personnel in the war, which, while tragic, stands in stark contrast to several *million* Vietnamese, Cambodians, and Laotians.

The Environmental Conference on Cambodia, Laos, and Vietnam, in a 2003 report titled "Long Term Consequences of the Vietnam War," attempted to quantify what a similar scale of destruction would have looked like for Americans, and the numbers are nearly impossible to comprehend. If the United States had experienced consequences equivalent to those wrought on the nations of Southeast Asia, the report shows, the figures would be as follows:

Bombs Dropped:	430 million tons
Occupying Troops:	12.5 million
Hectares Defoliated or Destroyed:	56 million
Chemical Agents Deployed:	2.24 trillion liters
Wounded:	70 million
Dead:	17,500,000[5]

Even these numbers, however, do not do justice to the scale of destruction to which they refer.

More importantly, however, the numbers do not indicate some of the most devastating aspects of the US War on Vietnam: the terrible legacies of the war that continued to harm the Vietnamese after the departure of the United States. For instance, 3.5 million land mines remained in the ground in Vietnam after 1975. Twenty-three million bomb craters littered the country's landscape. Since 1975, landmines and unexploded ordnance have killed more than 40,000 people throughout the Vietnamese countryside and have injured perhaps another 100,000.[6] Most significantly, however, the deadly chemicals dumped on the region remained in the ground, contaminating the water, the food supply, and thus future generations of Vietnamese children.[7]

While these and other horrible environmental legacies of the US War in Vietnam could not have been known to Americans in the immediate postwar era, the figures from the military war itself certainly were. There was little doubt about the devastation left behind by the United States. And yet, in the wake of the war, the United States chose not to move toward healing and reconciliation, but instead chose to continue war by other means against Vietnam, beginning with the imposition of a draconian set of economic sanctions. This general mindset would continue, mostly unabated, for the next twenty-five years. Although the discourse of "healing" the wounds of war would gradually take hold in the United States, the actual motivations for a gradual easing of the sanctions are less clear.

What came to be known commonly as the United States' "embargo" on Vietnam consisted of several measures put in place by the Ford administration during the final days and immediate aftermath of the war. In April 1975, the administration ordered that the Commerce Department freeze an estimated $70 million in South Vietnamese assets held by American-owned banks and their foreign subsidiaries.[8] A few weeks later, on 14 May the State Department recommended to the secretary of commerce that South Vietnam and Cambodia be placed in the most restricted category of export controls, under which even private US citizens were forbidden to send people in those countries any humanitarian aid. Within the year, the United States would be enlarging its sanctions program, denying the Vietnamese international aid, access to international capital, and membership in the United Nations. In more than one way, the US War on Vietnam continued; only the weaponry had changed.

As Robert Miller, assistant secretary of state for East Asian and Pacific Affairs, told Congress on 4 June 1975, the export controls, which had been placed on "the Communist-controlled areas of Vietnam" in 1958, were extended to South Vietnam because they "further[ed] significantly the foreign policy of the United States" and that such controls can be authorized by the president "for national security reasons."[9]

When originally put in place, "Communist-controlled Vietnam" was placed in Category Z of export controls, a category normally reserved for nations with which the United States was at war. North Korea and Cuba were the only other nations included in Category Z at the time. Under this distinction, even private shipments of humanitarian aid to those countries were subject to licenses granted by the federal government. Rarely, if ever, were such licenses granted. Category Y, a slightly less hostile category used to identify nations to which the United States sought to deny "strategically important goods," was at the time applicable to the Soviet Union and China, among others. Under that category, military aid and other supplies deemed strategic were subject to the same licensing procedures, but humanitarian aid was not. Ironically, this policy placed greater restrictions on aid than had been in place during the war. Over the next two decades, the US embargo would contribute significantly to the inability of the Vietnamese economy to grow, diversify, and integrate with regional and global markets.

The embargo was but one piece of the initial phase of the US War on Vietnam. While the export controls remained in place, the United States further demonstrated its ongoing obstinacy with regard to Vietnam in the international arena, first at the United Nations as the Vietnamese applied for membership and then with several international financial organizations, as they sought critical development funds. On 6 August 1975, the United Nations Security Council denied a hearing for South Korea's application for membership. Although the South Koreans had been repeatedly denied admission since their first application in 1949, the decision not even to hold a hearing on the matter was somewhat unusual. The standard UN position had been that divided nations, such as Korea, Germany, and Vietnam between 1954 and 1975 would not be admitted unless both parties agreed on entrance. East and West Germany were not admitted until 1973, when they signed a mutual recognition treaty.[10]

North Korea's continued intransigence on joining the United Nations effectively rendered void their southern counterparts' request. As it turned out, however, the refusal of the Security Council to consider the

Korean question provided the Ford administration the fodder it desired to take the unprecedented step of vetoing the two Vietnamese applications.

The Vietnamese applications provided an unusual case in their own right. At the time of the applications, the Democratic Republic of Vietnam (DRV; commonly known as "North Vietnam") remained clearly in control of the Republic of Vietnam (RVN; commonly known as "South Vietnam"), and there was little doubt in Southeast Asia, the United States, or the rest of the world that the two would soon be reunified. As the *Economist* opined at the time, "There are now about one and a half Vietnams," united politically and militarily and separate primarily only in economic planning. Given that the DRV had taken over the RVN by force, regardless of the politics involved, the dual applications from "two governments, one of which has just helped overthrow the other's predecessor in a war fought to decide, among other things, whether their countries should be two or one," certainly constituted a unique situation.[11] The United States, though, was not interested in a debate on the subtleties of UN procedure, as the White House quickly made up its mind to reassert its power over the process.

Even taking into consideration the unusual nature of the Vietnamese applications, the clear international consensus was to allow the admission of both states under the assumption that reunification was little more than a formality. Although it has become increasingly common since the end of the war in Vietnam for the United States to be on the short end of near unanimous UN votes, at the time it was a major departure.[12] While US ambassador to the United Nations Daniel Patrick Moynihan's comments in the Security Council justified the vetoes on the grounds that the simultaneous denial of the South Korean application constituted a procedural misstep, it seems clear that the administration's motivations were far less idealistic. President Gerald Ford and Secretary of State Henry Kissinger could easily have instructed Moynihan to abstain from the votes, voicing displeasure at the process without making such a radical shift in policy. By noisily, publicly, and solitarily denying Vietnamese membership in the UN, the Ford White House echoed its actions after the fall of Saigon, enacting unnecessary measures that only made the nation appear more like a "petty and frustrated tyrant."[13]

This view was borne out a year later, when the recently reunified and renamed Socialist Republic of Vietnam applied for United Nations membership and was promptly greeted with an announcement by the Ford administration that it would once again veto the application in the Security Council. Although understandably frustrated, the French persuaded the Vietnamese to wait to apply until after the upcoming US elections.[14] Public statements by Hanoi, echoed by many in the international press, suggested that the continued obstinacy of the United States was based more on the personal pettiness of Kissinger than anything else. These feelings were seemingly confirmed yet again when, after the 1976 presidential elections, the United States cast the lone vote against Vietnam's application. Yet again the General Assembly responded with an adamant message to the Security Council to reconsider, and yet again the United States used its veto power to deny the application, leaving Vietnam to wait until 1977, after the election of Jimmy Carter and, perhaps more importantly, the departure of Henry Kissinger, to be formally admitted to the UN.

Throughout this period, anti-Vietnamese sentiment continued to harden in the US Congress, as efforts at diplomatic and economic normalization waned. Given the sentiments of lawmakers and the relative indifference of the US public, direct bilateral aid from the United States to Vietnam was out of the question, buried under layer upon layer of prohibitive legislation, but that did little to ease the most vehement opposition to economic assistance. Many in Congress, identifying what they considered a possible loophole, moved to prohibit US funds from reaching Vietnam through international aid agencies or International Financial Institutions (IFIs). As numerous congressional investigations had made plain, even without direct assistance from the United States, Vietnam could still become the indirect recipient of US dollars funneled through these organizations. Although Congress had refused to seize many opportunities to reclaim the economic tools of foreign policy, many in the Capitol were determined to exercise control over the direction of foreign aid, particularly to IFIs.

In September 1976, the Socialist Republic of Vietnam assumed the place of the former South Vietnamese regime in the Asian Development Bank, World Bank, and International Monetary Fund. This was a very significant development for a number of reasons. Symbolically, it further legitimized the newly reunified nation and further demonstrated Vietnam's desire for independence and sovereignty. At the time, neither the Soviet Union nor China had agreed to participate in the institutions because they were unwilling to divulge all the economic data required by member nations. Vietnam's willingness to participate in the process confirmed both its independence from those nations and its need for international aid.

The Vietnamese would soon come to realize that the Bretton Woods institutions were not democratic, nor did they offer a particularly healthy path for developing nations. Despite their charters, these institutions were subject to the will of the United States, the largest contributor to the IFIs. The 1976 *Final Report of the Select Committee on Missing Persons in Southeast Asia* noted that through these agencies and the United Nations, the Vietnamese would be receiving around $34 million in indirect United States aid in 1977 as well as $24 million in low-interest loans and $10 million in grants. The Select Committee recommended that the administration not "lose sight of these indirect contributions to Vietnamese humanitarian projects."[15]

As Vietnamese diplomats negotiated toward possible normalization of relations with the Carter administration throughout 1977, access to some form of international aid and trade became a major sticking point, as it became increasingly clear that Congress would indeed not allow the Carter White House or the Vietnamese to lose sight of the contributions. Throughout the summer, Congress tacked on a number of amendments to foreign aid bills that put increasingly tight restrictions on US contributions to the IFIs and that to that point were unprecedented in US foreign economic policy.

While Congress looked for any possible excuse to block US aid or trade from reaching Vietnam, the Vietnamese were simply looking for an opening. Willing to compromise on many points, the Vietnamese rightly rejected any announcement of potential normalization that was not accompanied by some promise of US aid, which had been promised as part of the 1973 Paris Accords that ostensibly ended the US War in Vietnam. As Vietnamese diplomat Phan Hien replied when pressed to announce a tentative agreement on normalization, simply "No. Without aid it is impossible."[16] There is little, if any, evidence in any of the debates over normalization in the late 1970s that US policymakers could empathize with the devastation the war left behind in Vietnam. They bickered over inconsequential issues like IFI contributions instead of substantive reconciliation because the United States was a traumatized, but still safe, wealthy nation; the Vietnamese were attempting to rebuild after three million had died and a nation had been destroyed from thirty years of warfare that still refused to end.

The prospects for normalization, which had been plausible only a few months earlier, were now greatly diminished. As political scientist Steven Hurst describes it, the failures of normalization in 1977 should be chalked up to both Hanoi and Washington. Without question, the Vietnamese underestimated the level of aversion toward Hanoi felt by many in Congress and, given their need for US aid, could have played their hand much better in the face of such congressional animosity. Nevertheless, the ultimate responsibility for failure must be placed with the United States. The Vietnamese, despite their initial obstinacy on the matter of reparations, continually demonstrated their flexibility in achieving some form of aid that would be acceptable to the United States. Earlier, in spring of 1977, the same type of amendments restricting aid through IFIs had been defeated in Congress, and the Vietnamese had indicated their willingness to receive aid through those institutions. But, as Hurst argues, an "opportunity was missed," because of the Carter administration's "overconfidence and unwillingness to provide Vietnam with aid."[17]

By way of contrast, consider the actions of France and Japan, both of which had also occupied and fought brutal wars against Vietnam just decades earlier. In 1973, France began to provide aid to Vietnam through both loans and grants, with an initial $20 million (in US dollars) as a "contribution to the reconstruction and development of the country." Over the next five years, France would make another $350 million available.[18] After Japan and Vietnam normalized relations in 1975, Japan made an immediate contribution of $40 million in direct foreign aid to Vietnam, acknowledged by both sides as reparations for the brutal Japanese occupation during World War II.[19] Yet France and Japan, although central to Vietnam's economy as investors and trading partners, did not hold the keys to the global economy; they could not singlehandedly proscribe international aid or IFI funds from reaching Vietnam. The Vietnamese, and the rest of the world, were well aware that in their search for international aid no nation was more important than the United States. Thus, international aid from the United States would have to wait for the roadmap to normalization that began in earnest under the George H.W. Bush administration in the early 1990s.

Despite winning their decades-long war for independence, the Vietnamese were learning that the world had changed a great deal since their declaration of independence from the French thirty years earlier. Although finally a sovereign nation, with a new constitution and (eventually) a seat in the United Nations, the leaders in Hanoi were learning that independence in the late 1970s had more to do with their position in the regional and global economy than with their political hegemony in Indochina. Vietnam had cast off the yoke of several colonizing powers, at an unimaginable cost. They were much less prepared, and would be much less successful, in their battle against the neocolonial global economic order.

Humanitarian Crises and Yet Another Continuation of War

By 1978, the Vietnamese economy was in tatters. As historian Mark Bradley writes, "The war-ravaged Vietnamese economy suffered from low agricultural and industrial output, high unemployment, and, in the south, rampant inflation."[20] The newly reintegrated state took over major sectors of the economy, particularly agriculture, resulting in or worsening existing dislocations of the population throughout the countryside. While clearly constrained by the embargo, misguided economic policies from Hanoi had a particularly devastating impact on rural Vietnamese and ethnic Chinese, millions of whom began to flee the country as refugees, popularly labeled "boat people."[21]

At the same time, tensions between Vietnam and its neighbors to the west and south were also reaching a crisis point. Similar to its twenty-first century wars in the Middle East, the US war in Vietnam was part of a larger regional conflict, before, during, and after US intervention. In the same way that US policymakers, analysts, and leaders—blinded by a misguided and ill-defined "global war on terror"—all but ignored the long-standing Sunni-Shia rifts in countries such as Iraq and Syria, those same groups in the early Cold War—blinded by a misguided belief in the threat of "monolithic communism"—demonstrated a staggering lack of knowledge about the long-standing historical tensions between nations and ethnic groups throughout Southeast Asia. Failure to recognize and learn from, let alone leverage, these tensions caused the United States to falter strategically in these wars. After the US withdrawal from Southeast Asia in the mid-1970s, those long-simmering historical tensions once again rose to the surface in what would eventually become known as the Third Indochina War, involving Vietnam, Cambodia, China, and, as a proxy in its ongoing war against Vietnam, the United States.

The suppression of long-standing national disputes and coalescing of Asian communist and nationalist factions that had been engendered by the US war in Vietnam was quickly erased when the Americans left. The revolutionary forces of Vietnam and the Khmer Rouge of Cambodia, both of which had been supported by the Chinese during the wars to liberate their countries from American-backed regimes, had exchanged messages of congratulations for their victories in April of 1975. Less than a month later, the two nations were battling over disputed territories in the Gulf of Thailand. By the end of 1976, the Khmer Rouge had become *the* major threat to the stability of Southeast Asia, having aggravated tensions with Thailand and Vietnam and, unbeknownst to most of the world at the time, having slaughtered millions of its own people.[22]

What began as a series of territorial disputes and border skirmishes escalated into a full-fledged war when on Christmas Day, 1978, 150,000 Vietnamese troops invaded Cambodia. Before the end of January 1979, the Vietnamese were in control of the capital, Phnom Penh, beginning what would turn into a decade-long occupation. Vietnamese tensions with China also rose to the boiling point as a result of the Vietnamese invasion, with China briefly invading northern Vietnam to "teach it a lesson" in early 1979.

While there is little doubt that the Khmer Rouge was the primary instigator of the conflict, legitimate questions can and have been raised about the wisdom of the long-term occupation by the Vietnamese. What has often been obscured in the rush to judge the failures of the Vietnamese, however, has been the role played by the United States in the conflict. The United States, in concert with China and other regional allies, followed a policy of "bleeding Vietnam" during this period, needlessly prolonging the devastating war in Cambodia while using the war as a justification for its continued hostility toward Vietnam. Far from a response to the Vietnamese invasion and occupation of Cambodia, US strategy toward Southeast Asia during the late 1970s and 1980s was merely an extension of its previous policies of continuing war by other means.

Over the course of the 1980s, the stridently anticommunist Reagan administration consolidated its ongoing war against Vietnam, deepening and prolonging the Third Indochina War as part of what came to be known as the "Reagan Doctrine." Unlike the Carter administration, which maintained a stance—in word if not in deed—of neutrality toward the situation in Southeast Asia, the Reagan administration had fewer qualms about providing aid to the Khmer Rouge–led "coalition" in Cambodia. As Christopher Brady argues in his study *United States Foreign Policy Toward Cambodia, 1977–1992*, the administration's vision of the Third Indochina War fit perfectly the worldview promoted by the Reagan White House: an expansionist Soviet empire was actively promoting revolution around the globe and had to be turned back.[23]

In spite of this worldview, for the first several years of his administration, Reagan failed to articulate a clear vision of foreign policy, particularly with regard to Southeast Asia. While the White House continued to support the seating of the Khmer Rouge delegation for the Cambodian seat at the United Nations, it publicly refused to offer any aid commitment—military or otherwise—to the Khmer People's National Liberation Front (KPNLF), a coalition dominated by the Khmer Rouge. Behind the scenes, however, the United States had already begun covert funding to the group. In 1985, as Congress was debating a substantial increase in foreign aid to anticommunist insurgencies around the world, the *Washington Post* revealed that the KPNLF had been receiving US funds since at least 1982. The story revealed that "millions of dollars" over several years had been funneled to the group through Thailand.[24] These policies would remain in place throughout the Reagan administration as the bloody stalemate in Cambodia continued. Not until 1989 would Vietnam remove its troops from Cambodia, bringing an end to another decade-long war in Southeast Asia.

As with the embargo, the support of the Khmer Rouge during its war with Vietnam reflects not only the reality that the US war on Vietnam remained alive and well more than a decade after its nominal end but also the persistent lack of empathy upon which US foreign policy rested. While the Khmer Rouge slaughtered their own people, and while the Vietnamese fought to contain that threat along their border while still recovering from the previous four decades of warfare, US policymakers maintained a safe, detached distance, driven more by domestic politics and static, stale ideologies than by the realities on the ground in Southeast Asia.

The Third Indochina War exacerbated the existing regional humanitarian crisis, helping to create millions of refugees and Vietnam's economic crisis, as ongoing industrial and agricultural challenges were left to fester while the Cambodian occupation continued. By the mid-1980s, Vietnam embarked on a fairly radical series of economic "reforms." Commonly known as *doi moi*, or "renovation," these measures brought market forces increasingly to bear on its economy, privatizing significant amounts of agriculture and industry while opening up the country to increased foreign direct investment. While the results of these policies were mixed for many Vietnamese families, they helped set the stage for Vietnam to finally begin integrating into the regional and global economies and signaled perhaps a new period of engagement with the United States in the late 1980s.

At the dawn of a new decade, fifteen years removed from the victory over the United States by the revolutionary forces of Vietnam, the two nations remained locked in a state of hostility but poised for a thaw. As the Cold War dissipated and Vietnam removed its troops from Cambodia, the administration of George H. W. Bush embarked on a road map to normalization that would, by 1994, bring an end to the embargo and, by 1995, bring the normalization of diplomatic relations between the United States and the Socialist Republic of Vietnam. Even with this formal end to the ongoing US War on Vietnam, however, significant scars and legacies of the war remained.

The Last Ghost of War

There is no better, or more well-known, example of what the United States left behind in Vietnam than the long shadow of Agent Orange, a chemical defoliant used by the United States and its allies during the war. From 1961 to 1971 the United States and its South Vietnamese allies sprayed nearly seventy-three million liters (over nineteen million gallons) of chemical agents over two and a half million acres of southern and central Vietnam to defoliate the landscape and limit the access of the National Liberation Front (commonly known in the United States as the Viet Cong) to local food supplies. Of those seventy-three million liters, about 62 percent—more than forty-five million liters—of the chemicals deployed consisted of Agent Orange, a 1:1 mixture of the herbicides 2,4-D and 2,4,5-T that by the late 1960s was known to contain often dangerous levels of dioxin, specifically 2,3,7,8-tetrachlorodibenzo-p-dioxin (TCDD), one of the deadliest toxins ever created.[25]

Since the late 1960s, when the world became aware of Agent Orange and the other so-called rainbow herbicides used by the United States and its South Vietnamese allies during the war, veterans and civilians around the world have sought to understand the implications of this chemical war and its toxic legacies. In particular, the burdens of this legacy of the war have fallen largely on Vietnamese civilians, who have been forced to deal with the daily realities of long-term effects from Agent Orange while navigating the complex legal and scientific uncertainties surrounding the issue.

Throughout the war, scientists and activists in the United States and around the world added to the concerns being raised by Vietnamese civilians during the war about the harmful effects of the defoliants.[26] By 1970, the United States had phased out the use of Agent Orange in Vietnam, but US veterans began organizing later in the decade to expand service-related disability benefits to cover a variety of health conditions they believed were linked to exposure to dioxin. To this day, both the short- and long-term effects of these chemicals remain a great source of controversy in many nations, communities, and academic fields, but particularly in Vietnam. Soldiers and civilians who claim they were exposed to Agent Orange blame the US government and the chemical companies that produced it for a variety of medical conditions they and their families have experienced.

Many in Vietnam claim that the dioxin found in Agent Orange is responsible for birth defects and other conditions currently being found in the third and even fourth generation of exposed populations. At the same time, several ongoing scientific and epidemiological studies dispute many of these claims, and while the US Department of Veterans Affairs (VA) has consistently expanded benefits for US veterans claiming to have been exposed to Agent Orange, the US government continues to deny that those same conditions are caused by herbicide exposure when Vietnamese citizens experience them. Vietnamese veterans who served for the Army of the Republic of Vietnam (ARVN) were also left without any support and denied access to resources and to benefits regardless of whether they emigrated to the United States or remained in Vietnam.

Several major studies released in the early twenty-first century transformed the way scientists, historians, veterans, and other constituencies around the world think about, write about, and grapple with Agent Orange and its associated dioxin. None of the studies had a more powerful global impact than that published by Jeanne and Steven Stellman in 2003 in *Nature*. The outgrowth of a long-term study mandated by the Agent Orange Act of 1991 and supported by the National Academy of Sciences (NAS) and the VA, the Stellmans' piece offered dramatically revised estimates of the overall volume of herbicides and dioxins spread over Vietnam during the war.[27]

Returning to the original Air Force flight records from Operation Ranch Hand, the Stellmans identified major gaps in military records to add a sizable number of previously uncounted missions to the record. The results were staggering. The revised estimates showed that between 1961 and 1971 the US Air Force sprayed 7,131,907 liters (1,884,050 gallons) more than previously believed. The revised estimate showed the totals from the NAS examination in 1974 to be more than 10 percent off. The revised total brought the estimate of total herbicides sprayed to nearly seventy-three million liters, or more than nineteen million gallons. For Agent Orange alone the revised numbers were nearly forty-six million liters, or about twelve million gallons.[28]

Even more important to understanding the ongoing effects of Agent Orange were the development and confirmation of the "hotspot" theory, which demonstrated that the most contaminated areas in Vietnam were not those repeatedly sprayed during the war, but areas where the herbicides had been stored. The most notable work on dioxin hot spots was done by Hatfield Consultants, a Canadian environmental services firm that contracted with the Vietnamese government in the early 1990s to study the human and environmental impact of Agent Orange on the country. The hundreds of soil samples Hatfield collected from 1996 to 2004, as well as those from other teams, showed elevated levels of TCDD in the soil, blood, breast milk, and wildlife in areas of Vietnam near former storage sites, particularly Bien Hoa, Da Nang, Phu Cat, and A Luoi. Schecter's team, for instance, found elevated TCDD levels in the blood of a limited sample of residents of Bien Hoa, many of whom were born long after Operation Ranch Hand had ended.

Some of the samples showed levels as high as 271 parts per trillion (ppt), far above normal or safe levels. A control group from Hanoi showed far lower levels of dioxin in their blood. Schecter's team included the

Vietnamese doctor Le Cao Dai and the Agent Orange research pioneer John Constable, who had been on the NAS team in the 1970s. The findings, which contradicted the presumed dissipation of dioxin levels over time, suggested that the TCDD from Agent Orange had, in fact, remained in the environment much longer than expected and had likely entered the food chain.[29]

The key development in the hotspot hypothesis came in the isolated A Luoi valley in the central highlands above Da Nang. At this site, home to several Special Forces bases occupied by US troops between 1963 and 1966, Dwernychuk's team found noticeably higher levels of residual dioxin than at other areas nearby that had been heavily and repeatedly sprayed but had not served as storage sites. By taking extensive samples of soil, sediment, fish and duck tissues, human blood, and breast milk, Hatfield showed conclusively that dioxin was moving from heavily contaminated soil into sediment, where it entered the food chain through dioxin's location of choice: the fatty tissues of animals, especially fish and poultry, two staples of the Vietnamese diet. Once consumed by humans, the dioxin present in the animals could be passed on from parents, particularly through breastfeeding mothers, to children born decades after the war.[30]

The Hatfield research also showed that while the residual dioxin contamination was a threat to human and environmental health, it was a "manageable problem":

> The principal concern today, regarding dioxin in the environment of Vietnam, is that people living near some of the former military installations continue to be exposed to dioxin. People born after the war are also at risk of contamination. Through the use of dioxin-laden herbicides, the Vietnam War has left a legacy of environmental contamination that continues to this day; however, with simple mitigation measures this problem can be addressed and the probability of exposure significantly reduced.[31]

Unlike the ongoing uncertainty about particular effects on human health related to Agent Orange exposure, the scenario for at least seven major hotspots (and potentially several other, smaller ones) in Vietnam was fairly clear: dangerous levels of dioxin are present in the environment, humans are thereby at risk, but the knowledge about how to fix the situation exists. All that remained was the will and the financing to clean up the hot spots. These crucial ingredients, however, would prove elusive.

Given the common refrain heard in Vietnam that testing for dioxin contamination in humans was prohibitively expensive (about one thousand dollars per person), the prospect of a major environmental remediation project, which would involve the excavation and incineration of contaminated soil and would cost, at the very least, tens of millions of dollars, would not be possible without, as the Hatfield report noted, "international cooperation and international financial assistance."[32] Such cooperation and assistance would have been most effective had they come from the United States, in light of its financial and technological resources, not to mention its responsibility for the presence of the dioxin reservoirs in the first place. But such assistance was not readily forthcoming.

The Agent Orange issue had been a sticking point throughout the long, painful stages of postwar normalization between the United States and Vietnam. Ever since the war ended, the United States has maintained a consistent official line that there is no scientific evidence linking contemporary health concerns in Vietnam to the historic use of Agent Orange. US ambassador to Vietnam Michael Marine availed himself of this discourse of uncertainty in 2007 when he stated:

> [I] cannot say whether or not I have myself seen a victim of Agent Orange. The reason for that is that we still lack good scientific definitions of the causes of disabilities that have occurred in Vietnam. ... We just don't have the scientific evidence to make that statement with certainty.[33]

The Vietnamese point to the gradual increases in benefits paid to US veterans suffering from conditions presumed to be caused by Agent Orange.[34] For more than twenty years the United States refused to accede to any linking of Agent Orange remediation and normalization, trade, or easing of the draconian regime of economic sanctions it enacted against Vietnam during the war; in fact, the issue is conspicuous by its near total absence in talks between the countries until the early twenty-first century, once Vietnam enjoyed normal trade relations with the United States and membership in the World Trade Organization.

When President George H. W. Bush laid out his road map to normalization in 1991, for instance, he posited a mechanism for US humanitarian aid to Vietnam but made no mention of Agent Orange or dioxin. When President Bill Clinton made his historic visit to Vietnam in 2000, leaders there pressed him for increased assistance for Agent Orange victims as part of a larger aid package, but the US delegation agreed only to a joint scientific meeting.[35]

The joint meeting took place in 2002, but talks over future research projects quickly fizzled out, largely because of the rather crass and now infamous "embassy memo" from the US delegation in Hanoi, which became public in 2003. This sensitive but unclassified memo revealed that the US embassy believed the lack of progress on Agent Orange issues reflected

> the unwillingness of the GVN [government of Vietnam] to allow its scientists to engage in genuinely transparent, open rigorous scientific investigation to determine the true extent of the impact of AO/dioxin on health in Vietnam. We believe that the GVN will attempt to control, disrupt, or block any research project that could potentially produce scientific evidence that refutes the GVN's allegations of broad, catastrophic damage to the health of Vietnamese citizens, especially birth defects.[36]

Only in President George W. Bush's second term did the two nations make some headway on remediation efforts. Bush and President Nguyen Minh Triet signed a carefully worded joint statement in 2006 that read in part, "Further joint efforts to address the environmental contamination near former dioxin storage sites would make a valuable contribution to the continued development of bilateral relations."[37]

Building on that pledge, Congress appropriated a total of $3 million in both 2007 and 2009 for assistance with dioxin removal and "related health activities" in Da Nang. Most of the initial grant was directed to various nongovernmental organizations operating in Da Nang, but three years later only the Department of State had released a fraction of the original money, leaving the remediation efforts almost completely reliant on other sources of funding and international aid, including the United Nations, the Red Cross, and the Ford Foundation, which has maintained a multiyear, multimillion-dollar project related to Agent Orange.

Two sites, the Da Nang air base and the A Luoi valley, illustrate the dilemmas of environmental remediation in contemporary Vietnam, even when the money required is in hand. In late 2009, Hatfield completed its assessment and initial remediation plan for the Da Nang airport. As one of the main herbicide storage sites, the soil under the Da Nang airport runways as well as in the adjacent Lake Sen are among the most heavily contaminated hot spots in the country. Hatfield deduced that the most common pathway for exposure was for the dioxin to move from the soil located under the former loading, mixing, and storage areas at the airport into the lake, from the lake into the fish (particularly the popular tilapia fish), and from the fish into humans. In 2007 the government erected a barrier around the lake, prohibiting fishing and other forms of public use. A sizable population still lives within a stone's throw of the lake. Although other sources contribute to the contamination and other potential exposure pathways exist, above all for those working at or living near the site, Hatfield's research has shown a reduction in human dioxin exposure since the lake closure.[38]

To make the site safe for the surrounding community and ecosystem, Hatfield recommended the constructing of a secure, onsite landfill at the airport, consideration of incineration for the contaminated soil, and increasing the awareness of local residents to exposure pathways.[39] The onsite landfill, while a less costly option, has not yet proven to be a long-term solution. Previous episodes of dioxin contamination in the United States have proven that incineration is an effective way to eliminate the most dioxin in the safest manner, but it is also costly. The estimated cost of the cleanup at Da Nang rose steadily over the years from $10 million to $17 million to more than $20 million. The United Nations Development Program estimated in 2010 that the cost of cleaning up three major hot spots—Da Nang, Bien Hoa, and Phu Cat—would be over $50 million.[40]

In late 2010 the Vietnamese government and the United States Agency for International Development signed a memorandum of intent and began the long-overdue program of dioxin remediation at Da Nang. In June 2011, after years of wrangling, the United States and Vietnam launched the first phase of a joint cleanup effort at Da Nang. Having an estimated cost of $31 million to remove dioxin from up to seventy-one acres of land, the project is a large step forward, but the process had only just begun there in 2011 and has not yet started at other hot spots.[41]

The situation in the A Luoi valley is no less serious. Removed from the population and economic center of Da Nang, which is home to nearly one million people, this remote valley is populated largely by poor, rural residents, many of whom are members of various minority tribal groups that have strained relationships with the government. These people rely on farming as a means of survival, and there are no resources to support alternatives to breastfeeding among new mothers. Some human blood samples from the Hatfield research in the valley revealed dioxin levels as high as 15 ppt, nearly as high as those found in Da Nang (17 ppt). Soil samples taken by Hatfield found levels as high as 879 ppt.[42] At Da Nang, Bien Hoa, and other hot spots at former bases, concrete casings and incinerators could easily be built onsite, but the excavation of soil in A Luoi is a far greater logistical and financial challenge. The remote location of the valley and the narrow, winding roads leading to it do not favor onsite incineration or excavation.

A Luoi is not alone among poor, rural hot spots. Although most of the attention with regard to dioxin remediation has focused on major sites near urban areas like Da Nang and Bien Hoa, Hatfield has identified more than two dozen other potential hot spots throughout central and southern Vietnam. These sites, nearly all of which are former air bases or storage sites, have not all been tested for elevated dioxin levels in the soil and the local population, but given the historical patterns of use and the findings from places like A Luoi, Hatfield considers them potential hot spots in need of further study.

For Vietnamese citizens in and around these locations, the legacies of what they call the "US war" remain part of everyday life, fifty years after its ostensible end. The Vietnamese Association of Victims of Agent Orange/Dioxin (VAVA) estimate that there are more than three million victims of Agent Orange in Vietnam, a number that I and others have speculated elsewhere is likely inflated.[43] Even if inflated, however, it is difficult to underestimate the amount of suffering—both real and imagined—caused by the legacies of Agent Orange in Vietnam. As one VAVA representative from Vinh Long told me in in 2008, "Vietnam is a poor country. We have suffered long from war and have many needs. The government has a small budget and we rely on outside aid for support. The US government has a responsibility."[44] And yet, with so many issues, after so many wars, the United States has failed to live up to its responsibilities, in this case choosing to continue to ignore the long-term impact of Agent Orange on the landscape, and people, of Vietnam.

Conclusion

As the chapters in this collection make clear, the United States does not end wars well. While the aftermath of the US War in Vietnam may serve as a case study in how *not* to end wars, what best defines this period in US foreign policy is how the war was not, in fact, ended, but rather continued by other means. From the imposition of devastating economic sanctions and a debilitating trade embargo to the support of Cambodian forces (including the genocidal Khmer Rouge) during the Third Indochina War, to the failure to recognize and assist with the healing of ongoing wounds, both real and symbolic, from the continued effects of Agent Orange and ongoing deaths from unexploded ordnance, the United States actively, if not always intentionally, continued to shape the economic, political, and environmental future of Vietnam in the decades after the military conflict ended.

One of the common threads in all of these cases is that they focus attention on what the US war did to the people of Vietnam—the massive amount of violence it inflicted on them—as opposed to what the war in Vietnam did to US troops and to US society, which is so often how the war is portrayed in US culture. The result has been, as historian Christian Appy has so powerfully shown in his *American Reckoning*, that the United States still, fifty years on, has never fully come to terms with what it did to Vietnam. At the core of Appy's argument is the stubborn persistence of American exceptionalism and its core tenet that the United States was a force for good in the world.[45] With this worldview so firmly ensconced in US culture, it is perhaps no surprise that most Americans would focus their attention on what the war did to the United States. But the corollary of this myopia is a refusal to take seriously, to look directly at, or to understand the impact of that violence on the people most directly affected by it: Vietnamese civilians.

This, ultimately, is a failure of empathy. "If the legacy of the Vietnam War is to offer any guidance," Appy writes, "we need to complete the moral and political reckoning it awakened."[46] In order to do that, Americans must be able to empathize with the victims of violence carried out in their name. As Viet Thanh Nguyen has written, what is needed to move Americans beyond this is a concept of "just memory," which can lead "to a more complex understanding of our identity, of what it means to be human and to be complicit in the deeds that our side, our kin, and even we ourselves commit."[47]

There can be little doubt that this fundamental lack of empathy is thus a critical component in the perpetuation of violence inflicted by the United States in multiple wars since Vietnam, all of them, of course, waged far, far, away from US shores. Given the myriad similarities between United States-Vietnamese relations and the early twenty-first century conflicts in Afghanistan, Iraq, Syria, and elsewhere in the Middle East, one can only hope that US involvement in those wars not only ends quickly but actually ends at all. As long as those conflicts remain on the periphery of US culture, however, and as long as the suffering they engender—particularly for the civilians of those nations—remains far from Americans' field of vision, changes in US foreign policy and in how the United States ends its wars remain unlikely.

Edwin A. Martini is professor of history at Western Michigan University, where he currently serves as Associate Provost for Extended University Programs. He is the author and editor of several books, including *Invisible Enemies: The American War on Vietnam, 1975–2000* (University of Massachusetts, 2007); *Agent Orange: History, Science, and the Politics of Uncertainty* (Massachusetts, 2012); *Four Decades On: Vietnam, the United States, and the Legacies of the Second Indochina War* (coedited with Scott Laderman; Duke, 2013); and *At War: The Military and American Culture in the Twentieth Century and Beyond* (coedited with David Kieran; Rutgers, 2018).

Notes

1. "Report of the United Nations Mission to North and South Viet-Nam," reprinted in "Aftermath of War: Humanitarian Problems of Southeast Asia," Staff Report Prepared for the Committee on the Judiciary, Subcommittee to Investigate Problems Connected with Refugees and Escapees," 94th Cong., 2nd Sess., 17 May 1976.
2. "Preface," in "Aftermath of War," v.
3. Tim O Brien, *The Things They Carried*, 2nd ed. (New York: Broadway Books, 1998), 37.
4. Environmental Conference on Cambodia, Vietnam, and Laos, Long Term Consequences of the Vietnam War, 43–44, http://www.nnn.se/vietnam/ethics.pdf, accessed 1 July 2005. These numbers reflect bombing and casualty data not only for Vietnam, but for Laos and Cambodia as well.
5. Ibid.
6. George Black, "The Lethal Legacy of the Vietnam War," *The Nation*, 16 March 2015, 17.
7. "Long Term Consequences of the Vietnam War," 43; Arnold Schecter et al., "Food as a Source of Dioxin Exposure in the Residents of Bien Hoa City, Vietnam," *Journal of Occupational and Environmental Research* 45, no. 8 (2003); "Decades Later, Vietnam War Toxin Still Torments," *Washington Post*, 16 February 2004; "New Study into Agent Orange," BBC News Online, 10 March 2002; Edwin Martini, *Agent Orange: History, Science, and the Politics of Uncertainty* (Amherst: University of Massachusetts Press, 2012).
8. Adjudication of Claims against Vietnam, Hearing and Markup before the Subcommittees on Asian and Pacific Affairs and International Economic Policy and Trade, 96th Cong., 1st Sess., 27 July 1979, 3.
9. United States Embargo of Trade With South Vietnam and Cambodia, Hearing before the Subcommittee on International Trade and Commerce, House of Representatives, 94th Cong., 1st Sess., 4 June 1975, 3.
10. "Count Your Vietnams," *The Economist*, 9 August 1975, 14; Louis Halasz, "Stalemate in the Halls of Diplomacy," *Far Eastern Economic Review*, 22 August 1975, 20.
11. "Count Your Vietnams."
12. For a catalog of such votes since 1978, see William Blum, *Rogue State: A Guide to the World's Only Superpower* (Monroe, ME: Common Courage Press, 2000), chap. 20: "The United States versus the World at the United Nations," 184–99.
13. Louis Halsalz, "Washington Put on the Spot," *Far Eastern Economic Review*, 24 September 1976, 20.
14. Joseph Zasloff and MacAlister Brown, *Communist Indochina and US Foreign Policy: Postwar Realities* (Boulder, CO: Westview Press, 1978), 9.
15. Final Report of the Select Committee on Missing Persons in Southeast Asia, 94th Cong., 2nd Sess., 13 December 1976, 235.
16. Quoted in Elizabeth Becker, *When the War Was Over: The Voices of Cambodia's Revolution and Its People* (New York: Simon and Schuster, 1986), 324.
17. Steven Hurst, *The Carter Administration and Vietnam* (New York: St. Martin's, 1996), 44–45.
18. "More Francs for Vietnam," *Far Eastern Economic Review*, 20 May 1977.
19. Zasloff and Brown, *Communist Indochina and US Foreign Policy*, 20. Also see Henrich Dahm, *French and Japanese Economic Relations with Vietnam Since 1975* (New York: Routledge, 1999).
20. Mark Bradley, *Vietnam at War* (New York: Oxford University Press, 2009), 175.
21. Ibid., 176.
22. For more background on the Cambodian revolution and the rise to power of the Khmer Rouge, see Becker, *When the War Was Over*; William Shawcross, *Sideshow* (New York: Simon and Schuster, 1979) and *The Quality of Mercy* (New York: Simon and Schuster,

1984); Ben Kiernan, *The Pol Pot Regime* (New Haven: Yale University, 1996); several works by David Chandler, including *Brother Number One* (Boulder: Westview Press, 1999) and *A History of Cambodia* (Boulder: Westview, 1996); and Kenton Clymer"s *The United States and Cambodia, vol. 1: From Curiosity to Transformation, 1870–1969*, and vol. 2, *A Troubled Relationship, 1969–2000* (New York: Routledge, 2004).

23. Christopher Brady, *United States Foreign Policy Toward Cambodia, 1977–1992* (New York: St. Martin's, 1999), 74–75.
24. "CIA Covertly Aiding Pro-West Cambodians," *Washington Post*, 8 July 1985.
25. The full names for 2,4-D and 2,4,5-T are 2,4-dichlorophenoxyacetic acid and 2,4,5-trichlorophenoxyacetic acid, respectively. 2,3,7,8-tetrachlorodibenzo-para-dioxin, more commonly known as 2,3,7,8-TCDD, or simply TCDD, is one of dozens of toxins known collectively as dioxins. Its name is derived from the location of the chlorine atoms on the molecule (positions 2, 3, 7, and 8) and their position relative to the benzene and oxygen atoms. The configuration of these components on the TCDD molecule makes 2,3,7,8-TCDD by far the most toxic form of dioxin, thousands of times more toxic than other polychlorinated dioxins. TCDD can be produced by a number of processes, including the manufacture of herbicides such as 2,4,5-T. For more on the makeup, history, and characteristics of dioxins and of TCDD, see Alastair Hay, *The Chemical Scythe: Lessons of 2,4,5-T and Dioxin* (New York: Plenum Press, 1982).
26. On the critical role of scientists as activists, see David Zierler, *The Invention of Ecocide* (Athens: University of Georgia Press, 2011).
27. Jeanne and Steven Stellman et al., "The Extent and Patterns of Usage of Agent Orange and Other Herbicides in Vietnam," *Nature* 422 (April 2003): 681–87.
28. Ibid., 682.
29. Schecter et al., "Recent Dioxin Contamination from Agent Orange in Residents of a Southern Vietnam City," *Journal of Occupational and Environmental Medicine* 43, no. 5 (2001): 435–43.
30. Wayne Dwernychuk et al., "Dioxin Reservoirs in Southern Vietnam: A Legacy of Agent Orange," *Chemosphere* 47, no. 2 (2002): 117–37.
31. Dwernychuk et al., "A Manageable Problem," 1–2.
32. Ibid., 2.
33. Quoted in Michael Martin, "Vietnamese Victims of Agent Orange and US-Vietnam Relations," Congressional Research Service Report (Washington, DC: Congressional Research Service, 2009), 7.
34. Martin, "Vietnamese Victims of Agent Orange," 2.
35. Ibid., 9.
36. Memo, "AMEMBASSY HANOI to SECSTATE WASHDC," 13 February 2003, available at the Fund for Reconciliation and Development, www.ffrd.org.
37. "Joint Statement between the Socialist Republic of Vietnam and the United States of America," White House press release, 17 November 2006, available at http://www.warlegacies.org/Bush.pdf.
38. "Comprehensive Assessment of Dioxin Contamination in Da Nang Airport, Vietnam: Environmental Levels, Human Exposure and Options for Mitigating Impacts—Summary of Findings," report prepared by Hatfield Consultants, November 2009, available at www.hatfieldgroup.com.
39. "Comprehensive Assessment of Dioxin Contamination in Da Nang Airport, Vietnam: Environmental Levels, Human Exposure and Options for Mitigating Impacts—Final Report," 4–6.
40. Martin, "Vietnamese Victims of Agent Orange," 20.
41. "VN-US Cooperate in Dioxin Detoxification in Da Nang," Vietnam News Agency, 31 December 2010, available at http://english.vovne ws.vn/Home/

VNUS-cooperate-in-dioxin-detoxification-in-Da-Nang/201012/122787.vov; "Vietnam Starts Joint Agent Orange Cleanup with US," *USA Today*, 20 June 2011.
42. Dwyernychuk et al., "Dioxin Reservoirs in Southern Vietnam."
43. Martini, *Agent Orange*, 227.
44. Interview with the author, 21 April 2008, quoted in Martini, Agent Orange, 227, n92.
45. Christian Appy, *American Reckoning: The Vietnam War and Our National Identity* (New York: Viking, 2015).
46. Appy, *American Reckoning*, xvii.
47. Viet Thanh Nguyen, *Nothing Ever Dies: Vietnam and the Memory of War* (Cambridge, MA: Harvard University Press, 2016), 283.

Select Bibliography

Appy, Christian G., *American Reckoning: The Vietnam War and Our National Identity* (New York: Viking, 2015).
Becker, Elizabeth, *When the War Was Over: The Voices of Cambodia's Revolution and Its People* (New York: Simon and Schuster, 1986).
Bradley, Mark, *Vietnam at War* (New York: Oxford University Press, 2009).
Brady, Christopher, *United States Foreign Policy Toward Cambodia, 1977–1992* (New York: St. Martin's, 1999).
Blum, William, *Rogue State: A Guide to the World's Only Superpower* (Monroe, ME: Common Courage Press, 2000).
Chandler, David, *A History of Cambodia* (Boulder, CO: Westview, 1996).
_____, *Brother Number One* (Boulder, CO: Westview Press, 1999).
Clymer, Kenton, *The United States and Cambodia: A Troubled Relationship, 1969–2000* (New York: Routledge, 2004).
_____, *The United States and Cambodia: From Curiosity to Transformation, 1870–1969* (New York: Routledge, 2004).
Dwernychuk, Wayne et al., "Dioxin Reservoirs in Southern Vietnam: A Legacy of Agent Orange," *Chemosphere* 47, no. 2 (2002).
Halasz, Louis, "Stalemate in the Halls of Diplomacy," *Far Eastern Economic Review*, 22 August 1975.
_____, "Washington Put on the Spot," *Far Eastern Economic Review*, 24 September 1976.
Hay, Alastair, *The Chemical Scythe: Lessons of 2,4,5-T and Dioxin* (New York: Plenum Press, 1982).
Hurst, Steven, *The Carter Administration and Vietnam* (New York: St. Martin's, 1996).
Kiernan, Ben, *The Pol Pot Regime* (New Haven: Yale University, 1996).
Martini, Edwin, *Agent Orange: History, Science, and the Politics of Uncertainty* (Amherst: University of Massachusetts Press, 2012).
Nguyen, Viet Thanh, *Nothing Ever Dies: Vietnam and the Memory of War* (Cambridge, MA: Harvard University Press, 2016).
O'Brien, Tim, *The Things They Carried*, 2nd ed. (New York: Broadway Books, 1998).
Schecter, Arnold et al., "Food as a Source of Dioxin Exposure in the Residents of Bien Hoa City, Vietnam," *Journal of Occupational and Environmental Research* 45, no. 8 (2003).

Schecter, Arnold et al., "Recent Dioxin Contamination from Agent Orange in Residents of a Southern Vietnam City," *Journal of Occupational and Environmental Medicine* 43, no. 5 (2001): 435–43.

Shawcross, William, *Sideshow: Kissinger, Nixon and the Destruction of Cambodia* (New York: Simon and Schuster, 1979).

_____, *The Quality of Mercy* (New York: Simon and Schuster, 1984).

Stellman, Jeanne et al., "The Extent and Patterns of Usage of Agent Orange and Other Herbicides in Vietnam," *Nature* 422 (April 2003).

Zasloff, Joseph and MacAlister Brown, *Communist Indochina and US Foreign Policy: Postwar Realities* (Boulder, CO: Westview Press, 1978).

Zierler, David, *The Invention of Ecocide* (Athens: University of Georgia Press, 2011).

Chapter 3

"His Epitaph Is Also Ours"
Robert McNamara, the Iraq and Afghanistan Wars, and the Vietnam War's Contested Usable Past

David Kieran

In the United States, a former president's passing is an occasion for pomp and reflection. There are the trappings of ceremony, all of which are televised: the horse-drawn caisson, the riderless horse, the lines of patient citizens waiting to pay their respects before a flag-draped casket atop the Lincoln catafalque, funeral services in the National Cathedral, entombment at the presidential library. And then there are the retrospectives, the attempts to discern this person's impact on the nation and his legacy. When Ronald Reagan died in 2004, newspapers overflowed with assessments on his role in ending the Cold War and in forging modern conservatism; three years later, commentators debated the wisdom of Gerald Ford's having pardoned Richard M. Nixon.[1]

The deaths of the men and women who served under these presidents seldom receive such attention. Rather, the cabinet secretaries that manage the day-to-day functions of the executive branch tend to shuffle off this mortal coil in much the same manner that they toiled on it: with a brief notation of their service, but scant attention. This is hardly surprising. Most Americans would struggle to name most of the current administration's cabinet members. "Former cabinet secretaries" seems a more likely pub trivia category than a subject of quotidian knowledge. Their deaths are noted in major newspapers and with prominent obituaries in the *New York Times* and the *Washington Post*, but there is rarely prolonged discussion of their legacy and its implications for contemporary politics.

The 2009 death of Robert S. McNamara marks a singular exception to this reality. The former secretary of defense, who served in both the Kennedy and Johnson administrations and was one of the most prominent architects of the US War in Vietnam, died in the early morning of 6 July, and his death became an occasion not only to revisit the history of the Vietnam War but also to assess whether the country had taken appropriate lessons from that conflict. Within two hours of the announcement that he had succumbed, National Public Radio's *Morning Edition* had produced a segment that featured an interview with Robert Dallek, and by midmorning the *Washington Post*'s website announced the story with a bright yellow "Breaking News" banner; that night, *ABC Nightly News* reported the story in a lengthy segment replete with Vietnam era footage of McNamara.[2] On the following day, the story appeared on the front page of most major national newspapers, including an above-the-fold story in the *New York Times*.[3] In the *Post*, the front-page story led to a two-page spread in the front section that included five photographs, an editorial on the opinion page, and, in the Style section, a two-page human interest story that featured quotes from Jimmy Carter and Henry Kissinger.[4]

Over the next month, McNamara's life, legacy, and contemporary relevance would be the subject of over 180 articles, editorials, letters, and political cartoons in American newspapers. It was, in short, a moment in which the country took stock of what Vietnam had meant and what it continues to mean. And yet, this was not the only moment in the twenty-first century when the former defense secretary emerged as a prominent figure in contemporary policy debates. In the winter of 2003, as Americans were increasingly turning a skeptical eye toward the Iraq War, filmmaker Errol Morris released *The Fog of War: Eleven Lessons from the Life of Robert S. McNamara*, a documentary that consisted primarily of an aged McNamara recounting his experiences to the camera. As his death would six years later, the film's release prompted a consideration both of McNamara's life and of its lessons for contemporary politics.

In this chapter, I examine these two moments and argue that they reveal how the contested, malleable legacy of the Vietnam War continues to shape political discourse in the United States. The US war in Indochina, the historian Christian G. Appy maintains, vies for the dubious title of the most traumatic event in the nation's past. He writes:

> With the possible exception of the Civil War, no event in US history has demanded more soul-searching than the war in Vietnam ... provoked a profound national identity crisis, an American reckoning. The war made citizens ask fundamental questions: Who are we? What defines us as a nation and a people? What is our role in the world?[5]

The answers to these questions have remained contested. While nearly all Americans agree that the war was a disaster, they continue to debate precisely why this is so. H. Bruce Franklin has argued, "The three main competing American stories of the Vietnam War can be titled 'A Noble Cause,' 'Quagmire' and 'Imperialism.'"[6] In the first of these, he explains, the failure is explained by an insufficient commitment on the part of political leaders and the public, and it demands a recommitment to American militarism.[7] In the second, the failure is attributed to "years of errors, misunderstanding, and confusion as America lurches deeper and deeper into the mire of Vietnam."[8] In the last, the war was an explicit attempt to preserve US hegemony at the expense of the "anticolonialist and anticapitalist movements throughout Asia and Africa."[9]

Americans have debated which of these three narratives best explains where the United States went wrong in Vietnam, and what that means in the war's aftermath has been ongoing since 1975. Frequently, sites of remembrance have served as the forum for these debates.[10] As Jay Winter, the foremost scholar of war and public memory, reminds his readers, "To privilege 'remembrance'" in the debate over the vocabulary about public memory "is to insist on specifying agency, on answering the question who remembers when, where, and how? And on being aware of the transience of remembrance, so dependent on the frailties and commitments of the men and women who take the time and effort to engage in it."[11]

In this chapter, I want to think through the "frailties and commitments" that shaped McNamara's 21st-century remembrance and how that remembrance in turn served to shore up particular positions within debates about US foreign policy as a means of illustrating how the Vietnam War continues to provide a language and set of ideas for advancing competing—and often opposing—ideas about US foreign policy.[12] The shifting ways in which the memory of a single person—Robert S. McNamara—was deployed in the service of opposing narratives about contemporary foreign policy illustrate how the diverse "frailties and commitments" of 21st-century US culture have shaped how the Vietnam War has been remembered and those remembrances' evolving utility within contemporary political debates. In 2003, remembrances of McNamara as an egotistical and dishonest villain served as a cautionary tale for critics who argued that the Bush administration, and particularly then-secretary of defense Donald Rumsfeld, had misled the nation, offering a faulty rationale for the Iraq War and failing to foresee that the invasion would become an occupation far more complicated than the American people had been led to believe.

McNamara's association with Franklin's "quagmire theory" continued in the aftermath of his 2009 death, but to a significant degree the terms of the debate had shifted. Although Rumsfeld and the Bush administration still earned unfavorable comparisons to the former secretary, conservative commentators mobilized his legacy in efforts both to redeem Bush's handling of the Iraq War and to critique President Barack Obama's approach to Afghanistan and the financial crisis. In these remembrances, McNamara appeared as a bloodless, overconfident technocrat tragically unable to acknowledge his mistakes. This portrayal helped advance the "noble cause" theory of the war, as Bush became McNamara's antithesis: a leader who, by acknowledging his mistakes and deferring to military leaders, salvaged the Iraq War from a Vietnam-like defeat by embracing counterinsurgency tactics and a troop surge.

Now, it was Obama's intelligence and confidence that earned unfavorable comparisons to McNamara, as critics cautioned that the new president was repeating the former secretary's mistake of believing that every problem could be solved through the intervention of sufficiently skilled bureaucrats. Within a span of six years, then, the remembrance of Robert S. McNamara was invoked to both critique and defend the Bush administration, to endorse and condemn conservative and liberal policies. These remembrances thus illustrate that the legacy of the Vietnam War remains unsettled. Rather, Americans' diverse understandings of the war continue to shape their debate over the most significant issues in US culture. Together, they belie the notion that the war has truly ended.

2003: "The Follies of Vietnam Are Now Being Reenacted in Iraq"

Errol Morris's *The Fog of War* premiered in a moment when the US war in Iraq turned from an invasion to an occupation, as the promises of a speedy victory in which Americans would be "greeted as liberators" were being tested by a growing insurgency.[13] In the first week of December, Americans encountered disheartening reports of escalating violence. On the first, the *New York Times* reported that US troops had engaged in "the largest battle in the country since coalition forces toppled Saddam Hussein's regime," noting that "the attacks over the weekend concluded a month that was the bloodiest yet for American soldiers."[14]

As this violence increased, US troops adopted increasingly aggressive tactics. On 7 December the *New York Times* reported:

> As the guerilla war against Iraqi insurgents intensifies, American soldiers have begun wrapping entire villages in barbed wire. In selective cases, American

soldiers are demolishing buildings thought to be used by attackers. They have begun imprisoning the relatives of suspected guerillas, in hopes of pressing the insurgents to turn themselves in.[15]

In one village, "encased in a razor-wire fence after repeated attacks on American troops, Iraqi civilians line up to go in and out, filing through an American-guarded checkpoint, each carrying an identification card printed in English only."[16] Amid all of this violence, however, Bush administration officials promised a continued commitment to the war.[17] On 10 December, President Bush declared, "We're making good progress in Iraq."[18]

Despite these reassurances, many Americans were becoming increasingly critical of the war. In September, for example, journalist Tim Russert began *Meet the Press* by asking, "Did the Bush administration misjudge the level of organized resistance, the number of American troops needed, the cost of securing Iraq, and the existence of weapons of mass destruction?"[19] This sense that the Bush administration had either failed to plan for an insurgency, or misled the country, led to increasing comparisons to the War in Vietnam. In the *Washington Post*, Tom Ricks profiled retired Marine Corps General Anthony Zinni, a Vietnam veteran who "sees both conflicts as beginning with deception by the US government, drawing a parallel between how the Johnson administration handled the beginning of the Vietnam War and how the Bush administration touted the threat presented by Iraqi weapons of mass destruction."[20]

A few days later, Robert Kaiser opined in the same paper, "If we see that a neat military victory is impossible and the political goal is difficult to reach, then Iraq and Vietnam begin to have more in common."[21] Outside of the United States, *The Irish Times* analyzed US troop losses and declared, "For the US soldier on the ground, Iraq has become a latter-day Vietnam," while Singapore's *Straits Times* opined, "Commentators are drawing parallels between the country and Vietnam. The consequences are mind-boggling for all concerned; the writing is already on the wall."[22] In these articles, the hallmarks of the quagmire theory—a failure of vision, rampant dishonesty, and a continued commitment when a disastrous outcome seemed assured—were evident in Iraq.

These sentiments doubtless shaped Americans' responses to *The Fog of War*. In the months following the release of *The Fog of War*, reviewers connected Vietnam and Iraq and invoked McNamara's appearance and comments to critique the current war, and particularly then-defense secretary Donald Rumsfeld. In the *New York Times*, Frank Rich observed, "Since its release, *The Fog of War* has generated plenty of debate. ... over the degree to which the follies of Vietnam are now being re-enacted in

Iraq."²³ The consensus, in several dozen articles, was that it was; many echoed the Associated Press's comment that the film was "especially relevant now," with a piece circulated through the Copley News Service suggesting, "When McNamara talks about World War II or Cuba or Vietnam, he could just as easily be talking about Iraq."²⁴

In particular, reviewers asserted that McNamara had lacked the circumspection to avoid an unnecessary conflict that deteriorated into a disaster. This point was made most stridently in the *New York Times* by Samantha Power, who in an op-ed wrote:

> Revisiting Vietnam and the images of sprightly young G.I.'s so eager to serve, one is reminded how soldiers can be led astray by reckless ideology, shoddy intelligence, and liberal hubris ... and how our faith in our own good intentions and our ignorance of local culture can undermine our objectives.²⁵

In making this claim, Power does two things. She continues the narrative in which the war's greatest tragedy is that deeply patriotic young soldiers were betrayed by their government. Additionally, she reiterates the argument that Vietnam had been the product of policymakers' refusal to deviate from a rigid belief system and unwillingness to think critically about either their policy or their enemy that McNamara had himself been making for eight years.²⁶ Moreover, Power suggested, the war in Iraq illustrated that the country had failed to learn these lessons and that it may be too late to do so.

The article's closing image illustrates this point, referencing Rumsfeld's foreign policy aphorisms and noting that they "were not dissimilar to those Mr. Morris elicited from Mr. McNamara."²⁷ Power thus imagines Rumsfeld as having initially approached contemporary foreign policy crises with a clear sense of the errors of Vietnam only to repeat them; she points out that "the lessons, known as 'Rumsfeld's Rules,' were posted on the Pentagon website when Mr. Rumsfeld took office. They have since been removed."²⁸ Here, Power condemns Rumsfeld and, through him, the Bush administration's Iraq policy not as ignorant of Vietnam's lessons but rather as deeply aware of, and desperately seeking to obscure, the extent to which they have been explicitly disregarded.

Power's editorial is the most explicit example of a narrative that also appeared in other editorialists' work. In the *San Francisco Chronicle*, Ruth Rosen called McNamara's "remorseless confession ... a cautionary tale about the war in Iraq" and once again argued that the primary lessons are of cultural ignorance and the rigid adherence to inflexible doctrine: "The problem, says McNamara ... is that American leaders failed to see the world through the eyes of the Vietnamese ... . [and] blinded themselves by viewing the world through the limited lens of the Cold War."²⁹ Rosen drew further comparisons between Vietnam and Iraq through references to "exaggerated evidence and persistent propaganda ... that persuaded the American public to support a war in Iraq."[30] For Rosen, however, this misinformation paled in comparison to the larger "cultural and historical ignorance in which the Bush administration planned the war in Iraq."[31] Similar ideas appeared in editorials and reviews published in smaller newspapers. In an Associated Press story, Morley Safer established McNamara and Rumsfeld as analogs and extended the comparison to the entire administration, remarking that "there's a kind of pride in the ignorance."[32]

Humorist Art Buchwald pondered whether "Donald Rumsfeld would ever admit to making a mistake" before concluding:

> It would be a big mistake to do what McNamara did. Leaders can't afford for people to know they make mistakes. What kind of a world would we live in if we found out sometime down the road that they had a bad plan, or worse still, no plan at all?[33]

Like Power's editorial, these pieces mobilize the quagmire theory's emphasis on dishonesty and ignorance to provide a cautionary tale and a means of understanding what they assert is an already evident failure of current US foreign policy.[34] Amid all of this coverage, only one editorial, in the conservative *Washington Times*, complained, "Never considered is the possibility that Mr. McNamara learned the wrong lessons from Vietnam and the Bushies learned the right ones."[35] Yet even here McNamara's admissions of errors based in ignorance and overconfidence provided not a model to be avoided but rather the vocabulary through which the already extant critiques of the Iraq War as replicating the errors of Vietnam could be made with specificity.

These comparisons were strengthened by what some writers saw as physical and personal similarities between McNamara and his contemporary counterpart.[36] The *New York Times* review asserted, "It's hard to watch Mr. McNamara, with his combed-back hair and blunt didactic manner, without thinking of the man who currently holds his old government job, Donald H. Rumsfeld."[37] Somewhat more comically, Amanda Henry's review in the *Wisconsin State Journal* exclaimed, "Holy Rumsfeld! This guy could be the older brother of our current Secretary of Defense," while another reviewer condemned McNamara's "arrogance" as "uncannily like the briefing follies run today by Donald Rumsfeld."[38] Roger Ebert, perhaps the most respected movie reviewer in the United States, declared, "I cannot imagine the circumstances under which Donald Rumsfeld ... would not want to see this film about his predecessor, having recycled and even improved upon McNamara's mistakes."[39]

In these articles, one of the Bush administration's most prominent hawks became the literal embodiment of McNamara—or perhaps the even more complete embodiment of the former secretary's failings.

The reviews and commentary that surrounded McNamara's reemergence as a public figure in 2003 reveal one way in which his legacy was deployed to make Vietnam meaningfully signify on behalf of contemporary foreign policy debates. As the Iraq War devolved into a chaotic insurgency, it appeared to many critics a quagmire that, like Vietnam, was marked by ignorance, dishonesty, and a failure to consider the likely consequences of intervening. Robert McNamara personified those attributes, and invoking him helped facilitate claims that the Iraq War was a misguided disaster, the work of arrogant dissemblers. McNamara's meaning, however, was never stable. When he died six years later, the political situation in the United States had evolved, and the former secretary's legacy would be deployed differently and on behalf of a quite different political agenda.

"'The Best and the Brightest' Has Been Scrubbed of Its Intended Irony"

Robert McNamara died in July 2009, six months into Barack Obama's first term as president and in the midst of a protracted internal debate about what strategy the president should adopt in Afghanistan, a war to which he had promised to devote more resources.[40] Although some commentators continued the earlier narrative that characterized McNamara's hubris and dishonesty as the predecessor of the Bush administration's failures in Iraq, two other narratives emerged, this time from the political right. On the one hand, some conservative commentators invoked McNamara to redeem Bush's leadership during the Iraq War. This narrative was steeped in the noble cause theory of the Vietnam War, the revisionist discourse that posited the Vietnam War as having been winnable had politicians given military leaders a free hand to fight the war as they saw fit.

In 2009, Bush appeared as the antithesis of McNamara, an unintellectual and humble leader who had admitted his errors, trusted his military leaders, and adopted a winning strategy. Concurrent with this narrative, however, was one that invoked the quagmire theory to critique Obama as another overconfident, unemotional technocrat, one likely to repeat the error of believing that an activist government could resolve both foreign and domestic crises. The coexistence of these two narratives reveal the malleability of McNamara's cultural significance. Invoked now to defend the administration he had been mobilized to critique a few years earlier, it was no longer recollections of his perceived dishonesty that had political relevance; in 2009, he was damned for his intellect and arrogance.

Americans learned of Robert McNamara's death, and considered his legacy, in a moment when they were considering the conduct of two wars, the legacy of the president who began them, and the strategy advocated by his successor.[41] Editorials continued to compare McNamara's failures in Vietnam to the Bush Administration's approach to the Iraq War. The *New York Times* asked whether McNamara's claims about the Tonkin Gulf "remind[ed] anyone of the 'slam dunk' evidence of Saddam Hussein's Weapons of Mass Destruction"; a *St. Louis Post-Dispatch* cartoon showed Rumsfeld at McNamara's grave, declaring, "I guess this makes me the best and the brightest former defense secretary alive today"; and *USA Today* editorialized that "a chastened McNamara thought the [Iraq] invasion was a mistake, and had two of his successors at the Pentagon, Dick Cheney and Donald Rumsfeld, been as wise, that war would surely have gone better or not have been fought."[42] Noting that not enough attention had been paid to the mistakes of the Bush administration, one letter writer made a more sweeping condemnation: "Vietnam and Iraq may be different, but we have not changed. ... His epitaph is also ours."[43]

Yet McNamara's legacies were also invoked in a discursive effort to redeem Bush. By the end of Bush's term, many conservatives were praising his embrace of counterinsurgency tactics and the 2007 troops surge as having ended the bloody civil war in Iraq and allowing the United States to contemplate withdrawal.[44] In January 2008, for example, then-presidential candidate Senator John McCain (R-AZ) and his colleague Senator Joe Lieberman (I-CT) penned an op-ed in the *Wall Street Journal* claiming, "The Surge Worked."[45]

The popularity of counterinsurgency among military leaders, politicians, and conservative commentators was in part rooted in a revisionist remembrance of Vietnam as a war that could have been won had the proper strategy been adopted. Some revisionists have argued that the United States should have committed even more conventional military force. Others have argued that the failure to effectively embrace counterinsurgency led to the US defeat.[46] Still others have argued, as the historian Lewis Sorley put it, that as General Creighton Abrams and other leaders "raced to render the South Vietnamese capable of defending themselves before the last American forces were withdrawn ... [they] came very close to achieving the elusive goal of a viable nation and a lasting peace."[47]

McNamara's legacy was invoked on behalf of this argument. Implicitly endorsing the noble cause argument that the Vietnam War had been lost because of political leaders' cowardice and myopia, several articles cast George W. Bush as the antithesis of the former secretary—decisive, anti-intellectual, willing to acknowledge the failure of his previous strategy, deferential to his military commanders, and militarily successful. The argument that Bush had avoided McNamara's errors underlay Rumsfeld critic Bradley Graham's *Washington Post* piece "McNamara Apologized for Vietnam. Will Rumsfeld Do So for Iraq?"[48] Although the title recalled earlier critiques, Graham ultimately argues that the error had not been, as in 2004, the decision to go to war but rather the initial failure to develop a winning strategy and that "the shift in strategy and surge in US forces that occurred in early 2007, after Rumsfeld left, are credited with pulling Iraq back from the brink of total disaster."[49]

Both the *Wall Street Journal* and *Investor's Business Daily* presented George W. Bush as the antithesis of McNamara, with the *Journal* condemning liberals who "as with Vietnam ... also turned against the Iraq War after supporting it" and lauded the former president because he "never lost his nerve. ... He replaced his generals, sent more troops, and embraced a new counter-insurgency strategy."[50] Nearly identically an *Investor's Business Daily* editorial argued, "What McNamara did in losing Vietnam might best be called an 'antisurge.' Whereas President George W. Bush turned to the military's best in turning around Iraq, giving them the resources they needed, McNamara ignored them, then provided too little, too late."[51] Neatly, and prematurely, the *Journal* declared that "the insurgency was defeated, and Mr. Bush left office with Iraq as a united, self-governing ally."[52] Smaller papers made similar claims; the *Arkansas Democrat-Gazette* opined:

> [McNamara] never insisted on a change of strategy, or leaders, of generalship. That would have been way too dramatic, way too human. It was how an inarticulate, unsophisticated, unscientific George W. Bush might react. When that president was finally persuaded to change course in Iraq, he would fire his secretary of defense, get his unsuccessful generals out of there, find his US Grant in David Petraeus, order a surge and save the day—not to mention a whole country and American credibility in a crucial part of the world.[53]

McNamara's death thus presented the Bush administration's defenders with an opportunity to cast Iraq as a war in which the United States had learned appropriate lessons from Vietnam and avoided a similar defeat. Juxtaposing a remembrance of McNamara as cold, calculating, unapologetic, and ultimately ineffective and Bush, cast as unintellectual but successful, these pieces deployed McNamara's legacy to shore up revisionist narratives of Vietnam.

The corollary to the revision of the Bush administration as having heeded the appropriate lessons from McNamara's service in Vietnam was that the Obama administration risked repeating McNamara's errors, both at home and abroad. In conservative newspapers, opinion pieces and retrospectives invoked the arrogance and intelligence that had always been ascribed to McNamara to critique Obama and caution against any reluctance to unequivocally use force. The *Wall Street Journal* published "From McNamara to Obama" on the first day of a three-day editorial page salvo against McNamara, arguing that the former secretary "will go down as a cautionary tale for the ages, and perhaps none more than for the age of Obama."[54]

Reiterating the familiar argument that the United States could have won the War in Vietnam had it fought it with less restraint, this piece vigorously critiqued Obama's national security team, calling them "people deeply impressed by their own smarts, the ones for whom 'the best and the brightest' has been scrubbed of its intended irony" and closing with an admonishment to the president to "note that he, too is the whiz kid of his day."[55] Likewise, in a *Washington Post* piece that celebrated the Bush administration's troop surge as having "rescued US involvement in Iraq from a Vietnam-like collapse," Jim Hoagland wrote:

> President Obama has acted more thoughtfully on Iraq, and Afghanistan, than his campaign promises indicated would be the case. ... To succeed, Obama must persuade Americans to show strategic patience with these efforts. He must avoid the intellectual hubris and blindness that Robert McNamara, brilliant as he was, sadly came to personify.[56]

Similarly, two weeks after critiquing Obama, *Investor's Business Daily* alluded to McNamara while criticizing Secretary of Defense Robert Gates as one of many "defeatists put in charge of running wars."[57] For each editorialist, the chief lesson of McNamara's life was no longer the need to have the wisdom to avoid unwise interventions, but rather to maintain the capacity to endure them and maintain public support for them. Obama and Gates here became replicas of McNamara, men who didn't trust the military to develop a winning strategy and lacked the courage to see it through.

However, lack of will and unwillingness to adopt a winning strategy were not the only commonalities that McNamara and Obama were imagined as having in this moment. Critics also suggested that the president would struggle because he shared the former secretary's arrogance about the capacity of his unemotional, calculating intellect to solve complicated problems. These comparisons played on long-standing and not always flattering comparisons of Obama and Kennedy. The *Times* noted that Obama "doesn't shrink from comparison with Kennedy, another charismatic forty-something president with an attractive young family and a Harvard pedigree" but that "he vowed to avoid the stumbles of Kennedy's 'Best and the Brightest' by seeking a broad range of advice."[58] Between January 2009 and McNamara's death, articles, editorials, and letters regularly referred, with varying degrees of irony, to Obama's administration as including "the best and the brightest," a phrase of course deeply resonant with the legacy of Kennedy and, in particular, McNamara.[59]

Even before Obama's inauguration, *The Hill* described the president-elect's "unflappability and demeanor of cerebral reserve" and the *New York Times* described Obama's "cool, cerebral delivery."[60] But not all of these comparisons were complimentary. Just before Obama's inauguration, *New York Times* columnist Ross Douthat cautioned, "If his administration founders, his hypercerebral side will almost certainly take the blame."[61]

After McNamara's death, critics seized on the notion that no one better recalled the folly of "the best and the brightest" more than the former defense secretary to critique Obama. In Baton Rouge, an editorialist complained that "smart doesn't always count" before writing that "new generations of policy analysts, men not so different from McNamara, are again trying to break the will of people who are very, very different from all of us."[62] The *Arkansas Democrat-Gazette* editorial that had lauded Bush and referred to McNamara's youth and intelligence evoked Obama's near-celebrity status in its complaint that "we tend to forget how celebrated these masterminds were in their time." It declared that the chief lesson of McNamara's life was "never trust a technocrat with power"—a term that had special resonance in 2009 because of its frequent application to Obama, to whom it had also been frequently applied.[63]

Two days before the president's inauguration, for example, the *New York Times* described him in terms that could have been used to described McNamara: "an elegant, well-spoken technocrat who went to all the right schools."[64] A few months later, columnist David Rothkopf lamented, "Watching Obama at times, it seems that we've elected—despite their smarts and earnestness—a government of stumbling technocrats whose solutions either fall short or go too far."[65]

More directly, syndicated columns by John M. Crisp, David Ignatius, and George Will also asserted that McNamara's intellectual overconfidence could easily be applied to contemporary Washington. Drawing on a broader discursive linkage that had preceded Obama's inauguration, each implicitly linked the Kennedy and the Obama administrations.

Crisp, the most explicitly liberal of the three, argued that condemning McNamara "should be tempered by the fact of our continued willingness to use war in the service of our interests, rather than as a last resort."[66]

His column, however, is hardly a pacifist screed. Rather, he argues, "While the war in Afghanistan seemed like a worthy cause eight years ago, many Americans have only a vague sense of purpose now and no clear concept of how our current tactics can achieve that purpose" before closing with an implicit juxtaposition of McNamara and Obama: "Perhaps we know what we're doing in Afghanistan. But at one point the 'best and the brightest' thought they understood Vietnam perfectly. Years later we discovered, after great national cost, that unquestioning faith in our leadership was unjustified."[67] While Crisp is painting Afghanistan as a quagmire akin to Vietnam, he identifies the reason for McNamara's failure as quite different from those applied to Rumsfeld six years earlier; here, the issue is not dishonesty as much as a calculating intellectual hubris.

Similarly, while neither Ignatius nor Will references Afghanistan, both make evident their skepticism of Obama's foreign policy. Ignatius, who five years earlier had compared McNamara and Rumsfeld, in 2009 recalled both the title of Obama's campaign book and the slogan of that campaign in his references to the "sense of possibility McNamara conveyed in those first years—the audacity, not of hope but of reason."[68] More generally, his description of McNamara as someone who struggled against a bureaucracy that "resented [his] attempt to impose change" and of an administration filled with "men who had never known failure" and "charmed and brilliant people struggling with Vietnam" implicitly evoked Obama and his administration. And while he never mentions contemporary foreign policy, this language makes Ignatius's concluding plea to "be wary of the notion that smart people can solve any problem if they just try hard enough" and "to consider, even when we feel most confident, the possibility that we could be wrong" signify as a call to be skeptical of Obama's Afghanistan strategy.[69] Here again, the issue was not the failure to imagine the problem; it was having the arrogance to believe that it could be solved.

Will, a critic of expanding the Afghanistan War, likewise linked the two men on the basis of a simplistic hubris. "Seemingly confident that managing the competition of nations could be as orderly as managing competition among the three members of Detroit's oligopoly," he wrote, "McNamara entered government seven months before the birth of the current president, who is the owner and, he is serenely sure, the fixer of General Motors."[70] Will ostensibly aims his critique at the neoconservatives advocating a stronger response to Iran. However, his rhetoric ultimately identifies the overconfidence behind the Obama administration's aggressive agenda as his deepest concern: "Today, something unsettlingly familiar to McNamara's eerie assuredness pervades the Washington in which he died. The spirit is: have confidence, everybody, because we have, or soon will have, *everything*—really, everything—under control."[71]

Moreover, that Will's concern intersects with his critiques of Obama is likewise reflected in his referencing, as Ignatius does, Obama's campaign book and reaching a nearly identical conclusion, "the capital, gripped by the audacious hope of mastering everything, would be wise to entertain a shadow of a doubt about that."[72] Here, as it had been to the Bush administration six years earlier, the quagmire theory of the Vietnam War was applied to the Obama administration, but in this case the flaw that contemporary policymakers shared with McNamara was not a failure to imagine that the war might be difficult or a tendency to dissemble about its progress, but rather the hubris to assume that it was a problem that they could solve.

For some editorialists, Robert McNamara's death was imagined as something of a closing statement on the Vietnam War. The *Richmond Times-Dispatch*, for example, intoned, "Peace, we pray, comes to us all."[73] However, the uses to which McNamara's legacy was put in the twenty-first century reveal that the Vietnam War remains a potent metaphor in contemporary public life, even as the nation has hardly much less settled on a singular remembrance of that conflict. In 2003, the emergence of McNamara in Errol Morris's *The Fog of War* created a cultural moment in which the Iraq War's critics could mobilize a remembrance of the former secretary's arrogance and dishonesty to condemn a war that they felt had been started on false pretenses and an administration that they viewed as similarly dissembling. Six years later, upon McNamara's death, his legacy served quite different purposes. Then, he could serve as a foil to validate the Bush administration's increased commitment to Iraq and a cautionary tale as the Obama administration contemplated an increased commitment in Afghanistan.

The diverse and competing uses to which one figure's legacy was put in the first decade of the twenty-first century illustrates much about how wars end—or do not—in US culture. Robert McNamara's public remembrance reveals that Americans still struggle with what the Vietnam War means and apply competing narratives about it in debates over contemporary issues. As well, it reveals that the meaning of critical figures, events, and aspects remain unstable, able to be invoked in diverse ways to serve competing remembrances of the war. And perhaps most importantly, it illustrates that Vietnam's remembrance has become a defining, permanent aspect of American public life and the debate over the United States' role in the world. Indeed, while John Crisp's acknowledgment that with the exception of Henry Kissinger, McNamara was the last significant official of the Vietnam era points out the degree to which the Vietnam War is receding into history, what seems certain is that the passing of Kissinger's death will be another occasion to evaluate the war's legacy and contemporary relevance, but it will hardly be the last.[74]

David Kieran is assistant professor of history at Washington and Jefferson College in Washington, Pennsylvania. He is the author of *Forever Vietnam: How a Divisive War Changed American Public Memory* (University of Massachusetts Press, 2014), the editor of *The War of My Generation: Youth Culture and the War on Terror* (Rutgers University Press, 2015), and the coeditor of *At War: The Military and American Culture in the 20th Century and Beyond* (Rutgers, 2018). His articles have appeared in *American Studies, War & Society, Children's Literature Association Quarterly*, and several edited collections, and an article is forthcoming in *The Journal of American Studies*. His most recent book is *Signature Wounds: The Untold Story of the Military's Mental Health Crisis* (New York University Press, 2019). He holds a PhD from The George Washington University.

Notes

1. See, for example, Marilyn Berger, "Ronald Reagan Dies at 93," *New York Times*, 6 June 2004; Scott Shane, "Ford Is Remembered as Bringing 'Grace to a Moment of Great Doubt,'" *New York Times*, 3 January 2007.
2. "Former Defense Chief McNamara Dies at 93," *Morning Edition*, NPR News, 6 July 2009; "McNamara's Death," *ABC Nightly News*, 6 July 2009.
3. Tim Weiner, "Robert McNamara, Architect of Futile War, Dies," *New York Times*, 7 July 2009.
4. Thomas W. Lippman, "'Terribly Wrong' Handling of Vietnam Overshadowed Record of Achievement," *Washington Post*, 7 July 2009.
5. Christian G. Appy, *American Reckoning: The Vietnam War and Our National Identity* (New York: Viking, 2015), xii.
6. H. Bruce Franklin, *Vietnam and Other American Fantasies* (Amherst: University of Massachusetts Press, 2001), 41.
7. Ibid., 41–42.
8. Ibid., 42.
9. Ibid.
10. In this paragraph, I am revisiting the major claims of my earlier work, *Forever Vietnam: How a Divisive War Changed American Public Memory* (Amherst: University of Massachusetts Press, 2014), esp. 3–8.
11. Jay Winter, *Remembering War: The Great War between Memory and History in the Twentieth Century* (New Haven: Yale University Press, 2006), 3.

12. Kieran, *Forever Vietnam*, 3.
13. Qtd. in "Transcript for Sept. 14," *Meet the Press*, NBC News, 14 September 2003, available at http://www.nbcnews.com/id/3080244/ns/meet_the_press/t/transcript-sept/#.WZ3IJDPMwWo.
14. Edward Wong, "A Region Inflamed: Combat; 46 Iraqis Die in Fierce Fight between Rebels and G.I.'s," *New York Times*, 1 December 2003.
15. Dexter Filkins, "A Region Inflamed: Strategy; Tough New Tactics by U.S. Tighten Grip on Iraq Towns," *New York Times*, 7 December 2003.
16. Ibid.
17. Steven R. Weisman, "Bush Aides Say Attacks Won't Scare Allies into Leaving Iraq," *New York Times*, 2 December 2003.
18. George W. Bush, "Remarks Following a Meeting with Members of the Iraqi National Symphony," 10 December 2003, online by Gerhard Peters and John T. Wooley, The American Presidency Project, available at http://www.presidency.ucsb.edu/ws/index.php?pid=763.
19. "Transcript for Sept. 14," *Meet the Press*, NBC News, 14 September 2003. For a longer critique of how the Bush administration failed to plan for the war, see Thomas E. Ricks, *Fiasco: The American Military Adventure in Iraq* (New York: Penguin, 2006), 109–11.
20. Thomas E. Ricks, "For Vietnam Vet Anthony Zinni, Another War on Shaky Territory," *Washington Post*, 23 December 2003.
21. Robert G. Kaiser, "Iraq Isn't Vietnam, but They Rhyme," *Washington Post*, 28 December 2003.
22. "Iraq Has Become a New Vietnam for U.S. Combat Troops," *Irish Times* (Dublin), 8 December 2003; William Choong, "Iraq: America's New Vietnam?" *Straits Times* (Singapore), 20 December 2003.
23. "Oldest Living Whiz Kid Tells All," *New York Times*, 25 January 2004.
24. Christy Lemire, "At the Movies: 'The Fog of War,'" *Associated Press*, 17 December 2003; "Lessons about War and Peace," *Copley News Service*, 19 March 2004. See also Marc Cooper, "Hard Lines and Second Thoughts," *LA Weekly*, 19 December 2003.
25. Samantha Power, "War and Never Having to Say You're Sorry," *New York Times*, 14 December 2003.
26. On the location of the soldier within Vietnam memory, see Marita Sturken, *Tangled Memories: The Vietnam War, the AIDS Epidemic, and the Politics of Remembering* (Berkeley: University of California Press, 1998), 102.
27. Power, "War."
28. Ibid.
29. Ruth Rosen, "The Fog of Power," *San Francisco Chronicle*, 5 February 2004.
30. Ibid.
31. Ibid.
32. "Veteran Newsman Safer Sees Fault Line from Vietnam to Iraq," *Associated Press* State and Local Wire, 18 April 2004.
33. Art Buchwald, "The Fugue of War," *Washington Post*, 15 January 1004. Nonsyndicated writing made similar observations. See Mark Burger, "Two Oscar Winners for Fourth Documentary Pierces the Fog of War with McNamara on the Firing Line," *Winston-Salem Journal*, 21 March 2004; Barbara Peters Smith, "Insights Loom in the Fog of War," *Sarasota Herald-Tribune*, 18 February 2004; Brandt Ayers, "Cost of Vietnam Lingers," *Charleston Gazette* (West Virginia), 29 February 2004; James Ralston, "Gulf of Tonkin and WMD Lessons from Vietnam Apply Now," *Charleston Gazette* (West Virginia), 1 March 2004. See also "Lessons about War and Peace," *Copley News Service*, 19 March 2004; Jeri Rowe, "Plunging into 'Fog of War,'" *News and Record* (Greensboro), 25 March 2004; Jonathan E. Kaplan, "How Bush's Vulcans Arrived at Their Mind Meld," *The Hill*, 31 March 2004; Martin Gottleib, "Kerry, 'Fog of War' Stir Memory; Vietnam Was

Like 2004, Only Worse," *Dayton Daily News*, 31 March 2004; Stacy Taylor, Letter to the Editor, *San Francisco Chronicle*, 12 April 2004.
34. Significantly, each of these comments coincided with critiques of the Bush administration and its foreign policy apparatus that appeared elsewhere simultaneously. See, for example, Bob Woodward, *Plan of Attack: The Definitive Account of the Decision to Invade Iraq* (New York: Simon and Schuster, 2004), 80.
35. Scott Galupo, "Fog of War: Questionable Lessons Drawn from the Career of Robert McNamara," *Washington Times*, 26 December 2003. For defenses of the Iraq War as not like Vietnam, see Dan Rodricks, "Proud Army Parent Believes," *Oakland Tribune*, 18 April 2004; Jim Tierney, Letter to the Editor, *Oregonian* (Portland), 26 April 2004.
36. That there had been many comparisons between Rumsfeld and McNamara was also noted after McNamara's death; see Pete Yost and Mike Feinsilber, "Ex-Secretary of Defense Robert McNamara Dies at 93," *Lowell Sun* (Massachusetts) , 6 July 2009.
37. A. O. Scott, "Critic's Notebook; Searching for Modern Lessons in Films That Recall Old Wars," *New York Times*, 12 January 2004.
38. Amanda Henry, "Shrouded in Fog; Film Aims to Get Inside the Mind of Robert McNamara," *Wisconsin State Journal*, 7 March 2004; Marc Cooper, "Hard Lines and Second Thoughts," *LA Weekly*, 19 December 2003. See also J. Hoberman, "A '60s Mr. Death Explains the Calculus of Military Slaughter," *Village Voice* (New York), 23 December 2003; Tom Horgan, "'Fog of War' Describes Life through Deaths of Others," *University Wire*, 12 February 2004; Carrie Rickey, "A Veteran of War Cites Their Lessons," *Philadelphia Inquirer*, 13 February 2004; Philip Martin, "Mournful Documentary Gives Former Defense Chief His Say," *Arkansas Democrat-Gazette*, 27 February 2004; Sebastian Mallaby, "Legitimacy's Legacy," *Washington Post*, 12 April 2004; "Newsweek Cover: Crisis in Iraq: The Vietnam Factor—How This War Compares—and How It Doesn't," 11 April 2004; "Veteran Newsman Safer Sees Fault Line from Vietnam to Iraq," Associated Press State and Local Wire, 18 April 2004; Mark Sommer, "Lifting the Fog; McNamara Sheds Some Light on U.S. Policies," *Buffalo News*, 20 February 2004; Jim Tierney, "Letter to the Editor."
39. Roger Ebert, "'War' Horse Tells Riveting Tale," *Chicago Sun-Times*, 23 January 2004. See also Gina Kaufmann et al., "Tell the Truth; Film Festival Extracts Confessions, Some of Which Are Lies," *Pitch* (Kansas City).
40. For a narrative history of these debates, see Bob Woodward, *Obama's Wars* (New York: Simon and Schuster, 2011).
41. My thinking here is informed by Benedict Anderson's argument that seemingly coincidental appearance of unrelated news items is hardly inconsequential; Anderson notes that "their linkage is imagined," and yet he posits that they create the "imagined world" that is central to the individuals' sense of national consciousness (*Imagined Communities: Reflections on the Origin and Spread of Nationalism.* [London: Verso, 1983, rev. 1991], 33, 35).
42. Bob Herbert, "After the War Was Over," *New York Times*, 7 July 2009; "Matson's View," editorial cartoon, *St. Louis Post-Dispatch*, 7 July 2009; "McNamara's Hubris Holds Lessons for Today's Leaders," *USA Today*, 7 July 2009. See also Seam Legell, "Vietnam War Architect McNamara Dies; Ex-Defense Secretary Later Called Conflict 'Terribly Wrong,'" *Washington Times*, 7 July 2009; *Capital Times* (Madison), "Robert McNamara and the Burden of Being Wrong," 14 July 2009; Mark Russell, Editorial, *Grand Rapids Press*, 9 July 2009; Bill Kelly, Letter to the Editor, *Columbian* (Vancouver, WA), 14 July 2009; Dorian De Wind, Letter to the Editor, *USA Today*, 13 July 2009; Nathaniel Fick, "A Warrior Fighting the Wrong War," *Washington Post*, 26 July 2009.
43. Brian Santo, Letter to the Editor, *The Oregonian* (Portland), 9 July 2009.
44. The legitimacy of this claim has been hotly debated. For one critical perspective, see Gian Gentile, *Wrong Turn: America's Deadly Embrace of Counterinsurgency* (New

York: New Press, 2013), 88–89; Thomas E. Ricks, *The Gamble: General Petraeus and the American Military Adventure in Iraq* (New York: Penguin, 2010).
45. John McCain and Joe Lieberman, "The Surge Worked," *Wall Street Journal*, 10 January 2008.
46. I have detailed this debate in greater detail elsewhere. See David Kieran, *Forever Vietnam: How a Divisive War Changed American Public Memory* (Amherst: University of Massachusetts Press, 2014), 205–6.
47. Lewis Sorley, *A Better War: The Unexamined Victories and Final Tragedy of America's Last Years in Vietnam* (New York: Houghton Mifflin Harcourt, 1999), xv.
48. Graham writes, for instance, of the "string of miscalculations about the Iraq War" that included "false premise that Iraq had WMD stockpiles" ("McNamara Apologized for Vietnam. Will Rumsfeld Do So for Iraq?" *Washington Post*, 12 July 2009).
49. Ibid.
50. "McNamara and the Liberal's War," *Wall Street Journal*, 8 July 2009. The *Wall Street Journal* piece was followed the next day by an editorial that straightforwardly maintained that the Vietnam War had been lost because of McNamara's strategic mismanagement (Seth Lipsky, "McNamara in Purgatory: Setting the Record Straight," *Wall Street Journal*, 9 July 2009).
51. "The Smart Loser," *Investor's Business Daily*, 7 July 2009.
52. "McNamara and the Liberal's War."
53. Ibid.
54. "From McNamara to Obama," *Wall Street Journal*, 7 July 2009.
55. Ibid.
56. Jim Hoagland, "Brightness Cloaked in Hubris," *Washington Post*, 7 July 2009.
57. "Tired of Losers," *Investor's Business Daily*, 21 July 2009.
58. John Harwood, "Yes He Can, and He'll Tell You about it," *New York Times*, 12 January 2009.
59. An editorial in the *Deming Headlight* (New Mexico) reported, "The Center for Individual Freedom, a conservative Virginia 'think tank,' reported that the mainstream media initially described the president's new staff and Cabinet members as the 'best and brightest'" ("Setting the Bar," *Deming Headlight*, 16 February 2009). See, for example, Cheryl Hall, "Dallas Leaders Tell What They'd Do First If They Were Obama," *Dallas Morning News*, 4 January 2009; Stuart Rothenberg, "It May Not Be the Economy, Stupid, in the End," *Roll Call* (Washington, DC), 6 January 2009; Zachary Coile, "A Challenge Obama Chose; The Presidency in Transition; He's Tapped the Best, Brightest, and Now Has to Manage Them," *San Francisco Chronicle*, 11 January 2009; David Rogers, "Can Obama Seize the Moment?" *St. Paul Pioneer Press*, 12 January 2009; "Journalists Examine Possible Strengths and Weaknesses of Obama Presidency," *States News Service*, 16 January 2007; David Rogers, "Obama's Challenge; at This Breathtaking Moment in History, He'll Need to Rely on His Trademark Calm, Pick His Battles Carefully and Stay in Touch with the Little People," *Pittsburgh Post-Gazette*, 18 January 2009; Richard Wolf, "Obama's Style Shifts along with the Task at Hand; Critics Say Actions Not Always in Line with Image," *USA Today*, 24 April 2009; and Norma J. Neto, Letter to the Editor, *Contra Costa Times*, 9 May 2009.
60. Alessandra Stanley, "It Seemed Familiar, and Yet So Different," *New York Times*, 10 February 2009; "Obama's Deftness," *The Hill*, 15 January 2009.
61. "Obama's Deftness"; Ross Douthat, "When Buckley Met Reagan," *New York Times*, 18 January 2009.
62. "McNamara: Smartest Fool," *Advocate* (Baton Rouge), 13 July 2009.
63. "A Man for the Soulless Age; the Numbers Man: Robert Strange McNamara," *Arkansas Democrat-Gazette*, 9 July 2009.
64. Alessandra Stanley, "Vive le Wrestler," *New York Times*, 18 January 2009.

65. David Rothkopf, "Somebody Take Control (Anybody. Really. Please.); Where Are All the Leaders?" *Washington Post*, 29 March 2009.
66. John M. Crisp, "What We Learned from the Vietnam War," *Contra Costa Times*, 15 July 2009.
67. Ibid.
68. David Ignatius, "Scapegoat in Chief," *Washington Post*, 21 December 2004; David Ignatius, "Certainty That Hit a Wall," *Washington Post*, 7 July 2009.
69. Ignatius, "Certainty That Hit a Wall."
70. George F. Will, "The McNamara Mentality," *Washington Post*, 8 July 2009.
71. Ibid.
72. Ibid.
73. "Rest in Peace," *Richmond Times-Dispatch*.
74. Crisp, "What We Learned."

Select Bibliography

Anderson, Benedict, *Imagined Communities: Reflections on the Origin and Spread of Nationalism* (London: Verso, 1983).
Appy, Christian G., *American Reckoning: The Vietnam War and Our National Identity* (New York: Viking, 2015).
Franklin, H. Bruce, *Vietnam and Other American Fantasies* (Amherst: University of Massachusetts Press, 2001).
Gentile, Gian, *Wrong Turn: America's Deadly Embrace of Counterinsurgency* (New York: New Press, 2013).
Kieran, David, *Forever Vietnam: How a Divisive War Changed American Public Memory* (Amherst: University of Massachusetts Press, 2014).
Ricks, Thomas E., *Fiasco: The American Military Adventure in Iraq* (New York: Penguin, 2006).
_____, *The Gamble: General David Petraeus and the American Military Adventure in Iraq, 2006–2008* (New York: Penguin, 2009).
_____, *Obama's Wars: The Inside Story* (New York: Simon and Schuster, 2011).
Sorley, Lewis, *A Better War: The Unexamined Victories and Final Tragedy of America's Last Years in Vietnam* (New York: Houghton Mifflin Harcourt, 1999).
Sturken, Marita, *Tangled Memories: The Vietnam War, the AIDS Epidemic, and the Politics of Remembering* (Berkeley: University of California Press, 1997).
Winter, Jay, *Remembering War: The Great War between Memory and History in the Twentieth Century* (New Haven: Yale University Press, 2006).
Woodward, Bob, *Plan of Attack: The Definitive Account of the Decision to Invade Iraq* (New York: Simon and Schuster, 2004).

Chapter 4

After the Fall of Saigon
Strategic Implications of America's Involvement in Vietnam

Robert K. Brigham

The Vietnam War had a dramatic impact on the formulation and implementation of US foreign policy. Successive US presidential administrations felt the long shadow of Vietnam and adjusted their strategic outlooks accordingly. A Vietnam Syndrome, as it was described, circled every significant US foreign policy decision. That syndrome included new low-risk strategies and a limited commitment of American troop interventions around the globe. The United States would have to rein in its geopolitical objectives because the American public would not tolerate body bags and unending military commitments following Saigon's collapse.

The Vietnam syndrome actually began before the war ended. On 22 April 1975, President Gerald Ford told an audience at Tulane University that the Vietnam War was "finished as far as the United States was concerned."[1] One week later, on 30 April 1975, Saigon fell to combined PAVN (People's Army of Vietnam) and PLAF (People's Liberation Armed Forces) forces, and the US War in Vietnam was indeed over. Hanoi moved quickly to consolidate its power and unite Vietnam under the socialist banner. In Washington, the White House blamed Congress for refusing a request for $722 million in emergency military assistance for South Vietnam.

Ford and his secretary of state, Henry Kissinger, argued that additional aid might bring about the stalemate that all had hoped for in Vietnam and that would lead to a negotiated settlement between North and South Vietnam instead of an all-out communist victory. Kissinger publicly worried that pulling the plug on South Vietnam would have dire consequences for US prestige in the world and that it would doom the South Vietnamese to "lingering deaths."[2] Congress, in sharp contrast, claimed that South Vietnamese troops had abandoned more military equipment in late 1974 and early 1975 than all the emergency aid could buy. Published photographs of South Vietnamese soldiers fleeing Phuoc Long, Hue, and Da Nang ahead of the communists did not endear Saigon's cause to Congress.

Furthermore, congressional critics were quick to point out that Kissinger himself had negotiated the terms of the peace deal in Paris that had sealed South Vietnam's fate. He had purposefully separated political and military issues. He had negotiated a standstill cease-fire, which had given the PAVN an unfair advantage, allowing ten of its main force infantry divisions to remain south of the seventeenth parallel while the United States completed a unilateral troop withdrawal. Moreover, Kissinger had not included any implementation language in the peace agreement, and he had not insisted on workable enforcement mechanisms. If the Vietnamese communists violated the terms and conditions of the treaty, they suffered no penalty. Despite Kissinger's claims to the contrary, none of the significant political questions from the war were linked. All of this led Congress to see the emergency request for aid as little more than a fig leaf barely covering the underlying problems in Vietnam. It was time, Congress declared, to end US involvement in this "horrid war."[3]

Following the fall of Saigon, US policymakers dealt with the Vietnam Syndrome in a variety of ways. Some, like Kissinger, argued that the United States needed to abandon the reckless liberalism of the early Cold War and focus more on its realistic national interests. Shortly after the war, Kissinger concluded that "we probably made a mistake" by focusing single-mindedly on international communism and falling dominos when dealing with Vietnam. "We perhaps might have perceived the war more in Vietnamese terms," he conceded, "rather than as the outward thrust of a global conspiracy."[4] In his view, the United States had stretched itself too thin in Vietnam, and in the future, must define its interests more narrowly. Like the European statesmen he had written about, Kissinger believed the true responsibility of a great power was in "knowing when to stop."[5]

Kissinger claimed to recognize that the United States could not fight a protracted war again and maintain its other, more vital interests. The Soviet Union had reached nuclear parity while the United States was bogged down in the jungles of the Southeast Asia, some had claimed, and it had also greatly expanded its naval fleet. Both developments changed the power relationship between the superpower rivals, and this change worried Kissinger more than the loss of South Vietnam.

Kissinger's critics scoffed at his situational realism, however, claiming that he had failed to carefully calibrate military operations in Cambodia, Laos, and Vietnam with the negotiations taking place in Paris.[6] For someone who positioned himself as a clear-eyed realist following the war, he had been "an emotional statesmen"[7] during it and this had led to unnecessary death and destruction. Kissinger aided the Vietnam Syndrome and its influence on US foreign policy by claiming that a skilled policymaker could easily separate the soaring rhetoric used to defend US intervention in Vietnam from clear geopolitical goals. These false claims led successive US administrations to search for meaning and immutable truths from the Vietnam War.

Some suggested that the lesson of Vietnam was that the United States should not get involved in nationalistic struggles with no clear political goals in mind. Others were highly critical of this view, however, claiming that the United States could have won the Vietnam War and that the failure to do so was no reason to limit US global responsibilities. Nixon's secretary of defense, James Schlesinger, argued that the military had operated with too many restrictions.[8] US Army colonel Harry Summers agreed, advising that in the future the United States needed to bring all-out military force to bear in any conflict.[9] General William Westmoreland, commander of the Military Assistance Command-Vietnam, believed that his attrition strategy could have worked in Vietnam if only the American people had not suffered from a failure of will during the Tet Offensive.[10]

Some advisers suggested that the problem rested with the US allies in Saigon.[11] Without a viable government and a strong national army, how could the United States have achieved victory? McGeorge Bundy, national security adviser for presidents Kennedy and Johnson, warned that Vietnam taught no useful lessons because the war was unique and probably would not be repeated.[12] Americans, the Vietnam apologists all argued, should get over the war and turn their attention to the pressing international problems of the day.

But Congress still felt the limits on US power following Vietnam. Six months after Saigon fell, Portugal granted its former colony, Angola, independence following a bloody civil war. The announcement set off another internal conflict involving the Soviet-supported Popular Movement for the Liberation of Angola (MPLA). The Central Intelligence Agency (CIA) spent $32 million on covert aid to the MPLA's rivals, hoping to control the revolution and events in Africa. The US State Department official in charge of African affairs, Nathaniel Davis, urged the Ford administration to engage in trilateral diplomacy, bringing in neighboring Tanzania and Zambia to help negotiate a peaceful settlement. President Ford rejected Davis's advice, opting instead for more covert aid and a military solution. Davis resigned in protest and let several members of Congress know that the Ford administration had rejected the diplomatic path. As the MPLA made headway against its adversaries, Ford prepared to ask Congress for an additional $25 million for arms and covert aid. Congress balked, voting down the proposal by a wide margin. Kissinger immediately complained that Congress had been too traumatized by Vietnam, and Ford concluded that Vietnam had caused members of Congress to "lose their guts."[13]

The Carter administration also experienced the hangover effect from Vietnam. Jimmy Carter came into office in 1977 promising to cut military budgets, reduce US forces overseas, trim arms sales abroad, and support allies of his human rights agenda. He vowed there would be no more Vietnams. Carter was deeply troubled by the malaise that he thought had gripped the nation since Vietnam. He believed the American people would no longer accept US military intervention in faraway places for dubious reasons. He argued that the United States could not "prop up a series of regimes that lacked popular support" and that "there can be no going back to a time when we thought there could be American solutions to every problem."[14] Carter believed that newly emerging postcolonial nations were in revolt because of grinding poverty, social and racial problems, and political difficulties, not international communism. He wanted to reorient US relations with the southern world, erasing the "intellectual and moral poverty" of military interventions that had been demonstrated in Vietnam.[15]

Yet Carter was also a Cold Warrior. He insisted that détente had allowed the Soviets to increase their domination of Eastern Europe, and he was highly critical of grain sales to Moscow. He reinvigorated the containment doctrine by initiating new weapons systems and by cultivating friendly governments in the southern world. When the Soviets invaded Afghanistan in 1979, Carter launched a new phase of containment. He armed many of Moscow's neighbors, such as Pakistan, and created several new naval facilities in Oman, Kenya, Somalia, and Egypt. Carter also opened formal diplomatic relations with the People's Republic of China—a move that he was sure would make the Soviets think twice about more aggressive action. In his State of the Union address of 23 January 1980, the president announced the Carter Doctrine: "An attempt by any outside force to gain control of the Persian Gulf region will be regarded as an assault on the vital interests of the United States of America, and such an assault will be repelled by use of any means necessary, including military force."[16] Carter even declared a US boycott of the 1980 summer Olympics in Moscow to protest the Soviet invasion of Afghanistan.

Carter's bold words caused many in Washington to proclaim that the Vietnam Syndrome had already been cured. But others knew better. George F. Kennan, the father of the original containment policy, suggested that Carter was long on words and short on action. He concluded that the president was using "thundering" rhetoric but carrying "a very small stick."[17] Kennan knew what others knew. At the height of a devastating economic crisis at home, in the shadow of Vietnam, Congress was not likely to approve any bold plans that included direct military action against the Soviets. The United States could fight wars with proxies in the post-Vietnam era, but Congress would not go along with the full mobilization of US troops to save Afghanistan—or any other nation in the region, for that matter. When Carter promised $400 million to Pakistan for its defense against a potential Soviet invasion, the Pakistani prime minister called it "peanuts."[18] Indeed, Carter was trying to fight the Cold War with one hand tied behind his back. The knot was Vietnam. The hostage crisis in Iran simply underscored Carter's inability to move the nation to a war footing so soon after the fall of Saigon.

Other signs indicated that Carter and the country were still suffering from Vietnam Syndrome. In 1975 the Khmer Rouge took over Cambodia following a brutal civil war against the American-backed Lon Nol government. The Khmer Rouge not only were Maoists but were perhaps even more fanatical about the moral superiority of their ideas. Once they seized power, the communists emptied Phnom Penh and other Cambodian cities, creating a nation of refugees. They relocated urban Cambodians to rural areas and forced them to work at meaningless tasks in death camps.

Over time, the Khmer Rouge instituted one of the most reprehensible genocidal programs in history, killing over one-third of the entire Cambodian population. During this purge, the Carter administration sat on the sidelines. Of course, Washington's new relationship with Beijing made it difficult for the Carter administration to protest Khmer Rouge atrocities—China was the Khmer Rouge's major benefactor—but US officials turned their backs, fearing another Vietnam. Carter purposefully avoided the genocide in Cambodia, according to public policy expert John Mueller, because of "fears that paying too much attention might lead to the conclusion that American troops should be sent over to rectify the disaster."[19] Carter was not alone in ignoring the problems in Cambodia. The three television networks devoted less than thirty minutes of coverage to a genocide that lasted three years, and Congress failed to pass any resolutions condemning the Khmer Rouge and calling for united action by the US foreign policy establishment and the United Nations.

Carter and Congress did take note, however, when Vietnam invaded Cambodia and drove the Khmer Rouge from power. The administration condemned Vietnam's violation of Cambodian sovereignty and called on Hanoi to withdraw its troops. At the United Nations, the US representative did not object to the Khmer Rouge maintaining the official Cambodian seat because of Hanoi's actions. Furthermore, Carter called a halt to negotiations taking place in Hanoi to normalize relations between the United States and Vietnam. During his 1976 presidential campaign, Carter had made normalizing relations with Vietnam a priority. With the Cambodian invasion and with new US ties to China, it was now time to punish Vietnam for forcing an American withdrawal from Vietnam. Carter used the pretext of the Cambodian invasion, Hanoi's postwar treaties with Moscow, and the ongoing debate over the POW/MIA (prisoners of war/soldiers missing in action) issue to deflect criticism of his weak foreign policy directives.

Congress did go along with increased military budgets in the Carter years, however. If the president could not deploy US troops out of fear of another Vietnam, he definitely intended to beef up America's defense arsenal. This would give the appearance of strength, even if the shadows of Vietnam would not allow full mobilization to protect American national security interests. The president deployed the MX intercontinental missile and added $47 billion in new weapons systems. The Pentagon's budget jumped from $170 billion in 1976 to $197 billion in 1981, Carter's last budget year. Carter also doubled arms sales to US allies between 1977 and 1980, to $15.3 billion.[20] Some critics suggested Carter was trying to "remilitarize" the United States, but others concluded he had been "too soft" on the Soviets and America's enemies.[21] His public opinion polls in the area of foreign affairs were some of the lowest of the twentieth century. Only 17 percent of Americans polled in 1980 gave the president a satisfactory rating.[22]

For many Americans, Carter's mixed foreign policy agenda only enforced the desire to isolate themselves from the rest of the world. In retrospect, Carter's problem was that he did not want to get involved in another Vietnam-type conflict, but the world held only more of the same. Americans wanted a more robust response to global crises while avoiding the negative connotations of potential Vietnam-like quagmires. Afghanistan promised no easy solutions, and the civil wars in Central America offered only open-ended commitments. Given the reluctance of Congress and the American people to repeat the Vietnam experience, the only avenue available to the president other than military intervention was to build up America's deterrent capabilities.

This military buildup was a national salve for some, but Carter's fiercest critics claimed that this expansion was not enough to stop the Soviets. They feared that Ford, and then Carter, had not stopped the Soviets after Vietnam, claiming that Moscow had gone unchallenged in Ethiopia, Angola, and Mozambique. Furthermore, this group of hawkish Democrats argued that Ford and Carter had allowed the Soviets to gain superiority in nuclear weapons. This group of policymakers that gathered in US Senator Henry "Scoop" Jackson's (D-Washington) office for regular doses of anti-Soviet arguments became known as the "neocons." The neoconservative movement had deep roots in the early twentieth century, but its modern incarnation was led by people who believed that it was proper to promote democracy abroad without the aid and support of multilateral institutions, like the United Nations.

At the intellectual or abstract level, they represented a release from the Vietnam-style dependency on others or the reliance on allies that the Nixon Doctrine implied. They were Wilsonians who argued that the United States had the legitimate right to pursue its own agenda because it exerted a benevolent hegemony in the international system. They feared that Carter had failed to understand that the Soviets had used America's retreat from the world to make bold strikes in Africa and Central America following the US withdrawal from Vietnam. Despite the neoconservatives' calls for a more muscular US foreign policy, Carter remained committed to reorienting American power following the fall of Saigon.

Carter would never balance US fear of "more Vietnams" with broader foreign policy objectives, however. His opponent in the 1980 presidential election found a solution to this foreign policy dilemma through tough Cold War rhetoric denying that Vietnam had been a defeat. Candidate Ronald Reagan claimed that policymakers in Washington had gotten Vietnam all wrong. "For far too long," Reagan declared in August 1980,

> we have lived with the Vietnam Syndrome. This is a lesson for all of us in Vietnam. If we are forced to fight, we must have the means and the determination to prevail, or we will not have what it takes to secure peace. And while we are at it, let us tell those who fought in that war, that we will never again ask young men to fight and possibly die in a war our government is afraid to let them win.[23]

Reagan was hoping to revise America's understanding of Vietnam and its meanings in order to pursue a more aggressive foreign policy agenda. Carter's military budget increases and the neoconservatives' tough talk paved the way for the Reagan administration to fight the Cold

War using new weapons and covert CIA operations. Still, Reagan was as constrained by the ghosts of Vietnam as Carter, and his national security team took the Vietnam experience to heart no matter what the president claimed in public.

Despite Reagan's expansive rhetoric, his administration was the first to put formal parameters on US military operations. In a speech before the National Press Club in November 1984, Reagan's secretary of defense, Caspar Weinberger, announced the administration's new defense posture following the 1983 bombing of a US Marine Corps barracks at the Beirut airport in Lebanon. That stunning terrorist attack had caused the Reagan administration to withdraw all troops from Lebanon and the regional peacekeeping mission. The president did not want to isolate the United States from overseas actions, but he did want the Defense Department to prepare a plan summarizing the lessons learned in Beirut and Vietnam. These lessons were distilled into six major points that became known as the Weinberger Doctrine:

1. The United States should not commit forces to combat unless the vital national security interests of the United States, or its allies, is involved.
2. US troops should be committed only wholeheartedly and with the clear intention of winning. Otherwise, troops should not be committed.
3. US combat troops should be committed to conflicts with clearly defined political and military objectives.
4. The relationship between objectives and the force structure should be continually reassessed and adjusted if necessary.
5. US troops should be committed only when there is reasonable assurance that Congress and the American people will support the action.
6. The use of arms should be the last resort to protect US interests.[24]

After the attack at Beirut and against the backdrop of Vietnam, Weinberger was limiting where and when the United States would engage in military intervention. Reagan's secretary of state, George Shultz, was a staunch critic of the Weinberger Doctrine, arguing that diplomacy needed the constant threat of military force to succeed. Shultz did not believe that the nation was suffering from any Vietnam Syndrome, and he thought Congress would support US military intervention whenever and wherever it was needed.[25]

Given these parameters, the Reagan administration never asked the American people to make painful sacrifices to support its foreign policy agenda. Despite military intervention in several Central American countries, Reagan and Weinberger managed to keep US military action relatively limited on their watch. Few US soldiers died in combat during the Reagan years, and there was no full-scale mobilization of the armed forces. Despite claims from many quarters that US intervention in Nicaragua and El Salvador signaled new Vietnams, those conflicts never engulfed the United States as the war in Southeast Asia did.

Reagan did not use the US military to destabilize unfriendly regimes or to support friendly ones; instead, he used covert aid, CIA operations, and economic coercion to influence politics in the region. In Nicaragua Reagan supported proxy forces against the Sandinistas, in El Salvador he supported the authoritarian government rather than engage in direct US military intervention. Even the administration's support of the contras in Nicaragua did not match the Vietnam buildup. The CIA helped the contras mine three Nicaraguan ports and built large bases in neighboring Honduras, but there was no full-scale use of US forces against the Sandinistas as there had been against the People's Army of Vietnam (PAVN) and the People's Liberation Armed Forces of South Vietnam (PLAF).

Like Carter before him, Reagan increased US military spending to signal to allies and adversaries that the United States still held preponderant power. The president's bloated budgets included increasing military spending by 40 percent between 1980 and 1984. He believed he could outspend and outarm the Soviets with beneficial results. Reagan's flirtations with the Strategic Defense Initiative (SDI) were an outgrowth of this thinking. The missile shield was short on science but long on cost and publicity. The Reagan administration believed that such a shield would force the Soviets into even more expensive weapon systems that did not significantly alter the strategic balance. Reagan was gambling that the Soviets would not see past weapons production to policy implementation. That gambit left the United States with record budget deficits, nearly $7 trillion, and a soaring balance of trade deficit. Still, most Americans felt confident about the nation's place in the world, and few feared that the United States would be engaged in another Vietnam anytime soon.

After Reagan left office, many of his administration's views on military intervention survived with Colin Powell. Powell, a Vietnam veteran and disciple of Casper Weinberger, maintained that the United States must continue to use its economic power, diplomatic skills, and multilateral support as the cornerstone of all foreign policy actions. He warned that the United States should never lead with the use of armed force. He said the country had to ask itself a series of questions before it actively engaged in military conflict:

1. Is the political objective we seek to achieve important?
2. Does it have a clearly defined objective that is easily understood?
3. Have all other nonviolent policy means failed?
4. Will military force achieve the objective?
5. At what cost can the objective be reached?
6. Have the gains and risks been analyzed?
7. How might the situation that we seek to alter, once it is altered by force, develop further, and what might be the consequences?[26]

In short, the Powell Doctrine brought Weinberger's thinking into the 1990s.

Powell also outlined the military's willingness in the post-Vietnam era to ask hard questions and to make fundamental changes in its culture. Rejecting much of the academic thinking that had held sway during the Cold War, the services returned to the basics. One of the most significant changes was introducing courses on strategy in the service academies.[27] These courses emphasized history over academic theory. Students studied the classic battles and investigated writers long ignored. Sun Tzu and Carl von Clausewitz became familiar names at West Point and Annapolis once again. Along with this renewed emphasis on military history and strategy came a belief among the officers that the principal lesson of the Vietnam War was that the United States should never find itself in that position again. The military began to concentrate again on the Soviet threat in Europe and to prepare for a more conventional war on the continent. Military officers also came to reject many of the theories of protracted and limited war as applied in Vietnam. Instead, those with Vietnam experience insisted that there were limits to US power. They told their troops that there was not always a military solution to complex political problems.

Another significant development to ensure no more Vietnams was the move to make sure that service reserve troops were completely integrated into any mobilization scheme. During the Vietnam War, President Johnson refused Secretary of Defense Robert S. McNamara's requests to mobilize the reserves, fearing that the American public would see such a move as a sure sign that the war would require enormous sacrifice. Johnson wanted to limit public debate by fighting the war "in cold blood."[28] He worried that mobilizing the reserves might spark a heated debate about the war and its costs in Congress and among the American people. He also refused a war surtax, again not wanting to stimulate public examination of his policies. When Johnson introduced ground troops to Vietnam in March 1965, the reserves stayed home. Ultimately, this decision cost Johnson more than just a public debate. The draft became a focal point in the war because demand for new troops never abated. Even though Johnson claimed to have given General Westmorland everything he wanted to fight in Vietnam, most US commanders never believed that they had enough troops.

General Creighton Abrams, who served as US Army chief of staff in the last years of the Vietnam War, negotiated a new look for the Army with Secretary of Defense James Schlesinger. Abrams increased the Army's size to sixteen divisions without increasing the number of regular forces above 785,000.[29] He did so by assigning most support functions to an expanded reserve. The link with the regular Army became so tight that Abrams guaranteed there could be no future war without mobilizing the reserves. "They're not taking us to war again without calling up the reserves," Abrams was fond of saying.[30]

The impact of this policy was felt immediately. Coupled with the Goldwater-Nichols Act of 1986, which gave the head of the Joint Chiefs of Staff greater responsibility over all service branches and allowed coordinated and integrated training among the services, the new reserve force structure meant the Army would never be short of troops again. By the time of the first US Gulf War, 70 percent of the Army's support services, 60 percent of the Air Force's strategic airlift units, and 93 percent of the Navy's cargo handling battalions were with the reserves.[31] When George H. W. Bush took the nation to war in Iraq and Kuwait in 1991, he had no choice but to call up the reserves, and this arrangement made the president keep goals, objectives, and force structure in line. Of course, Colin Powell was a key member of Bush's strategic team, and this had a tremendous impact on the rules of engagement during the Gulf War.

Powell and National Security Advisor Brent Scowcroft shared with Bush the pragmatism that would mark the 1991 Gulf War. Following Saddam Hussein's refusal to follow a United Nations resolution demanding that Iraq withdraw from Kuwait, the Bush administration asked Congress for approval to enforce the UN mandate. The political goals were clear and limited, and the exit timeline precise. In just six short weeks, allied military actions forced Saddam Hussein to beat a heavy retreat out of Kuwait and back to Baghdad. In the process, thousands of Iraqis were killed, and Iraqi military equipment worth millions was destroyed. The use of force had been overwhelming, and military victory, decisive. President Bush, applauding the American-led effort, proclaimed, "By God, we've kicked the Vietnam syndrome."[32]

But the Bush administration had not kicked the Vietnam Syndrome. Instead, it had adopted a limited military strategy because of it. Bush, Powell, and Scowcroft faced Saddam's threat through a Vietnam lens.

They believed that Iraq could easily become a quagmire if they did not keep their political goals limited and the exit strategy clear. Following the parameters of a UN resolution, the Bush team did not follow Saddam's troops to Baghdad. Bush simply fulfilled the UN mandate: he removed Iraqi forces from Kuwait. In a touch of irony, those neoconservatives who criticized Bush for not marching on Baghdad would become the cornerstone of his son's national security team. Powell turned quickly on the administration's foes, claiming prophetically that if the war had not been limited, "the United States would be ruling Iraq today — at unpardonable expense in terms of money, lives lost, and ruined regional relationships."[33] Powell went on to suggest that a long-term nation-building project in Iraq was not in the US national interest. He argued that the undying faith in America's ability to alter political outlook would have been as misplaced in Iraq as it had been in Vietnam.

The Bush administration showed extreme caution in other areas of the world and in other conflicts too. During the 1990s Balkans crisis, the Bush administration refused to intervene directly to stop the slaughter in Bosnia. When a reporter asked why, the president responded:

> Everyone has been reluctant, for very understandable reasons, to use force. There are [sic] a lot of voices out there in the United States today that say 'use force,' but they don't have the same responsibility for sending somebody else's son or somebody else's daughter into harm's way. And I do. I do not want to see the United States bogged down in any way into some guerrilla warfare — we lived through that.[34]

The Bosnian Serbs seemed to understand Bush's comment perfectly. Serb leader Radovan Karadžić boldly proclaimed that his forces could have their way in the Balkans because the United States was paralyzed to act. He boasted that the Bush administration would have to send in two thousand marines to put down his forces, "then they have to send 10,000 more to save the 2,000. ... This is the best way to have another Vietnam."[35] Another Bosnian Serb leader claimed that the Balkans would be a "new Vietnam" for American troops should Bush intervene.[36] According to Samantha Power, then a journalist covering the Balkan crisis, "Vietnam became the ubiquitous shorthand for all that could go wrong in the Balkans if the United States became militarily engaged."[37]

The specter of Vietnam also hampered the Clinton administration. During the presidential campaign of 1992, Clinton had chided Bush over his decision not to intervene to protect human rights and promote democracy around the globe. Once in office, however, Clinton vowed that the United States would not send ground troops to the Balkans, even to stop genocide. As *New York Times* journalist Drummond Ayres reported in May 1993, there was an "abiding fear that the Balkans are another Vietnam, a deep-seated angst that tends to outweigh concerns that another holocaust is in the making."[38] This same fear kept the United States from intervening to stop the genocide in Rwanda that killed nearly one million people. Instead of military intervention, Clinton offered refugee camps on Rwanda's border and aid to rebuild the country.

Instead of military intervention around the world, Clinton hoped to engage nations as the movement toward globalization and democracy transpired naturally. Clinton and his advisers believed that the president had to supervise this development by removing the restrictions on the free flow of capital, labor, resources, and ideas. If this process could bind the nations of the world, the Clinton administration reasoned, the root causes of violence and interstate rivalry would fade away. There would be no reason to repeat the mistakes of Vietnam because the fundamental underpinnings of conflict would have been destroyed. When, in 1993, the United States got bloodied in Somalia, Clinton quickly pulled the troops out and left that region of the world to fend for itself.

At the end of the 1990s, however, some foreign policy analysts claimed that the pressing international questions were no longer about fears of another Vietnam, but about ethical dilemmas concerning military intervention to support human rights. They asked how and when the United States should intervene to stop major human rights violations and mass atrocity crimes. Others suggested that the move toward capitalism and democracy was irreversible and that US foreign policy should be aimed at helping that process along, not at seeking monsters to destroy.[39] Still, there was a growing feeling among many policy experts that the Clinton administration was indeed suffering from Vietnam Syndrome. Its inability to "pull the trigger" in Rwanda to stop the genocide was a product of that worldview. Clinton's top national security team, most of them Vietnam generation men and women, were hesitant to get involved in a complex situation that had elusive objectives and no easy answers. According to Samantha Power, Clinton administration officials were reluctant to get bogged down again, even if the cause was just.[40]

The Clinton administration never found a satisfactory answer to the Vietnam dilemma until it was too late for thousands of innocent people, and even then the answer was strategic bombing with no US ground troops. Critics of the Clinton use of force in Bosnia and Kosovo claimed that the United States could not support the principle of universal human rights with air power alone. Still, Clinton administration officials did not want to change the strategic thinking on the use of ground troops that they had inherited from four successive presidential administrations following the Vietnam War.

The Vietnam Syndrome was temporarily put aside, however, following the 9/11 terrorist attacks on the United States. The George W. Bush administration believed that the best defense against future terrorist attacks was to take the fight to them in Afghanistan and the states that supported them, like Iraq.[41] The United States had the right to defend itself, Bush reasoned, but it also had the responsibility to make the world safe for democracy. As the world's only superpower, the United States had the power and obligation to defend and promote democratic ideals. Leading neoconservatives William Kristol and Lawrence Kaplan agreed with the president, declaring that the United States was in the driver's seat and should drive the car: "What is wrong with dominance in the service of sound principles and high ideals."[42] With these words, the neoconservatives who supported the Bush administration wiped the memory of Vietnam from all policy discussions on Iraq and Afghanistan, including the heavy use of reserves. They also sidelined Colin Powell and others with Vietnam experience as a result.

Bush's new strategic thinking also embraced much of the neoconservatives' thinking on democracy promotion, and he came to believe that regime change was essential in Iraq and that promoting democracy through US military power was the key to stopping future terrorist attacks. The United States had to extend peace through military intervention in a troubled region, according to this thinking. This view separated the Bush administration from its predecessors. Although President Reagan had talked of tearing down walls and promoting democracy, he had rarely involved US troops. George H. W. Bush had used the military for a very limited objective and had purposefully ruled out regime change and democracy promotion through force. President Clinton believed that peace would naturally happen without America using its powerful military at all. But George W. Bush's policy line denied that Vietnam had happened at all. Ironically, just as in Vietnam, the Bush administration would use America's considerable power to influence events in a country far away and for a people it knew little about, because policymakers in Washington believed that such a policy would actually make Americans safer.

Promoting democracy or anticommunism promised to rid the world of the conditions that had created threats to American ideals. The appeal to ideals is what separated the George W. Bush administration from other post-Vietnam administrations. Other presidents had talked about ideals, but few had built military intervention around them. Policymakers had indeed restructured the use of military force to solve complex political problems in the post-Vietnam era. But many in the Bush administration thought that this had handcuffed American foreign policy. The president's speech at West Point's graduation ceremonies in 2002 included these telling words: "We must take the battle to the enemy. ... In the world we have entered the only path to safety is the path of action." Bush was clear about his moral certainty: "Moral truth is the same in every culture, in every time, and in every place. ... We are in a conflict between good and evil."[43] The appeal to American ideals did not go unnoticed by the cadets.

Shortly after the March 2003 invasion of Iraq, President George W. Bush further distanced himself from the lessons of the Vietnam War by publicly proclaiming, "America's vital interests and our deepest beliefs are now one."[44] Attacking Iraq, the president claimed, was in US national security interests, as was promoting democracy in the Middle East. Bush told the nation about US war aims in clear and concise language: "A liberated Iraq can show the power of freedom to transform that vital region. ... Success in Iraq could also begin a new stage in Middle East peace."[45]

Wesley Clark, former commander of all coalition forces in Europe, worried that the Bush administration's "quasi-imperial vision" would create "an army of empire." In his book, *Winning Modern Wars*, Clark warned that the Bush administration sought a new world order based on aggressive policy goals built on the back of a powerful military:

> This was to be a new America, reborn from adversity and defeat, reaching out constructively to the world, liberating peoples, reforming a vital region, enabling the emergence of a new, universal morality, and taking advantage of this unique window of American military dominance to secure into the foreseeable future our security and safety.[46]

For Clark and others, this vision was too grand. It required too much from the military, and its hubris was overwhelming.

The Bush administration's strategic thinking on Iraq got bogged down quickly, however, and the ghosts of Vietnam returned. Once again, the United States found itself engaged in a war characterized by no clear boundaries, no clear exit strategy, no definition of victory, little allied support, no UN authority, rising costs, and public pressure to withdraw. The nation-building experiment in Iraq was also quickly derailed as questions about the efficacy of counterinsurgency and the ability of the United States to change Iraqi political outlook surfaced. The Bush administration supported the Maliki regime in Iraq because its counterinsurgency program there relied on the Baghdad government to provide for the public welfare. This dependency gave the United States little power over Maliki and made it impossible to press for reforms that could have brought Iraq's Sunnis back into public life following Saddam's ouster. This failure showed the limits of American power, just as Vietnam had. Was Iraq George W. Bush's Vietnam? Perhaps, but maybe American diplomat George F. Kennan said it best when he stated that America's war in Vietnam reflected "a certain unfitness of the system as a whole for the conceiving and executing of ambitious political-military ventures far from our own shores."[47]

President Barack Obama, too young to have experienced Vietnam directly, engaged in the pragmatism of most post-Saigon presidents. Obama continued the phased withdrawal of American troops from Iraq as called for by the Bush administration's status of forces agreement with Baghdad. The president also kept the US footprint in Afghanistan stable with only slight increases as the conflict with the Taliban threatened that Afghan government. When Russia invaded Ukraine, Obama issued a stern warning and engaged in increased NATO exercises in the region, but he did not send in US ground troops. Perhaps most telling of all, after drawing a "red line" in the sand on the use of chemical weapons in Syria, the Obama administration did very little to stop the assault on rebels there or to confront ISIS directly. The administration used coordinated air attacks with its allies to hit ISIS in Syria, but the Russians have focused most of the military attention there on the Assad government's detractors. In Iraq today, US advisers helped the Iraqi National Army take control of key areas from ISIS, but the progress is painfully slow and there is little support for a larger American footprint.

The United States intervened in Vietnam hoping that a distinctively American story would emerge. Successive US presidential administrations believed that America's transformative power could create a counterrevolutionary alternative to Ho Chi Minh and the communists south of the 17th parallel. When this failed to materialize at acceptable cost and risk, the United States withdrew, leaving the Saigon government to its fate. Following the war, the lessons of Vietnam had a dramatic impact on US strategic thinking as the Vietnam generation assumed positions of responsibility in Washington. Few American policymakers in the immediate postwar period embraced open-ended military commitments with unclear or unattainable objectives. Following the George W. Bush administration's war in Iraq, the lessons of Vietnam resurfaced for all who wished to heed them. Only time will tell if Vietnam Syndrome will continue to shape US foreign policy.

Robert. K. Brigham, Shirley Ecker Boskey Professor of History and International Relations, joined the Department of History in 1994, Vassar College Poughkeepsie, New York. A specialist in US foreign policy, Brigham is author or coauthor of seven books, including most recently *American Foreign Relations: A History, Volume I & Volume II*, 8th ed. (along with Thomas Paterson, J. Garry Clifford, Michael Donoghue, and Kenneth Hagan; Cengage, 2015); *The United States and Iraq since 1990: A Brief History with Documents* (Wiley-Blackwell, 2013); *Iraq, Vietnam, and the Limits of American Power* (PublicAffairs, 2008); *Is Iraq Another Vietnam?* (PublicAffairs, 2006); and *Argument without End: In Search of Answers to the Vietnam Tragedy* (PublicAffairs, 1999), written with former secretary of defense Robert S. McNamara and James G. Blight of Brown University. Most recently, he is the author of *Reckless: Henry Kissinger and the Tragedy of Vietnam* (PublicAffairs, 2018).

Notes

1. "President Gerald R. Ford's Address at Tulane University Convocation," 23 April 1975, at https://www.fordlibrarymuseum.gov/library/speeches/750208.asp, accessed 15 December 2018.
2. Notes on Cabinet Meeting, 16 April 1975, Ron Nessen Papers, Box 294: Memorandum of Conversation, Kissinger, Ford, and Congressional Leaders, 5 March 1975, Kissinger/Scowcroft File, Box 1A, Gerald Ford Presidential Library.
3. *Congressional Record*, 94th Congress, 1st Session, 10101–8.
4. Quoted in Charles Neu, *America's Lost War* (Wheeling: Harlan-Davidson, 2005), 225.
5. Paul Kennedy, *The Rise and Fall of Great Powers* (New York: Random House, 1987), 408.
6. Greg Grandin, *Kissinger's Shadow* (New York: Metropolitan Books, 2015), 70–77.
7. Barbara Keys, "Henry Kissinger: The Emotional Statesmen," *Diplomatic History* 35, no. 4 (2011): 587.
8. Arnold Isaacs, *Vietnam Shadows, The War, Its Ghosts and Aftermath* (Baltimore: Johns Hopkins University Press, 1997), 72–73.
9. Harry Summers, *On Strategy: A Critical Analysis of the Vietnam War* (San Francisco: Presido Press, 1995).
10. William Westmoreland, *A Soldier Reports* (New York: Doubleday, 1976).
11. Roger Hilsman, *To Move a Nation: The Politics of Foreign Policy in the Administration of John F. Kennedy* (New York: Doubleday, 1967).
12. Gordon Goldstein, *Lessons in Disaster: McGeorge Bundy and the Path to War in Vietnam* (New York: Holt Paperback, 2009).
13. Quoted in Thomas Franck and Edward Weisbrand, *Foreign Policy by Congress* (New York: Oxford University Press, 1979), 46.
14. Quoted in "Vance Would Put Controls on US Covert Operations," *Washington Post*, 12 January 1977, 1.
15. Jimmy Carter, "Commencement Exercises at the University of Notre Dame," 22 May 1977, https://www.presidency.ucsb.edu/documents/address-commencement-exercises-the-university-notre-dame, accessed 15 December 2018.
16. *Department of State Bulletin*, 80 (February 1980): Special B.
17. As quoted in Thomas Paterson et. al., *American Foreign Policy*, 3rd ed. (Lexington: DC Heath, 1991), 641.
18. Quoted in Gaddis Smith, *Morality, Reason, and Power* (New York: Hill and Wang, 1986), 232.
19. John Mueller, "The Iraq Syndrome," *Foreign Affairs* 84 (November/December 2005), 53.
20. Walter LaFeber, *The American Age: United States Foreign Policy at Home and Abroad since 1750* (New York: W.W. Norton, 1989), 665–66.

21. Smith, *Morality, Reason, and Power*, 9, 81–84.
22. LaFeber, *American Age*, 666.
23. Neu, *America's Lost War*, 227.
24. "The Weinberger Doctrine," *Washington Post*, 30 November 1984, 1.
25. George Shultz, *Turmoil and Triumph: My Years as Secretary of State* (New York: Charles Scribner's Sons, 1993), 646, 650.
26. "About the Powell Doctrine," *Air Force Magazine*, August 1999, 1–4.
27. Edward Coffman, "The Course of Military History in the United States since World War II," *Journal of Military History* 61, no. 4 (1997): 769–70.
28. George C. Herring, *A Different Kind of War: LBJ and Vietnam* (Austin: University of Texas Press, 1994).
29. George C. Herring, "Preparing Not to Refight the Last War: The Impact of the Vietnam War on the US Military," in Charles Neu, ed., *After Vietnam: Legacies of a Lost War* (Baltimore: Johns Hopkins University Press, 2000), 65.
30. Lewis Sorley, *Thunderbolt: General Creighton Abrams and the Army of His Times* (New York: Simon and Schuster, 1992), 360–65.
31. Herring, "Preparing Not to Refight," 65.
32. Quoted in Neu, *America's Lost War*, 229.
33. Colin Powell, "US Forces Challenges Ahead," *Foreign Affairs* 71 (Winter 1992/1993): 37.
34. "News Conference with President Bush," *Federal News Service*, 7 August 1992.
35. As quoted in Samantha Power, *A Problem from Hell: America in the Age of Genocide* (New York: Perennial, 2002), 284.
36. Ibid.
37. Ibid.
38. "In American Voices, a Sense of Concern over Bosnia Role," *New York Times*, 2 May 1993, 4.
39. Francis Fukuyama, *The End of History and the Last Man* (New York: Free Press, 1992).
40. Power, *Problem from Hell*, 283–85, 294, 315.
41. While Iraq was supporting terrorists, it did not directly support those involved in the 9/11 attacks.
42. William Kristol and Lawrence Kaplan, *The War over Iraq* (San Francisco: Encounter Books, 2003), 112.
43. As quoted in Wesley Clark, *Winning Modern Wars: Iraq, Terrorism, and the American Empire* (New York: PublicAffairs Books, 2003), 163.
44. Second Bush Inaugural Address, White House Press Release, 19 January 2005.
45. Clark, *Winning Modern Wars*, 164.
46. Ibid.
47. George F. Kennan, *The Cloud of Danger: Current Realities of American Foreign Policy* (Boston: Little, Brown, 1977), 4–5.

Select Bibliography

Clark, Wesley, *Winning Modern Wars: Iraq, Terrorism, and the American Empire* (New York: PublicAffairs Books, 2003).

Coffman, Edward, "The Course of Military History in the United States since World War II," *Journal of Military History* 61, no. 4 (1997).

Franck, Thomas and Edward Weisbrand, *Foreign Policy by Congress* (New York: Oxford University Press, 1979).

Fukuyama, Francis, *The End of History and the Last Man* (New York: Free Press, 1992).

Goldstein, Gordon, *Lessons in Disaster: McGeorge Bundy and the Path to War in Vietnam* (New York: Holt Paperback, 2009).

Isaacs, Arnold, *Vietnam Shadows: The War, Its Ghosts and Aftermath* (Baltimore, MD: Johns Hopkins University Press, 1997).

Kennedy, Paul, *The Rise and Fall of Great Powers* (New York: Random House, 1987).

Keys, Barbara, "Henry Kissinger: The Emotional Statesmen," *Diplomatic History* 35, no. 4 (2011).

Kristol, William and Lawrence Kaplan, *The War over Iraq* (San Francisco, CA: Encounter Books, 2003).

Grandin, Greg, *Kissinger's Shadow* (New York: Metropolitan Books, 2015).

Herring, George C., *A Different Kind of War: LBJ and Vietnam* (Austin: University of Texas Press, 1994).

_____, *Thunderbolt: General Creighton Abrams and the Army of His Times* (New York: Simon and Schuster, 1992).

Hilsman, Roger, *To Move a Nation: The Politics of Foreign Policy in the Administration of John F. Kennedy* (New York: Doubleday, 1967).

Kennan, George F., *The Cloud of Danger: Current Realities of American Foreign Policy* (Boston, MA: Little, Brown, 1977).

LaFeber, Walter, *The American Age: United States Foreign Policy at Home and Abroad since 1750* (New York: W.W. Norton, 1989).

Mueller, John, "The Iraq Syndrome," *Foreign Affairs* 84 (November/December 2005).

Neu, Charles, *America's Lost War* (Wheeling, IL: Harlan-Davidson, 2005).

_____, ed., *After Vietnam: Legacies of a Lost War* (Baltimore, MD: Johns Hopkins University Press, 2000).

Paterson, Thomas, et. al., *American Foreign Policy*, 3rd ed. (Lexington, MA: DC Heath, 1991).

Powell, Colin L., "US Forces, Challenges Ahead," *Foreign Affairs* 71 (winter, 1992/1993).

Power, Samantha, *A Problem from Hell: America in the Age of Genocide* (New York: Perennial, 2002).

Shultz, George, *Turmoil and Triumph: My Years as Secretary of State* (New York: Charles Scribner's, 1993).

Smith, Gaddis, *Morality, Reason, and Power* (New York: Hill and Wang, 1986).

Summers, Harry, *On Strategy: A Critical Analysis of the Vietnam War* (San Francisco, CA: Presido Press, 1995).

Westmoreland, William, *A Soldier Reports* (New York: Doubleday, 1976).

Part II

Iraq and Afghanistan

When examining the United States' recent wars and the attempts to end them, we see similar frustrations and pathologies to those of the Vietnam era. In Iraq—in 1991, in 2003, and after 2009 when Obama began the withdrawal process—as well as in Afghanistan, the United States failed to find a way to end the war on its own terms. As with the Vietnam War, there was a profound myopia and inability to think through how local dynamics might affect American narratives. David Ryan demonstrates in his chapter on the ending of the Gulf War in 1991 that there were profound failures and missed opportunities even in the only major conflict since World War II that appeared to end on triumphant terms.

Despite US attempts to learn from Vietnam by applying the Powell Doctrine, with its implicit promise of a "clean exit" from war, the narrow exit strategy in the Persian Gulf was coupled with unrealistic dreams about a new world order and uprisings in Iraq that would transform the region in a positive way. When events did not go to plan, the Bush administration found itself caught between this expansive, if vague, vision and the imperatives of the Powell Doctrine and the politics of the coalition assembled to fight Saddam Hussein. As Ryan argues, though, the humanitarian disasters that unfolded in the aftermath of the war were not just a result of an administration surprised by events but were the consequence of an absence of clear thinking about the postwar order and the dynamics of the region evident throughout the buildup to war. Even as the Bush administration styled themselves as cautious realists, they displayed a remarkable degree of incautiousness in their approach to the end of the war in the Persian Gulf.

That this should have happened within sixteen years of the Vietnam War demonstrates in part how introspective the war and its victory were. Even as Americans celebrated with victory parades, the aftereffects were devastating for the Kurds and the Shia, which would affect the situation after 2003, as sectarian tensions built up in the wake of massacres perpetrated by Saddam Hussein's regime. Moreover, the unresolved war meant that the sanctions regime (1991–2003) also had devastating effects on all of the Iraqi population that also played itself out at various levels after 2003, as the American occupiers found themselves dealing with crumbling infrastructure and public health crises exacerbated by war and sanctions. Again, the point is that the US policymakers abjured deep historical and strategic thinking in favor of the possible within the cultural context of US and coalition politics.

Similarly, while the inadequacy of the George W. Bush administration's planning for postwar reconstruction in Iraq in 2003 is well known and has often been framed as a story of neoconservative hubris, we see the same symptoms of myopia in the actions of the Obama administration, a group that—like the first Bush administration—saw themselves as sober and cautious practitioners of foreign policy.

In their chapter on the costs of the Iraq War, Ryan and David Fitzgerald focus on the Obama administration's failed attempt to turn the page on Iraq after the withdrawal of American troops in 2011. The administration's strategy was not rooted in any deep understanding of the dynamics of Iraqi politics, and the failure to acknowledge those dynamics led to the dramatic unraveling of Obama's Iraq policy in 2014. Both the Bush and Obama White Houses operated from generic scripts at times rather than responding to existing conditions. For instance, the tendency to reinforce the position of Nouri Al-Maliki as prime minister seemed to be predicated on broad ideas about the need for a strong leader rather than an understanding of Iraqi politics. This is because unquestioning American support made him too strong to be kept in check by other coalition partners and helped to unbalance the ethnic politics of Iraq and lead to the unraveling of 2014.

This move to support Maliki was of a piece with longstanding practice: despite the sentiment within the region for extended democratic opportunities, the US sided with the strongman, the autocrat, echoing the myopic Cold War tactics of backing authoritarian regimes throughout the region,

Africa, and Latin America and losing credibility and the fidelity of generations growing up through these regimes. Likewise, in Afghanistan, there was a failure to understand local politics. In his chapter, Antonio Giustozzi argues that the Americans underestimated the military power of the Taliban, miscalculated the ability of the Taliban leadership to reach a political settlement, and overestimated the capabilities of the Afghan security forces.

The failure to understand local dynamics can be tied to a particular way of looking at the world that ignores the agency of the Other. Much as American support for Maliki seemed to be based on preexisting scripts, debate within the Beltway on withdrawal from Iraq and Afghanistan took place within a very narrow frame. For instance, discussion of the Obama administration's exit strategy made very little reference to Iraqi dynamics, and instead the debate over the US role in postoccupation Iraq was reduced to the narrow question of boots on the ground. For both the administration and its critics, the issue of the size of any "stay-behind" force seemed to be the sole metric on which to judge the success or failure of US strategy. While Obama certainly promised continued diplomatic engagement in Iraq and across the region, the fact that so much intellectual energy was expended on the question of troop numbers denotes a particularly narrow view of what the endgame in Iraq would look like.

Jeffrey Michaels identifies a very similar way of thinking when it came to the Obama administration's declaration of a "responsible end" to the War in Afghanistan. The actual meaning of a "responsible end" was somewhat unclear and, again, debate within the Beltway was reduced to the question of boots on the ground. As Michaels argues, the rhetoric of responsibility and the use of troop numbers as a barometer of progress meant that the administration and its critics were trapped by a narrow discourse in which success measured not by how quickly the Taliban would be defeated but by how slowly the Afghan government would be defeated. Here there are echoes of the "decent interval" that historians of the Vietnam War have identified: the idea was that the United States could within that narrative walk away with clean hands.

Ultimately, in both Iraq and Afghanistan, the United States decided not so much to end wars as to simply disengage from them. In many ways, the first disengagement was the mental one, when policymakers fell back on generic doctrines and discourses rather than consider the agency of others. This mental disengagement ended serious thinking on the war and the situation, which then in turn precluded deep consideration of the strategic (as opposed to tactical) lessons that might be derived from these failures.

Chapter 5

The Ironies of Overwhelming "Victory"
Exits and the Dislocation of the Gulf War

David Ryan

Before the year was out, as President George H. W. Bush geared up for the 1992 electoral campaign, the media increasingly asked how Bush had lost the Gulf War. General Tom Kelly, who retired a couple of weeks after the war, recalled that he was constantly asked why they had not gone further, why did they not finish Saddam off? He explained "that we did what we were sent to do, and that we had to stop."[1] In the infamous phrase of William Safire: "Bush snatched defeat from the jaws of victory."[2] The war was won; the peace was lost. The dilemmas were plain enough. The Weinberger-Powell strictures on the use of US force guided military planning in a political environment eager to implement the lessons of the Vietnam War; it was not that the public, the Congress, or the Senate agreed on the necessity of war, but if military action was conducted it had better be swift and decisive; public and congressional support were predicated on such a message—the antithesis of the Vietnam War. The demise of the Soviet Union reduced the external balance of power, the internal "check" pivoted on a short, sharp, decisive war. Besides the use of overwhelming force, the Vietnam War brought another lesson to the table in the words of Jeffrey Engel, "The virtues of speed and international support."[3]

If the lessons of the Vietnam War facilitated a return to the use of large-scale force in the Gulf War, the lessons remained relatively silent on the question of winning the peace; what comes after the exit strategy?

Yet the popular lessons of Munich and World War II also animated Bush, that dictators should not be appeased. And while Bush built up the Hitler analogy across the autumn of 1990, sometimes to the chagrin of his advisors,[4] Saddam Hussein was left in power.[5] He exacted vengeance against those who rose to oppose him in 1991, but this domestic violence did not mobilize the same level of response provoked by his international violence against Kuwait in August 1990. Inadequate strategic thinking characterized this phase of operations in 1991 and then again in 2003.[6] The local consequences were horrific.

The demise of the Soviet Union offered the United States an opportunity to craft a new order based on old ideals tempered by the cautious realism of the Bush administration. Had the Soviets remained a potent power, willing to exercise their veto at the United Nations Security Council (UNSC), it is unlikely the United States would have gone to war in Iraq in 1991. Saddam had been a Soviet client and recipient of their weapons; Syria also aligned with the Soviets during the Cold War; Iran had cultivated its own hostility to the United States since 1979. Moscow might have tempered US ambition at the UN or in the region; or they might have constrained Saddam, preventing the invasion.[7] There is little point in hypotheticals; suffice to say an opportunity, for good or ill, was created through Saddam's brutal ambitions. Within that context President Bush was clear: the United States had to stand for what was right and just. In the post–Cold War era, regimes would not be permitted to flagrantly transgress; Kuwaiti sovereignty had to be restored. The demonstration effect had to be reversed. Restoration of order was one thing, its preservation yet another. The selected institutional lessons of the Vietnam War only provided half answers.

Mid- to long-term US objectives were clear enough. The 1990 National Security Directive recognized that "US interests in the Persian Gulf are vital to the national security. These interests include access to oil and the security and stability of key friendly states in the region"; Washington was willing to defend these with force if necessary.[8]

Beyond access and order, could the United States stand for what was right and just *and* maintain order? And if it could not win the peace in Iraq, was leaving Saddam in power not merely pushing a problem down the road while generating animosity among certain sections of Iraqi society and regional neighbors? Yet to inflict an overwhelming military defeat and remove a dictator that had brutally maintained the sovereignty of Iraq might create a regional power vacuum. Saddam continued to balance Iranian power. Washington wanted to inflict a crushing defeat through overwhelming power, yet leave Iraq with sufficient strength to pose a credible balance against Iran, *hopefully* without Saddam Hussein, but still without a clear vision of who or how he would be replaced. Phase IV of the operations was opaque. The post-Saddam strategy relied on "hope," undermining one of the strictures of the Vietnam lessons, to define clear objectives; clearly ejecting Iraq from Kuwait, the pivotal objective at the heart of UNSC Resolution 660, did not secure peace.

The restricted objectives were clearly defined and sanctioned by the UNSC Resolutions, an international coalition was knit together and contributed to the war effort. The objectives were limited, and they were achieved, and the emerging Powell Doctrine advocated an exit strategy. The war stopped short of Baghdad. Saddam remained in power. Bush's famous call to the Iraqi people to take matters into their own hands was born out of frustration and circumscribed lessons, not strategy. The "Iraqi people" (as in most appeals to the concept of "the people") was a construct, not ignorant of the divisions, but an appeal eliding the difficulties of the internal divisions within Iraqi society, especially one that had been brutalized by the regime and might have scores to settle. US credibility was damaged after the exit strategy was exposed as Saddam crushed the Shia in the south and the Kurds in the north. The hasty decision regarding the war's end left Saddam with Iraq and left the United States and the region with Saddam.

Former national security advisor to President Jimmy Carter, Zbigniew Brzezinski, wrote shortly after the war that he believed a policy of sanctions was preferable to war, even though the victory "was easier than expected." Yet there was a growing risk that the "war may eventually come to be seen as having precipitated a geopolitical disaster and a moral disgrace." Iran would benefit from Iraq's demise, but an "American military presence in the region is now a necessity—a fact not automatically inimical to US interests, but potentially a source of new instabilities." Second, there was a "growing danger" that the war will exacerbate "barely suppressed ethnic, religious and tribal animosities." Brzezinski wrote: "The war against Iraq could become part of a prolonged chain reaction, eventually 'Lebanizing' the region as a whole while bogging the United States down in it." Finally, he argued, "the human misery produced by the war has subsequently been compounded by the abortive Shia and Kurdish revolts."[9]

Were there viable alternatives that might have involved options that fell short of UNSC Resolution 660, which demanded the complete and unconditional withdrawal of Iraq from Kuwait? When those objectives were achieved, Washington was left with a regime of sanctions, inspections, and diplomacy, which it had earlier argued were insufficient to deal with the situation prior to the Gulf War.[10] In Jeffrey Record's infamous phrase, the Gulf War produced a "hollow victory"; "The Gulf War was a magnificent victory barren of any significant diplomatic gains. It was fought to repel Saddam Hussein's challenge to the *old* order in the Persian Gulf, not to create a new one."[11] Yet Brent Scowcroft and Bush also had their eyes on the creation of a new world order.[12]

It was not just the absence of a countervailing power that made war possible: the administration's adoption of the Weinberger principles, first enunciated by the secretary of defense, Caspar Weinberger, in November of 1984, distilled further by his then assistant and future chair of the Joint Chiefs of Staff (later secretary of state), Colin Powell, appeased influential congressional leaders. As James Baker, secretary of state, indicated, the US invasion of Panama in December 1989 had broken the "mind-set of the American people about the use of force in the post–Vietnam era, Panama established an emotional predicate that permitted us to build the public support so essential to the success of Operation Desert Storm thirteen months later."[13] The Gulf War was supposed to be its consummation. Indeed, famously Bush declared that the syndrome had been kicked;[14] it was buried in the sands of Iraq.

Crucially, in the Weinberger principles, objectives were defined, limited, and achievable. Overwhelming power was used. Finally there was an exit strategy. To go further would be to succumb, in Warren Cohen's words on President Truman and Korea, "to one of the most treacherous temptations confronting any victor, the temptation to expand war aims."[15] Observance of the limited objectives was important for adhering to the prescriptions to maintain cordial civil-military relations, to build public support, to persuade Congress, to keep the international coalition intact. The Pentagon would be further appeased if operations were multilateral.[16]

This not only conferred an international legitimacy to use force against Saddam Hussein but also alleviated fears that the United States would not be the only country to bear the burden, pay the price. Yet a cost of that approach necessitated the adoption of the twelve UNSC Resolutions. As the war pressed on the United States had to balance its unilateralist inclinations with the need to adhere closely to the resolutions, especially as crucial allies, not least Moscow, the French, and Italians wanted to bring matters to an end sooner—to go beyond threatened to undermine the cohesion of the nervous alliance. Within all of these restrictions, the end of war and exit strategies were still predicated on US politics rather than Iraqi or regional dynamics.

So the United States had ultimately trapped itself within the limitations of the Powell Doctrine, the limitations of the UN Security Council resolutions, the need to maintain regional "security and stability," its inclination toward unipolarity,[17] and simultaneously a desire to use force as a means to resolve *this* crisis. In that sense a very strict reading of Resolution 660 had to be maintained; compromise or limited withdrawals could not be entertained. To compromise through diplomacy might convey the legitimacy of Saddam's claims on Kuwait or of the border dispute; to compromise would undercut the demonstration effect the response was supposed to have; to compromise might smack of Munich, of popular readings, of appeasement and accommodating aggression. Yet, after Bush had characterized Saddam as another Hitler on the Euphrates, it made it all the more galling that this Hitler should be allowed to remain in power, to crush the uprisings encouraged by Bush, and to ultimately consolidate his hold on power.

In his book *How Wars End* Gideon Rose relates how the memories of Vietnam pervaded the administration and the chain of command. The Third Army's official history observed, "This war would be everything the Vietnam War had not been." The "haunting legacy"[18] of the war had provided sufficient lessons to deal with both the operational and the tactical aspects of the Gulf. "But at the strategic level, it produced an allergy to long-term, open-ended military commitments that was neither relevant nor helpful." They feared another quagmire in the desert or embroilment in Iraqi politics. Bush did think about the postwar scenario but without sufficient strategic depth. Rose cites his diary entry of 15 February 1991:

> Now the question is, what comes next? But my emotion is not one of elation. We've got some unfinished business. How do we solve it? How do we now guarantee the future peace? I don't see how it will work with Saddam in power, and I am very, very wary.[19]

Memoirs and Memory

All memoirs and autobiographies need to be treated with circumspection; the horses' mouths shape the first official narratives. A revisionist autobiography is a rarity. Yet there is a credibility that diplomatic historians still accord to the memoir, a fascination with stories told by those who were "present at the creation," fraught and problematic as they are. If there has not been a historiographical turn on the Vietnam War since Iraq 2003, a byway in the literature was created to explore the impact of Iraq on our understanding of Vietnam.[20] Similarly with memoir, those written after 2009 absorbed the pathos not shared by those written after the Gulf War; consequences affect interpretation.

"After the Storm," chapter nineteen of President George H. W. Bush and his national security advisor Brent Scowcroft's shared memoirs, advances a paragraph much quoted by the media and others in 2004 when Scowcroft went public with his rebuke of George W. Bush during the Iraq War.[21] "Trying to eliminate Saddam, extending the ground war into an occupation of Iraq, would have violated our guideline about not changing objectives in midstream, engaging in 'mission creep,' and would have incurred incalculable human and political costs." In *A World Transformed*, published in 1998, they remembered the difficult pursuit of Manuel Noriega in Panama City in 1989 as they contemplated apprehending Saddam: "We would have been forced to occupy Baghdad and, in effect, rule Iraq."[22]

Cited by Brigham earlier in this volume, "Powell ... [claimed] prophetically that if the war had not been limited, 'the United States would be ruling Iraq today—at unpardonable expense in terms of money, lives lost, and ruined regional relationships.'"[23] The coalition, Arab and otherwise, would have collapsed. Bush and Scowcroft wrote, "Under those circumstances, there was no viable 'exit strategy' we could see, violating another of our principles." They reflected on the precedent that they were trying to set for the legitimate use of force after the Cold War. They knew they could not exceed the UN mandate. And finally, "Had we gone the invasion route, the United States could conceivably still be an occupying power in a bitterly hostile land. It would have been a dramatically different—and perhaps barren—outcome."[24]

As the country prepared for war, the White House drew up key themes to shape the public message. The president had clear goals; its objectives were defined and shared internationally. The forces called on to liberate Kuwait "will do their job quickly, massively and decisively. And when their mission is completed, they will go home."[25]

The message on limitations was frequently repeated to avoid any connotation of Vietnam and quagmire. It is important to remember that public opinion and the congressional vote on war was far more divided than postwar memory suggests.[26] Bush wrote in his diary on 17 October 1990 that he was "not sure where our country is," having observed that "the Brits are strong, and the French are French." But he believed that if the American public saw a provocation they would support "knocking the hell out of this guy. We can do it from the air. Our military is waffling and vacillating in terms of what we can do on the ground."[27]

Bush and Scowcroft reflected on the regional balance of power and were "determined not to destabilize the Gulf region in the future." Yet there was a balancing act: "The trick here was to damage his offensive capability without weakening Iraq to the point that a vacuum was created, and destroying the balance between Iraq and Iran, further destabilizing the region for years."[28] The plan was not just liberation but also destruction of the Republican Guard, "to reduce the threat Saddam posed to his neighbors."[29] The thinking was replete with conundrum. Powell had wanted to cut off and kill the Iraqi forces, yet at wars' end he wanted to avoid unnecessary slaughter; he was squarely behind the use of overwhelming power (for US political reasons), but Iraq had to remain a credible deterrent force (for regional purposes).[30]

In his memoirs, James Baker, in a chapter titled "A Postwar Vision for the Mideast," opens with an epigram from a Bush speech of 27 February 1991, to the effect that it would be necessary not only to win the war but also to secure "the peace."[31] Baker was keenly aware of the geopolitical necessities of an integrated Iraq. He notes in his testimony to the House Foreign Affairs Committee, 6–7 February, that the most controversial aspect was that Iraq (post-Saddam) should be included in the efforts to build a stable region: "The time for reconstruction and recovery should not be the occasion for vengeful actions against a nation forced to war as a result of a dictator's ambition. ... The secure and prosperous future everyone hopes to see in the Gulf has got to include Iraq."[32]

A disintegrated power would invite an enduring civil war; Iraq had to be sufficiently coherent. An integrated Iraq could remain a stabilizing force against the ambitions of either Syria or Iran. Baker wrote that the strategy had to be "designed with one overriding strategic concern in mind: to avoid what we often referred to as the Lebanonization of Iraq, which we believed would create a geopolitical nightmare." But he described "a strong emotional component" at play in presidential decision making, echoed by his surrounding staff on the decision to end the war after 100 hours of ground warfare.[33]

Powell received cables from Charles Freeman, US ambassador to Saudi Arabia: "We cannot pursue Iraq's unconditional surrender and occupation by us. It is not in our interest to destroy Iraq or weaken it to the point that Iran and/or Syria are not constrained by it." Powell added, "The only way to have avoided this outcome was to have undertaken a largely US conquest and occupation of a remote nation of twenty million people. I don't think that is what the American people signed up for."[34] Even though subordinates disagreed with swift termination, Gordon and Trainor point out, "Nobody with enough rank to change that decision objected." It was *hoped* that destruction of three Republican Guard divisions would result in toppling Saddam.[35] Robert Divine concluded, "In retrospect, it seems clear that the Bush administration found itself unprepared for the crucial process of ending the war. Having overestimated the military strength of Iraq all along, US officials were surprised by the success and speed of the ground offensive." Events spun out of control.

An advisor to Norman Schwarzkopf indicated that they never had a plan on war termination.³⁶

"Put to the ultimate test, the Powell Doctrine proved only partially valid," Divine argued. Overwhelming force coupled with public support was good at limiting the US loss of life and ending the war quickly, yet "Bush and Scowcroft failed to forge a clear link between the use of force and their political goals." They *hoped* Saddam would fall, but "this proved wishful thinking." Moving to Baghdad would have fractured the coalition, perhaps resulting in occupation, and Saddam might have retreated and fought a guerrilla war for years. Divine writes:

> In effect, the Bush administration waged a limited war for unlimited ends, and thus was doomed to disappointment once the heady euphoria of military victory passed. The Persian Gulf War appears to confirm the oldest of adages about US military involvement—the United States always wins the war but loses the peace.³⁷

Among the Robert Gates files in the Bush Presidential Library an eight-page document considered the "security structures" after the war. Dated 21 January 1991, it opens with the observation that "the Gulf crisis will affect Middle East dynamics for decades to come." The author considered the political, security dynamics, weapons of mass destruction, and economic issues, including the extremes of wealth and poverty in the region. It indicated that NSD-45 had set out US principles for the postwar period, including security and stability in the region, "more specifically, that means creating conditions in the region that collectively can deter future aggression against the GCC [Gulf Cooperation Council] states."

Iraq's invasion was made possible by the "collapse of a regional balance of power." Iraq's strength had grown over the 1980s, while Iran's had diminished. Therefore, "a key objective is to help reestablish a balance so that future aggression directed against the GCC states by either Iraq or Iran will be deterred." Apart from the regional balances, they worried about the US reliance on the UN in this crisis and on the president's concerns about "a permanent presence of American ground forces in the region." Its policy approaches included strengthening various deterrent capabilities, "containing and/or constraining Iraqi military power" and integrating Iran into the regional security environment.³⁸

The memorandum considered two scenarios. First, "unchanged capabilities" in which both conventional and nonconventional Iraqi capabilities remained intact. The second, "combat destruction" envisaged Iraqi capabilities "significantly attrited [sic] and its weapons of mass destruction largely destroyed." The first would obviously pose an ongoing Iraqi threat to US allies, Kuwait and Saudi Arabia in particular. The second, if Iraqi capability was destroyed, a US "peacetime presence of ground troops would not be necessary," its presence could be reduced and the visibility of foreign troops lessened.[39]

The problem was that "If Iraq voluntarily withdraws or its armed forces survive a conflict in relatively good order, its military power will have to be contained." This required the reduction or elimination of its WMD (weapons of mass destruction) and the reduction of its conventional forces to restrain regional capabilities. It pointed out that US leverage in any negotiation on levels of WMD or conventional force, "obviously depends upon the endgame case which applies." Various types of inspection regimes were considered. It observed that however the crisis ended, the future of Iran would need to be considered in a regional dimension. Immediately, however:

> Iran and the US share an interest in rolling back Iraq's aggression against Kuwait, and Iranian leaders have indicated they can tolerate the temporary presence of foreign forces in the Gulf to accomplish this goal. But this short-term convergence of interests is likely to diverge rapidly once the crisis is resolved.[40]

Iran considered the US presence a direct threat to its regional aspirations.[41]

Baker described ambitions to seize the momentum after the war ended to initiate the regional conference that would ultimately find expression in the 1992 Madrid meeting; but once Saddam remained in power, once he endured, the rationale was undermined.[42] If a key element of strategy should include agency, that is who will effect a particular operation that should contribute to the overall strategy it is somewhat lacking in the memoir material reflecting the politics of aspiration and *hope*. As Baker reveals in his thinking on transitions:

> We never embraced as a war aim or a political aim the replacement of the Iraqi regime. We did, however, *hope* and believe that Saddam Hussein would not survive in power after such a crushing defeat. Ironically, the uprisings in the north and the south, instead of lessening his grip on power as we felt they would, contributed to it, as he skillfully argued to his army that these events required his continued leadership in order to preserve Iraq. When he managed to consolidate his power, Saddam scrambled our strategic calculations. The result was a sobering reminder that the consequences of success are often far more intricate and unpredictable than anticipated [emphasis added].[43]

Washington did not aim to replace Saddam, but they hoped he would not survive. There were no specifics on who might replace him or how that regime might deal with the Kurds or the Shia.

After the devastating victory, there was "no operational reason to remain." Ironically, the "turkey shoot" destruction of retreating Iraqi forces on the highway furthered Soviet resolve to push for an end through the UNSC, revealing fractures in the coalition. Baker reflected that the destruction ran the risk of looking un-American—too easy:

> From the start of the crisis, we had said repeatedly that the United States had no motives beyond forcing compliance with the UN resolutions and ejecting Iraq from Kuwait. We had argued that we had no grand design for a substantial permanent military presence in the region. The simplest way to establish our credibility on this score with all parties was to remain true to our word and withdraw promptly from Iraq. In short, there was no reason to continue, from either a military or political standpoint.[44]

Baker was aware of the ongoing controversy, but there was no reason to think about exceeding the UN mandate; all believed that the president's decision was right—there was no debate on it. Panama was difficult enough and there was a democratic alternative to Noriega; no such alternative existed in Iraq. If Saddam was captured and the regime deposed, "American forces would still be confronted with the specter of a military occupation of indefinite duration to pacify the country and sustain a new government in power." Further casualties would eventuate; domestic controversy over the United States' purpose would have erupted; the coalition would have dissolved. Baker surmised, "Ironically, while Saddam was wrong in thinking that America's Vietnam and Lebanon hangovers would save him from a war, the painful lessons learned by US policymakers from those conflicts may have actually saved Saddam himself from capture."[45] In the midterm the media and the public would weary of news of Iraq. In the short term the cultural impact in the states was significant: "In six short weeks, the bitter legacy of Vietnam had been swept away by Desert Storm." Bring the boys home. Period.[46]

Writing four years after the conclusion of the Gulf War Baker reflected, "It's important to recall that, while it would have been welcome, Saddam's departure was never a stated objective of our policy." Yet as he reflected in his memoirs, he recalled that Tariq Aziz told Baker, in their final meeting days before the war, "We will be here long after you're gone."[47]

There was a pathos in the observation. In 1991 Baker was more assertive. He told Aziz, "Clearly, if there is a peaceful settlement and you withdraw, those in power in Iraq today will have a say in Iraq's future. If withdrawal takes place by force, others will determine that future."[48] He was temporarily incorrect. Pages later in the transcript of their January 1991 meeting in Geneva, Baker signaled that the United States had disproportionate power: the United States had "tremendous technological advantage" and "your forces will face devastatingly superior fire-power and forces." The United States would "destroy your ability to run the county. And they will destroy your ability to command your own forces."[49] Such was not to be.

Baker elaborated:

> We owe it to you to tell you that there will be no stalemate, in our opinion. If conflict follows, there will be no UN ceasefire or breathing space for negotiation. We have said in public over the past four or five months that if conflict begins, it will be massive. This will not be another Vietnam. We won't put forces into battle for which they are not equipped to do the job. Should war begin—God forbid—it will be fought to a swift decisive conclusion.[50]

Aziz was certain that they would remain in power "now and in the future."[51] Aziz, in a despondent diplomatic tactic, reminded Baker that Iraqi resistance to Iran contributed to US interests in a stable, balanced region.[52]

Powell recalled the exact time that the president decided to end the war: 5:57. Gathered in the White House after a briefing with Secretary of Defense Cheney on Capitol Hill, checks had been made to ascertain the concurrence of his "chiefs." Moreover, the commander in chief had now made the decision to suspend hostilities, and "every member of his policymaking team agreed." They were soon attracted to the description of the war as a Hundred-Hour War. Powell recalled the timing and the discussions reflecting on the need to halt, writing:

> The back of the Iraqi army had been broken. What was left of it was retreating north. There was no need to fight a battle of annihilation to see how many more combatants on both sides could be killed. Obviously, the President would have preferred total capitulation, the way World War II had ended. And we knew, barring a lucky bomb hit, that Saddam would likely survive the war. We further accepted that we would face criticism from some quarters for not continuing the fight. However, we had a clear mandate, and it was being achieved.[53]

Critics, including Admiral Crowe, suggested that they should have widened their war aims and removed Saddam. Powell considered moving the goal posts, but the mission had been accomplished; the coalition had to hold. The president "had promised the American people that Desert Storm would not become a Persian Gulf Vietnam, and he kept his promise."[54] But, the unstated *hope* of removing Saddam failed.[55]

The war was constrained by the UNSC, the coalition and domestic US politics and the goal to destroy Iraqi forces. In a later review, Zbigniew Brzezinski wrote, "Both goals, it was clear in advance, were attainable, and they were attained." The calculus was hard-nosed realism, balancing the costs of action against the costs of inaction. Yet before 1990 the United States had supported Iraq against Iran; as Brzezinski summarized Richard Haass, "The United States did not object to Iraq's using chemical weapons against Iran." Haass favored expanding relations with Iraq during the 1980s.[56]

Among the memoirs after 2009 was Donald Rumsfeld's *Known and Unknown*. Preceding the first chapter, "Smiling Death," on the US descent into Beirut, Donald Rumsfeld reprinted the Getty image of himself shaking hands with Saddam, his infamous meeting of 20 December 1983. At the time Saddam's Iraq was the bitter enemy "of the two nations that threatened the interests of the United States—Syria and Iran." Saddam was the "less bad." "Whatever misgivings we had about reaching out to Saddam Hussein, the alternative of Iranian hegemony in the Middle East was decidedly worse." He discussed with Tariq Aziz, the need to keep both countries contained and describes efforts to get Iraq to lean toward the United States. He did not realize Iraq would play such a prominent role in the US future, nor that Iran would prosper through the failures of US strategy after 2003. At that time their interests converged: the United States could discourage others selling arms to Iran; "Iraq could assist America by holding the line against an ascendant radical Islamist and terrorist-supporting regime in Iran." Stability was essential, Lebanon a key warning.[57]

Rumsfeld begins part ten of his memoirs with a three-page section preceding chapter thirty, "Washington, DC, January 16, 1991." He describes the crucial decision that Bush had to face, one that "would have lasting consequences," on whether to end war or topple Saddam. He recalls Powell and Gates on the slaughter and reiterated the belief that Saddam could not retain power. The Kurds had risen and Powell indicated, "It is not clear what purpose would have been achieved by getting ourselves mixed up in the middle of that." They were quickly crushed, "creating among many Iraqi dissidents a lasting sense of betrayal and distrust." In 2003, when Saddam was interrogated after capture, he reiterated his belief that the United States was a paper tiger. After the United States decided not to press on to Baghdad, he was emboldened. It was a missed opportunity, Rumsfeld recalled.[58]

When Robert Gates wrote his latest memoirs, *Duty* (2014), Iraq had dominated US foreign policy for over a decade. The Gulf War makes up a small part of a chapter titled "Iraq, Iraq, and Iraq." Reflecting on what he describes as Bush's ad-libbing on the Iraqi people to put Saddam aside, Gates indicates that the administration was convinced that the crushing defeat would lead to Saddam's replacement. They were dismayed when the Shia and Kurd uprisings began almost immediately after US operations ended: "They had interpreted the president's words—aimed at the Iraqi military—as encouragement of a popular uprising. We should have been more precise in saying what we were after."[59]

Indeed it was a curious objective. In Bush's correspondence with Saddam and his news conference of 12 January 1991, he argued that their resolve was strong and that they fully intended to reverse the situation. The objective was to stop Saddam because of his *international* aggression but not because of his *domestic* violence. Clearly Washington was not willing to intervene to stop the domestic repression. Yet Bush indicated, "The United States and the rest of the world have no quarrel with the people of Iraq. ... Saddam Hussein's aggression must be reversed."[60] Gates reflected, "Neither the Kurds nor the Shia—especially the latter—would forgive us for not coming to their assistance after they thought we had encouraged them to take up arms."[61]

War's End

There is little need to recount the importance of the Weinberger principles or the Powell Doctrine here, they have been succinctly covered in Brigham's chapter in this volume. Crucial to this discussion is the nexus between the clarity of objectives and the exit strategy. Put succinctly, once UNSC Resolution 660 had been accomplished, the war terminated. Such guidance was pivotal in facilitating the US passage to war. Powell was the consummate new type officer, at ease on Capitol Hill, in the White House, and on the battlefields. As Gordon and Trainor summarized, the Vietnam War influenced his vision of war: force would be overwhelming, decisive, and short and "military intervention should not be undertaken unless the outcome was all but guaranteed." Precise definition was required, US casualties kept to a minimum, and, once the objectives had been achieved, "American forces should be quickly extracted, lest the Pentagon risk sliding into a quagmire."[62]

Yet Hoagland, reflecting a year after the conclusion of the war, wrote that Saddam's survival indicates there was "something to his bet that whatever happened in Kuwait the United States still remembers Vietnam too vividly to have the patience and will to pursue him militarily to the bitter end."[63] Prior to the conflict, Powell argued against war within and outside the administration. He feared Kuwaiti liberation might not be as easy as it turned out to be, but once the decision for war was made Gordon and Trainor describe him as the "politico-military maestro, playing a pivotal role in shaping the war plan in light of his doctrine of decisive military force." The logic was to enter decisively, leave and eschew any commitment to potential insurgent groups that might rise to fight the dictator.[64] The emphasis was on order, stability, and international sovereignty, not on peace, individual security, or the Shia or Kurdish communities.

Ironically, the Weinberger strictures identified the need for "clearly defined political and military objectives." In the same paragraph, he quoted, as too many strategists do, Clausewitz: "No one starts a war—or rather, no one in his senses ought to do so—without first being clear in his mind what he intends to achieve by that war, and how he intends to conduct it."[65] As Powell later summarized, "Is the national interest at stake? If the answer is yes, go in, and go in to win. Otherwise, stay out."[66] Saddam also thought the war would be limited. In late February 1991, he and his advisors discussed resistance, arming the people and the Soviet peace initiative, among talk of how many casualties they might inflict. Saddam indicated, "I don't think this international coalition will continue to the end, and especially after the new political status that was stated."[67] Iraq had offered to comply with the Soviet diplomatic initiative.

The day before the war ended the conservative Heritage Foundation put out one of their *Backgrounder* reports. It started abruptly: "Saddam Hussein is in retreat. The question is, will he be defeated decisively or will he survive and claim a propaganda victory? There is an enormous difference between a military retreat and a geopolitical defeat." No one expected him to prevail against the United States and its allies, although the document argued that he sought to avoid a "geopolitical collapse that would threaten his rule over Iraq" and shatter his regional ambitions.[68]

The *Backgrounder* drew distinctions between 1956 and 1967. In 1956 Gamal Nasser survived the British, French, and Israeli invasion and moved on to become a dominant political and ideological force in the region. In 1967 the Israelis delivered a humiliating and crushing defeat. It was imperative to ignore the peace feelers and try to oust Saddam by separating him from the Iraqi military. Survival was his key objective, preferably through a prolonged conflict, but if not, one that avoided an explicit surrender. Heritage counseled the Bush administration to avoid the diplomatic landmines by insisting on an unconditional and total withdrawal, but it must not allow the Iraqi army to withdraw without surrendering. "The US must not only defeat Saddam Hussein's army but his political strategy. It must block Saddam's efforts to salvage political victory out of military defeat, as Nasser did in 1956." Moreover, and presciently, Saddam's removal would be a major victory:

> But such an outcome would be pyrrhic were it purchased at the price of occupying Baghdad and fighting a protracted guerrilla war inside Iraq that

would inflame the Arab world and turn Saddam into a martyr. As the Iranians found when they pushed Iraqi troops across the border in 1982, the Iraqis fight much better on their own territory, motivated by national defense rather than conquest. Occupying forces would be easy targets for truck bombs; it is not difficult to imagine Iraq turning into a super-Lebanon.[69]

It concluded the section with the observation that the "military costs and ensuing political costs that such an occupation would impose on US policy in the Arab world would offset the benefit of finishing off a mortally wounded Saddam."[70]

Richard Haass later recounted that they were looking for the "Goldilocks outcome." They wanted "an Iraq that could balance out other foes in the neighborhood without being so strong as to intimidate our friends."[71] Days after the war had started he drew up a paper on "war termination" in which he explored various scenarios. They ranged from Iraq signaling a desire to end hostilities through to third parties, such as the Soviets, putting on pressure to end hostilities, to the US desire to end the war. All produced various difficulties.

Haass observed early that Saddam would "try to 'win' by not formally 'losing' and by surviving." Various tests of the sincerity of an Iraqi offer were advanced, essentially looking for compliance with UN resolutions and on withdrawal within certain time limits. Haass questioned whether the United States wanted to stick to the strict reading of UNSC 660. With hostilities under way, should the United States require Iraq to take its forces and equipment out of Kuwait or should it be required to abandon major equipment in Kuwait? The latter "[has the] advantage of inflicting further penalty on Iraq ... and diminishes Iraq's ability to challenge regional peace in the future." However, to do so might complicate cease-fire discussions, might be seen as stretching beyond the UNSC remit, and, of course, might "have some impact on Iraq's ability to balance Iran in the post-crisis regional environment."[72]

The Vietnam analogy cropped up frequently in the contemporary discussion. Thus, it was important to constantly remind audiences that while the strategic goals were limited the operational plans and tactical instruments were overwhelming. The president had asserted that this war would not be "another Vietnam" and soon after explained to the US Reserve Officers Association in late January that he meant two things: First, "never again will our fighting men and women be sent in to do a job with one hand tied behind their back." And, second, they would not be sent to war without "the full backing of the folks back home."[73]

While Bush and Scowcroft were clear on the point of no occupation or march on Baghdad, Powell wanted the ground war delayed so they could see what would happen a day at a time. Powell wanted to see the Iraqis walk out of Kuwait; the cost in additional US lives was not worth it. Bush asked if he would prefer a negotiated end: "If it met our conditions totally, yes. They will crack," Powell argued. Bush retorted, "If they crack under force, it is better than withdrawal." And as quickly Powell returned, "But at what cost." Scowcroft sided with Bush though he saw Powell's concerns; yet the president "saw the dangers of an Iraqi withdrawal before its army had been destroyed."[74]

The dilemmas were clear enough and Haass was well aware that the end would not be as "clean" as a *USS Missouri* ending to World War II. But pressure mounted as Gorbachev pushed diplomatic options arising from bilateral Soviet-Iraqi talks. Ultimately, divisions emerged among the principals, with Cheney demanding a surrender and Baker suggesting that an early end ensured coalition cohesion. Among the administration, Haass relates, there was "widespread concern voiced by Powell and others, which I shared, that the images of Iraqi soldiers getting shot at while they were retreating in disarray was making us and our soldiers look bad" both regionally and globally. Soon after, the war was brought to a halt. It was assumed that the Republican Guard would have to abandon their equipment. In the White House there was no dissent on whether they should go onto Baghdad. Haass recounts, "We would have become an occupying force in a hostile land with no exit strategy."[75]

Haass continued to think about the postwar scenarios. In a paper, "Beyond the Gulf," he argued that the US presence would not be an anomaly; their relationship with Israel, oil dependency, and the outcomes of this war produced enduring interests. They needed to create a viable regional framework; essentially they needed stability without US troops stationed in the area, albeit a "transitional ground presence" in Kuwait and elsewhere might be required. Regional balance was important and the sources of instability were multiple and included "economic inequality, a lack of regime political legitimacy, arms imbalances, arms proliferation, religious extremism, and unresolved conflicts." Ironically they were about to leave yet another unresolved conflict. The high expectations at the time reveal ambitious US priorities. These, Haass argued, should include the pursuit of viable regional security arrangements; attempts to resolve disputes between Israel and the Palestinians; economic issues including trade, investment, and development; encouraging political pluralism and democratic institutions; and working toward regional approaches to WMD, oversized military powers, water, and other resource problems.[76] Few of these issues were resolved.

The US footprint was vital to the postwar scenarios. On the one hand, they were eager not to see Saddam rise from the ashes and reassert hegemony. On the other hand, they had to exit and reduce the US presence. Scowcroft wrote to Bush on 8 February 1991 in a memorandum titled "Restoring Liberated Kuwait." Technical issues were dealt with in terms of reconstruction and restoration of services and securing remnant areas. But crucially, Scowcroft's message was that "the last thing we need to do is follow up Iraq's occupation with one of our own. The model is thus post–World War II France, not Germany."[77]

Soon after, an internal discussion on "Security Choices after the Gulf War" identified ongoing threats including Iraq, Iran, and a third one that is redacted, probably Islamism or Islamist extremism, because solutions mention political and economic reforms, presumably to undermine the appeal of such ideologies associated with radicalism. Given the contemporary power structures, they knew the United States was required to back up its allies. Yet there was agreement that "we should avoid any stationing or basing of US air or ground forces in the region on a long-term or permanent basis." Exercises and rotation of troops "into and around the region" would provide the military benefits without the political costs. Yet if Saddam remains in power, the paper suggested, they might have to "maintain substantial air and ground forces in the region" to be phased out as conditions permitted.[78]

Again, the Powell Doctrine was operative. US airpower and troops would enter "in force and leave as soon as possible," avoiding entanglement. Powell persuaded the president to end after the five-day war (better than the Six Day War). Bush asserted, "We do not want to lose anything now with charges of brutalization." Gordon and Trainor argue that this crucial decision on war termination was made with "incomplete intelligence." Shortly after hostilities, a CIA plane discovered that half the Republican Guard forces, initially earmarked for destruction, had survived. The United States had planned to cut these forces off, but in the hasty conclusion they escaped. Soon, these forces would be used to crush the Shia and Kurdish uprisings.

Despite the overwhelming military victory, Saddam remained in power, unrepentant. Gordon and Trainor write:

> The way the war was planned, fought, and brought to a close often had more to do with the culture of the military services, their entrenched concept of warfare, and Powell's abiding philosophy of decisive force than it did with the Iraqis or the tangled politics of the Middle East.[79]

The United States certainly had the capability to crush the Iraqi forces, but they lacked the credibility to pursue the war to its logical regional and Iraqi conclusion. Ultimately, "The undermining of the post-Gulf War

Saddam Hussein regime—an implicit goal of the allied military campaign—was contradicted by the impulse to quickly withdraw, disengage, and avoid any military links to the insurgents. The disconnect between the military and political aims resulted in a confusing end."[80] At that point Saddam knew the United States was in a rush; they wanted an outcome before the Soviet-proposed ceasefire garnered strength. Aziz pointed out to Saddam, "Sir, George Bush has rushed into the ground attack [inaudible]." "Because of the political position," Saddam replied.[81]

A key element of both the Weinberger principles and the Powell Doctrine is that war should be the last resort. Of course there is an extensive literature on whether the diplomacy prior to the war—and, for current purposes, especially during the war—had been exhaustive. Could the war have been avoided? Or could the war have been brought to an earlier conclusion through Soviet diplomacy that might have been messy and incomplete, instead of the messy and incomplete victory that ensued? Senate Majority Leader George J. Mitchell pointed out in his response to Bush's State of the Union address that there was no disagreement on the ultimate objectives, but there was on the method. Was the war one of last resort? "No one will ever know if that other course would have worked." The United States would support the troops in war. But he pointed out that the United States had supported Iraq for ten years despite the character of the regime. And when the war ends, "there's one lesson we must never forget: The dictator we help today may turn his weapons on us tomorrow."[82]

Even as the air war continued, several commentators discussed concepts of victory and defeat. Iraq had offered to withdraw, which Bush had quickly dismissed as a "hoax."[83] Given their position on the UNSC, Soviet diplomacy with the Iraqis complicated US efforts to end the war on their terms. In a juxtaposition of two articles, the *Guardian* in London asked whether "Bush can lose by winning" and "how Saddam can win by losing." In the first, Martin Walker wondered why the Iraqi offer to withdraw was dismissed so quickly, why Bush had called on Iraqis to take matters into their own hands, and why they had not engaged positively with Soviet diplomacy.

Walker cited a discussion of a "nightmare scenario" in the White House that would leave Saddam in place without diminished forces, still large enough to threaten neighbors, "standing defiant and proud as a new rallying point for Arab nationalism." The article noted that the United States normally ended wars badly: the civil war with the "vengefulness of reconstruction," World War I with an idealism that subsided into isolationism, World War II with a divided planet and an arms race, and Vietnam with "introspective malaise."[84] Next, Hirst argued that

"Saddam has always stood to win a political victory that would offset, possibly even eclipse, military defeat, or an eleventh hour withdrawal designed to forestall one."[85]

The Ironies of Ends

Given the "cautious realism" frequently attributed to the Bush administration, the Gulf War was strategically incautious. Iraq had been ejected from Kuwait, but Saddam crushed the Shia and the Kurds in the war's "aftermath"; many Iraqis would remember the betrayal of 1991 as George W. Bush, Rumsfeld, and Cheney expected to be welcomed as liberators in 2003. The violence that Saddam exacted on internal populations of different ethnic and religious beliefs did not invoke a response on the scale of the violence associated with the "Hitler of the Euphrates" that had invaded a sovereign country. Yet in part the Gulf War was fought in pursuit of a new world order envisaged by Bush and Scowcroft—an order that was immediately questioned at war's end.

Despite the prewar fears of large numbers of US casualties, once the war started it was apparent the defeat would be crushing. H. Norman Schwarzkopf, the commanding general, belittled the Iraqi attacks as "no more significant than a mosquito to an elephant." By early February the death of eleven US Marines confirmed the consensus in the Bush administration to defer the ground war and continue with the air war. Yet, there was time pressure to bring offensive actions to an end, in deference to Arab coalition partners, before 17 March 1991, the start of Ramadan,[86] and before the Soviets or others might negotiate a ceasefire curtailing US objectives, mitigating the demonstration effects the war was supposed to instill. Bush outlined the gravity of the situation in his 1991 State of the Union address:

> I come to this House of the people, ... certain that we stand at a defining hour. Halfway around the world, we are engaged in a great struggle in the skies and on the seas and sands. We know why we're there. We are Americans: part of something larger than ourselves.[87]

In his historicism, Bush remarked:

> For two centuries we've done the hard work of freedom. And tonight we lead the world in facing down a threat to decency and humanity. What is at stake is more than one small country; it is a big idea: a new world order, where diverse nations are drawn together in common cause to achieve the universal aspirations of mankind: peace and security, freedom, and the rule of law.

> Our purpose in the Persian Gulf remains constant: to drive Iraq out of Kuwait, to restore Kuwait's legitimate government and to ensure the stability and security of this critical region. Let me make clear what I mean by the region's stability and security. We do not seek the destruction of Iraq, its culture, or its people. Rather, we seek an Iraq that uses its great resources not to destroy, not to serve the ambitions of a tyrant, but to build a better life for itself and its neighbors.[88]

He promised the families of the US forces that they would not "stay there one day longer than is necessary to complete their mission."[89]

So, on the one hand, you have this desire to construct a new world order, yet, on the other hand, quite limited postwar planning, much of which depended on a hope for a post-Saddam Iraq. Brent Scowcroft worried that US inaction might unleash a range of centrifugal forces; it would set a "terrible precedent." Other despots might be tempted by aggressive solutions, betting on US indecisiveness—the "fluidity of global politics might devolve into anarchy."

The Bush administration believed that decisive action would shape a very different order. The United States would be trusted by allies, feared by adversaries. The demonstration of its resolute force would deter future aggression. Yet these ambitions do not account for the paucity of postwar planning. Hal Brands suggests, "This expansive conception of US interests in the Gulf predisposed the administration to take strong, and virtually immediate, action to oppose Saddam's gambit."[90] Rose concurred:

> The Bush administration did not seek just to beat up Iraqi forces; it wanted to do so in a way that would send an unmistakable and humiliating message. The idea was to supplement the reduction of Iraqi capabilities with a crushing psychological burden of defeat. Aggression had to be punished and had to be seen to be punished, so that nobody could be left in any doubt about what just happened.[91]

When Gorbachev criticized Washington, suggesting that its operations might have exceeded UNSC Resolutions, the legal analysis prepared for Scowcroft by Nicholas Rostow argued that the defense of Kuwait as a practical consequence also necessitated "bringing Iraq's military establishment to a level consistent with the restoration of regional peace and security." Further, destroying its "capability for mounting other armed attacks against regional states is entirely consistent with the law governing the use of force in self-defense and the UN Security Council's mandate for Desert Storm."[92]

Seen within the context, Maureen Dowd, of the *New York Times*, suggests it was a part of Bush's attempt to control the war's endgame: "With the Iraqi leader facing military defeat, Mr. Bush decided that he would rather gamble on a violent and potentially unpopular ground war than risk the alternative: an imperfect settlement hammered out by the Soviets and Iraqis that world opinion might accept as tolerable." Bush was committed to a war that he had increasingly cast in moral terms; within the context of the Hitler analogy he had to stop the Soviets playing Chamberlain and providing a face-saving deal for Saddam. Given the limited casualties to date there was little domestic opposition to the ground war. Dowd cited a National Security Review from 1989: "In cases where the US confronts much weaker enemies, our challenge will be not simply to defeat them, but to defeat them decisively and rapidly," it argued. "For small countries hostile to us, bleeding our forces in protracted or indecisive conflict or embarrassing us by inflicting damage on some conspicuous element of our forces may be victory enough, and could undercut political support for US efforts against them." She concludes her report by observing that those close to Bush say he is "determined that this war's ending will not be ambiguous."[93]

The new world order was important to Scowcroft. It was not only associated with Franklin D. Roosevelt and the visions of internationalism interrupted by forty-five years of Cold War; it was also about setting a precedent for the future.[94] Scowcroft saw the Gulf crisis as a defining moment. He was dismayed at the initial lack of resolve in the Bush administration. US credibility was at stake in a vastly altered world landscape. Scowcroft had Haass prepare a memorandum for the National Security Council:

> Its main premises were that the United States had to properly understand how Iraq fit into the larger context of American foreign policy, and that diplomacy and economic sanctions, while necessary steps, would most likely fail, leaving the use of military force as the only option for reversing the situation.[95]

Early in the crisis Scowcroft worked on accentuating the importance of the situation to the region, to the United States, and to the world. Schmitz summarizes his rationale based on internationalist principles: stability, balance of power, unprovoked aggression, and the threat to oil supply.[96]

Bush added the moral dimension with comparisons to Nazi Germany; appeasement did not work. While fishing on 23 August 1990, Bush and Scowcroft discussed the "larger meaning of American policy" within the context of the crisis and memory of the Vietnam War. They believed the war was feasible, yet they did not want to get bogged down, they would not expand the conflict to overthrow Saddam, they would not get involved in open-ended nation building.[97] Soon after the war Robert

Kimmitt of the State Department wrote to Baker, urging him to have Bush include a key message to preempt the retrospectives Congress might indulge: "While we must all learn from the lessons of the past, we must not distract from the real challenge before us: to look to the future in a creative way to shape a new regional order that makes further aggression less likely."[98]

The lofty ambitions remained elusive. Toward the end of February Scowcroft wrote to Bush. He outlined two ways that wars had traditionally ended. The Gulf War will constitute a de facto rather than de jure end, "especially if Saddam stays in power." At that point, "the most likely scenario would be for the war to come to a somewhat 'messy' end with a massive tactical ... surrender, where unit by unit, defeated Iraqi forces in Kuwait and southern Iraq would raise the white flag to coalition forces." The "tidy" version would be if Saddam ordered all to stand down. The ability to declare war over rested on three criteria. First, Kuwait would be free of active Iraqi forces. Second, the Kuwaiti government would be restored. And, third, "no Republican Guard units in southern Iraq [would be] intact and perched to threaten Kuwait. When that comes about, we would be wise to withdraw most of our ground and air forces, work to ensure that Kuwait and Arab forces (mostly Egyptian and Saudi) are able to bear the principal security burden."[99] Still, negotiations at Safwan on 3 March 1991, which lasted a couple of hours, permitted the Iraqis continued use of their helicopters.[100]

With the inconclusive victory, enough of Saddam's forces escaped prosecution. Weeks earlier, Bush had indicated that an alternative end to war might require the "Iraqi people and the Iraqi military to take matters into their own hands, to force Saddam Hussein the dictator, to step aside." Allies were angered by the statement. Some "Western" diplomats suggested that this was a blatant interference in the internal affairs of Iraq. An Egyptian diplomat argued that it gave the impression that the United States was about to "dictate what kind of government would take over in Iraq, as it did in Panama after ousting General Manuel Noriega," the *Independent* reported.[101]

Bush's call was in part based on wishful thinking. Though written later, a Special National Intelligence Estimate of August 1991 indicated:

> We lack credible information on the political attitudes of the senior military officers, but most probably are conservative and intensely nationalistic in outlook. The brutality with which they suppressed the rebellions suggests they will remain loyal, at least while the prospect of internal rebellion exists. Saddam's pervasive security networks combined with the fear of purges, executions, and retribution against family members will also restrain senior military officials.[102]

They concluded that Saddam would probably be ruling a year from now.

Following Bush's invocation, the Shia in the south and the Kurds in the north did rise up. With his remnant forces, Saddam exacted a brutal revenge and suppression. Rose writes that survivors told of "mass public executions of hundreds of people by Saddam's revitalized troops." Yet Cheney thought the potential breakup of the country might be a worse outcome than Saddam staying in power. They decided to stand aside from the domestic wars.[103] The desire to withdraw precipitously left them unwilling to deal with the internal Iraqi aggression, even as they had fulfilled the international promise that the aggression against Kuwait would not stand.[104]

Engel rightly argues that as Bush laid out his vision, "the prospect of securing something truly historic ... beyond mere battlefield success, steeled his mind." Here was the opportunity, as Woodrow Wilson had recognized, to forge a world order. Not a perfect order by any means. Engel draws the distinction between the moderate aims of the administration and ultimate objectives. The world would be "freer," "stronger," and "more secure," but it would not attain "universal freedom," or full justice, or end wars and uncertainty completely.[105] Herein lay the cautious realism. Yet others, especially Slobodan Milošević, also drew the lesson that the United States would be reluctant to interfere in the internal affairs of countries; violence within borders was very different from violence across borders. Of course the Bush administration could not be held responsible for the "dithering" of the Clinton administration on Bosnia, yet the violence in Iraq after the conventional phase of the war and the ethnic cleansing in Bosnia and genocide in Rwanda pushed governments to examine their responsibilities to protect people within other sovereign states.[106]

When James Baker made an unauthorized foray into diplomacy with the Soviets that might have resulted in an early withdrawal, albeit with concessions, Bush wrote in his diary, as quoted above, that he did not know what would come next; he was not elated: "We've got some unfinished business. How do we solve it? How do we now guarantee the future peace?" He did not see how it would work with Saddam still in power.[107] By 2006 Baker indicated at the height of the US embroilment in Iraq that he was no longer asked why the United States had not pushed on to remove Saddam. Engel confirms that no one in the administration in 1991 had "any appetite" for occupation or reconstruction: "He'd gone to war to set a precedent, not to transform a region."[108]

Ironically, Dick Cheney was clear on the complexities in the Gulf War. Wary of going to Baghdad, he pointed out, "It's not clear what kind of government you would put in place of the one that's currently there now." Would it be Shia, Sunni, or Kurdish? Or would it be one that "tilts toward the Ba'athists or one that tilts toward the Islamic fundamentalists?" Would the government have any credibility if backed by US forces? How long would the United States have to stay to "protect the people that sign on for that government, and what happens to it once we leave?"[109]

Scowcroft and Haass had to impress upon Bush not to expand his war aims, not to go to Baghdad. To some extent the war had become personal for Bush;[110] he wanted to punish Saddam. The US intelligence community set about assessing such scenarios. The Defense Intelligence Agency warned of the regional implications; the Kuwait Task Force/US Army Civil Affairs Reconstruction Group concluded that "political and military collapse could make Iraq vulnerable to the predatory ambitions of its immediate neighbors." The United States could not manage the situation and they would watch as the region turned to chaos.

One assessment suggested, "The whole fertile crescent—Iraq, Syria, Lebanon, Jordan—is in question." Haass and Scowcroft ultimately persuaded Bush to limit his objectives; toppling Saddam was undesirable: Washington would be responsible for maintaining "order in a country on the verge of a multisided civil war, one in which all sides would view the Americans as occupiers."[111] Paul Wolfowitz had written to Cheney at war's end to push for an international force "to take control of southern Iraq as we pull out."[112] As Powell eventually put it in his *A Soldier's Way*: "[Bush] had promised the American people that Desert Storm would not become a Persian Gulf Vietnam, and he kept his promise."[113]

Yet the military strategy had not been calibrated with the postwar scenarios; they had not planned adequately for Phase IV. Rose contends:

> Policymakers were loath to sit back and watch as their supposedly defeated and humiliated enemy regained his footing and proceeded to engage in mass murder with impunity—but they were even more loath to get trapped in a desert Vietnam. So they froze and did nothing as events on the ground played themselves out.[114]

David Ryan is professor of modern history at University College Cork, Ireland. He has published extensively on contemporary history and US foreign policy, concentrating on interventions in the post–Vietnam era. His books include *Obama, US Foreign Policy and the Dilemmas of Intervention* coauthored with David Fitzgerald (Palgrave, 2014); *US Foreign Policy and the Other*, edited with Michael Cullinane (Berghahn, 2015); *Frustrated Empire: US Foreign Policy from 9/11 to Iraq* (Pluto and University of Michigan, 2007); *Vietnam in Iraq: Tactics, Lessons, Legacies and Ghosts*, edited with John Dumbrell (Routledge, 2007); *The United*

States and Europe in the Twentieth Century (Longman, 2003); *US Foreign Policy in World History* (Routledge, 2000); and *US-Sandinista Diplomatic Relations: Voice of Intolerance* (MacMillan, 1995). He is also the author of numerous articles.

Notes

1. John Bulloch, "How Bush Lost the Gulf War," *The Independent on Sunday* (London), 8 December 1991.
2. Jeffrey Record, *Hollow Victory: A Contrary View of the Gulf War* (Washington, DC: Brassey's, 1993), 156.
3. Jeffrey A. Engel, *When the World Seemed New: George H. W. Bush and the End of the Cold War* (Boston: Houghton Mifflin Harcourt, 2017), 397.
4. Spencer D. Bakich, *Success and Failure in Limited War: Information and Strategy in the Korean, Vietnam, Persian Gulf, and Iraq Wars* (Chicago: University of Chicago, 2014), 177.
5. Engel, 398–99; see also, Jeffrey Record, *Making War, Thinking History: Munich, Vietnam, and Presidential Uses of Force from Korea to Kosovo* (Annapolis: Naval Institute Press, 2002), 101–9.
6. Aaron Rapport, "The Long and Short of It: Cognitive Constraints on Leaders' Assessments of 'Postwar' Iraq," *International Security* 37, no. 3 (2012/2013): 133–71; Aaron Rapport, *Waging War, Planning Peace: US Noncombat Operations and Major Wars* (Ithaca: Cornell University Press, 2015).
7. On whether the war was avoidable, see Record, *Hollow Victory*, 15–42.
8. George H. W. Bush, "National Security Directive 45," 20 August 1990, National Security Archive, Washington, DC, http://nsarchive.gwu.edu/NSAEBB/NSAEBB39/document2.pdf, accessed 15 December 2018.
9. Zbigniew Brzezinski, "Three Ways America Can Save Its Honour," *The Observer* (London), 21 April 1991.
10. Record, *Hollow Victory*, 157.
11. Ibid., 159.
12. Engel, *When the World Seemed New*, 415–39. See also Bartholomew H. Sparrow, "Realism's Practitioner: Brent Scowcroft and the Making of the New World Order, 1989–1993," *Diplomatic History* 34, no. 1 (2010): 141–75; David F. Schmitz, *Brent Scowcroft: Internationalism and Post-Vietnam War American Foreign Policy* (Lanham: Rowman & Littlefield, 2011).
13. James A. Baker, *The Politics of Diplomacy: Revolution, War and Peace 1989–1992* (New York: Putnam's, 1995), 194.
14. George H. W. Bush, Remarks to the Legislative Exchange Council, 1 March 1991, George H. W. Bush Presidential Museum, Speeches, https://bush41library.tamu.edu/archives/public-papers/2754, accessed 15 December 2018.
15. Warren I. Cohen, *America in the Age of Soviet Power, 1845–1991*, vol. 4, Cambridge History of American Foreign Relations (Cambridge: Cambridge University Press, 1993), 68.
16. Stefano Recchia, *Reassuring the Reluctant Warriors: US Civil-Military Relations and Multilateral Intervention* (Ithaca: Cornell University Press, 2015), 16–33; Sarah E. Kreps, *Coalitions of Convenience: United States Military Interventions after the Cold War* (Oxford: Oxford University Press, 2011), 49–73.
17. David Milne, *Worldmaking: The Art and Science of American Diplomacy* (New York: Farrar, Straus and Giroux, 2015), 387–456.

18. Marvin Kalb and Deborah Kalb, *Haunting Legacy: Vietnam and the American Presidency from Ford to Obama* (Washington, DC: Brookings Institution Press, 2011).
19. Gideon Rose, *How Wars End: Why We Always Fight the Last Battle* (New York: Simon & Schuster, 2010), 220–21.
20. David Fitzgerald and David Ryan, "Iraq and Vietnam: Endless Recurrence or Stirrings Still," *Critical Asian Studies* 41, no. 4 (2009): 621–53; David L. Anderson and John Ernst, eds., *The War That Never Ends: New Perspectives on the Vietnam War* (Lexington: University of Kentucky, 2007).
21. Jeffrey Goldberg, "Breaking Ranks: What Turned Brent Scowcroft against the Bush Administration?" *The New Yorker*, 31 October 2005; Andrew Rice, "Brent Scowcroft Calls Iraq War 'Overreaction,'" *The Observer* (London), 6 September 2004.
22. George Bush and Brent Scowcroft, *A World Transformed* (New York: Alfred A. Knopf, 1998), 489.
23. Colin L. Powell, "US Forces, Challenges Ahead," *Foreign Affairs* 71 (winter, 1992/1993), 37.
24. Bush and Scowcroft, *World Transformed*, 489.
25. Gulf Strategy, January Themes and Messages, n.d., Office of Cabinet Affairs, John Sununu files, Persian Gulf War 1991, 03922-018 Persian Gulf (2), Bush Presidential Library.
26. Richard Sobel, *The Impact of Public Opinion on US Foreign Policy since Vietnam* (New York: Oxford University Press, 2001), 143–74.
27. Bush and Scowcroft, *World Transformed*, 383.
28. Ibid., 383–384; Robert A. Divine, "The Persian Gulf War Revisited: Tactical Victory, Strategic Failure," *Diplomatic History* 24, no. 1 (2000).
29. Bush and Scowcroft, *World Transformed*, 383.
30. Colin L. Powell, *A Soldier's Way: An Autobiography* (London: Hutchinson, 1995), 459–542.
31. James A. Baker, *The Politics of Diplomacy: Revolution, War and Peace 1989–1992* (New York: Putnam's, 1995), 411.
32. Ibid., 413.
33. Ibid., 435.
34. Powell, *A Soldier's Way*, 527.
35. Divine, "Persian Gulf War Revisited," 137; Michael Gordon and Bernard Trainor, *The Generals' War: The Inside Story of the First Gulf War* (London: Atlantic, 1995).
36. Divine, "Persian Gulf War Revisited," 137.
37. Ibid., 138.
38. Unknown, "Security Structures?" (NSC, Robert M. Gates files, Subject files, CF00946, Persian Gulf Conflict, 21 January 1991), George H. W. Bush Presidential Library.
39. Ibid.
40. Ibid.
41. Ibid.
42. Baker, *Politics of Diplomacy*, 414.
43. Ibid., 435, emphasis added.
44. Ibid., 436.
45. Ibid., 436–38.
46. Ibid.
47. Ibid., 442.
48. Secretary of State James Baker and Deputy Prime Minister and Foreign Minister Tariq Aziz, Memorandum of Conversation, 9 January 1991, Geneva, Switzerland, NSC, Robert Gates files, Subject files, CF00946, Persian Gulf Conflict January 1991 (2 of 2), Bush Presidential Library.
49. Ibid.

50. Ibid.
51. Lawrence Freedman and Efraim Karsh, *The Gulf Conflict 1990–1991: Diplomacy and War in the New World Order* (London: Faber and Faber, 1993), 410–27; Lawrence Freedman, *A Choice of Enemies: America Confronts the Middle East* (London: Weidenfeld & Nicolson, 2008), 251–53.
52. Secretary of State James Baker and Deputy Prime Minister and Foreign Minister Tariq Aziz, Memorandum of Conversation, 9 January 1991, Geneva, Switzerland, NSC, Robert Gates files, Subject files, CF00946, Persian Gulf Conflict January 1991 (2 of 2), Bush Presidential Library.
53. Powell, *Soldier's Way*, 523.
54. Ibid., 524–26.
55. Robert A. Divine, "The Persian Gulf War Revisited: Tactical Victory, Strategic Failure," *Diplomatic History* 24, no. 1 (2000), 129.
56. Zbigniew Brzezinski, "A Tale of Two Wars: The Right War in Iraq, and the Wrong One," *Foreign Affairs* 88, no. 3 (2009): 148–52; Ryan, "From the 'Tilt' to the Unintended 'Transformation': The United States and Iraq, 1975–1992," in *America and Iraq*, eds. Ryan and Kiely.
57. Donald Rumsfeld, *Known and Unknown: A Memoir* (New York: Sentinel, 2011), 3–8.
58. Ibid., 413–15.
59. Robert M. Gates, *Duty: Memoirs of a Secretary at War* (London: Allen, 2014), 26.
60. George H. W. Bush, "Statement by Press Secretary Fitzwater on President Bush's Letter to President Saddam Hussein of Iraq" (Public Papers, George H. W. Bush Presidential Library and Museum, 12 January 1991); George H. W. Bush, "The President's News Conference" (Public Papers, George H. W. Bush Presidential Library and Museum, 12 January 1991).
61. Gates, *Duty*, 26.
62. Gordon and Trainor, *Generals' War*, viii.
63. Jim Hoagland cited in Record, *Hollow Victory*, 160.
64. Gordon and Trainor, *Generals' War*, ix.
65. Caspar W. Weinberger, Secretary of Defense, "The Uses of Military Power," remarks at the National Press Club, Washington, DC, 28 November 1984, PBS, https://www.pbs.org/wgbh/pages/frontline/shows/military/force/weinberger.html, accessed 15 December 2018.
66. Powell, *Soldier's Way*, 303.
67. Kevin M. Woods, David D. Palkki, and Mark E. Stout, eds., *The Saddam Tapes: The Inner Workings of a Tyrant's Regime 1978–2001* (Cambridge: Cambridge University Press, 2011), 194–95.
68. Heritage Foundation, "Winning a Real Victory Over Iraq" (Heritage Foundation, 26 February 1991).
69. Ibid.
70. Ibid.
71. Richard N. Haass, *War of Necessity, War of Choice: A Memoir of Two Iraq Wars* (New York: Simon & Schuster, 2009), 126.
72. Richard N. Haass, "War Termination" (Memorandum to Bob Gates, Bob Kimmitt, David Jeremiah, Paul Wolfowitz, Dick Kerr, NSC, Robert M. Gates files, Subject files, CF00946, Persian Gulf Conflict, 19 January 1991), George H. W. Bush Presidential Library.
73. McNally/Simon, "Presidential Remarks: US Reserve Officers Association" (Office of Cabinet Affairs, John Sununu files, Persian Gulf War 1991, 03922-081, Persian Gulf (2), 23 January 1991), George H. W. Bush Presidential Library.
74. David F. Schmitz, *Brent Scowcroft: Internationalism and Post-Vietnam War American Foreign Policy* (Lanham: Rowman & Littlefield, 2011), 159.

75. Haass, *War of Necessity*, 122–33.
76. Richard N. Haass, "Beyond the Gulf War" (NSC, Robert M. Gates files, Subject files, CF00946, Persian Gulf Conflict January 1991, 25 January 1991), George H. W. Bush Presidential Library.
77. Brent Scowcroft, "Restoring Liberated Kuwait" (NSC, Robert M. Gates files, Subject files, CF00946, Persian Gulf Conflict February 1991, 8 February 1991), George H. W. Bush Presidential Library.
78. Unknown, "Security Choices after the Gulf War" (NSC, Richard Haass files, Conduct of the Persian Gulf War: Final Report to Congress, CF 01584-004, Iraq-February 1991(2), n.d.), George H. W. Bush Presidential Library.
79. Gordon and Trainor, *Generals' War*, ix–xv.
80. Ibid.
81. Woods et al., *Saddam Tapes*, 192.
82. George J. Mitchell, "Mitchell Stresses Need to Put 'Our Own House in Order,'" *Congressional Quarterly*, 2 February 1991.
83. George H. W. Bush, "Address to the American Academy for the Advancement of Science," *Congressional Quarterly* 49, no. 7, 15 February 1991).
84. Martin Walker, "Helping to Make a Martyr," *The Guardian* (London), 16 February 1991.
85. David Hirst, "In Search of a Safe Way Out," *The Guardian* (London), 16 February 1991.
86. Pat Towell, "Combat Reality Brought Home by Deaths of 11 Marines," *Congressional Quarterly*, 2 February 1991.
87. George H. W. Bush, "Bush Seeks to Inspire Support for His Persian Gulf Mission," *Congressional Quarterly*, 2 February 1991.
88. Ibid.
89. Ibid.
90. Hal Brands, *Making the Unipolar Moment: US Foreign Policy and the Rise of the Post-Cold War Order* (Ithaca: Cornell University, 2016), 301–2.
91. Rose, *How Wars End*, 216.
92. Nicholas Rostow to Brent Scowcroft, "The Gulf War: Gorbachev Statement on Exceeding the U.N. Mandate," Brent Scowcroft files, Desert Shield/Desert Storm files, 91146-009 (January 1991) (3), George Bush Presidential Library, 11 February 1991.
93. Maureen Dowd, "Bush Moves to Control War's Endgame," *New York Times*, 23 February 1991.
94. David F. Schmitz, *Brent Scowcroft: Internationalism and Post-Vietnam War American Foreign Policy* (Lanham: Rowman and Littlefield, 2011), 137.
95. Schmitz, *Brent Scowcroft*, 141.
96. Ibid., 143–44.
97. Ibid., 145.
98. Robert M. Kimmitt, "Iraq Retrospective" 4 March 1991 (document 01648, fiche 254), the National Security Archive, Washington, DC.
99. Brent Scowcroft, "Ending the Gulf War," NSC, Richard Haass files, Conduct of the Persian Gulf War: Final Report to Congress, CF 01584-005, Iraq—February 1991(3), 25 February 1991, George H. W. Bush Presidential Library.
100. Rose, *How Wars End*, 198.
101. Leonard Doyle, "Bush Call for Coup Angers US Allies," *The Independent* (London), 16 February 1991; Peter Pringle, "Gorbachev Manoeuvres for Diplomatic Gains," *The Independent* (London), 16 February 1991.
102. Special National Intelligence Estimate, "Iraq: Saddam Husayn's Prospects for Survival over the Next Year," September 1991.
103. Gideon Rose, *How Wars End: Why We Always Fight the Last Battle* (New York: Simon and Schuster, 2010), 199.
104. Ibid., 202.

105. Engel, *When the World Seemed New*, 415–19.
106. Gareth Evans and Mohamed Sahnoun, "The Responsibility to Protect" (Ottawa: International Commission on Intervention and State Sovereignty, December 2001).
107. Rose, *How Wars End*, 221; Engel, *When the World Seemed New*, 435.
108. Engel, *When the World Seemed New*, 438.
109. Cheney quoted by Adrian R. Lewis, *The American Culture of War: The History of US Military Force from World War II to Operation Iraqi Freedom* (New York: Routledge, 2007), 369.
110. Stephen R. Graubard, *Mr. Bush's War: Adventures in the Politics of Illusion* (London: I. B. Tauris, 1992).
111. Bakich, *Success and Failure in Limited War*, 177–78.
112. Paul Wolfowitz, "Memorandum for the Secretary of Defense" (NSC, Robert M. Gates files, Subject files, CF 00946, Persian Gulf Conflict, George Bush Presidential Library, March 1991).
113. Powell, *Soldier's Way*, 526.
114. Rose, *How Wars End*, 226.

Select Bibliography

Anderson, David L. and John Ernst, eds., *The War That Never Ends: New Perspectives on the Vietnam War* (Lexington: University of Kentucky, 2007).

Baker, James A., *The Politics of Diplomacy: Revolution, War and Peace 1989–1992* (New York: Putnam's, 1995).

Bakich, Spencer D., *Success and Failure in Limited War: Information and Strategy in the Korean, Vietnam, Persian Gulf, and Iraq Wars* (Chicago: University of Chicago, 2014).

Brands, Hal, *Making the Unipolar Moment: US Foreign Policy and the Rise of the Post-Cold War Order* (Ithaca, NY: Cornell University, 2016).

Brzezinski, Zbigniew, "A Tale of Two Wars: The Right War in Iraq, and the Wrong One," *Foreign Affairs* 88, no. 3 (2009).

Bush, George and Brent Scowcroft, *A World Transformed* (New York: Alfred A. Knopf, 1998).

Cohen, Warren I., *America in the Age of Soviet Power, 1845–1991*, vol. 4, Cambridge History of American Foreign Relations (Cambridge: Cambridge University Press, 1993).

Divine, Robert A., "The Persian Gulf War Revisited: Tactical Victory, Strategic Failure," *Diplomatic History* 24, no. 1 (2000).

Engel, Jeffrey A., *When the World Seemed New: George H. W. Bush and the End of the Cold War* (Boston, MA: Houghton Mifflin Harcourt, 2017).

Fitzgerald, David and David Ryan, "Iraq and Vietnam: Endless Recurrence or Stirrings Still," *Critical Asian Studies* 41, no. 4 (2009).

Freedman, Lawrence, *A Choice of Enemies: America Confronts the Middle East* (London: Weidenfeld & Nicolson, 2008).

Freedman, Lawrence and Efraim Karsh, *The Gulf Conflict 1990–1991: Diplomacy and War in the New World Order* (London: Faber and Faber, 1993).

Gates, Robert M., *Duty: Memoirs of a Secretary at War* (London: Allen, 2014).

Gordon, Michael and Bernard Trainor, *The Generals' War: The Inside Story of the First Gulf War* (London: Atlantic, 1995).
Graubard, Stephen R., *Mr. Bush's War: Adventures in the Politics of Illusion* (London: I.B. Tauris, 1992).
Haass, Richard N., *War of Necessity, War of Choice: A Memoir of Two Iraq Wars* (New York: Simon & Schuster, 2009).
Kreps, Sarah E., *Coalitions of Convenience: United States Military Interventions after the Cold War* (Oxford: Oxford University Press, 2011).
Lewis, Adrian R., *The American Culture of War: The History of US Military Force from World War II to Operation Iraqi Freedom* (New York: Routledge, 2007).
Milne, David, *Worldmaking: The Art and Science of American Diplomacy* (New York: Farrar, Straus and Giroux, 2015).
Powell, Colin L., "US Forces, Challenges Ahead," *Foreign Affairs* 71 (winter, 1992/1993).
_____, *A Soldier's Way: An Autobiography* (London: Hutchinson, 1995).
Rapport, Aaron, "The Long and Short of It: Cognitive Constraints on Leaders' Assessments of 'Postwar' Iraq," *International Security* 37, no. 3 (2012/2013).
Recchia, Stefano, *Reassuring the Reluctant Warriors: US Civil-Military Relations and Multilateral Intervention* (Ithaca, NY: Cornell University Press, 2015).
Record, Jeffrey, *Hollow Victory: A Contrary View of the Gulf War* (Washington, DC: Brassey's, 1993).
_____, *Making War, Thinking History: Munich, Vietnam, and Presidential Uses of Force from Korea to Kosovo* (Annapolis, MD: Naval Institute Press, 2002).
Rose, Gideon, *How Wars End: Why We Always Fight the Last Battle* (New York: Simon and Schuster, 2010).
Ryan, David, "From the 'Tilt' to the Unintended 'Transformation': The United States and Iraq, 1975–1992," in David Ryan and Patrick Kiely, eds., *America and Iraq: Policy-Making, Intervention and Regional Politics* (London: Routledge, 2008).
Rumsfeld, Donald, *Known and Unknown: A Memoir* (New York: Sentinel, 2011).
Schmitz, David F., *Brent Scowcroft: Internationalism and Post-Vietnam War American Foreign Policy* (Lanham, MD: Rowman & Littlefield, 2011).
Sobel, Richard, *The Impact of Public Opinion on US Foreign Policy since Vietnam* (New York: Oxford University Press, 2001).
Sparrow, Bartholomew H., "Realism's Practitioner: Brent Scowcroft and the Making of the New World Order, 1989–1993," *Diplomatic History* 34, no. 1 (2010).
Woods, Kevin M., David D. Palkki, and Mark E. Stout, eds., *The Saddam Tapes: The Inner Workings of a Tyrant's Regime 1978–2001* (Cambridge: Cambridge University Press, 2011).

Chapter 6

Failing to End
Obama and Iraq

David Fitzgerald and David Ryan

On 26 February 2012, the US Department of Defense issued a short statement noting that they had recovered the remains of Army Staff Sergeant Ahmed al-Taie, the last American service member unaccounted for in Iraq. The military's mortuary at Dover Air Force Base, Delaware, had positively identified his remains, which were being returned to his family in Michigan. Press coverage of this punctuation mark in America's war in Iraq was relatively muted, with most stories briefly recounting al-Taie's biography and the circumstances of his disappearance in 2006; little was made of the moment otherwise.[1]

Born in Baghdad, al-Taie emigrated to the United States in the 1980s; he later returned to Iraq as an Army reservist and married an Iraqi woman, frequently leaving the Green Zone to spend time with her. In October 2006, he was kidnapped at gunpoint during one of those visits, becoming the subject of a massive but fruitless manhunt by US forces in Baghdad. The Iranian-backed militia group Asaib Ahl al-Haq later claimed responsibility for the kidnapping. In 2010, Qais al-Khazali, the leader of their group declared on Iraqi TV that their duty to fight the Americans was over and that they would put down their weapons in order to join the Iraqi government. Eventually, in 2012, al-Taie's remains were handed over as part of an amnesty exchange agreement with Asaib Ahl al-Haq. The group would face no consequences for the killing. In 2016, the *Long War Journal* reported that US intelligence officials believed that the group were responsible for abducting three American contractors in Baghdad.²

The personal tragedy of al-Taie's story—an Iraqi-born American returned to his native land and a family in Michigan spending six long years enduring rumor and speculation as to his whereabouts before the final return of his body—is interlaced with the broader tragedy of the US disengagement with Iraq. Of course, al-Taie was not the last American body to come home from Iraq. Following the failure of the Obama administration's efforts to disengage from the region, there would be more dead and more missing. Indeed, the path followed Asaib Ahl al-Haq, the Shiite militant group who kidnapped and then killed al-Taie, gives some indication of the trajectories of Iraqi politics during this time: a violent campaign against US occupiers, followed by reconciliation with the Shiite-dominated government, followed by involvement in the Syrian war on the side of the Assad regime, a campaign against ISIS in Iraq and Syria and, allegedly, attacks on the Americans who had returned to Iraq.

This chapter sketches out the contours of the policy failures that helped lead to this state of affairs. The return of al-Taie's remains would not mark the definitive end to the period; at best, like the fall of Fallujah again in 2014, it would be a less definitive punctuation mark. Despite the wishes of the Obama administration to turn the page on Iraq, the choices they made from 2010 to 2013 meant that a return to a country more destabilized than ever was an inevitability.

Turning the Page on Iraq

Obama's desire for a recalibration of US power was clearly signaled from the time of his inauguration:

> Our nation is at war, against a far reaching network of violence and hatred. Our economy is badly weakened, a consequence of greed and irresponsibility on the part of some, but also our collective failure to make hard choices and prepare the nation for a new age. Homes have been lost; jobs shed; businesses shuttered. Our health care is too costly; our schools fail too many; and each day brings further evidence that the ways we use energy strengthen our adversaries and threaten our planet. ... Less measurable but no less profound is a sapping of confidence across our land—a nagging fear that America's decline is inevitable, and that the next generation must lower its sights.³

Famously, he indicated that nation building ought to begin at home. Derek Chollet, who served in various capacities in the White House, the Pentagon, and the State Department, indicated that Obama wanted his team to be more strategically creative: they needed to "do more to knit together the narrative of economic strength and global authority." His vision was not just to enhance the respect for the United States but to recover and grow its economy, to rekindle domestic vitality, and to set a moral example. Chollet cites Obama: "That's where I want to go, although we don't know if we can get there because history intrudes."[4]

Obama wanted to renew the United States, to stop squandering its power in wars like Iraq. He realized that Iraq had absorbed too much attention and wanted to widen the agenda, not only on the economy and nation building at home but by reengaging with allies and repairing the damage done to alliances, reducing the huge costs of military engagement, drawing down in Iraq and Afghanistan, pivoting to Asia and the Pacific, and dealing with a range of domestic issues as well as climate change, trade, and nuclear nonproliferation.[5] But of course history would intervene as the eight years of the presidency threw up a range of external challenges.[6] Not least, the rise of ISIS would compel a US return to Iraq.

While Obama's inaugural address made clear the extent of the crisis left behind by the Bush administration, it did not directly dwell on the specific legacies of the Iraq War. From a US perspective, there was little need to: the US public were thoroughly exhausted by war, even amid temporary optimism about the gains of the surge, and the costs of the war to the United States were clear for all to see. By 2014 there were 4,427 US personnel killed and 34,275 wounded, and Joseph Stiglitz and Linda Bilmes put the financial figure at $3 trillion by 2010.[7] Of course it would impact the national debt and hinder attempts to recover from the 2008 recession. Peter Hahn concluded his ironically titled *Mission Accomplished?* with this estimation: "From 2000 to 2010, the US share of global gross domestic product fell from 32 percent to 24 percent, a rate of relative national economic decline surpassed in world history only by the collapse of the Soviet Union in 1991."[8] Toward the end of the US war, Robert Gates thought it would have to be left to the historians to consider whether the efforts were "worth it."[9]

What was less visible to Americans was the cost of the war to Iraq. Estimates of civilian casualties vary wildly, but the Iraq body count database documented a minimum of 120,000 violent deaths up to 2011.[10] *PLOS Medicine* pointed out in 2013 that Iraqi fatalities had reached an estimated 461,000 up to 2011,[11] while a study in *The Lancet* in 2006 suggested a staggering 650,000 dead.[12] Neta Crawford noted, "As with the tendency to underestimate the budgetary costs of the Iraq war, there has been a tendency to minimize the harm of the war to Iraq." She claimed, "Official sources have not only been told, at the national level, to not make their figures public, local morgues have also underreported deaths due to war."[13] But even underreporting deaths could not hide the extent of the loss. Even using the Iraq body count's conservative estimates, more than four thousand Iraqi civilians were still being killed every year at the lowest ebb of the conflict in 2010–2012. The wounded remain essentially uncounted, but all studies agree that they far outnumber the dead. In 2007, UNCHR estimated that there were over 4 million Iraqis displaced throughout the world, including 1.9 million displaced in Iraq itself.[14]

The human costs of war were exacerbated by damage to Iraq's infrastructure. The 2003 invasion had badly degraded Iraq's electricity supply: in April 2003, Iraq's power generation capacity was 1.27 gigawatts, down from 4.3 gigawatts prior to the war.[15] Throughout the US occupation, the effort to surpass prewar levels of electricity generation was a central problem for military commanders, and Iraqi cities, even Baghdad spent much of their days without power. De-Baathification and the disbandment of the Iraqi army had meant that huge swathes of the civil and public service, along with the security infrastructure, needed to be rebuilt from scratch, and basic services, such as sewage and garbage collection, were rendered dysfunctional by the insurgency, especially as insurgents learned that targeting infrastructure was an effective way to undermine the Iraqi government.[16] The botched and rushed reconstruction effort allowed corruption to flourish. Iraqi doctors fled the country, one study estimating that eighteen thousand physicians, half the prewar total, had left the country. Amman and Beirut became medical destinations of choice for Iraqis who could afford to leave the country for medical care.[17]

This medical crisis, and indeed the overall state of Iraq's infrastructure, had been exacerbated by an earlier US failure to end war. The sanctions regime and Oil for Food Program, which had been put in place after the cessation of hostilities in the Persian Gulf War of 1991, had already caused an immense public crisis and degraded Iraq's infrastructure. In that earlier war, US air strikes had directly targeted Iraqi electricity generation nodes, causing a 70% reduction in electricity generation.[18]

Much of the damage caused to electricity, sewage, and transportation infrastructure caused by the 1991 war went unrepaired, leaving the country in a precarious position even before the 2003 invasion. Numerous studies indicated a severe childhood malnutrition problem in Iraq due to the sanctions regime. As with war deaths, estimates of fatalities varied wildly, from the 500,000 child deaths reported by *The Lancet* and UNICEF (United Nations International Children's Emergency Fund) to post-2003 studies that argued that there was no significant increase in childhood mortality caused by sanctions.[19] Regardless of imprecision in quantifying it, it was clear that the devastation of 1991 and 2003 was enormous and that the scale of reconstruction required in Iraq was immense. Bush era optimism that Iraqi oil revenue would pay for the war and that "cutting the head off" would be enough to unleash democratic reform and economic growth had long been proven to be a fantasy. Billions of dollars' worth of US reconstruction efforts had been lost to corruption or thwarted by insurgent attacks.

But the costs to Iraq were not uppermost in the minds of US strategists, focused as they were on US costs. The dilemma facing Obama was as old as writings on grand strategy: the need to balance commitments and capabilities—means and ends. There was a similar logic in Obama's early rhetoric to that of President Eisenhower. In Eisenhower's 1953 "chance for peace" speech he asked, "How many schools did a new bomber cost? How many hospitals did a new destroyer force the country to forego?"[20] Obama put it more prosaically: "Don't do stupid shit." The United States had engaged in wars of choice in Vietnam and Iraq that significantly undermined its strategic positioning not just in the region but also in the world. In the year after Obama's presidency, authors focused on his pragmatism, his caution, the prudence of the "long game."[21]

His reputation will certainly benefit from being bookended by George W. Bush and Donald Trump. While Obama did persist in Afghanistan and initiated a war in Libya, which he came to regret, he also realized that military intervention had rarely been successful, the costs were high and long term, US interests were frequently undermined, and alliances were disturbed. Andrew Bacevich concluded in a 2016 article for *Foreign Affairs*, "History offers few assurances that small wars stay small or that campaigns designed to be brief keep to schedule."[22] The long-term outcomes were usually unpredictable and negative. The CIA could not provide Obama with one good example for him to think about as he contemplated US support for the insurgencies in Syria—whether it was the Bay of Pigs, Vietnam, or the contras in Central America.[23] Obama was intent on staying out of Syria; but getting out of Iraq was a priority.

While Obama consistently focused on the costs of war throughout his entire political career, he did not reckon with the responsibility the United States generated by the costs its invasion had imposed on Iraq. Nor was there a reckoning with what the United States had created in Iraq through its intervention. Famously, Obama had described the war in Iraq as the "dumb" war. Saddam Hussein had for a time kept radicalism and Islamism at bay. As a senator during the electoral campaign of 2008, Obama visited Iraq and reportedly remarked that the country was not the center of gravity in the war on terror. General David Petraeus argued that al-Qaeda thought it was. They had not been in Iraq at the beginning of the war but now considered it a key location in which to expand their operations as well as a place in which they could impact US regional influence.[24]

Yet the destabilization of the country created opportunities, opening space for increasingly extremist radical politics associated first with al-Qaeda and later with ISIS. Of course, sectarian violence increased dramatically. If the reasons, as Obama understood, for going to war were "dumb" the conditions by 2009 had created a new issue of security for the United States. The US withdrawal was predicated on domestic issues, the war's unpopularity was a given by that stage, and withdrawal would reduce US commitments and costs. But the war was not ended responsibly in terms of Iraq or the region. Within years the United States would have to return, albeit with more limited forces. While the Status of Forces Agreement (SoFA) had been concluded between the United States and Iraq in 2008, Obama still sought an expedient exit from the country. A timetable was created, troops would withdraw from the field first in 2009, most from the country by 31 August 2010, and the remainder at the end of 2011.

The schedule was determined based on US politics and Obama's objectives, not on an assessment of Iraq, the viability of the Maliki government, or its dependence on the United States. Later, when the withdrawal had gone wrong, critics would point to a rushed timetable and military dissent to argue that Obama had thrown away the victory won by Bush. David Milne cites Wolfowitz's June 2014 observation that they had "won" the Iraq War "but that this hard-earned victory had been squandered by the Obama administration in its headlong rush to withdraw."[25] There seemed to be little remorse or regret among the principals of the Bush administration. Andrew Bacevich had challenged Paul Wolfowitz to respond regarding the lessons that could be learned from Iraq, especially, "so that we might extract from it something of value in return for all the sacrifices made there," but the nature of the debate over US withdrawal from Iraq indicated that few, if any, lessons had sunk in on either side of the partisan divide.

Simply put, that debate was reductive, focused solely on the question of troop numbers, and missed any detailed assessment of the state of Iraqi politics or of what the United States would be leaving behind. Obama's 2009 announcement of a withdrawal was broadly welcomed, with even Senator John McCain, Obama's opponent in the 2008 presidential election, calling the plan "reasonable" and declaring himself "cautiously optimistic that the plan as laid out by the president can lead to success." However, as the date for the final withdrawal of troops began to loom, Republicans began to critique the lack of plans for any residual force, while critics on the left skeptically noted the size of the planned new US embassy in Baghdad and the amount of personnel that would be required to guard it.[26] The debate over US strategy in postoccupation Iraq was reduced simply to the question of boots on the ground. While

Obama certainly promised continued diplomatic engagement in Iraq and across the region, the fact that so much intellectual energy was expended on the question of troop numbers denotes a particularly narrow view of what the endgame in Iraq would look like.

Moreover, the fixation on a "stay-behind" force and the criticisms of those who argued that the United States needed to keep troops in Iraq both to protect its interests and to ensure leverage with the Iraqis misread the politics of both Washington and Baghdad. In the first instance, Obama had won the election on a platform that explicitly promised withdrawal from Iraq, and polling consistently showed that Americans were tired of US efforts in Iraq, a sentiment that did not shift as time wore on. The proponents of a residual force also showed little understanding of Iraqi politics, the fact that US withdrawal was overwhelmingly popular with all Iraqi political parties, and that there was no constituency or desire for a continued US troop presence.

Finally, the argument that the sustained presence of large numbers of US troops would give the United States some leverage over the Iraqi government ignored Iraqi politics in a different way: despite the presence of over 100,000 troops in Iraq, the Maliki government had continually frustrated various generals and ambassadors. The mere presence of large numbers of US soldiers would not affect the calculus of Iraqi leaders in terms of acquiescing to US wishes. Critics overestimated US influence and power and underestimated Iraqi agency.

Writing in 2010, Toby Dodge noted these factors and the extent of the problems facing Iraq and asked, "If the US presence has failed to create a stable, sustainable post-war settlement in Iraq by now, why would the continued presence of 50,000 troops after 2011 make a difference?"[27] For Dodge, it was time for US troops to go home, but he cautioned the Obama administration not to underplay the vast scale of the challenges bequeathed to them by the Bush administration and not to claim victory in Iraq. He cited with some alarm Vice-President Joe Biden's ebullient declaration:

> I am very optimistic about Iraq ... this could be one of the great achievements of this administration. You're going to see 90,000 American troops come marching home by the end of the summer. You're going to see a stable government in Iraq that is actually moving toward a representative government.[28]

Even if the withdrawal of troops from Iraq was both inevitable and the correct decision, such confidence was not rooted in a consideration of the situation on the ground in Iraq, and it took little heed of what the United States would leave behind. Instead, the troops would come home, and the fact of their return would be victory enough.

A Temporal Withdrawal

Just as Obama spoke of a "new dawn," for the United States, violence in Iraq accelerated. Given the domestic imperative of reconstruction at home, reconstruction in Iraq was not a priority. There would be no major equivalent of the Marshall Plan, no investigations into US culpability for starting the war in 2003, no truth commissions or indictments.[29]

The 2007 surge in Iraq had lowered the levels of violence temporarily and crucially had lowered the levels of US casualties that provided Obama with an opportunity to leave without accusations of betraying the fallen. In any case, the 2008 SoFA mandated a US withdrawal, and given the inability to negotiate on the status of US forces and their potential legal liabilities Obama was keen to leave. Had the war continued at the violent presurge levels of 2006, leaving Iraq "would have appeared reckless, if not callous" according to Toby Dodge. Obama observed, "We must be as careful getting out of Iraq as we were careless getting in."[30] A Vietnam-style chaotic withdrawal had to be avoided for strategic and symbolic reasons; the ordered withdrawal had to make it appear as though they were not leaving as the vanquished yet again. Mohamed al-Dayni, a Sunni opponent of SoFA, thought that the formal agreement with the United States conveyed a legitimacy to the United States, which it had lacked throughout the war; he argued that the Iraqi government should not provide such legitimacy.[31]

There was little thought of what the United States was leaving behind. Of course, the discourse on *jus post bellum,* on justice after the war, was not a central factor. With some Iranian pressure, Maliki wanted the United States out. Local conditions were far from settled, and under Maliki the Shia-dominated government increasingly resorted to repressive violence and authoritarianism. Obama focused on rebuilding the United States.[32] The responsibilities *to* and *for* Iraq figured little in US discussion. But the region had been destabilized and there was little reflection on the situation in Afghanistan after the United States withdrew support for the Mujahedin after the Soviet withdrawal. The Taliban emerged as a political force soon after. Still, Obama had indicated in 2008 that when he came to office, he would "give the military a new mission: ending this war." Yet at that stage he argued it would not be precipitous and it would contribute to the wider US strategic goals.[33] A restrained realism was a necessary antidote to the Bush administration's fiasco.[34]

The strategic imperative was vital. Iraq could no longer be seen in isolation from other US priorities. Afghanistan, Pakistan, and the domestic economy needed essential attention, Obama told US troops at Camp Lejeune in February 2009.[35] They had fought intensely, and even after years of combat they could not be responsible for complete security in Iraq.³⁶ They had provided Iraq with an opportunity, they had ousted Saddam, the rate of violence was reducing, and elections had been held: "That is an extraordinary achievement." In this narrative, the country had some stability and Iraq would not be a haven for terrorists, "We can start bringing our folks home."³⁷ The US departure would be augmented by diplomatic engagement to stimulate a "more peaceful and prosperous Iraq" and a "comprehensive American engagement across the region."³⁸

On 31 August 2010 Obama marked the end of Operation Iraqi Freedom. The combat mission would end, but not the commitment. He observed, "Through this remarkable chapter in the history of the United States and Iraq, we have met our responsibility. Now, it's time to turn the page."³⁹ On the next page, the Iraqis would have to continue the script.⁴⁰ Obama did recognize that Iraq was "traveling through rough waters," but still "beyond the pre-dawn darkness, better days lie ahead."⁴¹ As Lloyd Gardner paraphrased John McCain, this was "defeat disguised as a timetable."⁴²

The key issue, though, was not so much military withdrawal, despite the focus on troop numbers in the Washington debate, as the extent to which the Obama administration was also conducting a diplomatic withdrawal in Baghdad. Despite speeches from Obama and Biden about continued US engagement in Iraq, events demonstrated that the Americans were no longer paying close attention to Iraqi politics and that the Obama administration didn't have a coherent vision for a postoccupation Iraq.⁴³ According to the *New York Times*, Biden argued that Maliki needed the United States to stick around to help prop up his government and that he would bet his vice-presidency that Iraq would extend the SoFA.⁴⁴ Concerns about human rights and democracy were overridden by a primary focus on building a security relationship with Iraq, renegotiating the SoFA, and enabling counterterrorist operations.

The consequences of this concern with building a relationship with Maliki became evident with the US reaction to the results of the 2010 parliamentary elections. The pro-Western al-Iraqiya coalition led by Ayad Allawi, a long-time critic of Iran, won the greatest share of the votes. According to one former US diplomat, "These were election results we could only have dreamed of. . . .The surge had worked. The war was winding down. And, for the first time in the history of the Arab world, a secular, Western-leaning alliance won a free and fair election."⁴⁵

Despite this result, Maliki refused to concede power, and in negotiations brokered by Iran, the Shiite movement led by Moqtada al-Sadr agreed to support him. Biden also favored Maliki, pushing for a power-sharing agreement that would give Allawi's party a role in the government but would keep Maliki as prime minister.[46] Despite the illusion of consensus provided by the announcement of a power-sharing government in December 2010, Maliki became acting minister of defense, interior, and national security in the new government, further consolidating his power. Allawi complained to US journalists that the outcome of the government-formation negotiations was due to the interference of Iran and the indifference of the Americans: "I needed American support ... they wanted to leave, and they handed the country to the Iranians. Iraq is a failed state now, an Iranian colony."[47]

Despite US assumptions that the SoFA would be renegotiated, no new agreement on a stay-behind force transpired, and the United States left behind an increasingly authoritarian Maliki regime and an increasingly rancorous Iraqi polity.[48] According to Vali Nasr, the timing of this disengagement was particularly poor:

> [Iraq's] fragile power-sharing arrangement ... required close American management. But the Obama administration had no time or energy for that. Instead it anxiously eyed the exits, with its one thought to get out. It stopped protecting the political process just when talk of American withdrawal turned the heat back up under the long-simmering power struggle that pitted the Shias, Sunnis, and Kurds against one another.[49]

While US diplomats remained in Baghdad and attempted to continue influencing Iraqi politics, the extent to which the United States was outmaneuvered by Iran in the aftermath of the 2010 elections spoke to the waning US leverage in Baghdad and its broader loss of regional dominance. After the US withdrawal, Iraq had turned from "bully to target," in the words of Toby Dodge.[50] Iran, Hezbollah, and Syria were the immediate beneficiaries. Ironically, not destabilizing the balance of power in the region had been an important concern for the Bush Sr. administration during the Gulf War, and the outcomes of the Iraq war had contributed to that condition.

True, Obama had inherited a very bad hand from his predecessor: two wars that were both expensive and inconclusive and a population that was tired of them, compounded by a deep recession that took hold just before his presidency.[51] In 2014 Julianne Smith, deputy national security advisor to Vice-President Biden, pointed out, "He genuinely believes that he was elected to get America off its war footing, that his legacy is to get the United States away from its over-reliance on the military instrument."[52] Despite the restrictions associated with SoFA, the withdrawal turned out to be driven more by political necessity than regional strategic calculus, even though it might have made sense for the long game, the long-term US strategic interests vis-à-vis the foundations of its powers.

The Return to Iraq

In 2014 the violence in Iraq continued, and as ISIS drew closer to Baghdad questions again emerged on the wisdom of withdrawal and on the prospects of return. Obama feared being dragged back into Iraq. Robert Gates, defense secretary from 2006 to 2011, reflected in his memoirs that domestic issues had been too prevalent in Obama's national security problems.[53] It is ironic that the 2010 National Security Strategy contained a section on "the Strategic Environment" subtitled "The World as It Is." It recognized that the "dangers of violent extremism" were connected to the "simmering conflicts" after the Cold War. Yet Obama had not recognized Iraq as it was—far from stable, filled with the extremism fueled by years of war and sectarian violence. Obama observed:

> Currently, the United States is focused on implementing a responsible transition as we end the war in Iraq, succeeding in Afghanistan, and defeating al-Qa'ida and its terrorist affiliates, while moving our economy from catastrophic recession to lasting recovery. As we confront these crises, our national strategy must take a longer view. We must build a stronger foundation for American leadership and work to better shape the outcomes that are most fundamental to our people in the twenty-first century.[54]

As Fallujah and Ramadi fell in early 2014, questions about the efficacy of Obama's withdrawal returned. In his memoirs, Robert Gates echoed Gerald Ford's line on Vietnam that as far as the United States was concerned the war was over. Gates writes, "For Americans, the war in Iraq was finally over."[55] In Iraq, the violence moved to new extremes after 2014. Gates had initially favored leaving a US presence in the country to ensure, as far as possible, an element of stability, to assist and train Iraqi forces and ultimately to send a clear signal, to US allies but also to Iran, that "we weren't abandoning the field." But the Iraqis wanted the United States out. Gates concluded, "It was a regrettable turn of events for our future influence in Iraq and our strategic position in the region. And a win for Iran."[56]

Despite Bush era intentions for a transformative foreign policy for the region,[57] the unintended consequence was to destabilize and weaken regimes and stability in the region, with the failures of the Arab Spring and the advance of ISIS that would ultimately compel a return and engagement beyond 2017. As those forces advanced across northern and western Iraq, the *New York Times* reported on the "unexpected crisis on the battlefield it thought it had left behind," which "has left a stunned White House groping for a response."[58]

This crisis stemmed directly from the authoritarianism that the United States had acquiesced to in their support of Maliki. As Toby Dodge documented, Maliki had centralized more and more power for himself, making use of "provisional command centers" to bypass ministerial control of security forces and to install commanders loyal to him while also stepping up arrests of political opponents, notably Sunnis from the western provinces who had been at the heart of the anti-American insurgency.[59] It was this latter move that precipitated Iraq's slide back toward large-scale violence. The Sons of Iraq initiative that co-opted Sunni tribes in Anbar into the fight against al-Qaeda had been one of the proudest achievements of the US military, but Maliki showed little interest in integrating them into the Iraqi armed forces or in pursuing national reconciliation. In April 2013, Maliki's security forces reacted to the killing of an Iraqi soldier near a protest in Huwija in Kirkuk province by encircling the site and then sending in SWAT (Special Weapons and Tactics) forces, who shot down forty-four protestors. Maliki's Christmas 2013 speech on Iraqi TV tried to tie Sunni protests to al-Qaeda, and he followed this by bulldozing an encampment of protestors in Ramadi.[60]

Soon after this, mass violence erupted in Anbar and across Iraq, with over one thousand Iraqis killed in car bomb attacks in Baghdad in January 2014. The cities of Fallujah and Ramadi, so central to US counterinsurgency efforts earlier in the war, fell to the newly resurgent Islamist insurgency led by ISIS. Maliki's response was to surround both cities and shell them. Sunni police in the cities abandoned their posts, and forty-four Sunni members of parliament resigned.[61] In the space of weeks, violence had returned to levels not seen since the height of the civil war in 2005/2006, even as the Obama administration continued to express confidence that al-Qaeda was on the wane globally.

Infamously, this was the moment that Obama referred to ISIS as al-Qaeda's JV (junior varsity) team in an interview with the *New Yorker*, but it was his specific remarks about the fall of Fallujah in the same interview that were the clearest articulation of the extent to which his administration had disengaged from Iraq:

> But let's just keep in mind, Fallujah is a profoundly conservative Sunni city in a country that, independent of anything we do, is deeply divided along sectarian lines. And how we think about terrorism has to be defined and specific enough that it doesn't lead us to think that any horrible actions that take place around the world that are motivated in part by an extremist Islamic ideology is a direct threat to us or something that we have to wade into.[62]

Critics of the conduct of US diplomacy after the withdrawal of US troops noted that while the political situation in Iraq had worsened, the embassy had undertaken a campaign to landscape the grounds and to add a bar and a soccer field to the existing suite of amenities, which included an Olympic-sized indoor swimming pool, a basketball court, tennis courts, and a softball field.[63] One of those critics, Emma Sky, who had been a political advisor to both generals Odierno and Petraeus, blamed the outcome on a simplistic US preference for strong leaders. Sky asked:

> Did we just get it wrong with Maliki and Karzai—were we that unlucky? ... No. Maliki wasn't like that in the beginning. The whole point of these places—of Iraq especially—is that the leaders need to do political deals. We make them so strong that they no longer need to do political deals. So we undermine any chance at stability. It's destroying Iraq. We're strengthening the guy who is creating the problem.[64]

The fruits of this approach, the dangers of which were apparent to critics as early as 2010, were apparent in June 2014, when the 2nd Division of the Iraqi army, charged with defending Iraq's second largest city, Mosul, melted away in the face of a much smaller ISIS force over the course of a few chaotic days of fighting. Analysts noted that while this collapse was shocking, it was the product of a deep-seated malaise within Iraqi Security Forces. High-ranking officers had been embezzling unit food budgets and the salaries of absent soldiers, leaving soldiers to fend for themselves on the black market. Maliki's politicization of the Iraqi military had had detrimental effects on combat effectiveness. One former senior US officer argued that the negative effects of purging Sunnis from the officer corps had long been apparent, noting, "Even as I was leaving [in 2008], those Sunni leaders were being replaced by people that didn't know Mosul; commanders that didn't know Tal Afar."[65]

In the face of ISIS attacks, Iraqi generals fled the battlefield, which caused a wholesale panic and the complete collapse of the 2nd Division. In short order, ISIS captured Mosul, Tal Afar, Tikrit, and Baji, with its major oil refinery, and they were within one hour's drive of Baghdad. ISIS executed at least 1,500 Air Force cadets at Camp Speicher in Tikrit and seized large amounts of military equipment.[66] The sight of ISIS driving American-supplied tanks and Humvees made plain the extent to which the US exit strategy of training Iraqi Security Forces, which had been a centerpiece of US efforts in the country for at least a decade, had been a failure.

In response to this crisis, there was a large-scale mobilization of Shiite militias to defend Baghdad and a Kurdish declaration that they would hold a referendum on independence. By August 2014, the US military had returned to Iraq, launching air strikes to prevent further massacres of the Yazidi minority surrounded by ISIS on Mount Sinjar. Obama was now paying attention. In a June 2014 press conference, he noted:

> It's not the place for the United States to choose Iraq's leaders. It is clear, though, that only leaders that can govern with an inclusive agenda are going to be able to truly bring the Iraqi people together and help them through this crisis. … There's no military solution inside of Iraq, certainly not one that is led by the United States. But there is an urgent need for an inclusive political process.[67]

In the face of immense pressure both from within Iraq and around the world, Maliki stepped aside as prime minister in favor of Haider al-Abadi, who moved to increase Sunni participation in the Iraqi government and began the long process of stabilizing the Iraqi Security Forces and planning to take back the territory lost to ISIS. The United States sent back combat advisors, special forces, and air support and began building a multinational coalition to fight ISIS.

For the remainder of Obama's tenure, his administration largely did the things that they had failed to do prior to 2014. Slowly, the Iraqi government recovered its capacity, and Iraqi Security Forces grew in confidence and competence until, in December 2017, al-Abadi could announce the total defeat of ISIS in Iraq. The cost of retaking lost ground was immense: the lengthy battle for Mosul, which stretched from October 2016 to July 2017, displaced over one million people, destroyed the city and, reportedly, cost Iraq's elite Special Forces units 40 percent of their strength.[68]

The campaign against ISIS had involved fighting that went far beyond the intensity of anything previously seen in Iraq and had involved fighting not just by the Iraqi army and an international coalition but also by Shiite militia groups and Kurdish peshmerga. Even on the approach to Mosul, the delicate politics of balancing ethnic groups was at play, with Kurdish and Shiite forces bidding for more prominent roles in the battle.[69] If ISIS had provided a spur for national unity in Iraq, then the underlying issues remained far from resolved, as was apparent in the overwhelming Kurdish vote for independence in September 2017 and the reluctance of Shiite groups to consider disarming in the aftermath of al-Abadi's declaration that ISIS had been defeated.

Now the Trump administration would have to face the same question: how to disengage from Iraq without further destabilizing the region. During his campaign, Trump had made similar promises to Obama about turning the page on an era of US intervention, albeit in much cruder terms. The actions of Trump once in office though, indicated no such desire for a retrenchment. The administration largely followed Obama's policy on ISIS, but with much less regard for civilian casualties. There was no indication that US troops would withdraw from the region any time soon. Indeed, any discussion of US strategy was again predicated on troop numbers and counterterrorism, with little hope for a more comprehensive investment in diplomacy. Indeed, the opposite was the case, with the State Department gutted under Rex Tillerson and regional policy seemingly invented on the fly.

Andrew Bacevich's hope for a reckoning with the lessons of Iraq seemed further away than ever. Yet, amid all of the justifiable criticism of Trump's lack of coherence on Iraq and so many other matters, it should not be forgotten that the US disengagement from Iraq was a bipartisan failure. Obama had been given a very poor hand by Bush, but—with its focus on a broader strategic rebalancing—his administration had failed to heed its own rhetoric on the centrality of diplomacy and development. By not engaging with what the United States had left behind in Iraq and by focusing solely on US exit narratives, the Obama administration ensured that the United States would return to Iraq and that the war would fail to end.

David Fitzgerald is lecturer in international politics in the School of History, University College Cork, Ireland. He has written numerous articles and books on military and foreign policy, especially counterinsurgency warfare and "small wars." His first book, *Learning to Forget: US Army Counterinsurgency Doctrine from Vietnam to Iraq* (Stanford, 2013) was a runner up in the Society for Military History's Edward M. Coffman first manuscript prize. His current research focuses on consequences of the All-Volunteer Force for US society and the rise of a 'warrior ethos' within the post-Vietnam US military. Together with David Ryan he is the author of *Obama, US Foreign Policy and the Dilemmas of Intervention* (Palgrave Macmillan, 2014).

David Ryan is professor of modern history at University College Cork, Ireland. He has published extensively on contemporary history and US foreign policy concentrating on interventions in the post-Vietnam era. His books include *Obama, US Foreign Policy and the Dilemmas of Intervention*, coauthored with David Fitzgerald (Palgrave, 2014); *US Foreign Policy and the Other,* edited with Michael Cullinane (Berghahn, 2015); *Frustrated Empire: US Foreign Policy from 9/11 to Iraq* (Pluto and University of Michigan, 2007); *Vietnam in Iraq: Tactics, Lessons, Legacies and Ghosts,* coedited with John Dumbrell (Routledge, 2007); *The United States and Europe in the Twentieth Century* (Longman, 2003); *US Foreign Policy in World History* (Routledge, 2000); and *US-Sandinista Diplomatic Relations: Voice of Intolerance* (MacMillan, 1995). He is also the author of numerous articles.

Notes

1. "Army Identifies Remains of Last Missing Soldier in Iraq," Stars and Stripes, accessed 18 December 2017, https://www.stripes.com/news/army-identifies-remains-of-last-missing-soldier-in-iraq-1.169973; "Remains of Last Missing US Soldier Return from Iraq," NPR.org, accessed 18 December 2017, https://www.npr.org/2012/02/27/147523337/remains-of-last-missing-us-soldier-return-from-iraq; Michael M. Phillips, "Last Missing Soldier in Iraq: Family Finally Learns Fate," *Wall Street Journal* (New York), 27 February 2012, https://www.wsj.com/articles/SB10001424052970204653604577247372298544072.
2. Bill Roggio, "US Officials 'Strongly Suspect' Iranian-Backed Militia of Kidnapping 3 Americans in Baghdad," *The Long War Journal*, 22 January 2016, https://www.longwarjournal.org/archives/2016/01/us-offiicals-strongly-suspect-iranian-backed-militia-of-kidnapping-3-americans-in-baghdad.php, accessed 15 December 2018.
3. Barack Obama, Inaugural Address, 20 January 2009, Washington, DC.
4. Derek Chollet, *The Long Game: How Obama Defied Washington and Redefined America's Role in the World* (New York: Public Affairs, 2016), x.
5. Ibid., xii.
6. Ibid., xix.
7. Gates, *Duty*, 472. Joseph E. Stiglitz and Linda J. Bilmes, "The True Cost of the Iraq War: $3 Trillion and Beyond," *Washington Post*, 5 September 2010. See also David Fitzgerald and David Ryan, *Obama, US Foreign Policy and the Dilemmas of Intervention* (London: Palgrave, 2014), 25–51.
8. Peter L. Hahn, *Mission Accomplished? The United States and Iraq since World War I* (New York: Oxford University Press, 2012), 197.
9. Gates, *Duty*, 473.
10. "Iraq Body Count," accessed 18 December 2017, https://www.iraqbodycount.org/database/.
11. Amy Hagopian et al., "Mortality in Iraq Associated with the 2003–2011 War and Occupation: Findings from a National Cluster Survey by the University Collaborative Iraq Mortality Study," *PLOS Medicine* (15 October 2013); BBC News, "Iraq Study Estimates War-Related Deaths at 461 000," 16 October 2013.
12. Gilbert Burnham et al., "Mortality after the 2003 Invasion of Iraq: A Cross-Sectional Cluster Sample Survey," *The Lancet* 368, no. 9545 (2006): 1421–28, https://doi.org/10.1016/S0140-6736(06)69491-9.
13. Neta Crawford, "Civilian Death and Injury in the Iraq War, 2003–2013," *Costs of War* (Providence, RI: Brown University, 2013), 9, http://watson.brown.edu/costsofwar/files/cow/imce/papers/2013/Civilian%20Death%20and%20Injury%20in%20the%20Iraq%20War%2C%202003-2013.pdf, accessed 15 December 2018.
14. United Nations High Commissioner for Refugees, "Statistics on Displaced Iraqis around the World," April 2007, http://www.unhcr.org/461f7cb92.pdf, accessed 15 December 2018.
15. Office of the Special Inspector General for Iraq Reconstruction, *Hard Lessons: The Iraq Reconstruction Experience* (Washington, DC: Government Printing Office, 2009), 145.
16. Ibid.
17. Richard Garfield, Sarah Zaidi, and Jean Lennock, "Medical Care in Iraq after Six Years of Sanctions," *BMJ* 315, no. 7120 (1997): 1474–75, https://doi.org/10.1136/bmj.315.7120.1474.
18. "United Nations/World Bank Joint Iraq Needs Assessment: Electricity" (UNDP/World Bank, October 2003), 1, http://siteresources.worldbank.org/INTIRAQ/Overview/20147658/ELECTRICITY%20final%20sector%20report%2016%20October.pdf, accessed 15 December 2018.

19. Sarah Zaidi, "Child Mortality in Iraq," *The Lancet* 350, no. 9084 (1997): 1105, https://doi.org/10.1016/S0140-6736(05)70470-0; Barbara Crossette, "Children's Death Rates Rising In Iraqi Lands, UNICEF Reports," *New York Times*, 13 August 1999, https://www.nytimes.com/1999/08/13/world/children-s-death-rates-rising-in-iraqi-lands-unicef-reports.html, accessed 15 December 2018.; Tim Dyson and Valeria Cetorelli, "Changing Views on Child Mortality and Economic Sanctions in Iraq: A History of Lies, Damned Lies and Statistics," *BMJ Global Health* 2, no. 2 (2017): e000311, https://doi.org/10.1136/bmjgh-2017-000311.
20. David Ryan, "Libertas or Fri? On US Liberty, Decline, Freedom and Pluralism," in *Challenging US Foreign Policy: America and the World in the Long Twentieth Century*, eds. Scott Lucas and Bevan Sewell (London: Palgrave, 2011),183–204.
21. Chollet, *Long Game*; David Milne, *Worldmaking: The Art and Science of American Diplomacy* (New York: Farrar, Straus and Giroux, 2015); Barry R. Posen, *Restraint: A New Foundation for U.S. Grand Strategy* (Ithaca: Cornell University Press, 2014).
22. Andrew J. Bacevich, "Ending Endless War: A Pragmatic Military Strategy," *Foreign Affairs* 95, no. 5 (2016), 41.
23. Chollet, *Long Game*, 144.
24. John Barry, "'The Endgame' Is a Well-Researched, Highly Critical Look at U.S. Policy in Iraq," *The Daily Beast*, 27 September 2013; Thomas E. Ricks, *The Gamble: General David Petraeus and the American Military Adventure in Iraq, 2006–2008* (New York: Penguin, 2009).
25. Milne, *Worldmaking*, 455–56.
26. Peter Baker, "With Pledges to Troops and Iraqis, Obama Details Pullout," *New York Times*, 27 February 2009, https://www.nytimes.com/2009/02/28/washington/28troops.html; "The Anti-Surge," *Foreign Policy*, accessed 18 December 2017, https://foreignpolicy.com/2013/10/30/the-anti-surge/; Tom Engelhardt, "Why We Won't Leave Afghanistan or Iraq," *Common Dreams*, accessed 18 December 2017, https://www.commondreams.org/views/2010/04/25/why-we-wont-leave-afghanistan-or-iraq.
27. Toby Dodge, "The US and Iraq: Time to Go Home," *Survival* 52, no. 2 (2010): 137, https://doi.org/10.1080/00396331003764660.
28. Dodge, 130.
29. Rachel Baig, "Amnesty: Serious Rights Abuses Continue in Iraq," DW, Germany, 11 March 2013, http://www.dw.de/amnesty-serious-rights-abuses-continue-in-iraq/a-16664671, accessed 15 December 2018.
30. Toby Dodge, "Iraq and the Next American President," *Survival* 50, no. 5 (2008): 38; Barack Obama, "My Plan for Iraq," *New York Times*, 14 July 2008.
31. Jonathan Steele, "This Is No Sop. It Is a Vote to End the Occupation of Iraq," *The Guardian* (London), 27 November 2008; Alissa J. Rubin and Campbell Robertson, "Iraq Backs Deal That Sets End of U.S. Role," *New York Times*, 28 November 2008.
32. Kathy Kiely, "Obama: 'To Rebuild America's Economy, Rebuild America,'" *USA Today*, 18 June 2010.
33. Obama, "My Plan for Iraq."
34. Thomas E. Ricks, *Fiasco: The American Military Adventure in Iraq* (London: Allen Lane, 2006).
35. Barack Obama, "Responsibly Ending the War in Iraq," Camp Lejeune, North Carolina, White House Press Office, 27 February 2009.
36. Seamus Milne, "To Free Iraq, Resistance Must Bridge the Sectarian Divide," *The Guardian* (London), 19 March 2009.
37. Barack Obama, "Remarks by the President to the Troops," Al Faw Palace, Baghdad, 7 April 2009, the White House Press Secretary.
38. Obama, Responsibly Ending the War in Iraq.

39. Barack Obama, "On the End of Combat Operations," Oval Office, White House, 31 August 2010.
40. Ibid.
41. Ibid.
42. John McCain paraphrased by Lloyd Gardner, *Killing Machine: The American Presidency in the Age of Drone Warfare* (New York: New Press, 2013), 18.
43. Emma Sky, *The Unravelling: High Hopes and Missed Opportunities in Iraq* (New York: Public Affairs, 2015).
44. Michael R. Gordon, "In U.S. Exit from Iraq, Failed Efforts and Challenges," *New York Times*, 22 September 2012, https://www.nytimes.com/2012/09/23/world/middleeast/failed-efforts-of-americas-last-months-in-iraq.html, accessed 15 December 2018.
45. Dexter Filkins, "What We Left Behind," *The New Yorker*, 21 April 2014, https://www.newyorker.com/magazine/2014/04/28/what-we-left-behind, accessed 15 December 2018.
46. Peter Beinart, "Obama's Disastrous Iraq Policy: An Autopsy," *The Atlantic*, 23 June 2014, https://www.theatlantic.com/international/archive/2014/06/obamas-disastrous-iraq-policy-an-autopsy/373225/, accessed 15 December 2018.
47. Filkins, "What We Left Behind."
48. Ned Parker, "The Iraq We Left Behind," *Foreign Affairs*, 1 March 2012, https://www.foreignaffairs.com/articles/iraq/2012-02-12/iraq-we-left-behind, accessed 15 December 2018.
49. Seyyed Vali Reza Nasr, *The Dispensable Nation: American Foreign Policy in Retreat* (New York: Doubleday, 2013), 146.
50. Dodge, *Iraq*, 181–95.
51. Fred Kaplan, "Obama's Way: The President in Practice," *Foreign Affairs* 95, no. 1 (2016), 46–47.
52. Kathleen Hennessey and Christi Parsons, "Obama's Mideast Airstrike Refrain: 'And Then What,'" *Los Angeles Times*, 19 June 2014.
53. Robert M. Gates, *Duty: Memoirs of a Secretary at War* (London: W.H. Allen, 2014), 584.
54. Barack Obama, "National Security Strategy," The White House, Washington, DC, May 2010; Toby Dodge, *Iraq: From War to a New Authoritarianism* (London: International Institute for Strategic Studies, 2012).
55. Gates, *Duty*, 472.
56. Ibid., 552–55.
57. David Ryan, *Frustrated Empire: US Foreign Policy, 9/11 to Iraq* (London: Pluto, 2007).
58. Mark Landler and Eric Schmitt, "U.S. Scrambles to Help Iraq Fight Off Militants as Baghdad Is Threatened," *New York Times*, 12 June 2014.
59. Toby Dodge, *Iraq—From War to a New Authoritarianism* (Abingdon: Routledge, 2012), 128–29.
60. Kirk H. Sowell, "Maliki's Anbar Blunder," *Foreign Policy*, accessed 18 December 2017, https://foreignpolicy.com/2014/01/15/malikis-anbar-blunder/.
61. Ibid.
62. Jeffrey Goldberg, "The Obama Doctrine," *The Atlantic*, April 2016, http://www.theatlantic.com/magazine/archive/2016/04/the-obama-doctrine/471525/, accessed 15 December 2018.
63. Ali Khedery, "Why We Stuck with Maliki—and Lost Iraq," *Washington Post*, 3 July 2014, https://www.washingtonpost.com/opinions/why-we-stuck-with-maliki—and-lost-iraq/2014/07/03/0dd6a8a4-f7ec-11e3-a606-946fd632f9f1_story.html, accessed 15 December 2018.
64. Filkins, "What We Left Behind."

65. Yasir Abbas and Trombly, "Inside the Collapse of the Iraqi Army's 2nd Division," *War on the Rocks*, 1 July 2014, https://warontherocks.com/2014/07/inside-the-collapse-of-the-iraqi-armys-2nd-division/, accessed 15 December 2018.
66. Rod Nordland and Alissa J. Rubin, "Massacre Claim Shakes Iraq," *New York Times*, 15 June 2014, https://www.nytimes.com/2014/06/16/world/middleeast/iraq.html, accessed 15 December 2018.
67. "Transcript: President Obama's Remarks on Iraq," CNN, accessed 18 December 2017, http://www.cnn.com/2014/06/19/politics/obama-iraq-transcript/index.html, accessed 15 December 2018.
68. Tamer El-Ghobashy, "Iraq's Elite Special Forces Struggle to Regroup after Bloody Fight for Mosul," *Washington Post*, 21 July 2017, https://www.washingtonpost.com/news/worldviews/wp/2017/07/21/iraqs-elite-special-forces-struggle-to-regroup-after-bloody-fight-for-mosul/, accessed 15 December 2018.
69. Luke Mogelson, "The Desperate Battle to Destroy ISIS," *The New Yorker*, 30 January 2017, https://www.newyorker.com/magazine/2017/02/06/the-desperate-battle-to-destroy-isis, accessed 15 December 2018.

Select Bibliography

Bacevich, Andrew J., "Ending Endless War: A Pragmatic Military Strategy," *Foreign Affairs* 95, no. 5 (2016).

Burnham, Gilbert et al., "Mortality after the 2003 Invasion of Iraq: A Cross-Sectional Cluster Sample Survey," *The Lancet* 368, no. 9545 (2006).

Chollet, Derek, *The Long Game: How Obama Defied Washington and Redefined America's Role in the World* (New York: Public Affairs, 2016).

Dodge, Toby, *Iraq: From War to a New Authoritarianism* (London: International Institute for Strategic Studies, 2012).

Dyson, Tim and Valeria Cetorelli, "Changing Views on Child Mortality and Economic Sanctions in Iraq: A History of Lies, Damned Lies and Statistics," *BMJ Global Health* 2, no. 2 (2017).

Fitzgerald, David and David Ryan, *Obama, US Foreign Policy and the Dilemmas of Intervention* (London: Palgrave, 2014).

Gardner, Lloyd, *Killing Machine: The American Presidency in the Age of Drone Warfare* (New York: New Press, 2013).

Garfield, Richard, Sarah Zaidi, and Jean Lennock, "Medical Care in Iraq after Six Years of Sanctions," *BMJ* 315, no. 7120 (1997).

Gates, Robert M., *Duty: Memoirs of a Secretary at War* (London: W. H. Allen, 2014).

Hagopian, Amy et al., "Mortality in Iraq Associated with the 2003–2011 War and Occupation: Findings from a National Cluster Survey by the University Collaborative Iraq Mortality Study," *PLOS Medicine* (15 October 2013).

Hahn, Peter L., *Mission Accomplished? The United States and Iraq since World War I* (New York: Oxford University Press, 2012).

Milne, David, *Worldmaking: The Art and Science of American Diplomacy* (New York: Farrar, Straus and Giroux, 2015).

Nasr, Vali, *The Dispensable Nation: American Foreign Policy in Retreat* (New York: Doubleday, 2013).

Office of the Special Inspector General for Iraq Reconstruction, *Hard Lessons: The Iraq Reconstruction Experience* (Washington, DC: Government Printing Office, 2009).

Posen, Barry R., *Restraint: A New Foundation for US Grand Strategy* (Ithaca, NY: Cornell University Press, 2014).

Ricks, Thomas E., *Fiasco: The American Military Adventure in Iraq* (New York: Penguin, 2006).

———, *The Gamble: General David Petraeus and the American Military Adventure in Iraq, 2006–2008* (New York: Penguin, 2009).

Ryan, David, *Frustrated Empire: US Foreign Policy, 9/11 to Iraq* (London: Pluto, 2007).

———, "Libertas or Fri? On US Liberty, Decline, Freedom and Pluralism," in *Challenging US Foreign Policy: America and the World in the Long Twentieth Century*, edited by Scott Lucas and Bevan Sewell (London: Palgrave, 2011).

Sky, Emma, *The Unravelling: High Hopes and Missed Opportunities in Iraq* (New York: Public Affairs, 2015).

Zaidi, Sarah, "Child Mortality in Iraq," *The Lancet* 350, no. 9084 (1997).

Chapter 7

A "Responsible End" to the Afghan War
The Politics and Pitfalls of Crafting "Success" Narratives

Jeffrey H. Michaels

On 23 January 1973, Richard M. Nixon announced "peace with honor" in Vietnam, ostensibly fulfilling a campaign pledge he made while running for president years earlier. Two months later, the remaining US combat forces withdrew from Vietnam, leaving a relatively small US embassy presence behind. Two years after that, the US embassy had to be evacuated amid the complete collapse of South Vietnam. A number of questions arise from this sequence of events. Did the Nixon administration believe its own rhetoric about "peace with honor"? Was "peace with honor" merely a short-term cover to allow a "decent interval" to elapse between the US withdrawal and the "inevitable" collapse of South Vietnam? And even if it was merely a cover, could the United States have left without making such a claim? Put another way, did US policymakers feel that for domestic political reasons, and possibly for international prestige purposes, the United States had to be seen as leaving Vietnam on a high note, regardless of the reality of the conflict? Most crucially, did these policymakers foresee any consequences *if*, or more likely *when*, this success narrative would inevitably collapse, or did they merely hope it could be inevitably postponed?[1]

Answers to these questions are highly debatable on both conceptual and empirical grounds, and it is not the intention here to enter any further into the Vietnam "quagmire." The purpose of asking them at all is to provide a starting point for trying to understand how the Obama administration sought to bring the war in Afghanistan to a responsible end, similarly characterized by the withdrawal of US combat forces and the retention of a relatively small residual presence—or at least to portray itself as achieving this end. Until October 2015, it had been Obama's intention to end the war before he left office in January 2017. However, for reasons that remain contested, that month Obama announced his decision to retain 5,500 US combat troops in Afghanistan through the end of his presidency, leaving it to his successor to determine whether or not to withdraw them, maintain the status quo, or re-escalate US involvement.

This chapter will explore why Obama's reasons for keeping US combat troops in Afghanistan remain contested. Several motives were attributed to his October announcement, which on the surface, appear plausible. The collapse of Afghan government control over the northern city of Kunduz at the end of September had brought the conflict back into the media spotlight, having continually receded into the background over the previous several years. A somewhat larger al-Qaeda presence in that country than previously estimated had also been discovered around the same time. Moreover, the near collapse of the Iraqi government in 2014 at the hands of ISIS raised the prospect that a similarly embarrassing development could occur in Afghanistan if the United States withdrew its combat forces prematurely.

The problem with these and similar explanations that highlight the Obama administration's response as reflecting the reality of the conflict is that they fail to discuss the connection the reality of the conflict actually had—or didn't have—for US policy in the years leading up to the October announcement. Furthermore, to what degree was the decision to keep 5,500 troops in Afghanistan through the end of 2016 based on a realistic approach to the conflict given that less than a year later Obama changed this to 8,400 troops into 2017? To examine these issues, this chapter will cover three main themes. First, it will provide an overview of the key decisions to increase the number of US troops in Afghanistan, then reduce them to an embassy presence, and finally to retain thousands of combat troops there indefinitely. Second, it will set Obama's decisions and rhetoric against the backdrop of the reality of the conflict, as perceived through the lens of relevant bureaucratic actors. Finally, it will review the Obama administration's rhetoric about bringing the conflict to a responsible end.

Getting down to Zero

The numerous debates and decisions about troop numbers, and the important place these numbers have held in the discourse of US policymakers when discussing Afghanistan, suggest that they merit some investigation when attempting to assess the Obama administration's efforts to exit from that country. In many respects, this issue was central to the policy debate, much more so than many other issues that might have received more attention.

Throughout the course of the post-9/11 conflict, troop numbers proved to be highly contentious, but given the relative importance of the Iraq War prior to Obama taking office, this issue had received less public attention than in later years, apart from some critics of the Iraq war who argued that this was a distraction from the Afghan war. Beginning with then-senator Obama complaining that the Bush administration had not dedicated enough troops to Afghanistan and continuing through the first year of the Obama administration, when two decisions were made to substantially increase the number of US troops, this issue began to receive considerable public attention and was the focus of much internal debate, especially during the autumn of 2009.

After the numbers peaked in 2010, the debate gradually focused on reducing these numbers eventually to zero or, more precisely, a 1,000-strong embassy presence. The role of these numbers is important because they became a barometer of progress, irrespective of the reality on the ground, and a major point of contention between hawks and doves. Interestingly, as will be discussed, when it came to deciding on troop numbers, Obama consistently chose some variation of the middle ground. Thus, Obama's being seen to take the middle ground on troop numbers would appear to be an important causal factor when examining the US military effort in Afghanistan during his administration, with the waging of that war being fundamentally linked to this issue rather than to some other political or strategic one.

Upon taking office in 2009, Obama's main foreign policy priority was to withdraw US combat forces from Iraq and to increase the US military presence in Afghanistan. Prior to the November 2008 presidential election, Obama had already made a number of references to the need to commit additional "badly needed" resources to Afghanistan. For example, in August 2007, Obama stated that if he was elected president, he would send "at least two additional brigades" to Afghanistan.[2] One year later, Obama still spoke of two additional "combat brigades" that would be needed to "make the fight against al-Qaeda and the Taliban the top priority that it should be."[3] It is notable that these proposed troop increases were not tied to any concept of how they would be employed or why two brigades were selected, as opposed to one, three, four, and so on. At this point, prior to the election, it seems that Obama's main objective in referring to the two brigades was limited to demonstrating additional commitment to the

Afghan conflict and did not reflect a more sophisticated appraisal of the sort of military presence that could provide the United States and its allies with success over its al-Qaeda and Taliban adversaries.

Curiously, despite the prioritization Afghanistan supposedly needed, Obama avoided substantive engagement with the topic until after his inauguration in January 2009. It was only when he arrived in the White House that he appointed Bruce Riedel to head a sixty-day review of US policy toward Afghanistan and Pakistan, the results of which were presented at the end of March 2009.[4] As the review was underway, Obama announced on 17 February 2009 that he was going to increase US forces in Afghanistan by seventeen thousand troops, based on still outstanding requests from the previous year.[5] Then, on 27 March, after the completion of Riedel's review, Obama announced, "Later this spring we will deploy approximately 4,000 US troops to train Afghan security forces. For the first time, this will truly resource our effort to train and support the Afghan army and police."[6] Obama insisted, at least rhetorically, on the need for an exit strategy, stating, "There's got to be a sense that this is not perpetual drift."[7] However, at this early stage, the emphasis of Obama's policy was to escalate, with little discussion of an exit strategy, much less the timing of one.

Within months of this first Afghan surge and policy review, the administration embarked on a second review followed by a second surge. In contrast to the first review, conducted in relative secrecy and with little outside scrutiny, the second review was highly controversial within the US government and so generated a great deal of media attention. The troop numbers were the main issue causing friction, with Obama's hesitancy to make a decision aggravating the process. According to numerous accounts of this second policy review, Obama was fixated on fine-tuning the numbers rather than focusing on more substantive issues.[8] Moreover, he insisted that there would be no more troops beyond those sent as part of this latest Afghan surge and also demanded that these extra troops begin withdrawing after eighteen months.

It is at this point that a clear distinction must be made about the withdrawal timetable. Whereas some commentators criticized Obama's policy on the grounds that announcing a withdrawal timetable would aid the enemy, a close look at the wording of this announcement should have laid to rest any fears of an early US withdrawal. In the first place, the announcement was limited to reducing the troop numbers only to the level they had been at before the surge. In no way was there an indication of a complete withdrawal. Moreover, there was the question of the timing of withdrawal of these troops—was it to be completed within eighteen months after Obama's December 2009 speech, or was the process of their withdrawal only to *begin* at this time? Again, many commentators failed to look closely at the wording.

In the administration's internal deliberations, most notably at a high-level meeting on 29 November 2009, Obama specifically mentioned that the withdrawal process would only begin in July 2011, with the pace of withdrawal still up for negotiation. The key point Obama insisted upon was that his generals would not be asking for yet more troops. By contrast, there was little discussion about the longer-term withdrawal, which was put off.[9] In typical fashion, US commanders would attempt to keep as many troops in the country for as long as possible. As such, the vast majority of troops would be scheduled to withdraw close to the withdrawal deadline. US commanders would therefore no doubt have felt confident that they could maintain a large military presence in Afghanistan for a number of years, even though many critics of Obama's policy suggested this would not be the case.

Though not framed in terms of a large-scale open-ended military commitment, in practice this is what Obama's 2009 decision amounted to. Initially, no withdrawal deadline was set—only a date for commencing the drawdown. In due course, references to 2014, specifically the end of 2014, were made in relation to the end of the combat mission, though not necessarily of the US military presence as a whole.[10] Again, the language employed was paradoxically both precise and misleading. Technically speaking, the term "combat mission" means any sort of military activity involving the use of kinetic force. It is used to distinguish from other noncombat activities, such as training and advising. Revealingly, when the Obama administration talked about the end of the combat mission, it not only talked about a long-term training and advisory mission but also used the term "counterterrorism mission" to mean a separate long-term activity. In this sense, the terminology reflected a disingenuous and confusing approach to the conflict that attempted to placate different audiences but ended up causing confusion.

By the administration's own logic, counterterrorism was not a combat mission, but this failed to explain why combat was occurring as part of this activity, especially after 2014. On the other hand, the administration was not using this terminology in a technically precise way but as a convenient shorthand. Thus, "combat mission" meant the activities of large-scale conventional forces, such as regular Army and Marine Corps brigades. Training and advisory related to noncombat activities, with the possible exception of some advisors to the Afghan military that engaged in combat incidentally. Counterterrorism was used to characterize the activities of Special Forces and intelligence personnel. After 2014, US spokespersons would attempt to explain US military involvement in combat activity as being part of counterterrorism.[11]

On 22 June 2011, roughly one and a half months after Osama bin Laden was killed, Obama stated that beginning in July, the United States would begin removing ten thousand troops from Afghanistan by the end of 2011 and an additional twenty-three thousand by the summer 2012, "fully recovering the surge I announced at West Point" (in December 2009).[12] Obama's announcement came at a time when there was a great deal of speculation that bin Laden's death would lead to a much quicker withdrawal.[13] Yet as this measured timetable demonstrates, US commanders recognized that the security gains they claimed to have achieved were "fragile and reversible," and they therefore argued it was essential to keep as many US troops in the country for as long as possible.[14] Perhaps by coincidence, these troops would be returning ahead of the 2012 presidential election. The next round of withdrawals was announced in February 2013, when Obama stated that an additional thirty-four thousand troops would be home within a year. Obama spoke of this withdrawal as "the next step to responsibly bringing this war to a close."[15]

In May 2014, Obama announced a further reduction of twenty-two thousand troops by the end of 2014 and also declared that the United States would not have a combat role in Afghanistan after 2014. However, he said that ninety-eight hundred troops would remain but that by the end of 2015 this number would be reduced by roughly half, and that by the end of 2016, "we will draw down to a normal embassy presence in Kabul."[16] According to Obama, this would "bring America's longest war to a responsible end."[17] Meantime, the US commander in Afghanistan, General Joseph F. Dunford Jr., sought to delay the pace of withdrawal and to keep as many US troops as possible in Afghanistan through the 2015 fighting season. At the time of Obama's announcement, it was observed that his decision meant that he would leave office "having extricated the country from the longest war in US history." This announcement sparked criticism from Republicans, who argued that leaving too early might provide an opportunity for the Taliban just as the US withdrawal from Iraq had supposedly facilitated the rise of ISIS.[18]

The problem with this unilaterally imposed timetable was that it was to be carried out regardless of the changing military situation on the ground. Moreover, as the Taliban had not been defeated, the shrinking US military presence was almost certain to result in an increase in Taliban activity. In other words, it was easily foreseeable that a significant US military presence was likely to be indefinitely required to maintain the relatively favorable military situation that had been achieved. Therefore, it should not have come as a surprise that Obama's plans to reduce the US footprint in Afghanistan to an embassy presence were highly unlikely to come to fruition. Indeed, they were effectively a nonstarter. Shortly before Obama declared the end of the combat mission in late December 2014, the Pentagon announced that roughly one thousand more troops than were originally planned would stay in Afghanistan into 2015.[19] In addition, Obama approved new guidelines that would allow the US military to continue targeting the Taliban, effectively giving it a combat role separate from the counterterrorism role originally envisioned.[20]

Until August 2015, the administration refused to consider altering its earlier plans to reduce the US military presence to one thousand troops. Suggestions to keep more troops in the country were dismissed due to the prevailing mantra that there was no military solution. For reasons that remain unclear, it was only during a high-level meeting that month that Obama did not dismiss a request by the chairman of the Joint Chiefs of Staff, General Martin E. Dempsey, to keep some five thousand troops in Afghanistan.[21] Presumably, between August and mid-October, the details of this option were discussed further. Then, in mid-October, Obama announced that instead of reducing to an "embassy-only presence in Kabul by the end of 2016, we will maintain 5,500 troops" in Kabul, Bagram, Jalalabad, and Kandahar.[22] Less than a year later, Obama again reversed his position. In early July 2016, he stated that instead of reducing US troops to fifty-five hundred by the end of the year, the United States would maintain some eighty-four hundred troops into 2017.[23] Furthermore, US forces in Afghanistan were given a broader mandate to target the Taliban since the Afghan forces operating more or less on their own were unable to contain their growing presence.[24]

Trouble Facing Reality

In a January 2013 weekly address that the White House titled "Ending the War in Afghanistan and Rebuilding America," Obama stated, "Over the past four years ... we've dealt devastating blows to al-Qaeda. We've pushed the Taliban out of their strongholds."[25] Obama subsequently went on to use this upbeat description of the Afghan conflict to justify his decision to bring US troops home and to begin transitioning the lead for security to the Afghan forces. Was this a reflection of reality — defined in this instance as the way the conflict was perceived inside the US government and by expert commentators? To answer this question, it is necessary to discuss the conclusions reached by the US intelligence community about the conflict and to highlight the way these conclusions were often politicized. In addition, it is essential to ask whether expertise had an impact on how policymakers viewed the conflict and whether it influenced the decisions to withdraw US troops, or if this knowledge was mostly immaterial.[26]

To a large extent, the consequences resulting from the misrepresentation of the Afghan conflict from 2001 until early 2012 have been extensively covered elsewhere and will only receive a brief mention here. As one military officer who compiled a list of optimistic official statements explained, "US military leaders have so distorted the truth ... in regards to conditions on the ground in Afghanistan that the truth has become unrecognizable."[27] During the first years of Obama's presidency, there were several high-level intelligence reports that cast doubt on the progress being made. At the same time, US military officials were keen to show progress and to downplay the pessimism of the intelligence community.[28] Arguably the most important issue being debated was the extent to which the Taliban was being defeated. Whereas military officials would make optimistic statements about the gains being made, intelligence officials tended to emphasize that these gains had "failed to fundamentally undermine the Taliban as a fighting force."[29] One year after Obama announced his surge, senior officials such as Secretary of Defense Robert Gates were keen to characterize this policy as a success, despite the pessimism of the intelligence community.[30]

An additional case in point was Obama's 24 January 2012 State of the Union address, which noted, "The Taliban's momentum has been broken."[31] This statement contrasted with a National Intelligence Estimate that concluded that the Taliban remained resilient.[32] Later that year, it was reported that US commanders "are offering glowing reviews of their 2012 war campaign, upbeat assessments that could be interpreted as leeway for President Obama to order another round of troop withdrawals next summer."[33] At that time, the ISAF (International Security Assistance Force) deputy chief of staff for operations, Major General Larry Nicholson, said that US Marines in Helmand were complaining of boredom because there was so little fighting to do.[34] Meantime, both the White House and senior military commanders were unwilling to accept a pessimistic National Intelligence Estimate that warned that security gains were not sustainable.[35]

Gradually a divergence emerged between the White House and the military. Whereas US military leaders in Afghanistan had previously been providing optimistic reports, giving the impression of the Taliban suffering significant losses, and demonstrating the success of their counterinsurgency strategy, the policy debates about the speed of the post-surge drawdown added a new dimension to the way the conflict was portrayed. Increasingly, US military officials would refer to gains that were reversible if a military drawdown occurred too quickly.[36] The argument was made that the surge had not defeated the Taliban, though it had reversed the Taliban's momentum.[37]

Curiously, whereas Obama administration officials were trying to make the case that their Afghan policy had been successful or good enough, thereby facilitating a drawdown, they were simultaneously being warned by their military and intelligence officials about the consequences of a resurgent Taliban, which presumably would be viewed as a policy failure. In the end, Obama accepted the pessimistic assessments and the need for a slower military drawdown but continued to publicly emphasize progress despite the evidence to the contrary. Ultimately, the administration was unable to resolve its key dilemma, namely that the Taliban remained resilient despite the US surge.[38] According to a US military spokesman in May 2016, "We typically believe there's probably about 30,000 or so Taliban fighters out there … you've probably heard that term before. We don't have any reason to think that it has significantly changed."[39] Actually, the US estimate of Taliban strength had increased from the twenty-five thousand figure continually cited by officials since 2009.[40]

Regardless, as US forces began to withdraw from Afghanistan, it was difficult to argue that a larger and emboldened Taliban was more likely to be defeated with fewer US troops or that the United States would be negotiating from a position of strength.[41] Apart from the resilient Taliban, another major policy problem was the assessment of the size of al-Qaeda's presence in Afghanistan. This was a problem because al-Qaeda was the original reason for invading Afghanistan; denying it a secure base in that country in the future had been one of the main justifications for not withdrawing.

Since at least 2010, US officials claimed that al-Qaeda had been decimated and estimated that there were some fifty to one hundred al-Qaeda operatives remaining in Afghanistan. This number remained consistent throughout the surge and after bin Laden's death in 2011. Yet this raised questions about why the United States was not more successful in making progress against al-Qaeda since their numbers never went down. In October 2015, a raid in Kandahar province uncovered a large al-Qaeda training camp and identified some 160 of its operatives—all reportedly killed in the raid. As a result, the official estimate changed to one hundred to three hundred.[42] The embarrassment about this discovery and the prospect of an al-Qaeda comeback might have contributed to Obama deciding to keep more US forces in Afghanistan into the next presidency. In his July 2016 statement about leaving eighty-four hundred troops in Afghanistan, Obama called the security situation "precarious" and specifically referred to the country as "where al-Qaeda is trying to regroup."[43]

A Responsible End?

Obama announced the end of the combat mission on 28 December 2014. In his statement, he said "Our combat mission in Afghanistan is ending, and the longest war in US history is coming to a responsible conclusion."[44] This was not the first time this sort of language was used, nor would it be the last. Time and again, the Obama administration used some variation of the words "bringing the war to a responsible end." How does one interpret such presidential statements that appear divorced from reality? With respect to the date of Obama's announcement, this had been agreed to by the United States and its allies several years earlier. Thus, the combat mission was expected to conclude at the end of 2014 irrespective of the security situation on the ground, though as mentioned earlier, a limited combat mission continued under the heading "counterterrorism operations."

Nevertheless, even if one were to accept the official line that the combat mission had ended, it is difficult to understand what was meant by a responsible end to the conflict. What was the administration's motivation for using this sort of language? Was it anything more than a soundbite? Did administration officials really think that the United States had ended the war—and in a responsible way? If they did believe it to be true, what did this say about the mentality of the officials themselves and their understanding of the conflict? If they did not believe it to be true, then what value did they see in communicating this message, especially if others were unlikely to buy it either? Although I was unable to trace the origins of this language in the administration or gain any direct insights into the thinking of officials, it is possible to make some useful inferences about these matters.

As a soundbite, the idea that the war had come to a responsible end did hold an obvious appeal. For one thing, it provided a simple positive sounding narrative that says nothing of substance but does not go so far as to claim outright victory. As a goal of the military action that needed to be achieved, this language could serve a useful purpose. In other words, the administration could make a legitimate claim that the purpose of US military action in Afghanistan was to bring the conflict to a responsible end, provided of course that the definition of what was considered a responsible end was enunciated. This was a difficult case to make for

Afghanistan. Unlike other conflicts that end, there was no negotiated settlement and no immediate prospect of one. No military victory had been achieved—at best there was a military stalemate in which the insurgents and the counterinsurgents were unable to defeat one another. The Taliban had proved that even with the presence of more than 100,000 US troops, plus thousands more from other countries, they could remain a "force in being."

As a description of reality, this language also fell short on several levels. For one thing, the United States and its allies may have unilaterally concluded their combat mission, but no similar declaration of an end to hostilities was made by either the Afghan government or the Taliban. Hostilities thus continued regardless of Obama's announcement. Thus, the war had not concluded for two of the three key actors. Of course, another interpretation of the administration's language was that they were not claiming that the war had actually ended but that it was in its final stages.

Yet such a claim did not correspond with reality either, as there was no indication that the war was winding down—indeed, there was plenty of evidence of precisely the opposite. A third interpretation is that when Obama unilaterally ended the war he was referring to US involvement only. From this perspective, the United States could exit wars at times of its own choosing, with the aftermath—including ongoing conflict—constituting someone else's problem. Here again, the fact that the United States remained militarily engaged in the conflict contradicted the idea that the United States was no longer involved. Therefore, with respect to ending, there was little room for misinterpretation, unless of course officials were simply uninterested in facts.

If one pursues this line of inquiry a step further and takes it for granted that the war had not ended, then logically it could not have been responsibly ended. But suspending disbelief for a moment, let us forget the fact that the war had not ended and consider what was meant by the use of the word "responsible." Judging by the lack of discussion by US officials about the prospect of some sort of substantive military victory over the Taliban, or a favorable negotiated settlement between the Taliban and Afghan government, one can only conclude that the notion of responsible had more modest connotations.

At best, US officials referred to leaving Afghanistan with a functioning government still in control of most of the country's territory and, perhaps more importantly, a military system able to prevent any major military defeats—though admittedly unable to take significant offensive action. By being able to deny any major Taliban victories in the short term, US officials hoped that this might lead to a negotiated settlement at some point. This best-case scenario was consistently discussed by officials in the most abstract terms. In any event, it was predicated on continued financial and military support to the Afghan government, without which the system was expected to collapse. Therefore, judging by the way US officials have discussed the matter, the mainstream notion of responsible conduct was for the United States to substantially reduce its military and, to a lesser extent, financial commitments to Afghanistan, in such a way as to avoid a government collapse. But this still implied that military support would be provided to Afghanistan, even if at a more modest level than before.

The inherent problem with this notion of a responsible end was that as long as the conflict continued, there would always be the risk of the United States being dragged back in. If this occurred, it would be politically embarrassing to explain that the conflict that had been responsibly ended remained active and would continue to directly involve the US military. Curiously, despite Obama's October 2015 decision to keep US troops in Afghanistan going into the next presidency, in the run-up to the January 2016 State of the Union address, the spokesperson for the National Security Council tweeted about the United States ending two costly wars in Iraq and Afghanistan, pointing to a document on the White House website about Obama's foreign policy record. This document notes that the United States had "responsibly ended the US combat missions in Iraq and Afghanistan" and is linked to Obama's December 2014 statement.[45]

It is notable that the ending referred to in both conflicts does not describe the status of those conflicts as such but is linked to "bringing home some 90 percent of the nearly 180,000 US troops deployed in those countries when President Obama took office." By contrast, in Obama's actual State of the Union speech, Afghanistan received only a passing mention in the context of "instability that will continue for decades in many parts of the world."[46] When the statements are taken together, it appears as though achieving a responsible end has more to do with reducing US involvement and little to do with the fact that years of US military action had produced an indefinite state of instability.

It is difficult to ascertain why, after October 2015, Obama administration officials continued to make the case that they had responsibly ended the war, when they had already reversed their policy on troop withdrawals on the basis that the war was continuing and not going well. Perhaps one explanation is that officials did not see a contradiction. US troops could still be portrayed as leaving Afghanistan, but just not at a rate as quickly as previously expected. This might also explain why the administration in July 2016 was insistent on only reducing the US presence to eighty-four hundred instead of fifty-five hundred. Obama compromised on the precise numbers to avoid criticism of withdrawing too quickly while simultaneously demonstrating that the United States was still withdrawing troops. Meantime, the debates between Obama and the military about how many troops to withdraw and how quickly to do so had little basis in military strategy. Reductions reflected political compromises rather than military logic. Nevertheless, military logic seems not to have played much of a role throughout the entire course of the conflict going back to 2001. It is perhaps unsurprising, therefore, that it should have played much of a role fifteen years later.

Conclusion

In October 2016, one commentator described Obama's strategy in Afghanistan as "just enough to lose slowly."[47] This characterization is reminiscent of the so-called decent interval thesis used to explain Nixon's strategy in Vietnam. According to this thesis, the Nixon administration sought to exit from South Vietnam knowing that it would eventually collapse but leaving enough of a gap between the exit and the collapse to deflect the short-term political embarrassment. As this chapter has attempted to highlight, such a characterization is seemingly an apt one for Obama and Afghanistan. The problem faced by Nixon and Ford, and then Obama, was how to abandon any prospect of success — defined even in the most limited terms of ensuring no significant military threat to the existence of a friendly government — and at the same time indefinitely postpone the defeat of an increasingly weak government by a resilient adversary. This is a difficult balancing act, if not an impossible one. Or to put it slightly differently, it is a difficult balancing act in the short term and probably an impossible one in the long term.

Obama's Afghan exit strategy seems to have been predicated on two assumptions. The first assumption was the one based on forlorn hope and delusions that have been underpinned by one's own optimistic narratives. In other words, there was a belief held among key US decision makers that regardless of Taliban strengths and Afghan government weaknesses the Taliban was still too weak to score large victories, at least not in the immediate term, and particularly if a limited US military presence was maintained, albeit possibly augmented in a crisis. The second assumption was that the public, and probably allied governments as well, would lose interest in the conflict but were generally content with a status quo in which external military involvement was kept to a minimum.

Whereas in 2009 there was significant interest in doubling or tripling the size of the US military presence in Afghanistan, the situation several years later became one of war weariness and little appetite for further escalation, even if such an escalation would be considered necessary (based on relative Taliban gains compared with the strength of the government forces) to stave off military defeat based on the 2009 standards for escalation. A related assumption is that the reasons for escalating in the first place and for justifying the sacrifices made are not examined too closely and so don't become a political embarrassment.[48] This, in turn, is predicated on a further assumption that serious criticism is unlikely because there is a shared interest among the political class in not making this a major political issue.

For then-Senator Obama, the war in Afghanistan served a useful political purpose. Iraq was Bush's war, or the bad war. Afghanistan was the good war and would be *his* war. At the time of the 2008 election, Obama's interest was in getting the United States more involved in the Afghan conflict, though it is doubtful he foresaw the extent to which his administration would become involved. At that point, success was defined in quite vague terms, and Obama stressed that it was necessary to have a more focused mission to ensure Afghanistan never again became a base for al-Qaeda, an outcome that first required degrading or defeating the Taliban insurgency and building a relatively stable government in control of its territory. Other goals, such as improving women's rights, promoting democracy, reducing corruption, and so forth, were also often mentioned, but these tended to be talked about as subsidiary goals.

At some point after Obama's 2009 surge, a further goal emerged that would trump the aforementioned goals. Success in Afghanistan became increasingly tied to the US withdrawal—regardless of the extent to which any of the other goals had been reached. Instead, the new success metric was not whether the Taliban would be defeated but rather how slowly the Afghan government could be defeated. Success became associated, at least unconsciously, with a gradual defeat. This in practical terms meant that the Afghan government still controlled the major cities and that the Taliban took control over much of the countryside—with a minimal foreign military presence acting to delay the defeat of the government in the district and provincial capitals in the short term and to delay the Taliban capture of the major cities and capital in the long term. That this was likely an unconscious policy had to do with the lack of any hope that the Afghan government could actually succeed where the large-scale foreign military presence had failed for so many years. At best, it was hoped that there might be a negotiated settlement with the Taliban or perhaps that the Taliban would splinter internally, but these remained possibilities rather than probabilities.

The main impediment to achieving this type of responsible end was that it depended on two actors the United States had little or no control over: the Afghan government and the Taliban. As conditions on the ground worsened after the so-called end of combat operations in 2014, Obama faced the dilemma of risking a quicker disintegration—particularly problematic following the Iraqi government's disintegration in 2014—if the United States reduced its military forces to an embassy presence as originally envisaged. The resulting policy shift in October 2015 reflected a realization and a compromise. Obama realized that leaving Afghanistan no longer constituted success but was likely to be viewed as a policy mistake. He therefore compromised, accepting that the US military would continue to maintain thousands of troops in Afghanistan beyond his presidency.

The Afghan legacy for Obama's presidency is therefore likely to be one of policy disappointment rather than failure, particularly as the latter characterization would have required a collapse of the Afghan government, whereas the former could encompass a situation in which the Kabul authorities continued to survive even though they failed to prosper. On the other hand, the numerous attempts to craft positive narratives characterizing US policy under Obama as successful or claiming that the conflict had been ended responsibly held little credibility, particularly through the last year or so of his presidency, even among those who had previously accepted this narrative. In this sense, the August 2017 announcement by the Trump administration to send thousands of additional US troops to Afghanistan, based largely on the advice of US generals, served to drive the last nail into the coffin of the earlier success narratives.

Jeffrey H. Michaels is senior lecturer in defense studies based at the Joint Services Command and Staff College, UK. He has also held visiting research fellowships at the Oxford Changing Character of War Centre at Pembroke College and the Egmont Institute in Brussels. Earlier experience included working for the US Defense Department and NATO. He is the author of *The Discourse Trap and the US Military: From the War on Terror to the Surge* (Palgrave, 2013).

Notes

1. For more details, see Jeffrey H. Michaels, "Delusions of Survival: US Deliberations on Support for South Vietnam during the 1975 'Final Offensive,'" *Small Wars and Insurgencies* 26, no. 6 (2015), 957–75.
2. Barack Obama, "Remarks at Woodrow Wilson Center: The War We Need to Win" 1 August 2007, https://www.presidency.ucsb.edu/documents/remarks-washington-dc-the-war-we-need-win, accessed 15 December 2018.
3. "Obama's remarks on Iraq and Afghanistan," *New York Times*, 15 July 2008, http://www.nytimes.com/2008/07/15/us/politics/15text-obama.html?_r=0), accessed 15 December 2018.
4. "Press Briefing by Bruce Riedel, Ambassador Richard Holbrooke, and Michelle Flournoy on the New Strategy for Afghanistan and Pakistan," The White House, 27 March 2009, https://obamawhitehouse.archives.gov/realitycheck/the-press-office/press-briefing-bruce-riedel-ambassador-richard-holbrooke-and-michelle-flournoy-new-, accessed 15 December 2018.
5. "Statement by the President on Afghanistan," 17 February 2009, https://obamawhitehouse.archives.gov/the-press-office/statement-president-afghanistan, accessed 15 December 2018. See also Julian E. Barnes, "Obama Team Works on Overhaul of Afghanistan, Pakistan policy," *Los Angeles Times*, 11 February 2009.
6. "Remarks by the President on a New Strategy for Afghanistan and Pakistan," The White House, 27 March 2009, https://obamawhitehouse.archives.gov/the-press-office/remarks-president-a-new-strategy-afghanistan-and-pakistan, accessed 15 December 2018.
7. Helene Cooper, "White House Wants Exit Plan for Afghanistan," *International Herald Tribune*, 24 March 2009.
8. In late September 2009, US military leaders offered Obama three options for more troops, with 80,000 at the high end, 10,000–15,000 at the low end, and 40,000 as a middle option. Eventually, Obama settled on a variation of the middle option in which the United States deployed 30,000 additional troops. See Peter Baker, "How Obama Came to Plan for 'Surge' in Afghanistan," *New York Times*, 5 December 2009.
9. Anne Mulrine, "Mixed Messages from Obama, Petraeus on Afghanistan Pullout," *Christian Science Monitor*, 23 September 2010; Bob Woodward, *Obama's Wars: The Inside Story* (New York: Simon and Schuster, 2010), 325; Jeffrey H. Michaels and Matthew Ford, "Bandwagonistas: Rhetorical Re-description, Strategic Choice and the Politics of Counter-insurgency," *Small Wars & Insurgencies* 22, no. 2 (2011), 352–84.
10. See, for instance, Fact Sheet: Chicago Summit—NATO's Enduring Presence after 2014, The White House, 21 May 2012.
11. Michael S. Schmidt, "US Combat Missions May End but Fighting Goes On," *New York Times*, 14 May 2016.
12. "Remarks by the President on the Way Forward in Afghanistan," The White House, 22 June 2011.
13. See, for instance, Liz Halloran, "Bin Laden Death Fuels Afghan War Debate," NPR, 3 May 2011.
14. "Afghanistan: Obama Orders Withdrawal of 33,000 Troops," BBC, 23 June 2011.
15. "White House Fact Sheet: Afghanistan," 12 February 2013, https://obamawhitehouse.archives.gov/the-press-office/2013/02/12/fact-sheet-afghanistan, accessed 15 December 2018.
16. "White House, Fact Sheet: Bringing the US War in Afghanistan to a Responsible End," 27 May 2014, https://obamawhitehouse.archives.gov/the-press-office/2014/05/27/fact-sheet-bringing-us-war-afghanistan-responsible-end, accessed 15 December 2018; Mark

Landler, "US Troops to Leave Afghanistan by End of 2016," *New York Times*, 27 May 2014.
17. "White House, Statement by the President on Afghanistan," 27 May 2014, https://obamawhitehouse.archives.gov/the-press-office/2014/05/27/statement-president-afghanistan, accessed 15 December 2018.
18. Steve Holland, "Obama Plans to End US Troop Presence in Afghanistan by 2016," Reuters, 27 May 2014.
19. Anna Mulrine, "Symbolic 'End' to Afghanistan War Overshadowed by New Obama Plans," *Christian Science Monitor*, 8 December 2014.
20. Allen McDufee, "Obama Orders Expanded US Role in Afghanistan to Avoid Another ISIS," *The Atlantic*, 22 November 2014.
21. Greg Jaffe, "Hope Fades on Obama's Vow to Bring Troops Home before Presidency Ends," *Washington Post*, 12 October 2015.
22. "On-the-Record Conference Call on Afghanistan," *The White House*, 15 October 2015, https://obamawhitehouse.archives.gov/the-press-office/2015/10/15/record-conference-call-afghanistan, accessed 15 December 2018.
23. "Statement by the President on Afghanistan," *The White House*, 6 July 2016, https://obamawhitehouse.archives.gov/the-press-office/2016/07/06/statement-president-afghanistan, accessed 15 December 2018.
24. Missy Ryan and Thomas Gibbons-Neff, "US Widens War in Afghanistan, Authorizes New Action against Taliban," *Washington Post*, 10 June 2016; Jessica Donati and Habib Khan Totakhil, "US Adds Forces in Afghanistan to Fight Islamic State," *Wall Street Journal* (New York), 27 July 2016; Josh Smith, "US Air Strikes Spike as Afghans Struggle against Taliban, Islamic State," Reuters, 26 October 2016.
25. "Weekly Address: Ending the War in Afghanistan and Rebuilding America," The White House, 12 January 2013. Interestingly, the figure of 8,400 troops did not include an additional 400 troops stationed in the region that were available for immediate deployment to Afghanistan. See Dan Lamothe, "US Shifts Emphasis of New Operations against Taliban to Eastern Afghanistan," *Washington Post*, 12 July 2016.
26. Due to the nature of this subject, it is impossible to cite documentary evidence, such as the minutes of meetings or classified intelligence reports. Nevertheless, useful inferences can be made from at least two sources. First, numerous media reports focusing on this issue include interviews with serving officials and often cite passages from key documents such as National Intelligence Estimates. Second, even without privileged access to these estimates, any number of other open source analyses of the conflict, as well as information about it, such as casualty figures, can at least provide a general indication of how the conflict was progressing.
27. Lt. Col. Daniel Davis, "DRAFT: Dereliction of Duty II: Senior Military Leader's Loss of Integrity Wounds Afghan War Effort," 27 January 2012, https://wikispooks.com/wiki/File:Dereliction_of_Duty_II.pdf, accessed 15 December 2018.
28. Douglas A. Wissing, *Hopeless but Optimistic: Journeying through America's Endless War in Afghanistan* (Bloomington: Indiana University Press, 2016), 20–21; Mark Hosenball, "US Intelligence Pessimistic on Afghan War Success," Reuters, 15 December 2010; Josh Rogin, "Petraeus' Optimism Not Shared at CIA," *Foreign Policy*, 27 April 2011; Ken Dilanian and David S. Cloud, "US Intelligence Reports Cast Doubt on War Progress in Afghanistan," *Los Angeles Times*, 15 December 2010; Steve Coll, "Let's Hear from the Spies," *The New Yorker*, 23 November 2011.
29. Ken Dilanian, "Petraeus Cites Successes in Afghanistan," *Los Angeles Times*, 16 March 2011.
30. Adam Entous, "Gates Sees Afghan Progress," *Wall Street Journal* (New York), 9 December 2010.

31. Obama cited in Helene Cooper and Matthew Rosenberg, "NATO Sets Exit from Afghanistan," *International Herald Tribune*, 23 May 2012.
32. John Walcott, "Intelligence Doesn't Support Obama's Upbeat View of Afghanistan," Bloomberg, 2 February 2012.
33. Robert Burns, "US Commanders Are Upbeat on Afghan War Progress," Associated Press, 15 December 2012.
34. Ibid.
35. Jonathan S. Landay and Nancy A. Youssef, "Intelligence Report: Taliban Still Hope to Rule Afghanistan," *McClatchy Newspapers*, 11 January 2012. This report specifically mentions the objections of General John Allen, head of ISAF, US ambassador to Kabul Ryan Crocker, and General James Mattis, head of US Central Command.
36. See, for instance, David S. Cloud, "New Pentagon Report Paints Mixed Picture of Afghanistan Security," *Los Angeles Times*, 8 November 2013.
37. See Ernesto Londono, Karen DeYoung, and Greg Miller, "Afghanistan Gains Will Be Lost Quickly after Drawdown, US Intelligence Estimate Warns," *Washington Post*, 28 December 2013.
38. References to Taliban resilience can be found in Lynne O'Donnell, "The Taliban Now Hold More Ground in Afghanistan Than at Any Point since 2001," *Military Times*, 16 June 2016; Lolita C. Baldor, "US General: 10 Percent of Afghanistan under Taliban control," Associated Press, 23 September 2016; Sarah Almukhtar and Karen Yourish, "More Than 14 Years after US Invasion, the Taliban Control Large Parts of Afghanistan," *New York Times*, 19 April 2016.
39. "Brigadier General Charles H. Cleveland, Deputy Chief of Staff for Communications, Resolute Support Mission, Holds a Defense Department News Briefing via Teleconference from Afghanistan," 5 May 2016, http://www.defense.gov/News/Transcripts/Transcript-View/Article/721738/department-of-defense-press-briefing-by-general-cleveland-via-teleconference-fr, accessed 15 December 2018.
40. Adam Entous, "Taliban Growth Weighs on Obama's Strategy Review," Reuters, 10 October 2009.
41. Vali Nasr, "The Inside Story of How the White House Let Diplomacy Fail in Afghanistan," *Foreign Policy*, 4 March 2013.
42. Bill Roggio and Thomas Joscelyn, "US Military Admits al Qaeda is Stronger in Afghanistan than Previously Estimated," *The Long War Journal*, 13 April 2016, http://www.longwarjournal.org/archives/2016/04/us-military-admits-al-qaeda-is-stronger-in-afghanistan-than-previously-estimated.php; Anne Stenerson, "Al-Qaida's Comeback in Afghanistan and Its Implications," *CTC Sentinel*, 7 September 2016, https://www.ctc.usma.edu/posts/al-qaidas-comeback-in-afghanistan-and-its-implications, accessed 15 December 2018; Eric Schmitt and David E. Sanger, "As US Focuses on ISIS and the Taliban, Al Qaeda Re-emerges," *New York Times*, 29 December 2015.
43. "Statement by the President on Afghanistan," The White House, 6 July 2016.
44. "Statement by the President on the End of the Combat Mission in Afghanistan," The White House, 28 December 2014, https://obamawhitehouse.archives.gov/the-press-office/2014/12/28/statement-president-end-combat-mission-afghanistan, accessed 15 December 2018.
45. "American Leadership in the World," The White House, undated, https://obamawhitehouse.archives.gov/the-record/foreign-policy, accessed 15 December 2018.
46. Nancy A. Youssef, "Team Obama Brags: We 'Ended' Two Wars (Just Don't Count the Dead Troops)," *Daily Beast*, 12 January 2016; see the link to the original tweet, https://twitter.com/Price44/status/686710984468217856, accessed 15 December 2018. Missy Ryan, "Afghan War Grinds On, But It's Mostly Absent from Obama's Final State of the Union," *Washington Post*, 12 January 2016; "Remarks of President Barack Obama—State of the Union," 13 January 2016, https://obamawhitehouse.archives.gov/

the-press-office/2016/01/12/remarks-president-barack-obama-%E2%80%93-prepared-delivery-state-union-address, accessed 15 December 2018.
47. Douglas Ollivant cited in Thomas Gibbons-Neff, "'Band-Aid on a Bullet Wound': What America's New War Looks Like in Afghanistan's Most Violent Province," *Washington Post*, 16 October 2016.
48. In a 2012 study of Obama's rhetoric on the Afghan War, Trevor McCrisken raised the prospect that the president's references to "sacrifice" would hinder US withdrawal from the conflict by making it more difficult to demonstrate those sacrifices had been worthwhile. The notion of a "sacrifice trap," while useful, can also be slightly misleading if taken out of a wider context. See Trevor McCrisken, "Justifying Sacrifice: Barack Obama and the Selling and Ending of the War in Afghanistan," *International Affairs* 88, no. 5 (2012), 993–1007.

Select Bibliography

McCrisken, Trevor, "Justifying Sacrifice: Barack Obama and the Selling and Ending of the War in Afghanistan," *International Affairs* 88, no. 5 (2012).
Michaels, Jeffrey H., "Delusions of Survival: US Deliberations on Support for South Vietnam during the 1975 'Final Offensive,'" *Small Wars and Insurgencies* 26, no. 6 (2015).
Michaels, Jeffrey H. and Matthew Ford, "Bandwagonistas: Rhetorical Re-description, Strategic Choice and the Politics of Counter-insurgency," *Small Wars & Insurgencies* 22, no. 2 (2011).
Wissing, Douglas A., *Hopeless but Optimistic: Journeying through America's Endless War in Afghanistan* (Bloomington: Indiana University Press, 2016).
Woodward, Bob, *Obama's Wars: The Inside Story* (New York: Simon and Schuster, 2011).

Chapter 8

Flawed Afghanization
Underestimating and Misunderstanding the Taliban

Antonio Giustozzi

Introduction

President Obama started his first mandate with an agenda to increase American investment in Afghanistan in order to successfully resolve what he considered a conflict in which the United States had underinvested. Hence the widely discussed "surge" of 2009–2011. By early 2010 if not earlier, however, Obama was convinced that his generals would not deliver the quick, resounding victory that he needed and that they were instead getting bogged down in the conflict, lacking a clear idea of how to tackle it except demanding more and more resources. With his July 2011 announcement that the surge had expired and that the additional troops deployed to Afghanistan in 2009–2010 would now start pulling out, it was clear that Obama was now shifting fast toward the opposite end of the spectrum of options as far as Afghanistan was concerned: disengagement. Obama duly followed up with his May 2014 announcement, that no US troops should be left in Afghanistan by the end of 2016, except for a small contingent to protect the US embassy. Although Obama later reneged on this commitment and agreed to leave 5,500 troops in 2017, the aim of disengaging quickly was not in question.[1]

With the political decision to disengage made, what was left to do was framing a strategy that would make disengagement look like an achievement and not an admission of defeat. Key to the strategy as it was being worked out in Washington was the assumption that the Afghan security forces could protect the pro-American Afghan regime and achieve at least a stalemate on the battlefield; a parallel diplomatic effort, which was already being hammered together by US diplomats, would hopefully deliver a political settlement after the armed opposition of the Taliban realized that a military victory was not achievable. Engagement or reengagement with regional powers, particularly Pakistan and later even China, should have created a regional environment conducive to a political settlement, because Pakistan was (rightly) believed to have leverage with the Taliban, and China to have leverage with Pakistan. Engaging Pakistan was supposed to get the Pakistani authorities to deliver the Taliban to the negotiating table.[2]

In this chapter we will explore why the American plan did not work as expected, focusing in particular on how the Americans underestimated the military power of the Taliban, miscalculated the ability of the Taliban leadership to reach a political settlement, and overestimated the capabilities of the Afghan security forces.

The Overestimation of the Afghan Security Forces

Throughout their experience in Afghanistan, the US military has tried to boost the image of their trainees, the Afghan army and to a lesser extent the Afghan police, and claim a much greater role in the conflict than they actually played. Operations were regularly claimed to be Afghan led or to have a strong Afghan participation, even if there was just a token Afghan presence in them. While this might have worked to produce a more positive image of the Afghan security forces internally and externally, it led to a dramatic overestimation of the capacity of the Afghan security forces to operate autonomously. After having long stagnated, American assessments of the capabilities of Afghan units showed a very dramatic improvement in 2014, the year when Americans disengaged from combat operations.[3]

The most obvious limitation of the Afghan security forces in 2015 was the lack of any close air support capability. Even transport and medevac capabilities were vastly inferior to what the Afghan security forces had experienced under the patronage of the International Security Assistance Force (ISAF). On the other hand, all the way to 2014 the Afghan security forces and particularly the army had been trained to fight the American way, that is relying on air-delivered firepower to defeat its enemies. During 2015 the Afghan army, lacking close air support, adopted a very passive attitude and ceded substantial ground to the insurgents. At one point in October 2015 the army seemed close to implosion around Kunduz in the northeast and in Helmand in the south, forcing the Americans to redeploy some "expeditionary teams" to provide close air support and stop the Taliban's advance. From that point onward, the Americans have been providing close air support and recommitted a few hundred troops to the battlefield in areas of highest Taliban pressure; they were still there in December 2016.[4]

Although the Afghan air force took delivery of a handful of combat helicopters and strike aircraft in early 2016, its capability to provide close air support remained very limited as of December 2016 and the Afghan army remained dependent on US-provided air capabilities; it will be so for the foreseeable future, despite plans drafted at the end of the Obama administration to reequip the air force with larger numbers of US helicopters and a few more strike aircraft.[5] There was uncertainty over the intentions of the future Trump administration, but following the inclusion of several Afghan veterans in its ranks it seemed likely that it would maintain the existing commitments. Many army and police officers cannot read maps and therefore are unable to provide anything resembling accurate coordinates to pilots providing air cover. The Taliban, by contrast, are used to fighting against Western military forces fully supported by air assets and are likely to barely notice the activities of the Afghan air force in the future.

The lack of close air support is not the only weakness of the Afghan security forces. The logistics of the army is severely limited by lack of capability and by the limited road network of Afghanistan, reducing the ability of the army to operate far from the main highways. Even along the highways the Afghan army only has the capability to support one major operation at a time. The Taliban, by contrast, have the potential ability to mount four major attacks at any given time; the army could therefore end up being stretched very thin very quickly.[6]

During 2015 the problem of ghost policing and ghost soldiering emerged as major issues. Although not on the same scale as the Iraqi army, the practice of keeping on the payroll nonexistent soldiers and patrolmen while officers pocketed their salaries was widespread in Afghanistan too and contributed to its poor performance against relatively modest numbers of attacking Taliban in Helmand. The army looked big and powerful on paper, but that was only serving the purpose of keeping US donors satisfied (until the problem was reported by SIGAR [Special Inspector General for Afghanistan Reconstruction]).[7]

Finally, both army and police have been suffering from poor and incompetent leadership, which in turn is the result of widespread patronage practices and of political appointments. Very few of the Afghan generals have any ability to maneuver their troops on the battlefield, and even fewer displayed any initiative or creativity in confronting the threat. Particularly in the police, many officers even at senior level were illiterate or nearly so.[8]

All these limitations and weaknesses of the Afghan security forces were well known to American advisers to the army and the police, but the top level of ISAF and NATO Training Mission (NTM) opted to sweep these issues under the carpet, rather than confront them decisively, with the result that they were still largely unresolved in 2015 despite many years of American and Western engagement there.[9] During early 2016 a number of appointments of more qualified senior officers were made in the army and police, although as of April 2016 it was too early to say whether this was having an appreciably positive impact on the performance of either police or army.[10]

The Military Underestimation of the Taliban

As the American surge in southern Afghanistan had reached its peak, the US military assessed that the Taliban had been weakened to the point that the Afghan security forces could take the lead in the fight. This assessment assumed that the Taliban considered the provinces of Kandahar and Helmand, where the surge was concentrated, as their turf. The surge undoubtedly succeeded in pushing the Taliban out of the relatively densely populated areas of central Helmand and central Kandahar. The Taliban had also undoubtedly viewed reaching the outskirts of Kandahar city in 2006 as a major achievement and even a prelude to victory. Being pushed back did hurt the Taliban and kick-started acrimonious internal debates about strategy and organization. Some of the leaders, led by de facto operational leader Mullah Baradar, argued that time was ripe for a political settlement, while others argued for a deep reform of the Taliban's military apparatus to meet the new challenge. Personal rivalries also emerged as the existing leadership started being delegitimized.[11]

However, the assessment that the Taliban had been permanently wounded by the surge and by the new kill and capture tactics adopted from 2007 onward was flawed. The Taliban instead proved resilient for a number of reasons. The first and most obvious one was that they had the option of pulling back into their Pakistani safe haven and to recover or reorganize there. The mobile forces of the Taliban were not seriously damaged by the surge, although the local Taliban militias suffered much more and in many areas were de facto crushed. Because of their local character they could not easily withdraw into Pakistan, lest their members abandon families and property. Taliban political leaders connected to the local communities felt the pressure as their associates complained to the Taliban about their failure to protect communities that they had encouraged to rise. The idea of some form of political reconciliation, mentioned above, derived in part at least from the situation created by the surge.[12] Those political leaders, however, turned out not to have sufficient leverage to impose their policy line.

Had the Pakistani safe haven been the only source of Taliban resilience, the damage done by surge and kill and capture would still have seriously weakened the Taliban for the long term in the south. The Taliban, however, had at least four other sources of resilience.

The first one was the Taliban's convoluted and redundant command system. Organized in a number of parallel and even competing networks, each with its own command system, the Taliban were inefficient, but also able to absorb massive casualties among their field leaders and still continue to operate. The Americans and their NATO allies did not realize the implications of fighting a decentralized organization like the Taliban, as they were still basing their counterinsurgency tactics on previous experiences of fighting Marxist insurgencies.[13]

Another source of resilience was external support. The Americans badly misunderstood the attitude of regional powers toward their intervention in Afghanistan and particularly toward the escalation that had already started toward the end of the Bush administration. They thought they could handle the Pakistanis despite early evidence of their support for the insurgents and of meddling in Afghan affairs; Gen. Barno of the Combined Forces Command, for example, intervened early to stop operations against Pakistani intelligence support for the Taliban.[14] They did not believe that Iranian support for the Taliban made their strategy unviable. And not just the Pakistanis or the Iranians (routinely accused of supporting the Taliban), but several other countries in the region started supporting the Taliban in response to the Taliban surge, or increased their level of support if they had already been supporting them. In particular a crucial amount of support came from Saudi Arabia.[15]

The third source of Taliban resilience worth mentioning is the emergence of new Taliban networks outside their traditional southern turf, which had been marginal before the surge. The growing amount of external support available did not accrue mainly to the southern Taliban network, but mostly to new networks developing in eastern Afghanistan. The new development was not particularly welcomed by the southern Taliban, who came under pressure to share leadership positions with the eastern Taliban, but Taliban gains in the east and then gradually even in the north more than offset losses in the south, therefore reducing the impact of the surge.[16]

Finally, the Taliban responded to the kill and capture tactics of the Americans and of their allies with various forms of military adaptation. Initially very naïve in the use of such technologies as radios and mobile phones, the Taliban had to become more sophisticated in order to survive. Their command and control system had to become more secretive as well. The Taliban gradually learned how to fight a guerrilla war, using asymmetric tactics with which they had initially not been familiar. Their most successful effort in this regard was the use of mines (mostly improvised ones) on a massive scale. By 2010, 54% of all American troops killed in Afghanistan were victims of IEDs (improvised explosive devices).[17]

All combined, these sources of resilience meant that the Taliban's military power continued to grow even as they underwent the greatest military pressure they had ever met in 2009–2011. The Pakistan safe haven allowed them to develop reserves and to deploy them according to tactical requirements and opportunities; until 2014 the Taliban were essentially limiting themselves to harassing the Americans and to training their forces, while deploying a relatively limited portion of them at any given time. Even during the peak of the fighting season, the Taliban were not deploying much more than half of their mobile fighting forces. But their human resources were growing.[18]

This meant that by the time the Afghan security forces were left to fight essentially on their own at the beginning of 2015, they faced Taliban forces that were much larger and powerful than expected.

Misunderstanding the Taliban

The American disengagement strategy was also flawed because of the failure to understand the internal political dynamics of the Taliban, or at least to factor them into the strategy. The Americans rightly perceived perhaps already during 2009 that within the Taliban political leadership there was appetite for a negotiated solution to the conflict. However, they failed to detect major political struggles going on between different factions of the political leadership and between the political and military leaders, which affected efforts to kick-start a reconciliation process. The emergence of new Taliban networks as discussed above also weakened the hold and cohesion of the old political leadership, as did the growing number of foreign supporters of the Taliban, which distributed their funds to different actors within the leadership.[19]

Key elements of the Quetta Shura political leadership started showing an interest in political negotiations in 2009–2010; at the time, the Americans seemed to have been uncertain about how to deal with this and were even coopted in an attempt by the Pakistani authorities to thwart such effort by arresting the top figure involved, Mullah Baradar, the operational leader of the Quetta Shura. Following this arrest, efforts to bring the Taliban to the negotiating table were driven by efforts first of the Qatari government (2010–) and then of the Pakistani government (2014–). These two efforts eventually converged and started seeing a growing involvement of American diplomats in seeking options to bring the Taliban back into the mainstream political fold of Afghanistan. Contrary to the early 2009–2010 efforts, the priority in this case was for Taliban-United States talks, as opposed to Taliban-Kabul talks, but Washington had to agree to increasingly involve the Afghan government as well, despite Pakistani misgivings.[20]

In 2010–2012 the efforts centered on Qatar ran into deep trouble as the Quetta political leadership came under strong criticism by other components of the Taliban, such as the Haqqanis and the Peshawar Shura, which had not been given much representation in the Qatar-based Taliban delegation that was handling the pretalks. It also ran into trouble when the Afghan government discovered the talks between the Taliban and the Americans. It took until June 2013 to relaunch the Qatar-based talks, this time with all the main components of the Taliban on board and Kabul as well. The Pakistanis remained unenthusiastic about talks that might not take place in Pakistani territory and under some kind of Pakistani management and managed by 2015 to hijack the agenda, relegating the Qatar track to a marginal role. Through their delaying tactics and outright sabotage of everybody's else efforts, the Pakistani authorities managed to delay negotiations until a worn-out Obama administration eventually agreed to a Pakistani sponsorship of the talks, but they had by then lost five precious years.[21]

Although the different components of the Taliban all had some representation in the pretalks and in the only formal talks that took place in July 2015 in Pakistan, they did not necessarily agree to reconciliation with Kabul or with Washington, at least not with the same conditions. Hardliners like the Haqqanis were not the only ones to resist the attempt of the leader of the Quetta Shura, Akhtar Mansur, to accelerate the reconciliation process by dropping some Taliban preconditions, such as the preliminary withdrawal of foreign troops and a preliminary agreement to revise the Afghan constitution. Many senior members of the Quetta-based political leadership also did. The July 2015 meeting saw the Taliban delegation imploding even before the meeting was over, due to a revolt against Mansur's attempt to force through a decision on talks without the consent of the Taliban leadership. The backlash prompted Mansur to try to consolidate his position by announcing the death of the supreme leader of the Taliban, Mullah Omar, and get himself appointed as a successor, but he only made things worse, causing an open revolt against his leadership. The Quetta Shura split, with several senior political leaders openly rejecting Mansur's selection as successor to Mullah Omar.[22]

Pakistani and US pressure on the Quetta Shura to get reconciliation finally going therefore backfired, producing an even more complex situation to handle, with an acrimonious split that eventually resulted in the anti-Mansur Mullah Rasool being selected as alternative leader of a parallel Quetta Shura. Rasool made clear that even if he was not against reconciliation in principle, he would never sit at the same table with the impostor Mansur.[23]

Through 2015 it also became clear that Mansur and the Quetta Shura political leaders did not control the military leaders of the Taliban, whether before or after Mansur claimed the succession to Mullah Omar. Despite Mansur's commitment until the summer to contain military operations against Kabul forces, the two main military leaders of the Taliban, Qari Baryal in the northeast and Abdul Qayum Zakir in the southwest, committed their forces to the battlefield with a violence and a determination never shown before by the Taliban. The result was the first seizure of a city by the Taliban at the end of September (Kunduz) and a direct threat to the cities of Lashkargah and Girishk.[24]

The heavy fighting inevitably made it difficult for the Kabul government to accept Mansur's declarations of serious intent on negotiations. In addition, Mansur was by the second half of the summer feeling that he could not afford to let loose military commanders score successes on the battlefield, without risking his leadership. During autumn and winter Mansur also committed his forces to the battlefield, trying to gain credibility as the leader of an insurgency. Under pressure from his own loyalists, in early March he had to pull out of negotiations altogether and start planning for more military operations. The sense was that going further down the road of reconciliation with Kabul without major concessions from Kabul would wreck the Taliban without achieving anything substantial. The hardliners seemed well positioned to attract the bulk of the fighting forces of the Taliban to their side and to be well positioned to retain sufficient funding for continuing to fight even if the political leadership acceded to reconciliation with Kabul. Many military commanders of the Taliban could not see any gain for themselves in reconciliation, quite the contrary.[25]

Perhaps advocates of reconciliation with the Taliban in the State Department deliberately brushed aside intelligence about the Taliban's internal divisions in order to remove the temptation (strong in circles close to the Pentagon) to exploit Taliban divisions for merely tactical purposes.[26]

A specific aspect of Taliban politics that was overlooked when framing Washington's disengagement strategy was the relationship with al-Qaeda. From 2011 onward the Americans and some of their allies, notably the British, tried to recast the rationale for the intervention in Afghanistan as exclusively focused on destroying al-Qaeda's presence there. It was hoped that such a recasting would ease negotiations with the Taliban and justify disengagement after the large expenditures and significant loss of human life. Arguably the presence of al-Qaeda in Afghanistan was probably never enough to require a massive military intervention to handle it, but the problem in this narrative was that after having almost been wiped out in 2001, al-Qaeda was resurgent in Afghanistan after 2012. Although as of 2016 its presence was still more than modest, the trend made it difficult to justify disengagement in terms of "we have won and we can leave," as Washington and London were doing. The Pentagon, unable to directly confront President Obama on the issue after the sackings of a few prominent generals, tried to undermine a reconciliation/disengagement policy it did not like by highlighting the presence of al-Qaeda and its splinter organization Daesh (another name for ISIS) with statements and military operations.[27]

Perhaps more importantly, al-Qaeda maintained relations with some prominent Taliban leaders, a fact that could have cast doubt on the sincerity of their intention of focusing exclusively on the Afghan jihad. According to sources within al-Qaeda itself, until 2015, among the beneficiaries of al-Qaeda funding were some of the key players in the reconciliation process, like Akhtar Mansur. Al-Qaeda dropped support for Mansur in late 2015 and his motives for accepting al-Qaeda's aid might have been pragmatic, such as accessing funding. Nonetheless, a comprehensive assessment of the reconciliation/disengagement policy by American diplomats should have featured this risk as well.[28]

In sum, because of the failure to consider divisions within the Taliban leadership, the Americans were trapped in an uneasy situation as of spring 2016, with a commitment to withdraw entirely by the end of 2016 that could not be honored and without the political will to recommit sufficient forces to definitely prevent further Taliban military gains. The risk of a collapse of a client government in Afghanistan was looming.

Conclusion

Despite the huge resources committed to Afghanistan after 2001 and particularly from 2008 onward, American intelligence on the Taliban remains weak and too focused operationally, largely missing not just the internal political dynamics of the Taliban but also the evolution of its military organization and the incorporation of new networks into the Taliban. The US military also regularly misreported and overstated the capabilities and the progress being made by the Afghan security forces. On this basis, the framing of a disengagement strategy could hardly have been very successful. On the other hand, the Americans (or at least President Obama) did understand perhaps as early as 2009 that committing more resources (human and financial) to Afghanistan would not win the conflict per se; what was needed was to get America's Afghan partners to start playing a more proactive role in the war.

Obama also understood that complex regional politics would have prevented the Americans from gaining a decisive upper hand and that moving toward a political settlement was the only way of potentially appeasing the regional powers. However, he managed neither to get the Afghans to successfully take control over the conflict nor to fully engage the regional powers. The Pakistanis did not manage to establish a productive relationship with Kabul, despite some efforts and Chinese support for reconciliation, while the Iranians were never engaged in the reconciliation agenda.

As of 2016 the Americans were betting on committing the least possible amount of resources to the battlefield required to avert the collapse of the Afghan security forces, while at the same time trying to improve the capabilities of those forces, mainly by putting pressure on the Afghan government to replace some of the more incompetent commanders. However, such a line of action was incompatible with making progress on reconciliation: the key proreconciliation figure among the Taliban, Akhtar Mansur, had concluded by March 2016 that he could not afford to make any move in that direction as long as US troops were engaged in combat operations.[29] From the American perspective the risk was not just an inconclusive conflict dragging on, but it also gave the different factions of a badly splintered Taliban a common agenda: committing to the battlefield against the beleaguered Afghan security forces, even if for different reasons (achieving military triumph or improving leverage at the negotiating table). Considering how badly bruised the Afghan security forces were during the 2015 fighting season, when only in October the Taliban had committed a large portion of their resources to the battlefield, the threat of a general Taliban offensive was a serious one.

In Afghanistan as in a number of other conflicts before it, the conflict might end with the Americans who have not so much ended the war as disengaged from it. The war in Afghanistan was continuing in 2016, despite attempts to reach a negotiated settlement. The Americans dramatically reduced their commitment by 2015 and planned in early 2016 to reduce it further in 2017, even if complete disengagement had not been decided yet. The Trump administration was, as of the end of 2016, going to include several veterans of Afghanistan, including generals Flynn and Mattis, and despite Trump's stated intention of disengaging during the presidential campaign, it seems likely that his administration will decide to stay put. As might have been the case elsewhere too, the Americans did not opt for disengaging without producing a transition plan to empower their local allies, which was termed "Afghanization."[30] However, the plan was flawed because it was based on false premises. It is too early to say why the Americans, despite their huge and unrivaled intelligence assets, failed to put together a more solid transition plan. It has been argued that Obama, negatively impressed by the costs of achieving progress in Afghanistan, decided that he needed to cut the costs no matter what.[31]

Friction between the Obama administration and the US military might have played a role in the latter misreporting about progress in the preparation of the Afghan security forces, although the problem had existed even under the Bush administration. It is not surprising that the US military might have portrayed the military capability of the Taliban has having been eroded by the surge of 2009–2011, given that they had strongly advocated the surge and led it. The Obama administration should, however, have had access to other assessments by a host of intelligence agencies, which should have been able to question the Pentagon's view. From time to time, press reports suggested that different assessments did circulate in Washington and that the civilian intelligence agencies tended to be less optimistic than the military ones. The belief that hurting the Taliban in Helmand and Kandahar would be enough to force them to bow continued to stick.

It is not known (and might not be known for a long time) what the intelligence agencies were reporting about the inner politics of the Taliban, but some of the ongoing friction and infighting was reported even in the media, so it would be surprising if agencies like the CIA had completely missed it. The Pentagon appears to have stressed the persistent presence of al-Qaeda and the newly established presence of Daesh, in contrast to a tendency of the State Department to minimize the residual role of al-Qaeda and to dismiss the presence of Daesh as spurious. The purpose might have been to undermine the administration's line of negotiation and disengagement.

In sum, an administration eager to disengage picked the suitable elements of the analysis and of the intelligence provided by a host of agencies in order to justify its policy to Congress and the public. This is not unusual in liberal democracies, of course, but as Afghanistan once again demonstrated, there is no guarantee that policy making of this kind would result in coherent or viable strategy.

Antonio Giustozzi is an independent researcher born in Ravenna, Italy, who took his PhD at the London School of Economics and Political Science (LSE). He is the author of several articles and papers on Afghanistan, as well as of five books, *War, Politics and Society in Afghanistan, 1978–1992* (Georgetown University Press, 2000), *Koran, Kalashnikov and Laptop: the Neo-Taliban Insurgency, 2002–7* (Columbia University Press, 2009), *Empires of Mud: War and Warlords in Afghanistan* (Columbia University Press, 2012), *Policing Afghanistan* (with M. Ishaqzada, Columbia University Press, 2013), and *The Army of Afghanistan* (Hurst, 2016). He also authored a volume on the role of coercion and violence in state building, *The Art of Coercion* (Columbia University Press, 2011), one on advisory missions (*Missionaries of Modernity,* Hurst, 2016) and edited a volume on the Taliban, *Decoding the New Taliban* (Columbia University Press, 2009), featuring contributions by specialists from different backgrounds, and one on DDR processes, *Post-conflict Demobilization, Disarmament and Reintegration: Bringing State-Building Back In* (Ashgate, 2012). He carried out various unpublished research projects on drug smuggling and corruption. He is currently publishing a new book on the Islamic State in Afghanistan, Pakistan, and Central Asia and is starting a new project on people smuggling from Afghanistan.

Notes

1. Mark Landlermay, "US Troops to Leave Afghanistan by End of 2016," *New York Times,* 27 May 2014; Greg Jaffe and Missy Ryan, "Obama Outlines Plan to Keep 5,500 Troops in Afghanistan," *Washington Post,* 15 October 2015.
2. Department of Defense, "Enhancing Security and Stability in Afghanistan: Report to Congress in Accordance with Section 1225 of the Carl Levin and Howard P. 'Buck' McKeon National Defense Authorization Act (NDAA) for Fiscal Year (FY) 2015 (P.L. 113–291)," Washington, Department of Defense, 2015.
3. See Antonio Giustozzi and Artemy Kalinovsky, *Missionaries of Modernity: Advisory Missions and the Struggle for Hegemony, from the 1940s to Afghanistan* (London: Hurst, 2016); Antonio Giustozzi, *The Army of Afghanistan: A Political History of a Fragile Institution* (London: Hurst, 2016); Antonio Giustozzi and Mohammad Ishaqzadeh,

Policing Afghanistan: The Politics of the Lame Leviathan (London: Hurst, 2013); Antonio Giustozzi and Ali Mohammed Ali, "The Afghan National Army after ISAF," Kabul: AREU, March 2016.
4. Giustozzi and Mohammed Ali, "Afghan National Army after ISAF."
5. Sayed Sharif Amiry, "Afghan Air Power Developed after Security Agreement: MoD," TOLOnews, 7 April 2016.
6. Giustozzi and Mohammed Ali, "Afghan National Army after ISAF"; Giustozzi, *Army of Afghanistan*; Antonio Giustozzi, *The Taliban at War, 2001–2018* (Oxford: Oxford University Press, 2019).
7. Ibid.
8. Giustozzi, *Army of Afghanistan*.
9. For commentary from US sources on the Afghan army and police, see Giustozzi, *Army of Afghanistan* and Giustozzi and Kalinovsky, *Missionaries of Modernity*.
10. Lynne O'Donnell, "US Official: Major Changes underway in Afghan Army Units Battling Taliban in Helmand Province," Associated Press, 25 January 2016.
11. Paul D. Miller, "The Long War: Obama's Failed Legacy in Afghanistan," *The American Interest* 11, no. 5, 15 February 2016.
12. Theo Farrell and Antonio Giustozzi, "The Taliban at War: Inside the Helmand Insurgency, 2004–2012," *International Affairs* vol. 89, no. 4, July 2013; Giustozzi, *Taliban at War*; "The Taliban and the "Pakistani Reservoir": On the Importance of the Afghan Community in Pakistan for the Taliban's Military Effort," in S. Gregory, ed., *Democratic Transition and Security in Pakistan* (London: Routledge, 2015).
13. Giustozzi, *Taliban at War*.
14. Anthony Shaffer, *Operation Dark Heart: Spycraft and Special Operations on the Frontlines of Afghanistan* (Edinburgh: Mainstream, 2010), 180ff.
15. Giustozzi, *Taliban at War*.
16. Ibid.
17. Antonio Giustozzi, "The Military Adaptation of the Taliban, 2002–2011," in *Fighting the Afghanistan War: States, Organisations and Military Adaptation* (Stanford: Stanford University Press, 2013).
18. Giustozzi, *Taliban at War*.
19. Ibid.
20. Ewen MacAskill and Simon Tisdall, "White House Shifts Afghanistan Strategy towards Talks with Taliban," *The Guardian* (London), 19 July 2010.
21. Mona K. Sheikh and Maja T. J. Greenwood, "Taliban Talks Past, Present and Prospects for the US, Afghanistan and Pakistan," (Copenhagen: DIIS, 2013); Giustozzi, *Taliban at War*.
22. Antonio Giustozzi and Silab Mangal, "The Taliban in Pieces: The Internal Struggle behind the Announcement of Mullah Omar's Death," *Foreign Affairs* Snapshot, 3 August 2015; Barnett Rubin, "What Could Mullah Mohammad Omar's Death Mean for the Taliban Talks?" *The New Yorker*, 29 July 2015; Barnett Rubin, "Turmoil in the Taliban," *The New Yorker*, 31 July 2015.
23. Antonio Giustozzi and Silab Mangal, "An Interview with Mullah Rasool on Reconciliation between the Taliban and the Afghan Government," RUSI Commentary, 16 March 2016.
24. Interviews with Taliban leaders and commanders in Pakistan, Helmand and Kunduz, September–November 2015, January 2016.
25. Ibid.
26. See, for example, Jeffrey Dressler, "Reconciliation with the Taliban: Fracturing the Insurgency," Washington, DC: Institute for the Study of War, 2012.
27. Interviews with Taliban and al-Qaeda Cadres, February 2016; Putz Catherine. "Is al-Qaeda Back in Afghanistan?" *The Diplomat*, 15 April 2016.

28. Ibid.
29. Sources in the Quetta Shura, contacted in March 2016.
30. Hasse Holmberg, "Exit by Afghanisation," Copenhagen: Royal Danish Defence College, 2014.
31. Miller, "The Long War".

Select Bibliography

Farrell, Theo, and Antonio Giustozzi, "The Taliban at War: Inside the Helmand Insurgency, 2004–2012," *International Affairs* 89, no. 4 (2013).

Giustozzi, Antonio, "The Military Adaptation of the Taliban, 2002–2011," in *Military Adaptation in Afghanistan*, ed. Theo Farrell, Frans Osinga, and James A. Russell (Stanford, CA: Stanford University Press, 2013).

―――, *The Army of Afghanistan: A Political History of a Fragile Institution* (London: Hurst, 2016).

Giustozzi, Antonio, *The Taliban at War, 2001–2018* (Oxford: Oxford University Press, 2019).

Giustozzi, Antonio and Mohammad Ishaqzadeh, *Policing Afghanistan: The Politics of the Lame Leviathan* (London: Hurst, 2013).

Giustozzi, Antonio and Artemy Kalinovsky, *Missionaries of Modernity: Advisory Missions and the Struggle for Hegemony, from the 1940s to Afghanistan* (London: Hurst, 2016).

Miller, Paul D., "The Long War: Obama's Failed Legacy in Afghanistan," *The American Interest* 11, no. 5, 15 February 2016.

Shaffer, Anthony, *Operation Dark Heart: Spycraft and Special Operations on the Frontlines of Afghanistan* (Edinburgh: Mainstream, 2010).

Sheikh, Mona K., and Maja T. J. Greenwood, "Taliban Talks Past, Present and Prospects for the US, Afghanistan and Pakistan," (Copenhagen: DIIS, 2013).

Part III

The Cultural and Strategic Costs of War in the Early Twenty-First Century

In reading the preceding sections, readers may be struck by the extent to which the United States repeated the same errors time after time and showed the same lack of interest in both regional political dynamics and the local consequences of their actions. It is fair to ask why this should be the case. After all, wasn't one of the major consequences of the Vietnam War that, despite their best efforts, policymakers could not turn the page? As ably demonstrated by David Kieran and Robert K. Brigham, the Vietnam War did not end in the minds of policymakers and the American public. There seems to be very few signs of a reckoning with the lessons of Iraq and Afghanistan. What lessons are emerging are, in many ways, simplistic extensions of the instrumental lessons of Vietnam, which were crafted with US culture rather than local particulars in mind. Indeed, in some ways, the ability to comprehend local dynamics has been *worse* in more recent conflicts. Famously, Robert McNamara was torn by guilt over his decisions on Vietnam; it seems unlikely that Donald Rumsfeld suffers similar pangs of guilt.

In this final section, our contributors attempt to make sense of this continuity by offering some broader reflections on American failures to end wars in the twenty-first century. Andrew Bacevich and Scott Lucas locate this failure in the realm of the strategic imagination. In his chapter on how the United States has responded to strategic failure in these wars, Bacevich focuses on civil-military relations and failures to understand the political dynamics of wars. Bacevich argues that civil-military harmony is not a sign of a relationship that is working well, but rather marks a fundamental evasion of the responsibility for critical self-reflection. Policymakers and military leaders have prioritized a focus on operations and tactics that refuses to confront more difficult political questions on the misuse of American power or continuities between the various military campaigns being waged all around the world in perpetuity.

In his essay on the challenges for 21st-century US foreign policy and intervention, Scott Lucas offers a pessimistic analysis and argues that one of the reasons that Americans have failed to confront these political questions is because the very concept of "ending wars," as framed by US policymakers and by analysts, is obsolete. Conflicts no longer operate according to top-down, state-centric conceptions of the United States in the world. Indeed, these "new wars" follow scripts that are in many ways unintelligible to Americans, with the kaleidoscope of events, actors, and motivations on the ground meaning that these conflicts cannot be understood through American-centered narratives or solved by American-led solutions. Even as the character of warfare has changed dramatically, American thinking is still stuck in old ways. Perhaps here, even the idea of "exit" represents the traditional lowering of the flag and departure without reflection on the strategic impact on US credibility and reputation. Lucas instead argues for a much more ambitious vision of a cosmopolitan political response to these conflicts, one that goes beyond American-centric visions of war.

Yet in asking why the United States has failed to end its wars in the twenty-first century, it is not enough to focus on the inadequacies of American strategy. What has been striking about these contemporary wars is just how long they have run and how little public protest they have sparked. Indeed, there is an echo of earlier imperial histories in that the wars felt distant; the blood and violence was beyond the realm of recognition so domestic dissent could be contained and the wars could grind on. Thus, the final two essays in the volume reflect on how US culture has both influenced and absorbed the failures to end war in order to understand the ways in which these wars have been able to continue relatively undisturbed in a way that was not true for the war in Vietnam.

David Fitzgerald's chapter examines how US society has welcomed soldiers home from war and argues that with the notable exception of the Gulf War, the absence of victory in post-World War II conflicts often has made the experience of homecoming, and particularly its public celebration, a fraught one. The changing nature of these celebrations, however, reflects the ways in which the American public has begun adapting itself to an era of unending war. "Support for the troops" has become a reflexive, passive act that fails to paper over the cracks between the All-Volunteer Force and the society it serves. Few Americans now understand war or its consequences, and the rush to display gratitude to returning soldiers elides any broader public debate about American wars and the failure to end them.

Finally, through an analysis of the coverage of Vietnam War anniversaries, Marilyn Young demonstrates how outcomes short of victory have been obscured, denied, and transformed in elite discourse. Echoing Wolfgang Schivelbusch's work on the "culture of defeat," Young shows how the "transmogrification of defeat" in Vietnam into Reagan's celebration of a "noble cause" and the erasure of both Vietnamese perspectives and the question of American culpability for the war offers a model for how the United States handles defeats more broadly.[1] Young concludes her essay by noting that with "the task of historic erasure complete, the health of the state guaranteed, the future is safe for eternal war." The ambition of this collection of essays has been to help reflect on that historic erasure and to argue that the United States must confront the long-term consequences of its wars and reckon with what it has left behind.

Note

1. Wolfgang Schivelbusch, *The Culture of Defeat: On National Trauma, Mourning, and Recovery*, trans. Jefferson Chase (New York: Picador, 2004).

Chapter 9

Changing the Subject
How the United States Responds to Strategic Failure

Andrew J. Bacevich

A successful marriage is one in which partners find ways of reconciling their own individual needs with those they share as a couple. The challenge is to enable *me* and *you* to coexist with *us* in relative harmony. To indulge in wedding day illusions of being exempt from such challenges—to fancy that a new *us* transcends *me* and *you*—is to guarantee mutual disappointment. The sooner all parties jettison such illusions the better.

Similar challenges are infused into civil-military relations. There, harmonizing the interests of political leaders with those of the armed services in ways that serve the well-being of the nation as a whole requires more than solemn pledges of fealty and mutual respect.

Failed wars exacerbate such challenges. A marriage plunged into crisis due to the loss of a job or of a child may find partners unable to provide one another with solidarity and support precisely when they are most needed. So too with civilian and military leaders faced with confronting a military enterprise gone badly awry. In such circumstances, incentives to dodge painful truths by denying responsibility or offloading blame can become irresistible. As a consequence, problems contributing to failure fester, almost guaranteeing their recurrence at some future date.

The way the American political establishment and the US military responded to serial failures first in Vietnam and then in its post-9/11 "War on Terrorism" offers a case in point. In both instances, civil-military dysfunction adversely affected the war's actual conduct. In both, continuing dysfunction impeded efforts to discern why that failure had occurred and what corrective action might be in order.

The contemporary US civil-military relationship emerged during the early years of the Cold War, a direct result of a tradition-shattering decision to maintain on a permanent footing a large and powerful military establishment, pursuant to President Harry Truman's 1950 approval of NSC 68 ("United States Objectives and Programs for National Security") as a blueprint for rearmament. Prompting this break from past practice was the emergence of "national security" as an organizing principle of US policy, transcending mere "national defense" and consigning diplomacy to the status of afterthought.

The armed forces of the United States now became instruments of global power projection.[1] As a result, questions related to recruitment, composition, equipping, and employment of those forces acquired unprecedented political significance. The increased salience attributed to military matters—along with the money and prerogatives at stake—drew senior admirals and generals into issues previously beyond their purview. The divide once separating the military and civilian realms blurred.

Renegotiating the rules governing civil-military relations played itself out in a series of contentious issues and often crises that occurred between 1946 and 1951. The issues involved related to the control of nuclear weapons, the size of the Pentagon budget, racial and gender integration, defense "unification," the adjudication of service roles and missions, and the conduct of the Korean War.

Breached and battered, the principle of civilian control survived these crises, but in attenuated form. Without anyone paying much attention, the relationship between senior civilian officials and senior military officers had become deeply politicized. By the 1960s, mutual manipulation had long since displaced mutual respect as its defining characteristic.[2]

Although the factors that made Vietnam such a debacle are legion, the absence of honest dialogue between President Lyndon Johnson and Defense Secretary Robert McNamara on the one hand and the Joint Chiefs of Staff (JCS) on the other made a mighty contribution. Rather than providing their civilian bosses with unvarnished and forthright professional advice, members of the JCS fancied that they might game their civilian bosses into fighting the war their way. For their part, Johnson and McNamara viewed the brass not as a source of wisdom and counsel, but as a problem to be managed. In that regard, the JCS fell into the same category as the Congress, the press, or public opinion. While going through the motions of consultation, the real aim for Johnson and McNamara alike was simply to keep the JCS on board.[3]

Much the same can be said of the post-9/11 wars, especially during Donald Rumsfeld's tenure as Pentagon chief. Determined to prosecute the Global War on Terrorism his way without interference, Rumsfeld effectively marginalized the JCS and suppressed dissenting opinion coming from within the officer corps, most notoriously by his de facto silencing of army chief of staff General Eric Shinseki for daring to express reservations about US plans to invade Iraq in 2003. Although the defense secretary got his way, the results were not pretty. If the art of war requires that effective military action align with judiciously defined political purpose, then the conflicts in Iraq and Afghanistan stand on a par with Vietnam as examples of how not to do it.

The ultimate test of any system is how it responds to failure. Here too, it must be said, the existing American civil-military relationship leaves much to be desired.

Evading Vietnam

The US military responded to failure in Vietnam by effectively changing the subject. Institutionally, it turned its back on the type of warfare that Vietnam represented. There, on battlefields far from home, the massing of materiel, the lavish use of firepower, and the application of advanced technology—the methods that then defined the American way of war—had not sufficed to provide a positive outcome. The enemy had stubbornly refused to abandon its cause. Among the factors enabling the North Vietnamese to prevail were geographic proximity, historical legitimacy, helpful allies, discipline ruthlessly enforced from above, and a willingness to die for their cause in very large numbers. In the end, the outcome turned on which side cared more about the ultimate fate of Vietnam.

There was much here worthy of reflection, not least of all why the United States allowed itself to be drawn into the war in the first place and how the commanders who presided over it so badly misconstrued the problem at hand. Yet the chief lesson that the US military took away from Vietnam was this very simple one: Never again. With something close to unanimity, members of the officer corps agreed that never again would US forces allow themselves to become entangled in a "dirty war" pitting conventional forces against irregulars with the people for whom the war was ostensibly being waged present on the battlefield and thereby becoming active participants, whether as victims, hostages, or combatants.

Rather than forgetting Vietnam, the American officer corps evaded it. Through the 1970s and 1980s the US military remained haunted by all that had gone wrong with its Southeast Asian misadventure. Vietnam had been a nightmare and as such was never to be revisited. Asserting that henceforth US forces would engage exclusively in conventional conflicts pitting army against army with civilians on the sidelines obviated the need for any such visitation.

In November 1984, Secretary of Defense Caspar Weinberger codified the military's own "lessons" of Vietnam by promulgating what subsequently became known as the Weinberger Doctrine. The doctrine's purpose was to establish clear-cut criteria for when and how US forces were henceforth to be used. Among its provisions were the following: that the United States should commit forces only if vital national interests are at stake; that it should do so only if fully committed to winning and with military and political objectives clearly defined; that in the event of objectives changing, the size and composition of the forces committed be adjusted accordingly; that any commitment of US forces occur only after ensuring full public and congressional support; and, finally, that the United States resort to force only after exhausting all other alternatives.

With this aim in mind, the US military refashioned itself into an instrument optimized for high-intensity, decision-oriented combat against forces that were more or less a mirror image of itself. By refining a conception of combined arms warfare dating from World War II, senior officers leading America's ground, air, and naval forces sought to achieve supremacy in any future conflict that pitted state against state and army against army. Given such aims and expectations, the American officer corps wasted little time in contemplating the challenges inherent in fighting irregulars, much less in people's war more broadly. These were contingencies that officers viewed as too remote to be worth the bother.[4] To the extent that such contingencies nonetheless presented themselves, military leaders handed them off to the Central Intelligence Agency or looked to local indigenous forces to do the fighting with the role of American regulars limited to providing advice and training.

In political circles, a similar strategy of evasion took hold. The Vietnam War was one factor among several undermining the liberal consensus that had defined American politics since the advent of the New Deal. At home, that consensus had found expression in a regulated form of corporate capitalism that promised (and to some degree delivered) widely shared abundance. Abroad, it took the form of "liberal internationalism," a euphemism for a pattern of interventionism that depending on circumstance could be overt or covert, multilateral or unilateral, sustained or episodic, adhering to or casually flouting legal and moral norms. The bureaucratic apparatus erected to regulate the domestic political economy found its counterpart in a sprawling national security state of which the military itself was the largest and most generously supported component.

Imparting to these arrangements a seeming impregnability was the overriding importance assigned to the ongoing Cold War as a contest pitting freedom against slavery. The seeming omnipresence of the Cold War in the US global encounter bolstered the ostensible requirements of the national security state and its apparatus, thus privileging the militarization of the Cold War US culture.

Beginning in the mid-1960s, however, these arrangements fell from favor. With startling abruptness, the prevailing cultural winds shifted. Whether this shift was to be welcomed, opening the door to greater authenticity and self-expression, or lamented, sanctifying vulgarity and self-indulgence, depended on one's point of view. Cultural upheaval drew its energy from seemingly unrelated events such as assassinations, race riots, revelations of misconduct at the highest levels of government, and increasing sensitivity to the processes of decolonization and revolution that were having a transformative impact on the developing world. Above all, there was Vietnam itself, the ultimate "war of liberation," which ground on seemingly without end. In any event, protest infused with calls for radical change became the order of the day.

As a consequence, by the beginning of the 1970s, the disciplinary authority of the Cold War had eroded badly. The depiction of the Soviet-American rivalry as a Manichean struggle, once all but taken for granted, no longer commanded broad assent, especially among those for whom assent carried the prospect of combat in Indochina. That *we* were as responsible as *they* for the afflictions and injustices besetting humankind now gained credence, at least in some quarters.

What made the critique coming from the far left particularly worrisome was the way that it aggregated complaints into a single, semicoherent package. Evil done abroad in places like Vietnam (or Cuba or the Congo) stemmed directly from arrangements at home that if not evil were at the very least hypocritical. Democracy was a charade, American ideals fraudulent. Rather than a beacon of liberty, Amerika stood with the imperialist oppressors. So radical leftists forcefully insisted.[5]

Restoring political consensus meant disaggregating this critique and draining radicalism of its energy. This stands as the principal, yet seldom recognized, achievement of the Reagan era. Ostensibly a totem of conservatism, President Reagan rescued and revived postwar American liberalism. Revolutionary ferment subsided. While there was no repealing the sixties—sex, drugs, and rock and roll remained central to the American scene—a semblance of normalcy was restored. Corporate capitalism returned to the ascendancy. The seat of Evil Empire became once more a reference to the Kremlin rather than to Washington, DC. Above all, Reagan's designation of Vietnam as a "noble cause" transformed that war from a symbol of all that was wrong with America into a subject of solemn remembrance, with those who had served there elevated to the status of honored heroes. Reagan thereby drained the war of its political significance.

Testifying to his success in doing so was the abbreviated existence of the Vietnam Syndrome—the widespread conviction that the United States should refrain from further armed intervention abroad lest it find itself mired in another Vietnam-like quagmire. Within a mere handful of years, Reagan was chipping away at Vietnam-induced constraints on the use of force, sending the Marines into Lebanon, "liberating" Grenada, bombing Libya, and jousting with Iran in the Persian Gulf. Reagan's successor, George H. W. Bush, built on his legacy, invading Panama and then fighting an abbreviated, but large-scale war against Iraq. In early 1991, barely a decade and a half after the fall of Saigon, Bush happily declared, "By God, we've kicked the Vietnam syndrome once and for all."[6]

At that moment, the political effort to evade Vietnam—to deny its significance—achieved success. For proof, one need look no further than the record of Bush's successor, a Democrat. As a young man, Bill Clinton had opposed the Vietnam War and had successfully avoided military service there. As commander in chief, he used force with greater frequency than either Reagan or Bush. As a reference point in the formulation of policy, the relevance of Vietnam had begun to fade. By extension, the war itself—why the United States had intervened, what it did there, and what had resulted—had nothing or nearly nothing essential to say about America or Americans.

By the 1990s, the American political establishment and the American military establishment found themselves on the same page: Vietnam had lost its capacity to teach. On this point at least, a superficial form of civil-military harmony existed.

Evading the "Global War on Terrorism"

Something similar has occurred (and continues to occur) with regard to the US military actions undertaken in the wake of 9/11. Once more, in circumstances calling for critical self-reflection, both military and civilian elites have studiously avoided serious examination of what the episode once known as the Global War on Terrorism has actually wrought and at what cost.

In this case, the evasion finds expression in military hostilities that drag on in something approximating perpetuity. Today authorities in Washington no longer refer to a Global War on Terrorism. The hostilities in which the United States remains involved have no official name, even though they are generically referred to as "overseas contingency operations." Nor do they have any clearly identifiable purpose. There too generic language prevails. US troops fight, for example, "to keep us safe" or to "defeat terrorism."

Indeed, in elite circles and more generally with the American public, the current tendency is to classify recent and ongoing US military operations, largely concentrated in the Islamic world, as an open-ended series of more or less unrelated campaigns. In that sense, the fighting in Iraq stands apart from fighting in Afghanistan, not to mention from turmoil in Libya, Somalia, and elsewhere in the Greater Middle East. Many dots exist. Authorities in Washington, civilians and military alike, show little inclination to connect them.

Furthermore, according to this view, prior US military involvement in these countries (and others in the Islamic world) that predates 9/11 has no bearing on US participation in the ongoing violence in these countries today. So, for example, Americans willfully discount or simply ignore the possibility of a causal relationship linking the First Gulf War of 1980–1988 (Washington supporting Saddam Hussein), the Second Gulf War of 1990–1991 (Washington punishing Saddam), the Third Gulf War of 2003–2011 (Washington ousting Saddam and occupying Iraq), and the Fourth Gulf War dating from 2014 (Washington attempting to pull Iraq back from the abyss of disintegration).

We may compare this studied myopia to pretending that the European war of 1939–1945 had nothing to do with the European war of 1914–1918 that preceded it or the Cold War that followed swiftly on its heels—that each of these three events stands alone. Few thoughtful observers would find such a claim persuasive. Yet when it comes to the varied and sundry US interventions in the Islamic world over the past several decades, American political and military elites alike indulge this tendency. Rather than considering connections and continuities, their preference is for treating each campaign as sui generis.

This disregard for continuities is not without its benefits. Slicing and dicing history into bite-sized morsels makes serious self-reflection unnecessary or confines it to the narrow realm of operations and tactics. Larger questions related to purpose, costs, and prospects of success—to the very concept of strategy itself—go unattended.

Since the onset of the Global War on Terrorism in 2001, for example, the US military has cycled through as least four distinctive approaches to waging that war.

During the first phase, running from 2001 through 2003, belief in the so-called Revolution in Military Affairs (RMA) exercised a dominant influence on US military practice. Speed, agility, and accuracy derived from exploiting advances in information technology would provide ensured victory. So the officer corps persuaded itself and so the rapid ouster of the Taliban in Afghanistan and of Saddam Hussein in Iraq seemed to affirm.

When pacifying those two countries proved more difficult than the United States and its allies had expected, the RMA lost much of its luster. As an alternative, US forces turned to counterinsurgency, or COIN—a methodology seemingly discredited by Vietnam but now revived, first tentatively but eventually with full-throated enthusiasm. Yet this love affair with COIN proved to be brief, peaking in Iraq during the period 2007–2008 and in Afghanistan during the period 2009–2010. Whether or not COIN *might have* enabled the United States eventually to prevail in Iraq and Afghanistan is a moot point. In practice, the American people lacked the patience and the US military the requisite number of troops to test that proposition. A serious commitment to COIN would have required some version of mobilization—and nobody, either civilian leaders or uniformed ones, had the stomach for that. So by the summer of 2010, enthusiasm for COIN had already begun to wane. It soon thereafter joined the RMA on the heap of fashionable ideas found wanting when put into actual practice.

Without missing a beat, the Pentagon devised yet another approach. Since invading countries (using the RMA as a template) and occupying them (adhering to COIN "best practices") had proven a bust, the US military now opted for a variant of attrition. This third methodology emphasized the use of air power, to include missile-firing drones, and special operations forces employed as a hit-and-run strike force. Together air attacks and small-scale ground operations would—so it was assumed—take out jihadist leadership cadres and reduce the capacity of militant organizations to launch attacks, the object of the exercise having tacitly shifted from winning conflicts to keeping them within manageable limits.

By 2013, events in Iraq and Syria revealed the limitations of decapitation. The rise of the Islamic State (also known as ISIS or ISIL) prompted the administration of Barack Obama to extemporize yet another approach. With the Islamic State seizing vast swathes of territory, to include Mosul, Iraq's second largest city, and with Obama himself loath to reintroduce large numbers of American ground troops, the anti-ISIS campaign emphasized an amalgam of aerial bombardment, commando raids, and a reliance on proxies to do most of the actual fighting and dying. The principal role of US forces, aided by coalition partners, was to equip, train, and motivate Iraqi Kurds, Iraqi Shiites, and Iraqi Sunnis, not to mention Syrian "moderate rebels" to take on ISIS directly.

Results proved mixed. The announced timetable for liberating Mosul, a key US objective, and the Syrian city of Al Raqqa, capital of the Islamic State, slipped repeatedly. And while Iraqi forces made gradual progress in regaining captured territory, the Islamic State demonstrated a troubling ability to persist and to expand, with new "franchises" created in Egypt, Libya, Nigeria, and elsewhere. ISIS also sowed considerable panic in the West by orchestrating or inspiring successful terrorist attacks in France, Belgium, and even the United States itself.

By the summer of 2016, for Americans a presidential election year, it was impossible to say whether the anti-ISIS campaign was going to end successfully or indeed how long it was likely to last. Candidates for the presidency vied with one another in vowing, if elected, to escalate US efforts to destroy the Islamic State—suggesting the possibility that a *fifth* approach to "shaping" events in the Persian Gulf might be in the offing.

The importance that all candidates (and most media commentators) attributed to eliminating ISIS carried with it implied expectations that doing so would somehow eliminate or at least substantially reduce anti-Western jihadism itself and thereby restore stability to the Greater Middle East. In fact, such thinking was entirely fanciful. ISIS was not the problem. It was merely a symptom.

For the American national security apparatus, the Global War on Terrorism had, in effect, evolved into a series of operational experiments conducted in an environment devoid of overarching political purpose. In simple terms, America's decades-long military enterprise in the Greater Middle East continued without any end in sight, policymakers lacking the imagination to conceive of an alternative. In that regard, US military leaders served as tacit enablers for their civilian counterparts. Both parties in the civil-military relationship steered clear of first-order questions such as "what is the overall aim?" and "how exactly will we win?" Tactics—along with an unwillingness among senior civilians and senior officers alike to shoulder responsibility for disappointing outcomes—took precedence over strategy.

In sharp contrast to the Vietnam era, a public largely insulated from the war's negative effects did not rise up in protest against Washington's demonstrated inability either to win wars or to end them. To a remarkable extent, by the second decade of the twenty-first century, Americans had come to accept engagement in armed hostilities as a normal condition. By extension, those responsible for actually conducting war, civilian and military leaders alike, got a pass. Accountability became little more than a theoretical proposition—not for the first time in modern American history.

This is not to say that American citizens had been rendered entirely passive. Indeed, on both the left and the right, episodes of dissent and even outrage erupted—the Tea Party, the Occupy Movement, Black Lives Matter each in its own way demonstrating that Americans retained a capacity for large-scale and, indeed, angry political mobilization.

Unlike the protests of the 1960s, however, none of these movements yielded a comprehensive critique of the US approach to national security and the misguided military interventions undertaken pursuant to that approach. During the Vietnam era, domestic concerns and national security concerns intersected. During the first and second decades of the twenty-first century, they seemingly occupied two distinct and quite separate spheres.

The rise of Donald Trump, who in 2016 successfully captured the Republican Party itself, illustrates the point. "Trumpism" represents a revival of right-wing populism, an expression of profound discontent with the political, economic, and cultural status quo. Trump's success stemmed in considerable part from his instinctive talent for channeling antielite resentment. Yet Trump's legions pay remarkably little attention to the elites responsible for the conduct of America's wars, a point illustrated by public concurrence in Trump's appointment of an unprecedented number of recently retired senior officers to fill top positions in his administration.

Trump and his supporters subscribe to a sort of petulant nationalism captured by the phrase "America First," which Trump appropriated as a campaign slogan. But Trump himself showed no greater inclination to offer a broad-gauged critique of US military activism in the Islamic world than did his opponent Hillary Clinton—a reticence shared by ranking generals and admirals by no means interested in a public stocktaking of the campaigns over which they have presided.

Here too, in other words, an ironic and deeply pernicious civil-military harmony was forged—a steadfast refusal shared by all parties to probe too deeply into how the misuse of American military power may have contributed to the mess in which the United States finds itself today across much of the Islamic world.

Looking ahead to the further application of American military might—what US forces can or must do next year or the year after in confronting the Islamic State—provides a handy excuse to avoid examining what the armed forces of the United States have been doing for the previous several decades and with what results.

Whether the aim of American policy in the Islamic world has been to liberate, dominate, or pacify, US military exertions there have failed. Arguably, US military interventions have actually made matters worse. In Washington, however, that failure remains off-limits for discussion as do the costs incurred as a result, bowing before a blind determination to press on.

As in Vietnam so too in the Greater Middle East, the American response to failure has been to pretend otherwise, thereby in all likelihood laying the basis for yet further failures to come.

Andrew J. Bacevich graduated from West Point and Princeton, served in the army, became an academic, and is now a writer. He is the author, coauthor, or editor of a dozen books, among them *American Empire* (Harvard University Press, 2002), *The New American Militarism* (Oxford University Press, 2005), *The Limits of Power* (Henry Holt, 2008), *Washington Rules* (Metropolitan, 2010), and *Breach of Trust* (Metropolitan, 2013). His latest book, *The Age of Illusions: How America Squandered Its Cold War Victory* (Metropolitan Books), was published in 2020.

Notes

1. This argument is developed in greater detail in Andrew J. Bacevich, *Washington Rules: America's Path to Permanent War* (New York: Metropolitan, 2010).
2. Michael J. Hogan, *A Cross of Iron: Harry S Truman and the Emergence of the National Security State, 1945–1954* (Cambridge: Cambridge University Press, 1998). Regarding the implications for US civil-military relations, see Andrew J. Bacevich, "Elusive Bargain: The Pattern of US Civil-Military Relations Since World War II," in Andrew J. Bacevich, ed., *The Long War: A New History of US National Security Policy since World War II* (New York: Columbia University Press, 2007), 207–64.
3. See the now classic account by H. R. McMaster, *Dereliction of Duty: Johnson, McNamara, the Joint Chiefs of Staff and the Lies That Led to Vietnam* (New York: Harper Collins, 1998).
4. For further elaboration, see Andrew J. Bacevich, *The New American Militarism: How Americans Are Seduced by War* (New York: Oxford University Press, 2005), especially chap. 2.
5. "You Don't Need a Weatherman to Know Which Way the Wind Blows," 18 June 1969, rchive.org/stream/YouDontNeedAWeathermanToKnowWhichWayTheWindBlows_9 25#page/n0/mode/2up, accessed 10 January 2017.
6. George H. W. Bush, "Remarks to the American Legislative Exchange Council," 1 March 1991.

Select Bibliography

Bacevich, Andrew J., "Elusive Bargain: The Pattern of US Civil-Military Relations since World War II," in Andrew J. Bacevich, ed., *The Long War: A New History of US National Security Policy Since World War II* (New York: Columbia University Press, 2007).

———, *The New American Militarism: How Americans Are Seduced by War* (New York: Oxford University Press, 2005).

———, *Washington Rules: America's Path to Permanent War* (New York: Metropolitan, 2010).

Hogan, Michael J., *A Cross of Iron: Harry S Truman and the Emergence of the National Security State, 1945–1954* (Cambridge: Cambridge University Press, 1998).

McMaster, H. R., *Dereliction of Duty: Johnson, McNamara, the Joint Chiefs of Staff and the Lies That Led to Vietnam* (New York: Harper Collins, 1998).

Chapter 10

How Wars Do Not End
The Challenges for Twenty-First Century US Foreign Policy and Intervention

Scott Lucas

In 2010 Gideon Rose published his highly regarded explanation of *How Wars End*.[1] In his fluent narrative, he moved through cases from World War I to the 2003 Iraq War to remind US policymakers that "he who does not learn from history is doomed to repeat it." Specifically, he proclaimed that American officials had not thought through the political endgame of conflict.

Rose's goal might be admirable, but his guide fell into the same trap that, in his rendering, had caught politicians and generals. Just as US leadership was always fighting the last war, so was Rose as he wrote his preface to invoke the contemporary challenges of Libya and Afghanistan. His 432 pages depicted a concept of "war" that had been surpassed amid the carnage after the US invasion of Iraq in 2003.

That war may well have been the last that follows the script of a defined casus belli—even if it was based on the falsehood that Saddam Hussein's Iraq possessed weapons of mass destruction—for the defined end of toppling or forcing the surrender of the enemy's leadership. It may also have been the last that was the result of a deliberate "grand strategy," in this case the Bush administration's pursuit of a global dominance, a "preponderance of power" against any rival or group of rivals.[2] It may have demonstrated that, in contemporary warfare and politics, there is no possibility of such a preponderance.

With the quick collapse of Mission Accomplished into protracted chaos, resistance to occupation, and civil war, the Bushian vision of dominance evaporated. Its conception of a US-led order in which others followed an American center—the mythical "unipolar moment," the term promoted by the conservative columnist Charles Krauthammer[3]—was shattered. So was the notion of a war in which the United States led a Coalition of the Willing to conquer a foe opposed to its values and threatening to its interests. It was replaced by the interventions fought, even before Iraq, not against a state but for the slogan "War on Terror"; by the internal risings that defied the criteria of war or peace; by the morphing of transnational movements with no state center;[4] and by a full spectrum of twenty-first century covert operations that replaced the idea of overt military aggression.

This range of phenomena, part of Mary Kaldor's framing of "new wars"[5] but also beyond Kaldor's depiction, undermines the "war" of both American leaders and the analysts like Rose who critique them. This is because they do not operate according to the top-down conception of the United States in the world. They start with the ground-level patterns of tension, conflict, and possible cooperation. The invocation of learning is misapplied; it is not about the United States, its presidents, and its generals. It is about the kaleidoscope of movements on the ground.

Misleading Scenarios

In the Rose-ian conception of American policy, the US leadership finds itself in the middle of a war but then encounters—or rather fails to cope with—important political decisions. In World War I, Woodrow Wilson and his advisors dither over the postwar German system. In Rose's representation of World War II, Franklin Roosevelt and his agencies do not plan for postwar confrontation with the Soviet Union. In the Korean conflict, bureaucratic haggling over voluntary repatriation extends the war by eighteen months. In the first Gulf War, the George H. W. Bush administration looks for the "magical Iraqi" solution of an internal rising to depose Saddam. In the second, the George W. Bush administration repeats the magical Iraqi exercise—but this time flying a small group into Iraq from the United States and US bases—rather than carrying out effective postwar planning.

Some of this is useful for the historian's reconsideration. Some is superficial, as in failure to connect the issue of voluntary repatriation to the psychological and ideological dimension and aims of US foreign policy; some is misleading, as in the failure to acknowledge the planning during World War II that envisaged the next conflict with the Soviets. Much of it is divorced from wider recognition of the strategic, such as George W. Bush administration's pursuit of a "war of choice" for its aim of preponderance.

But the larger and more important challenge is that the cases may be peripheral to the issues of intervention faced today by the US government. In part, this is because they are far from complete. From 1945 to 2003, most consideration was of strategies and actions outside wartime, offering a range of counterpoints to Rose's hypothesis. The occupation of Japan and Germany and the Marshall Plan for European recovery can be posited as interventions in which the outcome was supported by planning that envisaged the local challenges. US covert action can be framed as effective or as destructive and counterproductive. Decades of economic and military assistance, under banners such as Alliance for Progress, pursued the notions of "modernization" and "security" that pursued political tactics to avoid "hot war" while still maintaining superiority over the enemy. While the programs often had limited or counterproductive outcomes, they were an approach beyond Rose's framing of war and peace.

After 2003, there has been no case of war to test Rose's hypothesis. Considering Iraq from civil war to surge to withdrawal is beyond *How Wars End*. Afghanistan—which was never a conventional war—presents questions of political reconstruction, counterinsurgency, and economic and social development. The Arab Spring conflicts such as those in Libya, framed inaccurately by Rose, are distinctive precisely because they offer situations and thus lessons for intervention or nonintervention outside war. They are political and social shifts, often violent, that will not and cannot end until a complexity of economic, cultural, and religious concerns and aspirations are either marginalized or pacified beyond existence.

The Demise of the "Old War"

One response to Rose is to widen the frame of war and thus the perspective on US policy and decision making, a possibility first offered by Mary Kaldor in 1999 through her presentation of "New and Old Wars." She suggested:

> a blurring of the distinctions between war (usually defined as violence between states or organized political groups for political motives), organized crime (violence undertaken by private organized groups for private purposes, usually for financial gain), and large-scale violations of human rights (violence undertaken by states or politically organized groups against individuals).[6]

She also noted "a myriad of transnational connections so that the distinction between internal and external, between aggression (attacks from abroad), and repression (attacks from inside the country), or even between local and global, are difficult to sustain." Thus, for Kaldor "new wars" are a revolution in the "social relations of warfare," rather than technologies, to be understood in the context of globalization.[7]

In this framing, the Iraq War of 2003—and the US intervention that launched it—is an exception rather than the rule, at least in its construction by Washington for the period between the first bombings of 20 March and George W. Bush's false declaration of "Mission Accomplished" on 1 May. In the administration's conception of the conflict, this was an exercise of overwhelming air and ground power to topple a regime led by an iconic figure, primarily to prevent the tyrant's use of weapons of mass destruction but also to liberate an undifferentiated, homogeneous "Iraqi people." The war was framed in the terms of World War II, with a clear mission against a single threatening foe, with an American power representing both the security and the values of an international order—even if much of the international community was skeptical about the intervention or even opposed to it.[8]

However, this construction of the war soon collapsed in reality. It was not just, as Rose portrays, that the American conception of an Iraqi administration led by exiles such as Ahmed Chalabi lacked legitimacy. A series of social, political, and economic conditions—exacerbated but not solely caused by the missteps of the US-led Coalition Provisional Authority—immediately fueled an insurgency against the American occupation. Those conditions also fed a conflict in which Iraqi groups, some influenced by foreign and transnational actors, turned on each other. By August 2003, as bombers attacked both the embodiment of the international (the UN offices in Baghdad, with the diplomat Sérgio Vieira de Mello and other staff among at least twenty-two fatalities) and of national factions (Ayatollah Mohammad Baqir al-Hakim of the Supreme Council for Islamic Revolution in Iraq), Kaldor's scenario of "new war" appeared to be fulfilled.

That scenario did not just arise as an aftermath of the US invasion. Its conditions were present in Iraq before March 2003, and indeed before the Gulf War of 1991, even if the multiplicity of groups and the transnational connections were contained to a great extent by the repression of Saddam Hussein's regime. But this diversity of local, ethnic, religious, and political factions—some with ties to outside actors with interests in Iraq—was largely ignored by the Bush administration, which blithely thought the vast majority of grateful Iraqis would have "flowers in their minds" as they welcomed US soldiers and officials,[9] and which apparently showed no cognizance of the hundreds of thousands of Iraqis whose deaths before 2003 were connected with US-led sanctions. The State Department's Future of Iraq Project did not effectively consider Iraq's future, despite the mythology that the detailed approach to a postconflict country—largely dismissed by the administration as it went to war—could have provided legitimacy, stability, and rehabilitation.

If only by default, the breakdown of the US invasion of Iraq, and the accompanying difficulties in Afghanistan after the operations to remove the Taliban from Kabul in November 2001, forced Washington policymakers back to a world in which the conventional notion of war was largely discarded. The Bush administration covered up the complications with phrases expanding the War on Terror to the Long War or the Global War on Terror,[10] but the option of starting and thus ending wars through the large-scale deployment of US forces was all but off the table. The Obama administration rhetorically buried the concept in March 2009 with this instruction to officials, "This administration prefers to avoid using the term Long War or Global War On Terror (GWOT). ... Please pass this on to your speechwriters." They replaced it with "overseas contingency operations."[11]

But of course the dismissal of the old war offered no concept of how—and whether—to fight any new ones. How did US policymakers, their agencies, and their militaries in overseas contingency operations get to grips with the "blurring of the distinctions" that encompassed transnational groups and organized crime as well as authoritarian regimes that could inflict mass killing upon their populations?

Even before its departure, the Bush administration used revised if incomplete constructions to address the question. For Iraq, the presentation was of a surge that could both defeat the transnational threat and cope with sectarian civil war by uniting local groups against the common menace of "al-Qaeda in Iraq." The Obama administration went further by invoking the transnational "terrorists" that justified a buildup of US forces in Afghanistan—even though the challenge was from the locally based Taliban.[12] Obama increased the use of drone warfare against transnational groups in Afghanistan, Pakistan, Yemen, and Somalia, expanding not only the conception of geographical space but also the frame of legitimacy of a war, notions that were peripheral—if relevant at all—for many as the campaign against al-Qaeda finally brought the demise of Osama bin Laden in 2011.

The military operations against the reality or illusion of the transnational terrorists did not engage the local conditions of the new wars. For this, the Obama administration introduced the Quadrennial Diplomacy and Development Review in 2010. The elevated rhetoric of the "common purpose"—"to harness our civilian power to advance America's interests and help make a world in which more people in more places can live in freedom, enjoy economic opportunity, and have a chance to live up to their God-given potential"—was deployed through areas such as "Diplomacy for the 21st Century," "Transforming Development to Deliver Results," "Preventing and Responding to Conflict and Crisis," and "Working Smarter."[13]

The QDDR (Quadrennial Diplomacy and Development Review) was still a mechanistic approach rather than one building up from a recognition of the specific local conditions. It was beholden, as was the accompanying Web 2.0 strategy, to Joseph Nye's vision of a soft power—now represented as "smart power" to include a "hard" military component[14]—in which the United States would persuade others to do what America wanted, rather than the United States beginning with what local constituencies desired. This ran counter to supposed lessons of the Vietnam War, such as a definition of objectives with relation to the desires of local constituencies, but if the combination of military operations, diplomacy, and development could contain challenges on the ground, there might be enough space to extricate the United States from its post-2003 bind. The timetable was set for an American withdrawal of combat forces from Iraq by the end of 2010 and a drawdown in Afghanistan, even though deadlines for full withdrawal were moved from the end of 2014 to December 2016 to an indefinite terminal point.

What this scenario could not anticipate were local conditions elsewhere that might escape containment and—in the regional as well as Kaldor's conception of globalization—interact with each other to escalate political, social, and economic disruption. In this case, the unexpected began in the town of Sidi Bouzid in Tunisia, with the self-immolation of an unemployed vegetable vendor named Mohammad Bouazizi on 17 December 2010.

New Conflicts, New Interventions

Four weeks after Bouazizi set himself on fire, Tunisian leader Zine El Abidine Ben Ali ended his 23-year rule. Four weeks after that, Egypt's Hosni Mubarak left after thirty-one years. Within the next four weeks, there were mass protests in Yemen and Bahrain and signs of discontent in Iraq, Jordan, and Algeria. Libya's Muammar Gaddafi—the second-longest serving head of state after the United Kingdom's Queen Elizabeth II, as he would proclaim to his citizens—faced an uprising. And the detention of a group of boys spraying graffiti in the city of Daraa in southern Syria started the first demonstrations against the Assad family, who had held power since 1970.

The range of local but intersecting rallies across the Middle East and North Africa offered an unprecedented challenge to a post-Cold War United States. The George W. Bush administration invoked a "Freedom Agenda" in 2005, exalting the "color revolutions" in former Soviet states and the Cedar Revolution in Lebanon, but this was more of an attempt to impose optimism on the imminent catastrophe in Iraq than the expression of a developed policy. Secretary of State Condoleezza Rice proclaimed in a speech at the American University in Cairo in June 2005:

> The principles enshrined in our Constitution enable citizens of conviction to move America closer every day to the ideal of democracy. Here in the Middle East, that same long hopeful process of democratic change is now beginning to unfold. Millions of people are demanding freedom for themselves and democracy for their countries. To these courageous men and women, I say today: All free nations will stand with you as you secure the blessings of your own liberty.[15]

However, this soon faded even if some nongovernmental organizations (NGOs) persisted with the idea.

In 2011, the Obama administration, having only just claimed its end to combat in Iraq, faced situations that were not about entry into, or exit from, war. They were not further expressions of the transnational that had occupied the rhetorical center of US foreign policy since 2001. They were local demonstrations that might bring the repression constitutive of the "large-scale violations of human rights" in Kaldor's construction of new wars, but in some cases this would be a repression by regimes the United States had supported for decades. Did these events constitute a case for intervention beyond diplomatic representation? Did they raise a "responsibility to protect," the doctrine considered by the international community after the 1990s experiences of the Balkans and Africa?

The administration's response, after weeks of indecision, was to try to manage the situation while limiting any overt American intervention. With the Egyptian protests growing despite attempts to repress them, Washington sent an envoy to try to persuade President Hosni Mubarak to give up power. When Mubarak defied the envoy with two televised speeches promising to fight to the death, the Americans turned to the Egyptian military.[16] The United States backed Saudi Arabia in its support of the Bahraini regime to quell mass demonstrations: in March 2011 as the monarchy carried widespread detentions and used force against the protests, Riyadh sent in armored vehicles and personnel.[17] In both

Yemen and Syria, it encouraged leaders—Ali Abdallah Saleh and Bashar al-Assad, respectively—to pursue reforms to temper public opposition.[18]

However, in March 2011, the administration faced a decision that would bring out the complexities of intervention. With the Gaddafi regime's ground forces, including armored units, on the verge of moving into the second city, Benghazi, with more than one million residents, the United States joined others—including European allies and the Arab League—in supporting a protected area in eastern Libya. Officially, the step was an extension of a "no-fly zone" authorized by the UN Security Council; however, in practice, the decision allowed immediate attacks on Gaddafi's army, not only to secure the zones but also to remove the capacity for any future assault.[19]

There were multiple convergent reasons that produced the American shift. A bureaucratic union was forged between Hillary Clinton, the former presidential candidate and now secretary of state who believed that the United States had acted too slowly in the Egyptian case and thus had been on the wrong side of history for not supporting protesters against an oppressive regime; National security official Samantha Power, who rose to prominence with high-profile scholarly work on genocide; and UN Ambassador Susan Rice. In part, looking to perceived international failures in the 1990s, they believed that Benghazi was a case for humanitarian intervention and a case that they had the responsibility to protect. President Obama's caution was addressed by the presentation of alliance politics—with the Arab League, NATO, and the UN—in which the United States was leading from behind.

But beyond all these motives was a lack of clarity over whether intervention constituted war. While this was a state-based confrontation of another state, both the nature of that confrontation and the context for it were ill defined. Would the defense of Benghazi and then of eastern Libya lead to an effort to defeat and remove the Gaddafi regime? Or was the de facto outcome to be an effective partition of the country, with Gaddafi retaining control in Tripoli and western areas and a new government for the east? If the external allies of the United States had been carefully established, the internal dynamics were not. The Libyan situation involved a series of political factions, militias, and armed groups, many based on local interests rather than a national conception. The United States threw its weight behind the creation of the National Transitional Council (NTC), but it was unclear if that council had legitimacy across the east, let alone enough for any effort to replace Gaddafi.[20]

This was a case that was more a Kaldorian new war than a state on state military conflict. It involved multiple political groups and private armed forces as well as the allegations of systematic violations of human rights fueling an uprising. Having entered this new war, the US government and NATO appeared to be uncertain in its prosecution. Even if the intervention in Afghanistan from 2001 offered a model, with aerial and covert support of armed factions used to topple the regime in the capital, this offered a far from hopeful vision. So the aerial operations gradually expanded across Libya, but with no clear political approach. The injunction of the 1980s Weinberger Doctrine to intervene only with defined objectives, capabilities, and public assent were left behind.

When Moammar Gaddafi suddenly fell in October 2011, soon to be lynched by a militia, this vacuum in planning was exposed. The NTC was unable to establish itself as a legitimate ruling authority at the national level. Efforts to organize a Libyan Army were challenged by the sustained power of the local militias working with local political factions. Those militias in turn complicated efforts to establish infrastructure, including the revival of the oil industry, on a national basis.[21]

The Case of Nonintervention

If Libya exposed the complexities of intervention—and thus the difficulties of it—in a situation that did not fit a Rose-ian conception of war, it was far from the end of the challenge. The Obama administration was also in the midst of a deliberation culminating in the damaging effects of nonintervention.

Immediately after the start of the uprising against Syria's Assad regime in March 2011, the administration hoped Damascus would carry out reforms to meet some of the demands of protesters. But as the regime responded with force—and as the Libyan and Yemeni risings gathered momentum—Washington reevaluated its position. In August, President Obama asserted:

> The future of Syria must be determined by its people, but President Bashar al-Assad is standing in their way. His calls for dialogue and reform have rung hollow while he is imprisoning, torturing, and slaughtering his own people. We have consistently said that President Assad must lead a democratic transition or get out of the way. He has not led. For the sake of the Syrian people, the time has come for President Assad to step aside.[22]

As with Libya, the Syrian case was marked by a diversity of local groups—political, military, and religious. By the autumn, those communities were beginning to arm in self-defense, with a Free Syrian Army declared by regime defectors as well as local men taking up weapons. Yet there was the prospect of a national force, if the international community could support its establishment in Turkey. This could have defined a war with an organized political and military structure to confront the Assad regime. However, before this emerged, the regime exploited a vital difference from the Libyan conflict. Unlike Gaddafi, President Assad could call on an air force that began to bomb against the threat of an opposition taking control. In February–March, the intense bombing scored its first major success by securing—at the cost of widespread devastation and several hundred civilian deaths—most of Syria's third-largest city, Homs.[23]

Facing a regime that was willing to use all aerial means in a new war—by August 2012, the regime was resorting to barrel bombs, oil canisters filled with explosives—administration officials such as Secretary of State Clinton and CIA Director David Petraeus returned to the concept of no-fly zones. This time, however, Obama balked because of his concern over unforeseen consequences. Invoking the mantra, "Don't do stupid shit," he vetoed the plan.[24]

The CIA did give limited assistance to some rebel factions, but Obama's rejection of the no-fly zone set a decisive pattern in restricting US action. The president had said that the use of chemical weapons was a red line, but when the Assad regime's military did so by spring 2013, Washington did not react. And when Assad's forces resorted in August to using sarin nerve agent near Damascus, killing at least 1,400 people, the president made a U-turn after a walk in the White House's Rose Garden as his advisors waited for an expected decision for intervention.[25]

Instead of offering an alternative to the Libyan case, the US nonintervention fed further fragmentation of the conflict. Local rebel factions proliferated, with outside backers such as Turkey, Saudi Arabia, and Qatar favoring different groups. Transnational groups entered the arena: in 2012, the Islamic State sent in the Syrian Abu Mohammad al-Jolani and fighters as Jabhat al-Nusra, and in 2013 ISIS crossed the Iraqi border in its attempt not only to be involved in the conflict but to reshape it.

Far from acknowledging its inaction, the United States tried a tangential approach. Obama and Secretary of State John Kerry followed a Russian lead in requiring that the Assad regime give up its chemical stockpile. Damascus eventually handed over the large majority of its stock but continued the chemical warfare through the use of chlorine, which is not banned by international conventions. Washington then accompanied Moscow in a purported political process to resolve the crisis, only for Russia to change the dynamics with its military intervention to prop up Assad, including thousands of attacks on opposition territory, from September 2015.[26]

Meanwhile, Obama and his advisors pursued another diversion. Rather than focusing on the dynamic between the opposition rebel factions and the regime, they identified the primary threat as the Islamic State. In September 2014, three months after ISIS's lightning offensive took much of neighboring Iraq, the administration began bombing ISIS. At the same time—in a testament both to the fragmentation of the conflict and to the move to the tangential approach—US warplanes began striking Jabhat al-Nusra. The move from the regime to extremists and jihadists as the center of activity continued with the creation of the US-supported, Kurdish-led Syrian Democratic Forces to push back ISIS in northeast Syria.[27]

None of this brought any prospect of a resolution, particularly of Syria as a unitary state. Instead, the gathering possibility was of a de facto partition of a country. The Assad regime controls most urban areas, including Syria's largest city Aleppo after ground assaults, bombing, and a siege led by Russia, Iran, and Hezbollah. The opposition and rebels, despite the loss of Aleppo, hold almost all of Idlib Province in northwest Syria, as well as some southern areas. In addition, Turkey's intervention alongside rebels from August 2016 has seized much of Aleppo Province from the Islamic State. The Kurds have effective autonomy over much of north and northeast Syria after the success of the SDF (Syrian Democratic Forces) and American backing, despite Turkey's wariness about the ties of the leading Kurdish faction PYD (Partiya Yekîtiya Demokrat, Syria's Democratic Union Party) and its YPG (Yekîneyên Parastina Gel, People's Protection Units) militia with the Turkish Kurdish insurgency PKK.

But the approach sidelined the United States as an actor in the conflict. Having pulled Washington along, first to get space for its military intervention and then to buy time for offensives eroding the opposition rebel position, Russia linked up with Turkey and Iran to broker its preferred political and military system. Excluded from the renewal of indirect negotiations between the regime and the opposition rebels, Washington's relevance was reduced to a minority section of the country, as the backer of the SDF.[28]

Failing in the "New Wars"

Both the US government and those such as Rose who purport to critique it have been exposed by the kaleidoscope of conflict in twenty-first century areas, such as Libya and Syria, because of an outdated conception of the nature of the state in war. The political and military confrontation of a state or group of states confronting another unitary state or group is the exception—marked by Iraq between March and May 2003—rather than the new rule. Rather, an American administration faces multiple factions within and beyond national boundaries. The relations between those groups cannot be engaged simply by proposing the restitution of a state with the trappings of a constitution, a legislature, and nation building.

Confronted by this, the Obama administration pursued a variety of sometimes incoherent, often incomplete strategies. It promised to curb involvement in Iraq and Afghanistan—although this was soon overtaken in the latter case by the perceived threat of the Taliban—for the national government to establish and extend legitimacy. It initially watched the surges of the Arab Spring before framing a case for humanitarian intervention, but without considering what lay beyond that immediate protection across the rest of Libya. It chose indecision, behind the rhetoric of a red line as the Syrian conflict escalated.

Perhaps most significantly, it chose diversion. Not only in Syria but in other insoluble cases like Yemen, the administration created a false center of the Islamic State or Al Qa'eda as the primary challenge. Obama held up "ISIL"—not even using the full name of the group, "Islamic State of Iraq and the Levant [Syria]"—to detach it from local contexts. Instead of situating ISIL in the complexities of the Syrian conflict to define US intervention, Obama abstracted the group as another variant of the global terrorist menace: "It is recognized by no government, nor by the people it subjugates. ISIL is a terrorist organization, pure and simple." As the military increasingly sought to portray airstrikes as ways of decapitating the enemy, and thus the supposed answer to the threat, officials spoke of extremists and jihadists rather than of the local factions involved in the conflict.[29]

Thus Obama and his officials removed the United States from the new war, replacing the local with a caricature. Months before the surprise ISIS offensive that captured Iraqi cities such as Mosul and Tikrit, the president belittled the organization, "If a jayvee [junior varsity basketball] team puts on [professional Los Angeles] Lakers uniforms, that doesn't make them [star player] Kobe Bryant." Only when pressed by interviewer David Remnick that the Islamic State had just taken over the city of Fallujah in western Iraq did Obama address the local context, only to immediately deviate:

> Fallujah is a profoundly conservative Sunni city in a country that, independent of anything we do, is deeply divided along sectarian lines. And how we think about terrorism has to be defined and specific enough that it doesn't lead us to think that any horrible actions that take place around the world that are motivated in part by an extremist Islamic ideology is a direct threat to us or something that we have to wade into.[30]

In the case of Syria, Obama tried to defend the US refusal to provide rebels with weapons with the derisory label of "an opposition made up of former doctors, farmers, pharmacists, and so forth."[31]

The Trump administration, which took office in January 2017, has offered even less of an indication that it will reengage with the core of the Syrian conflict. In its headline intervention in April 2017, US missiles struck the Assad regime airbase from which a sarin attack was launched on a town in northwest Syria, killing at least ninety-two people and injuring hundreds. However, beyond that single event, the military's sustained effort is still limited to support of the Kurdish-led SDF in the north of the country in their campaign against the Islamic State. US support has been withdrawn from rebels unless they commit solely to operations against ISIS and not against pro-Assad forces.[32]

Politically, the US presence is even more marginal than in the latter Obama years. Washington has been excluded from the Astana and Geneva processes, led by Russia, which have set out deescalation zones but at the same time permitted Moscow and regime aircraft to continue striking opposition areas. The Russians have brought in the United States only when convenient for the Kremlin's interests, for example, in a jointly proclaimed deescalation zone in southern Syria near the Israeli demilitarized zone in the Golan Heights.[33] Trump's priority, beyond claiming credit for the April missile strikes and "killing ISIS" has been ensuring that Syrian refugees do not enter the United States but instead remain in the region, suggesting that Gulf States can pay for this as "they have nothing but money."[34]

Confronting the Locals

Kaldor's new wars point to the necessity of US officials beginning with a recognition of the multiple local forces and contexts. However, US administrations usually start with a focus on an opposing state, or even an individual leader of the state, while setting aside the consideration of what lies beyond the president and the capital. In the case of Syria, it was Obama's decision in August 2011 to announce sanctions on Damascus with the demand that Assad step aside. There have been numerous lost opportunities to remedy this deficiency, options forsaken in part of the specter of fighting the last war in Iraq in 2003. There was the lack of reaction to the devastation of Homs as Assad turned to reliance on airpower. There was the rejection of no-fly zones in summer 2012, and the passivity before the Assad regime's chemical attacks in 2013. There were the repeated failures to establish effective links with local opposition groups and rebel factions from 2012 through the end of 2013, when forces realigned in blocs such as the Islamic Front, through the successful rebel offensive of spring 2015. There was the acceptance of Russia's military intervention in September 2015 while paradoxically working with Moscow in pursuit of a mythical ceasefire.

It was too late to regain any of these opportunities, but with the looming partition of Syria, there was another possibility, maybe the last, for the United States. A study by Lucas, Wolff, and Yakinthou argued:

> [The challenge is to] connect the legitimacy recently conferred on various Syrian actors by the Geneva negotiations and other international discussions to existing and future local arrangements establishing stability and security on the ground. These, in turn, are necessary conditions for a credible and sustainable transition from the current civil war. Arrangements put in place now for governance, reconstruction, provision of services, justice and civic engagement will lay the foundation for, and shape the direction of, the political, legal, economic and social constructions that will be necessary if there is ever again to be a meaningful "Syria" in the sense of a single state, or even if several entities emerge in the aftermath of the civil war. These arrangements must be made now, rather than waiting for a terminal moment in the conflict. They must be based on recognition of the necessity of a "bottom-up" approach, establishing connections with local groups rather than imposing a preconceived international model of the proper, "moderate" procedures and actors.[35]

This was only the start of an engagement facing difficult challenges. With President Assad rejecting a transitional process in which he might have to give up power, both the past accountability of the regime for abuses and measures to prevent these from recurring had to be considered. In opposition areas, tensions across the range of political and military factions, which often hold disparate views on governance and justice, should have been addressed with provision for recovery and reconstruction. Kurdish autonomy had to be approached to mitigate clashes both among Kurdish groups and between Kurdish factions and actors such as Turkey. However, this start with recognition of the local was better than the alternatives of inaction, withdrawal, or a counterproductive alliance with the Syrian state.

Rethinking War and the End

Returning to new wars in 2013, Kaldor responded to critiques with the summary, "The aim of describing the conflicts of the 1990s as 'new' is to change the way scholars investigate these conflicts and thus to change the way policy makers and policy shapers perceive these conflicts." She restated her hypothesis of the "main new elements" in "the destructiveness and accuracy of all forms of military technology," globalization's effects through communications and the changing state, and the significance of identity politics.[36]

This conceptual approach is still valuable, but it fails to offer any insight into the place and manner of intervention—and thus of the challenges for US foreign policy—in this twenty-first century environment. Indeed, Kaldor's framework appears to culminate in a fatalist portrayal: "The inner tendency of such [new] wars is not war without limits, but war without end. Wars, defined in this way, create shared self-perpetuating interest in war to reproduce political identity and to further economic interests." On the one hand, this appears to reduce any outside response to passivity; on the other hand, it reduces local actors to an inescapable role in a long-term, possibly perpetual, conflict. It is a reduction that Kaldor seems to acknowledge in her conclusion: "What is still lacking in the debate is the demand for a cosmopolitan political response."[37]

In her book *Cosmopolitan Peace*, Cécile Fabre argues for this response through attention to "just ... transition from war to peace and peace after war." This exposition on *jus post bellum* tries to establish the philosophical cosmopolitanism to recognize and support the local: "All human beings wherever they reside have rights to the resources and freedoms that they need in order to live a flourishing life, against all other human beings."[38] Still, the large obstacle remains, highlighted by conflicts in Syria and elsewhere: what if we never get to a position of just transition?

The 1990s notion of "responsibility to protect" developed in large part to address this notion of "just transition." However, it foundered on the same fallacy that besets Rose's *How Wars End*: both assume that the mission must culminate in an endpoint centered on the state. Whether it is reinforced, reformed, or retracted, there is a presumed stability in which threat is met and legitimacy is restored.

But oftentimes the answer to General David Petraeus's "tell me how this ends"—uttered with respect to the unraveling of US intervention during and after the 2003 Iraq War—is "It doesn't." When considered not from the top down of challenging a threatening state but from the ground up of providing what can be a long-term—but still an interim—shelter for Fabre's "rights to resources and freedoms," the challenge is a reconstructed notion of intervention for the local.

Barack Obama's "Don't do stupid shit" was not a cautious, considered response to that challenge, but an evasion of it. Paradoxically, through that evasion, the response in Syria sidelined the United States from the military and political center and buttressed the Assad regime that was supposed to be confronted. It left the United States, apart from the support of a Kurdish-led force to battle the sideshow of the Islamic State, with only one answer to how this conflict ends: disengagement. Rose's approach is now peripheral; Kaldor's new wars fatalism becomes a default position.

Derek Chollet, an Obama administration official, gave the game away in a December 2016 interview, when he explained that the US focus was soon not on the conflict between Assad and the opposition or on any effect on the Syrian people:

> By 2012 and 2013, [the issue of chemical weapons] was certainly the overriding concern of the administration. What do we do to ensure that 1,300 tons of Syrian chemical weapons are not used or end up in the wrong hands? It was a concern of ours, but also of the Israelis, and of others in the region.[39]

Analysts such as Joshua Landis erased those Syrians as they reduced the situation to *"extremists v. the Assad regime"*: "We are strategically allied with Assad. He is a bulwark against the spread of ISIS [the Islamic State]. ... If America destroyed Assad ... who's going to take Damascus? It's going to be ISIS and [Jabhat al-] Nusra."[40]

In 2009, accepting the Nobel Peace Prize, Barack Obama hailed "America, the world's sole military superpower" acting out of "enlightened self-interest": "The plain fact is this—the United States of America has helped underwrite global security for more than six decades with the blood of our citizens and the strength of our arms."[41]

Eight years later, Obama's cosmopolitan declaration is an artifact of the past rather than a marker of the present. Unless war and intervention are reconsidered, both by US policymakers and those who study them, it will remain so.

Scott Lucas is professor of international politics at the University of Birmingham and a journalist who is founder and editor of EA WorldView (www.eaworldview.com). His academic work includes eleven books, such as *Divided We Stand: The US, Britain, and the Suez Crisis* (Scepter, 1996); *Freedom's War: The US Crusade against the Soviet Union, 1945–1956* (New York University Press, 1999); *The Betrayal of Dissent: Orwell, Hitchens, and the New American Century* (Pluto, 2004); and *Challenging US Foreign Policy: America and the World in the Long Twentieth Century* (Palgrave Macmillan, 2011). He has authored more than fifty major articles, primarily on post-1945 and contemporary US foreign policy, international relations, and the Middle East and Iran. His journalism includes the day-to-day news and analysis on EA WorldView, one of the leading sites for coverage of Iran, Syria, and the wider Middle East as well as US foreign policy.

Notes

1. Gideon Rose, *How Wars End: Why We Always Fight the Last Battle* (New York: Simon and Schuster, 2010).
2. See Maria Ryan and Scott Lucas, "Against Everyone and No One: The Failure of the Unipolar in Iraq and Beyond," in David Ryan and Patrick Kiely, eds., *America and Iraq: Policy-Making, Intervention, and Regional Politics* (London: Routledge, 2008).
3. Charles Krauthammer, "The Unipolar Moment Revisited," *The National Interest*, Winter 2002/2003, https://www.belfercenter.org/sites/default/files/legacy/files/krauthammer.pdf, accessed 17 December 2017.
4. Wolfgang Schivelbusch argues that, after the illusive pursuit of "the enemy" in Vietnam, it was necessary to act against a Taliban "state" in Afghanistan because the "War on Terror" against al-Qaeda once more threatened. While Schivelbush's analogy may be strained, given that the US did try to destroy a North Vietnamese "state" as well as the insurgency in South Vietnam, his assertion of the necessity of a fight against institutions and a territory supposedly fixed by boundaries—a "containable" war—is apropos (Wolfgang Schivelbusch, *Culture of Defeat: On National Trauma, Mourning, and Recovery* [New York: Metropolitan, 2003]).
5. Mary Kaldor, *New & Old Wars: Organized Violence in a Global Era* (Cambridge: Polity, 2012).
6. Ibid., 2, 4, 220.
7. Ibid.
8. "Bush compares Iraq, terror wars to World War II," CNN, 3 June 2004, http://edition.cnn.com/2004/ALLPOLITICS/06/02/bush.speech, accessed 17 December 2017.
9. Former assistant secretary of defense Douglas Feith, quoted in Jeffrey Goldberg, "A Little Learning," *The New Yorker*, 9 May 2005, https://www.newyorker.com/magazine/2005/05/09/a-little-learning-2, accessed 17 December 2017.
10. Donald Rumsfeld memorandum, 16 October 2003, https://fas.org/irp/news/2003/10/rumsfeld101603.pdf, accessed 17 December 2017.
11. Oliver Burkeman, "Obama Administration to End Use of Term 'War on Terror,'" *The Guardian* (London), 25 March 2009, http://www.theguardian.com/world/2009/mar/25/obama-war-terror-overseas-contingency-operations, accessed 17 December 2017.
12. "Transcript of Obama Speech on Afghanistan," CNN, 2 December 2009, http://edition.cnn.com/2009/POLITICS/12/01/obama.afghanistan.speech.transcript/index.html, accessed 17 December 2017.
13. Leading through Civilian Power: The First Quadrennial Diplomacy and Development Review, https://www.state.gov/documents/organization/153108.pdf, accessed 17 December 2017.
14. Center for Strategic and International Studies, "CSIS Commission on Smart Power," 2007, https://carnegieendowment.org/files/csissmartpowerreport.pdf, accessed 17 December 2017.
15. Condoleezza Rice, "Remarks at the American University in Cairo," 20 June 2005, https://2001-2009.state.gov/secretary/rm/2005/48328.htm, accessed 17 December 2017.
16. Sheryl Gay Stolberg, "Frank Wisner, the Diplomat Sent to Prod Mubarak," *New York Times*, 2 February 2011, http://www.nytimes.com/2011/02/03/world/middleeast/03wisner.html, accessed 17 December 2017; Chris McGreal and Jack Shenker, "Hosni Mubarak Resigns—and Egypt Celebrates a New Dawn," *The Guardian*

(London), 11 February 2017, https://www.theguardian.com/world/2011/feb/11/hosni-mubarak-resigns-egypt-cairo, accessed 17 December 2017.
17. Martin Chulov, "Saudi Arabian Troops Enter Bahrain as Regime Asks for Help to Quell Uprising," *The Guardian* (London), 14 March 2011, https://www.theguardian.com/world/2011/mar/14/saudi-arabian-troops-enter-bahrain, accessed 17 December 2017.
18. Christopher Boucek and Mara Revkin, "The Unraveling of the Salih Regime in Yemen," Carnegie Endowment for International Peace, 31 March 2011, http://carnegieendowment.org/2011/03/31/unraveling-of-salih-regime-in-yemen-pub-43356, accessed 17 December 2017; Center for Prevention, "American Options in Syria," Council on Foreign Relations, 24 October 2011, https://www.cfr.org/report/american-options-syria, accessed 17 December 2017.
19. Kevin Sullivan, "A Tough Call on Libya That Still Haunts," *Washington Post*, 3 February 2016, http://www.washingtonpost.com/sf/national/2016/02/03/a-tough-call-on-libya-that-still-haunts, accessed 17 December 2017.
20. See, for example, Micah Zenko, "The Big Lie about the Libyan War," *Foreign Policy*, 22 March 2016, http://foreignpolicy.com/2016/03/22/libya-and-the-myth-of-humanitarian-intervention.
21. Mahmoud Abdelwahed, "Chaos and Conflict Plague Libya Six Years after Gaddafi's Demise," *Al Jazeera* English, 23 October 2017.
22. Obama speech, 18 August 2011, White House Archives, https://obamawhitehouse.archives.gov/blog/2011/08/18/president-obama-future-syria-must-be-determined-its-people-president-bashar-al-assad, accessed 17 December 2017.
23. Lyse Doucet, "Inside Homs: Syrian 'Ghost Town' Divided and Destroyed," 9 May 2012, http://www.bbc.co.uk/news/av/world-18013789/inside-homs-syrian-ghost-town-divided-and-destroyed, accessed 17 December 2017.
24. Jeffrey Goldberg, "The Obama Doctrine," *The Atlantic*, April 2016, https://www.theatlantic.com/magazine/archive/2016/04/the-obama-doctrine/471525, accessed 17 December 2017.
25. Scott Lucas, "Obama's Legacy Will Be Forever Tarnished by His Inaction in Syria," *The Conversation*, 25 November 2016, https://theconversation.com/obamas-legacy-will-be-forever-tarnished-by-his-inaction-in-syria-67030, accessed 17 December 2017.
26. Scott Lucas, "Why Putin Gambled on Airstrikes in Syria—and What Might Come Next," *The Conversation*, 1 October 2015, https://theconversation.com/why-putin-gambled-on-airstrikes-in-syria-and-what-might-come-next-48414, accessed 17 December 2017.
27. See Asaf Siniver and Scott Lucas, "The Islamic State Lexical Battleground: US Foreign Policy and the Abstraction of Threat," *International Affairs* 92, no. 1 (2016), https://www.chathamhouse.org/publication/ia/islamic-state-lexical-battleground-us-foreign-policy-and-abstraction-threat, accessed 17 December 2017.
28. Scott Lucas, "Syria is on the Brink of Partition—Here's How It Got There," *The Conversation*, 11 January 2017, https://theconversation.com/syria-is-on-the-brink-of-partition-heres-how-it-got-there-70825, .
29. See Siniver and Lucas, "Islamic State Lexical Battleground."
30. "Obama to Chuck: ISIS Not a JV Team," Meet the Press, 7 September 2014, http://www.politifact.com/truth-o-meter/statements/2014/sep/07/barack-obama/what-obama-said-about-islamic-state-jv-team, accessed 17 December 2017.
31. Nick Gass, 'Obama Rebukes Syrian "Fantasy", *Politico*, 10 August 2014, https://www.politico.com/story/2014/08/barack-obama-rebukes-syrian-fantasy-109890, accessed 6 November 2019.
32. Scott Lucas, "Syria Daily: US Strikes Assad Regime for 1st Time, Hits Chemical Weapons Airbase," *EA WorldView*, 7 April 2017, https://eaworldview.com/2017/04/

syria-daily-us-strikes-assad-regime, accessed 17 December 2017; Scott Lucas, "Syria Daily: Rebels—CIA Have Frozen Military Aid," 22 February 2017, *EA WorldView*, https://eaworldview.com/2017/02/syria-daily-rebels-cia-frozen-military-aid/, accessed 17 December 2017.
33. Suleiman al-Khalidi, "Russia, Jordan Agree to Speed De-Escalation Zone in South Syria," Reuters, 14 November 2017, https://uk.reuters.com/article/uk-mideast-crisis-jordan-russia/russia-jordan-agree-to-speed-de-escalation-zone-in-south-syria-idUK-KCN1BM2A2, accessed 17 December 2017.
34. Stephanie Ebbs, "President Trump Says He Will Create 'Safe Zones' in Syria and Get Gulf States to Pay for Them," ABC News, 18 February 2017, http://abcnews.go.com/Politics/president-trump-speaks-campaign-rally florida/story?id=45584942, accessed 17 December 2017.
35. Stefan Wolff, Christalla Yakinthou, and Scott Lucas, "Syria: Laying the Foundations for a Credible and Sustainable Transition," *RUSI Journal*, 22 June 2016, https://rusi.org/publication/rusi-journal/syria-laying-foundations-credible-and-sustainable-transition, accessed 17 December 2017.
36. Mary Kaldor, "In Defense of New Wars," *Stability*, 7 March 2013, https://www.stabilityjournal.org/articles/10.5334/sta.at.
37. Ibid.
38. Cécile Fabre, *Cosmopolitan Peace* (Oxford: Oxford University Press, 2016), 3.
39. Quoted in Aron Lund, "The Long View," 6 December 2016, Carnegie Middle East Center, http://carnegie-mec.org/diwan/66343, accessed 17 December 2017.
40. Quoted in "The President Blinked: Why Obama Changed Course on Syria," PBS Frontline, May 2015, https://www.pbs.org/wgbh/frontline/article/the-president-blinked-why-obama-changed-course-on-the-red-line-in-syria, accessed 17 December 2017.
41. Barack Obama, Nobel Prize Lecture, 10 December 2009, https://www.nobelprize.org/nobel_prizes/peace/laureates/2009/obama-lecture_en.html, accessed 17 December 2017.

Select Bibliography

Fabre, Cécile, *Cosmopolitan Peace* (Oxford: Oxford University Press, 2016).
Kaldor, Mary, *New & Old Wars: Organized Violence in a Global Era* (Cambridge: Polity, 2012).
Rose, Gideon, *How Wars End: Why We Always Fight the Last Battle* (New York: Simon and Schuster, 2010).
Ryan, Maria and Scott Lucas, "Against Everyone and No One: The Failure of the Unipolar in Iraq and Beyond," in David Ryan and Patrick Kiely, eds., *America and Iraq: Policy-Making, Intervention, and Regional Politics* (London: Routledge, 2008).
Schivelbusch, Wolfgang, *Culture of Defeat: On National Trauma, Mourning, and Recovery* (New York: Metropolitan, 2003).

Chapter 11

Coming Home
Soldier Homecomings and the All-Volunteer Force in American Society and Culture

David Fitzgerald

One of the more astute chroniclers of the experiences of the American GI in World War II and the Korean War, the Pulitzer Prize–winning cartoonist Bill Mauldin reflected on the differences between the two wars in 1952. Writing of the American soldier in Korea, Mauldin complained that "he fights in a battle in which his best friends get killed and if an account of the action gets printed at all in his home town paper, it appears on page 17 under a Lux ad." Further, the GI was not guaranteed a warm welcome home: "There won't be a victory parade for his return because he'll come home quietly and alone, on rotation, and there's no victory in the old-fashioned sense, anyway because this isn't that kind of war. It's a slow, grinding, lonely, bitched-up war."[1]

Mauldin's complaints would be deeply familiar to veterans of the United States' wars in Afghanistan and Iraq: there too the homecoming has been muted, the wars' outcome unclear, the public's attention to these long wars flickering in fits and starts. Indeed, the difficulties in defining victory or even an end point to the conflict has confounded even those who wish to celebrate the American soldier. With the notable exception of the Gulf War, the absence of victory in post–World War II conflicts often has made the experience of homecoming, and particularly its public celebration, a fraught one.

The figure of the returning veteran is a recurring theme in American culture, from the War of Independence to the Civil War, World War II to Vietnam, the soldier coming home from war has often been a figure onto which broader anxieties about America's wars have been projected. Civil War veterans were linked to an upsurge in crime and opiate addictions, while even demobilizing the "Greatest Generation" of World War II was not without its difficulties, as impatient draftees led mass protests about delays in demobilization and returning veterans were frequently depicted as troubled souls with a drinking problem.[2]

Veterans returning from Korea and, especially, Vietnam faced an often muted or hostile reception, and the figure of the troubled Vietnam veteran became a cultural trope that symbolized the toll that participation and defeat in that war had wrought on American society. This chapter explores contemporary iterations of those anxieties by focusing on the nature of public celebrations of soldier homecomings. It examines how returning soldiers have been welcomed home from America's wars in the late twentieth and early twenty-first centuries and reflects on the relationship between those celebrations and the evolving place of the all-volunteer force in American society. The wars that the United States has fought in the twenty-first century are characterized not only by their indeterminate ends but by the fact that these lengthy conflicts have been fought exclusively by volunteers, a fact that has affected how soldier homecomings have been enacted.

From the triumphant Desert Storm victory parades of 1991 to the contemporary figure of the lone soldier being thanked for her service in an airport terminal coffee shop, how returning soldiers have been greeted can tell us much about how Americans have viewed both their wars and the role of their armed forces more broadly. In an era when fewer and fewer Americans have experience of service in the military, these occasions, when soldiers are at the forefront of public attention, are all the worthier of attention.

The Shadow of Vietnam

To understand how returning soldiers were celebrated in the era of the all-volunteer force, it is crucial to understand the particular influence of the Vietnam War and the mythology surrounding the veterans of that war. Famously, veterans of that conflict did not get a homecoming parade and, like their counterparts in Korea, they often came home alone and on rotation.[3] Descriptions of disoriented soldiers arriving home and feeling alienated from broader US society, particularly the antiwar movement—are common in both oral histories and memoirs of the war.[4] The isolated veteran, no longer at home in the land that sent him to war, became a familiar theme in US popular culture from Robert De Niro's portrayal of a working-class veteran haunted by the loss of his friends in *The Deer Hunter* to Sylvester Stallone's betrayed and angry drifter in *First Blood*.[5] The veteran became a central symbol of—and participant in—the remediation of collective memory of America's war in Vietnam.[6]

In 1980, presidential candidate Ronald Reagan argued that that United States had "been shabby in our treatment of those who returned. They fought as well and as bravely as any Americans have ever fought in any war. They deserve our gratitude, our respect, and our continuing concern."[7] Even if Reagan's broader lessons of Vietnam were contested, there was a bipartisan consensus that Vietnam veterans had not been welcomed home and had indeed been poorly treated. Veterans themselves had begun to organize politically and to make the case for better access to healthcare and counseling services and for treatment for those who were exposed to Agent Orange.[8]

The emergence of veterans as a political force, as actors as well as symbols, accelerated throughout the 1980s. In particular, the public reaction to the release of the hostages from the US embassy in Tehran in January 1981 drew the anger of many veterans. Throughout the crisis, homes across the United States had been festooned with yellow ribbons in anticipation of their safe return, the first time that particular symbol was used on a mass scale.[9] On their release, the fifty-two hostages, who had been held captive for 444 days, were greeted with parades in Washington, DC and New York and given lifetime passes to baseball games, in stark contrast to Vietnam veterans, who had received no such public adulation.

While the hostages' repatriation in many ways echoed some of the spectacle of Operation Homecoming (the 1973 return of 591 POWs from Vietnam), both of those events lent themselves to spectacle in a way that the return of the vast majority of Indochina veterans did not. Business at veterans counseling centers dramatically increased at the height of the crisis, and the contrast between the two homecomings did not go unnoticed. In a column titled "We Already Had Heroes," Jeremiah Murphy of the *Boston Globe* wrote, "Well we had our heroes, the veterans of the Tet offensive, Hamburger Hill, Marine firebase Ross in the DMZ [demilitarized zone], but we didn't recognize them. We turned our backs on them ... and blamed them for the policies that were actually set in the White House."[10]

Thus, the Iran hostage crisis created a newfound sympathy for Vietnam veterans. An eight-page *Time* cover story, "The Forgotten Warriors," in July 1981 reflected this shift in tone. The article quoted Doug Kamholz, a former antiwar activist who said, "I have been feeling guilty about blaming the war on the warriors. I never yelled 'baby killer,' but I didn't oppose it either. It was a moral and political mistake for the antiwar movement not to see the difference. I hope it's not too late."[11] This sympathy was channeled into the already under way task of memorialization, with veteran-led projects such as the Vietnam Veterans Memorial on the National Mall and hundreds of other smaller monuments springing up across the country.

By the mid-1980s, the Vietnam veteran had gone from pariah to hero, or if not a hero then at least a victim worthy of sympathy. While *Time*'s story on the veterans concluded with a veteran's wife, "with a wan smile," declaring, "I'd love to see a great big parade—one time—national," those parades were not in fact long in coming. On the tenth anniversary of the war's end, twenty-five thousand Vietnam veterans, many of them dressed in remnants of their uniforms, received a ticker tape parade in New York City in May 1985, belatedly following the footsteps of the Iran hostages; 200,000 marched in Chicago a year later, cheered on by 500,000 spectators; 100,000 marchers, led by retired General William C. Westmoreland, turned out in Houston in March 1987.[12]

These belated homecomings also coincided with both extensive military reforms and an increasing regard among the US public for their military. Ronald Reagan's embrace of Vietnam as a "noble cause" was followed by a large increase in defense spending and a facile victory with the 1983 invasion of the tiny island of Grenada. The combination of increasing military confidence, defense reforms, and the cultural shift symbolized both by the embrace of the Vietnam veteran and Reagan's rhetoric meant that Gallup polling showed that by August 1990, 68 percent of Americans had a "great deal" or "quite a lot" of confidence in the military, up from a 1979 nadir of 50 percent.[13] Thus, on the eve of the Persian Gulf War, the US military had been restored to its place as one of the most trusted institutions in the United States, and Vietnam veterans had been given their welcome home, at least in terms of public celebrations.

The Gulf War and Operation Welcome Home

When the United States deployed troops to Saudi Arabia in the autumn of 1990 and began to build up forces in anticipation of war with Iraq, the repertoire for public support for the troops was now in place. Even after a relatively close vote in Congress on the question of war, there was a huge upsurge of support for the troops, from the now-familiar yellow ribbons displayed in front yards and as lapel pins to the thousands of care packages and letters sent to soldiers stationed in the Gulf to numerous celebrity displays of support; from the Voices That Care supergroup to Whitney Houston's Super Bowl performance and later welcome home concert in Norfolk, Virginia. Even Todd Gitlin, leader of the antiwar Students for a Democratic Society during the Vietnam War era, was filmed donating blood for the troops.

This wave of public support was predicated on the notion that, regardless of the politics of the war, US soldiers must be supported loudly and publicly and that the experience of the Vietnam veterans must not be repeated. What made this all the more important in the buildup to war in Kuwait was the fact that this would be the first major test of the all-volunteer force. US troops had performed well in Grenada and Panama, but much of the prewar commentary noted that Iraq had the fourth largest army in the world, one that had been hardened by nearly a decade of war with Iran. The Veterans Administration made arrangements to clear hospital beds for the anticipated flow of wounded. Analysts estimated that the war would result in between ten thousand and twenty thousand American casualties.[14]

Given this atmosphere, it is no surprise that on the day that President George H. W. Bush declared a ceasefire in the Gulf, ending a short, sharp, and seemingly victorious war with far fewer casualties than had been anticipated, the author Tom Clancy took to the opinion pages of the *Los Angeles Times* to call for victory parades in honor of the troops. Clancy argued that the armed forces were the true measure of any society, as "In uniform you will find the best and worst, the tools, the people, the ideas, all distilled in one place," Clancy closed his article with this appeal:

> How about a few parades? How about the collective thank you that was cruelly denied to the last class of American warriors? We give parades *to* baseball and football teams who win at games. These kids now finishing their job are America's Team. They wear our colors. Can we do any less *for* them? The military has learned its lessons from Vietnam. What about the rest of us?[15]

These appeals were not just being made in newspaper opinion pieces. The Bush White House was inundated with advice from political operatives and supporters on how to make maximum political use of the impending victory celebrations, which could, in the words of one advisor, "lay extremely solid foundations for 1992."[16] House minority whip Newt Gingrich wrote to Bush offering ideas for the president's upcoming address to a joint session of Congress, arguing that Bush should use the volunteer ethos of the military to advance conservative policy ideas by urging Americans to "join with that volunteer Army of freedom" to "make the twenty-first century the next American century."[17]

The all-volunteer force could thus be a model for the rest of American society. The public relations firm Hill and Knowlton suggested that Bush appoint either General Schwarzkopf or General Powell to run Operation Domestic Prosperity, a 100-day push to make the United States a "home for heroes" by passing the administration's domestic policy agenda.[18] Other PR (public relations) firms, such as Burson-Marsteller suggested having the Department of Defense handpick returning veterans to "maintain and expand in a meaningful way the national sense of pride, accomplishment and good feeling generated by Operation Desert Storm." These volunteers would be carefully selected and then be given media training before being sent out to various media markets to promote the administration's agenda.[19] The vice-president of General Electric wrote to Bush to suggest that the administration train the more than 500,000 Gulf War veterans as "Desert Storm community volunteers." The purpose of this organization was somewhat unclear, but it was predicated on the notion that military service was inherently heroic. The memorandum's authors argued:

> America's young people desperately need heroes—real heroes. Real people in real walks of life who do the real things that make America what it is. People who serve their country. People who earn their money, people who have a commitment to excellence and competence, people who believe in the value of service.[20]

The spectacle of returning troops could also be linked to this policy agenda. The same firm suggested a "victory train" and a "freedom flotilla," both of which would be stocked with Desert Storm veterans who would tour the nation and celebrate the men, women, and technology of Operation Desert Storm.[21] The Department of Defense was eager to cooperate with the White House in planning spectacles, and their Public Affairs Office planned to emphasize such themes as "We proved ourselves the best fighting force that has ever been fielded by our nation"; "America's half million heroes are coming home"; "Post-Vietnam syndrome is definitely over"; and, most tellingly, "Technology works—investment in a strong defense remains important—there are future threats that are impossible to predict."[22] For the Department of Defense, the parades were a chance to showcase their military technology and promote that investment in a strong defense.

The Pentagon's Public Affairs Office also noted the general groundswell of support for the troops and in a memorandum to the White House argued, "The homecoming should not be planned and managed by centralized government agencies, including DoD [Department of Defense] and the White House. Our role is to be responsive to what is clearly an outpouring of local, state and national-level support, and to provide assistance and guidance."[23] This approach was in tension with White House staffers who wanted to maintain a tight control on events and called for the White House to be intimately involved:

> In the planning and the coordination of events to be sponsored by the private and public sectors throughout the Nation to assure that: (i) the President is given every opportunity to participate in selected local events; (ii) the local planners have the benefit of White House advice and resource management; and (iii) the celebrations coincide with National events, including Armed Forces Day, Memorial Day, July 4th, and Veterans Day.[24]

Ultimately, the White House took the Pentagon's advice, keeping tabs on the various celebrations being planned but taking a step back to allow others to run them "while paying particular attention to events that might offer political benefit to the administration." In his 6 March 1991 address to Congress, Bush called for "every community in this country to make this coming Fourth of July a day of special celebration for our returning troops. They may have missed Thanksgiving and Christmas, but I can tell you this: For them and for their families, we can make this a holiday they'll never forget."[25] Americans, in both big cities and small towns were quick to respond to Bush's request, and parade committees sprang up across the country. In their own way, although they were not centrally planned, these parades all echoed the themes the White House had identified even before the end of the war: soldiers and veterans (including Vietnam veterans) as heroes, American technology triumphant, and the strength of the all-volunteer military.

The Mother of All Parades

While many small towns across the United States held Gulf War homecoming parades for the returning troops, in terms of media coverage (and White House focus), the efforts of larger cities loomed large. As the home of the ticker tape parade, New York City's parade would be a central part of the homecoming. Promising "the mother of all parades," Mayor David Dinkins enlisted corporate sponsorship from American Express to help the budget crisis-ridden city pay for the celebration. Twelve million pounds of paper were prepared for the parade, while American Express succeeded in getting over $10 million in donated advertising time to look for contributions and setting up a toll-free hotline through which citizens could donate to the parade by credit card. After initial worries, the parade organizers evidently had no trouble raising the $4.3 million needed to stage the parade.[26] The parade, which took place on 10 June, attracted between 1 and 4.7 million spectators.

While the troops, who came into the city via a combination of bus convoy, subway, and landing craft, were certainly the centerpiece of the celebrations, they were in a minority in the parade itself, with the five thousand soldiers—led by General Colin Powell—only the head of a 24,000-strong parade featuring various veterans' organizations and diverse community groups and bands.[27] Representatives of over fifty allied nations also marched in the parade, which caused some diplomatic problems. The Israeli Defense Forces were invited to send a color party (and duly did so) despite Israel not formally being part of the coalition that fought Iraq.[28]

The parade organizers also initially invited Syria to send a delegation, although they quickly backtracked once there was outcry among the families of the victims of the Lockerbie bombings.[29] Vietnam veterans did attend the parade, as they did in every other major city, but the *Washington Post* reported that they were relegated to the back of the parade, "behind celebrities such as boxer Thomas Hearns and rock legend Bo Diddley" and reported that the lone Korean War veteran who turned up at the parade assembly area gave up in frustration and rode the subway home before the start of the festivities.[30]

Washington, DC faced no such danger of forgetting the veterans of other wars, as the parade was organized by the Desert Storm Homecoming Foundation, which consisted of the three major veterans' organizations—Veterans of Foreign Wars, the American Legion, and Disabled American Veterans. In terms of troops participating, the Washington parade would certainly upstage the New York City one, with more than ten thousand troops marching, led by General Norman Schwarzkopf, who would also join President Bush on the reviewing stand. The Pentagon paid $7 million toward the cost of the parade, with private donations (including $1 million from the Saudi and Kuwaiti governments) making up another $5 million.[31]

The centerpiece of this celebration would not be the troops themselves, but rather the technology used to win the war. The parade would feature a twelve-minute-long flyby of over eighty aircraft, led by a lone F-117 stealth fighter, an icon of the war, and would feature thirty-one heavy military vehicles, including the M1A1 Abrams main battle tank and the Patriot Missile system. Not only that, but seven blocks of the National Mall were dedicated to what reporters jokingly called a "military petting zoo," where weaponry and equipment were displayed. One exhibit tent had every type of bomb and missile used in the war while others allowed visitors to try on a gas mask or practice laying a howitzer on the Washington monument. Indeed, such was the scale and bulk of the hardware on display that National Park Service personnel worried about tanks tearing up the Mall and damaging the sprinkler system underneath, while the parade route had to be modified so that the weight of the seventy-ton M1A1 Abrams tanks would not cause a bridge or a metro tunnel to collapse.[32]

The eventual parade route selected was just over two and a half miles long, but the event only attracted around 200,000 spectators, far below the 1,000,000 that parade organizers had hoped for. Interestingly, the crowd featured a heavy contingent of federal employees and defense contractors, a group that one reporter observed was "tightly connected to the military and the bureaucracy, closer than most of the country to weapons and the workaday of war."[33] If the "military petting zoo" on the Mall and the hardware-heavy parade and flyby were not enough, the Pentagon chose to use the week following the parade to promote their budget priorities. They proclaimed an Air Force Stealth Week at nearby Andrews Air Force base, where reporters could visit the base and see a selection of the Air Force's stealth aircraft; these included a prototype of the F-22 Raptor, the F-117 Nighthawk, and the B-2 Spirit, whose building program, not coincidentally, was under threat of cancelation by Congress.[34] For the Pentagon, then, the Washington parade was a chance not just to welcome home the "half million heroes" that their Public Affairs Office had talked about in discussions with the White House but to aggressively push for their budget priorities in the pending post–Cold War spending drawdown.

Los Angeles echoed Washington, DC's focus on military hardware, and its display included a flyby by four F-117 Nighthawks and fireworks display that simulated the shootdown of an Iraqi Scud by a Patriot Missile. Raytheon Corporation also provided a seventeen-foot, 2,000-pound simulated Patriot Missile for the parade, "symbolizing the partnership of technology and the traditional role of the citizen soldier."[35] The missile was also to hold a time capsule containing military memorabilia and unit flags. More than four thousand troops took part in the parade, which took place in Hollywood, and these troops led two thousand veterans of other wars, bands, color guards, and celebrities such as Roseanne Barr, Tony Curtis, and Gene Autry. The honorary cochairs were Jimmy Stewart and Bob Hope, who declared of the war that "That's the way all wars should be, real fast like that and get the hell out and get home."[36]

Veterans featured even more prominently in the Hollywood parade than they had in New York or Washington, with the large contingent of Vietnam veterans being led by none other than General William Westmoreland, the former commander of US forces in Vietnam. "Any time I can be with the troops it's an exhilarating experience," he said. "There's lots of camaraderie." He also noted that "I don't think we've ever seen a time in history when the country is so elated and so happy about the great success of a war." Westmoreland received loud cheers from Vietnam veterans when he appeared in the parade.[37]

What was somewhat unique about the Hollywood parade was not just the high level of involvement by celebrities, who rode along in vintage cars, but the explicit commercialism of the celebration. While New York had enlisted the help of corporate sponsors, the Los Angeles organizers put commercialism into the head of the parade itself. A float honoring the US Department of Veterans Affairs was sponsored by a new soft drink called Combat Cooler, which came in a desert camouflage can, while Kodak's float carried the newly crowned Miss Universe. When the US Air Force finished their show, civilian aircraft hauled banners over the route with such messages as "Welcome Home Troops from Downey Toyota" and "Welcome Home Troops-Pick-Your-Part Auto Wrecking."[38]

The TV coverage of the parade, which was to be syndicated nationally, was the most commercialized of all. Parade organizer, Johnny Grant, informally known as the mayor of Hollywood, was a vice-president of local TV station KTLA, which claimed exclusive broadcasting rights to the event and announced plans to charge rivals $250,000 each for the footage. Other TV stations, such as KCAL-TV announced that since it was a public event, they intended to turn up with their cameras anyway and threatened legal action. The dispute was only resolved when the city of Los Angeles became uneasy about subsidizing a profit-making venture. KTLA dropped their $250,000 charge, even as they claimed they were entitled to make such a levy, given that they had been the initiators of the parade and had planned to put $695,000 of their own money into it.[39]

The parade organizers' problems did not end with disputes over TV rights. Antiwar group Sane/Freeze decided that rather than protesting the parade from the outside, as others had done in New York, Washington, DC and other cities, they would participate in it as marchers. Activist Jerry Rubin argued that antiwar sentiment was an American tradition, claiming, "We want to participate in the parade to put forth our peace message. ... Peace people shouldn't be left on the periphery, as outcasts." Antiwar activist Grace Aaron said she considered the show of military hardware "obscene," but added, "It's more appropriate for us to be part of the parade than to be simply a counterdemonstration—from the outside looking in. ... We have every right to march. We are citizens. We do pay taxes."[40]

Initially, the parade organizers indicated that they might be able to accommodate the antiwar protestors before finally deciding that they would not, as this would be disrespectful to the veterans the parade was intended to honor. Indeed, it was fear of what the veterans might do to the protestors that seemed to have tipped the balance in favor of not letting the protestors march. One of the parade organizers argued that the activists simply did not understand the degree of hostility many veterans had toward them. He said:

> We have some Vietnam veterans who have a great deal of hostility toward the peace movement because of the way they were treated when they got back from Vietnam. ... One motorcycle veterans' group said put them in front of us. Another veterans group said put them behind us. I think they had an ulterior motive for wanting them close by.[41]

In many ways, the Hollywood parade encapsulated some of the key themes of the Gulf War homecoming parades: there was celebrity, commercialism, and a propensity toward celebrating American military technology and battlefield prowess. But there was also a repeated celebration of the professional soldier (occasional references to "citizen soldiers" aside) as inherently heroic and an elevation of the soldier and veteran as symbols that needed to be unquestioningly celebrated. Ostensibly apolitical, this move was in fact deeply ideological, as seen in the parade organizers' eventual decision not to allow antiwar protestors to march lest such as decision be seen to disrespect veterans. In New York, Washington, DC, and Los Angeles, US soldiers and US technology were at the heart of the festivities, as the White House and Pentagon intended them to be. Nonetheless, popular responses to the troop homecoming did not always accord with the agendas of public relations planners. The end of the war was celebrated because it was a short, sharp victory, in which US forces could win "real fast like that and get the hell out and get home," in the words of Bob Hope. Despite the wishes of Hope and others, such endings were not to become commonplace in later US wars.

Coming Home during the "Long War"

Eleven years later, many of the same themes could be seen again as Americans began to welcome troops home from the wars in Afghanistan and—just under a year later—Iraq. In one sense, even the people involved were the same. Bangor International Airport in Maine had been a transit point for more than sixty thousand veterans returning from the Gulf. The returning veterans had been met by a locally organized welcome committee that made a point to greet every single military flight that touched down in Bangor, sometimes with crowds of thousands, but always with handshakes, food, and free phone calls.⁴² This committee was activated again in 2003, and a mix of veterans groups and ordinary citizens again began the practice of greeting every military flight and of welcoming the troops home. The difference was that rather than a relatively concentrated burst of activity, as in the summer of 1991, the greetings would be extended over years, and indeed even decades, as the Long War saw over 1.4 million troops and seven thousand flights land in Bangor.⁴³

These figures point to a different sort of homecoming during the Long War that has endured in various guises since 2001. The veneration of the American soldier has continued, but often in smaller, more intimate settings. Occasionally, units returning from war have staged parades in public, but by and large, the homecomings have happened behind the fences of military bases as units rotate home or in airport arrival halls as individual soldiers return. Writing of the experiences of military families in Fort Hood, Texas, Kenneth MacLeish has captured the constant coming and going that has characterized these wars. Looking to the base gymnasiums as sites where departure or return events (known as "manifests") are held, he notes:

> [The gyms] do so much duty for manifests that there are signs hanging up permanently with big block-letter messages specific to the occasion, but serving as constant reminders, it would seem, to soldiers playing basketball or lifting weights. Above the doors out to the parking lot there are signs proclaiming "COME HOME SAFE"; on the opposite wall, so that the first thing you see when you enter, is a large "WELCOME HOME" sign. The rooms are configured for coming from and going to war.⁴⁴

This normalization of deployment can now be seen throughout American popular culture, from the holiday and Super Bowl advertisements that feature troops coming home to the viral homemade videos of surprise soldier homecomings that began to appear on sites like YouTube from 2006 onward. Sites such as welcomehomeblog.com collate and categorize the most popular videos, which typically garner millions of views and fit into categories such as "holiday reunions," "dog reunions," and "proposals."⁴⁵ Occasionally these videos depict the return of a wounded or maimed veteran from hospitals like Walter Reed in Bethesda, Maryland, or Landstuhl, Germany, but these rarely garner the same viewership and seldom go viral. The popularity of these homemade videos is instructive, as it points to a form of civic engagement with war that Laura Silvestri has termed "vicarious sacrifice."⁴⁶

In a context where so little has been demanded of American citizens in wartime, the videos serve as a way to participate, by allowing people to like, share, or comment on them. The passivity of this engagement is noteworthy, as is the intimacy of the videos themselves. Typically featuring a father surprising his child in some domestic everyday setting such as the home, the classroom, or a school sporting event, the videos are sentimental and patriotic in tone but also, as Silvestri notes, intentionally devoid of political content. She argues that by focusing on such intimate settings, the videos intentionally leave much out:

> Centered on traditional, apolitical themes grounded in the private realm of family life, the homecoming videos downplay the role of war and politics. The actual act of warfare is not depicted or even addressed in these videos. The only indicator that a war is occurring in a foreign land is the return of the warrior in uniform. These videos emphasize the emotional sacrifice of the household rather than the blood sacrifice of the battlefield.[47]

Thus, these wildly popular videos combine emotional identification with the service members and their family with political passivity or even powerlessness.

This move to depoliticize support for the troops by focusing on the personal is one that has also inevitably appealed to commercial interests. Along with homemade viral videos, there has been an upsurge in corporate support for the troops. Typical of these efforts is Budweiser's 2005 Super Bowl commercial.[48] Titled "Welcome Home," it opens with everyday scenes of a busy airport concourse. Suddenly, off-camera, applause breaks out and grows to a crescendo as people turn to look before rising to their feet to join the ovation. The camera then cuts to the object of acclaim, a company of soldiers in desert camouflage fatigues who silently walk through the arrivals hall, nodding and smiling at the applause. The piece then fades to a simple "thank you" and the Anheuser-Busch logo.

The soldiers depicted here are thankful, silent, and inherently heroic. This scene, however, can also be read in another way: the returning troops are not only objects of veneration but also almost dreamlike in their sudden apparition and disappearance; and, indeed, the inevitable aftermath of this scene, where the airport must have returned to its everyday rhythms, is not depicted in the commercial. They are loved by their airport audience but also separated from them, both by their uniform and their experiences. Their interactions with the public involve gratitude, but, beyond applause and a few handshakes, nothing more. The notion of "vicarious sacrifice" that Silvestri identifies in homemade videos is also present in more professional productions.[49]

This concept of civic duty expressed through passive support for returning troops is one that has been embraced by the US military itself. Not only has the Pentagon frequently cooperated with public spectacles intended to honor returning troops and "hometown heroes," particularly at sporting events, where salutes to the troops are commonplace, they have gone further and directly paid for these events as promotional opportunities. Indeed, a 2015 government oversight report released by senators John McCain and Jeff Flake noted that the Department of Defense spent over $53 million on marketing contracts with sports teams between 2012 and 2015, with a large portion of those funds going to pay for pregame or halftime salutes to the troops, particularly at NFL or NASCAR events.[50] These payments ranged from the $450,000 paid by the Georgia National Guard to the Atlanta Braves to allow on field presentations that could include a surprise homecoming to a $20,000 payment from the New Jersey National Guard to the New York Jets to recognize two New Jersey National Guard soldiers as "hometown heroes" at each Jets home game.[51]

Beth Bailey has written about the challenges that the Army has faced since the advent of the all-volunteer force in selling military service and competing with other employers in the labor market, but the difficulties of doing so during wartime mean that the Department of Defense had to embrace the concept of paid patriotism as a way to venerate the American soldier.[52] This has meant that the soldier has become an object that has branding value, as the Pentagon pours money into elevating the notion of the soldier as inherently heroic; commercial interests then seek to capitalize on this burnished image by associating themselves with it.

Perhaps the most interesting example of the confluence of patriotism, commercial interests, and a soldier's return home is the case of Lieutenant Chuck Nadd of the 10th Combat Aviation Brigade, whose homecoming was the centerpiece of a Budweiser 2014 Super Bowl commercial titled "Hero's Welcome." Nadd was stationed in Afghanistan as a helicopter pilot when he got notice that he would deploy home earlier than expected in order to assist with a public affairs effort and to give a speech in his hometown. On arrival at Fort Drum, a Budweiser private jet picked him up and flew him to his home town of Winter Park, Florida, where he was surprised by his girlfriend Shannon Cantwell at the airport while being secretly filmed by a film crew. The couple then drove downtown, where a ticker tape parade in his honor had been organized. Nadd and Cantwell were pulled along the parade route by Budweiser Clydesdales before a crowd of hundreds of cheering citizens, led by the local Veterans of Foreign Wars outpost. The subsequent film was made into a sixty-second commercial and aired at the 2014 Super Bowl.[53]

However, journalist Dan Lamothe uncovered a more complex story behind the saccharine and reductive patriotism of the "Hero's Welcome" spot.[54] Budweiser had originally approached the Army in the hope of organizing a similar event around National Lager Day on 10 December but were turned down due to unspecified legal concerns and fears of the Army being seen to endorse alcoholic beverages. Only when Budweiser approached the Veterans of Foreign Wars, who then contacted the Department of the Army to make the case for the project, did the event go ahead. Even after he was selected for the assignment, Nadd was unaware that he would be featured in a commercial.

The internal correspondence on the issue, revealed due to a Freedom of Information Act request by Lamothe, reveals not only the unease within Army Public Affairs at the project but the specific vision of the American soldier that Budweiser was attempting to sell to the Army and the broader public. The advertising agency responsible for the film sent a list of "casting considerations," which included the need for the soldier selected for the homecoming to be "camera-friendly in demeanor," laid-back and OK with surprises, and "vetted as PR-friendly by the military." The wife or girlfriend of the soldier was to be "devoted and strong," and the firm was interested in "family and/or friends who can talk about the troops coming home in a positive, hopeful light."[55]

Budweiser also preferred a soldier without children, as there were concerns with featuring anyone younger than twenty-one in a commercial related to alcohol. An email to Nadd's Public Affairs Officer in Afghanistan from a researcher with the film's production company made the claim that the project could help spur a broader movement to welcome troops home. The researcher wrote, "We are looking for all types of soldiers coming home and the emotional transition of returning to their communities. We think that by sharing their stories we will help empower others across the country to work with soldiers to achieve a truly community supported transition." Further, like its viral amateur equivalents, the film would focus on the personal in order to avoid the political: "While there are already a lot of documentaries out there on the subject matter, they tend to focus on systematic social problems and American policy. Our film instead seeks to focus on how individuals and communities can work together to celebrate and support those returning home." [56] That the documentary would in fact be a commercial for Budweiser was not made clear to Nadd or many within the chain of command.

The open commercialization of soldier homecomings has contributed to a growing cynicism about the sincerity of such efforts. Ben Fountain's novel *Billy Lynn's Long Half-Time Walk* (later made into a film directed by Ang Lee) tells a darker version of Nadd's story, in which a squad of soldiers responsible for heroic actions in a firefight in Iraq are brought back to the United States for a week-long victory tour culminating in an appearance at a Dallas Cowboy's halftime show.[57] As seen through the eyes of Lynn, who suffers from PTSD (posttraumatic stress disorder) and, unbeknownst to the public, is due to return to Iraq immediately after the game, the patriotism on display is shallow, jingoistic, and far removed from the lived experiences of those who served. Similarly, the title of David Finkel's *Thank You for Your Service*, which tells the story of the costs of war for the soldiers and families of the 2-16 infantry battalion who fought in Baghdad during the 2007 troop surge, is utterly ironic in its expression of gratitude.[58]

Indeed, several veterans have written about the emptiness of the phrase "thank you for your service" and argued that all of the public displays of gratitude toward soldiers coming home has not helped bridge the widening gap between the military and civilians.[59] In an address to the West Point graduating class of 2011, the chair of the Joint Chiefs of Staff Admiral Mike Mullen worried about the divide: "I fear they do not know us. I fear they do no not comprehend the full weight of the burden we carry or the price we pay when we return from battle." Mullen argued, "A people uninformed about what we are asking the military to endure is a people inevitably unable to fully grasp the scope of the responsibilities our Constitution levies upon them."[60]

The answer for some commentators and veterans has been a return to the spirit of 1991. Starting in 2011, with the official end of combat operations in Iraq, there have been calls for a large-scale parade in New York City or elsewhere to honor the veterans of Iraq and Afghanistan. In December 2011, New York City councilmen Vincent Ignizio and James Oddo called for a ticker tape parade of Iraq War veterans down Broadway, a proposal rejected by the Pentagon in part due to the ninety thousand US troops, many of them Iraq veterans, deployed to Afghanistan at the time.[61]

In April 2014, as the Afghanistan mission wound down, Senator Charles Schumer repeated the call for a Broadway parade. The newly formed Iraq and Afghanistan Veterans of America (IAVA) also pushed for a parade, and CEO and founder of IAVA, Paul Rieckhoff, hoped for a parade in New York City that "shines a spotlight on the sacrifices of veterans, galvanizes public support and inspires other cities to follow."[62] Writing in the *New Republic*, Lawrence Kaplan recognized that the 1991 parades were "shows of self-congratulatory bravado" but nonetheless invoked them in arguing that a parade for Iraq and Afghanistan veterans would help bridge the growing gap between the military and civilians. Invoking Jules Michelet's work on civic participation in public festivals during the French Revolution, Kaplan imagined an occasion of healing and civic pride:

> And so it should be when the returned march up Broadway, with maneuver battalions and high school bands each taking their turns, the crowds entertaining and being entertained, soldiers finally within reach of the civilians for whom they sacrificed so much in Iraq. All of the garbage of the past decade— the reluctance to abide any measure that might constrain personal autonomy, the subordination of the public good to private wants, the war itself—ought, if even for a moment, to give way to a modest display of civic vigor.[63]

Despite the hopes of Kaplan and others, these parades have not yet happened. The wars in Iraq and Afghanistan have not ended, even if US participation in them has changed in terms of intensity. The end of war parades have been impossible to schedule, absent an end of war.

Nonetheless, Kaplan's hopes for "a modest display of civic vigor" ignore the actual ways American soldiers have been welcomed home in the late twentieth and early twenty-first centuries. These homecoming celebrations have, perhaps understandably, not been used to actively reflect on how the United States fights and ends wars. The nature of the celebrations, though, do reflect an evolving attitude toward war in the twenty-first century. In these public displays of gratitude, there is no good war or bad war, only the ever-present imperative to support the troops. Aside from these acts of gratitude and occasional crises, the general public is free to ignore these unending wars. Despite good intentions, they have not served in any meaningful way to close the gap between the all-volunteer force and the society that it serves. Concerns about the "real 1 percent," that percentage of the population that serves in the military, abound now as much as ever.

Despite, or perhaps because of, that gap, the profusion of thanks to those who serve has become louder and more widespread. From the ticker tape parades and massed ranks of victorious troops in the summer of 1991 to the viral video of the Air Force technician being welcomed home by his happy dog, Americans have celebrated and elevated their soldiers and elevated them to heroic status. It is ironic then that with calls for a parade to thank those who served in Iraq and Afghanistan and stories about the growing number of veteran suicides, American soldiers and veterans find themselves in some ways in a similar position to their counterparts from the Vietnam era, isolated from a society that does not understand them, even if the mechanism of isolation is one based on adulation rather than scorn.

David Fitzgerald is lecturer in international politics in the School of History, University College Cork, Ireland. He has written numerous articles and books on military and foreign policy, especially counterinsurgency warfare and "small wars." His first book, *Learning to Forget: US*

Army Counterinsurgency Doctrine from Vietnam to Iraq (Stanford, 2013) was a runner-up in the Society for Military History's Edward M. Coffman first manuscript prize. His current research focuses on consequences of the all-volunteer force for American society and the rise of a "warrior ethos" within the post-Vietnam US military. Together with David Ryan, he is the author of *Obama, US Foreign Policy and the Dilemmas of Intervention* (Palgrave Macmillan, 2014).

Notes

1. Bill Mauldin, cited in Andrew J. Huebner, *Warrior Image: Soldiers in American Culture from the Second World War to the Vietnam Era* (Chapel Hill: University of North Carolina Press, 2008), 126.
2. David T. Courtwright, "Opiate Addiction as a Consequence of the Civil War," *Civil War History* 24, no. 2 (2012): 101–11; Susan L. Carruthers, *The Good Occupation: American Soldiers and the Hazards of Peace* (Cambridge, MA: Harvard University Press, 2016), 191–200.
3. Accusations that veterans were spat on upon their return to the United States have been the subject of some dispute. See Jerry Lembcke, *The Spitting Image: Myth, Memory, and the Legacy of Vietnam* (New York: New York University Press, 2000).
4. Tim O'Brien, *The Things They Carried* (London: Flamingo, 1991); Philip Caputo, *A Rumor of War*, reprint ed. (New York: Holt Paperbacks, 1996); Robert Mason, *Chickenhawk*, reissue ed. (New York: Penguin Books, 2005).
5. Ted Kotcheff, *First Blood* (1982); Michael Cimino, *The Deer Hunter* (1979); Marita Sturken, *Tangled Memories: The Vietnam War, the AIDS Epidemic, and the Politics of Remembering* (Oakland: University of California Press, 1997).
6. The literature on collective memory and the Vietnam War is extensive. For an introduction, see Patrick Hagopian, *The Vietnam War in American Memory: Veterans, Memorials, and the Politics of Healing*, reprint ed. (Amherst: University of Massachusetts Press, 2011); David Kieran, *Forever Vietnam: How a Divisive War Changed American Public Memory* (Amherst: University of Massachusetts Press, 2014); David Ryan, "Vietnam in the American Mind: Narratives of the Nation and the Sources of Collective Memory," in *Cultural Memory and Multiple Identities* (Berlin: Lit Verlag, 2008).
7. Ronald Reagan, "Peace: Restoring the Margin of Safety," Veterans of Foreign Wars Convention, Chicago, 18 August 1980, https://www.reaganlibrary.gov/8-18-80, accessed 16 December 2018.
8. Paul Camacho, "The Future of the Veterans' Lobby and Its Potential Impact for Social Policy," in *The American War in Vietnam*, ed. Jayne Susan Werner and David Hunt (Ithaca, NY: Cornell University Press, 1993).
9. Gerald E. Parsons, "How the Yellow Ribbon Became a National Folk Symbol," *Folklife Center News* 13, no. 3 (1991): 9–11; Jack Santino, "Yellow Ribbons and Seasonal Flags: The Folk Assemblage of War," *Journal of American Folklore* 105, no. 415 (1992): 19–33.
10. Jeremiah Murphy, "We Already Had Heroes," *Boston Globe*, 8 February 1981, cited in Camacho, "The Future of the Veterans' Lobby and Its Potential Impact for Social Policy," 114.
11. Lance Morrow, "The Forgotten Warriors," *Time*, 13 July 1981, http://content.time.com/time/subscriber/article/0,33009,1212934,00.html.

12. Jane Gross, "New York Pays Homage to Vietnam Veterans," *New York Times*, 7 May 1985, http://www.nytimes.com/1985/05/07/nyregion/new-york-pays-homage-to-vietnam-veterans.html, accessed 16 December 2018; special to *New York Times*, "Vietnam Veterans in Chicago Parade Cheered by Crowds," *New York Times*, 14 June 1986, http://www.nytimes.com/1986/06/14/us/vietnam-veterans-in-chicago-parade-cheered-by-crowds.html, accessed 16 December 2018; "Vietnam Veterans March in Houston," *Washington Post*, 24 May 1987, https://www.washingtonpost.com/archive/politics/1987/05/24/vietnam-veterans-march-in-houston/b996ba33-eb80-45c5-92c3-7281de2428ec/?utm_term=.20b495702189, accessed 16 December 2018.
13. Gallup Inc., "Confidence in Institutions," Gallup.com, accessed 6 March 2017, http://www.gallup.com/poll/1597/Confidence-Institutions.aspx .
14. "Potential War Casualties Put at 100,000: Gulf Crisis: Fewer US Troops Would Be Killed or Wounded Than Iraq Soldiers, Military Experts Predict," *Los Angeles Times*, 5 September 1990, http://articles.latimes.com/1990-09-05/news/mn-776_1_military-experts.
15. Tom Clancy, "How about a Few Parades?" *Los Angeles Times*, 28 February 1991; Persian Gulf Working Group, Paul McNeill Files, White House Office of Communications, George H. W. Bush Presidential Records, George H. W. Bush Presidential Library (GBPL).
16. Michael Bayer to Jim Pinkerton, "Coordination of Desert Storm Homecoming Events," 4 March 1991, Folder 04733-005, Sig Rogich Files, White House Office of Public Events and Initiatives, George H. W. Bush Presidential Records, GBPL.
17. Newt Gingrich to John Sununu, "Suggested Rhetoric for 3/6 Joint Speech," 4 March 1991, Persian Gulf War [2], Issues File, John Sununu Files, White House Office of the Chief Staff, George H. W. Bush Presidential Records, GBPL.
18. Craig L. Fuller to John Sununu, 27 March 1991, Folder 04733-005, Sig Rogich Files, White House Office of Public Events and Initiatives, George H. W. Bush Presidential Records, GBPL.
19. Thomas D. Bell to Ed Rogers, "Expanding the Spirit of Desert Storm," 2 April 1991, Folder 04733-005, Sig Rogich Files, White House Office of Public Events and Initiatives, George H. W. Bush Presidential Records, GBPL.
20. Ken Smith to David Demarest, "Desert Storm Heroes as Community Service Leaders," 15 March 1991, Folder 07637-09, White House Office of National Service, George H. W. Bush Presidential Records, GBPL.
21. Craig L. Fuller to John Sununu, 27 March 1991.
22. Daniel J. Kalinger to David Demarest, David Carney, "Homecoming Planning," 4 March 1991, Folder 04733-005, Sig Rogich Files, White House Office of Public Events and Initiatives, George H. W. Bush Presidential Records, GBPL.
23. Ibid.
24. Michael Bayer to Jim Pinkerton, "Coordination of Desert Storm Homecoming Events." 4 March 1991, Folder 04733-005, Sig Rogich Files, White House Office of Public Events and Initiatives, George H. W. Bush Presidential Records, GBPL.
25. George H. W. Bush, "Address before a Joint Session of the Congress on the Cessation of the Persian Gulf Conflict," Online by Gerhard Peters and John T. Woolley, The American Presidency Project, 6 March 1991, http://www.presidency.ucsb.edu/ws/?pid=19364.
26. Robert D. McFadden, "Fund-Raising on Target for Whopping Victory Parade," *New York Times*, 13 May 1991; Jerry Gray, "A Gulf Parade with Six Tons of Ticker Tape," *New York Times*, 6 June 1991.
27. Scot J. Paltrow and Josh Getlin, "Manhattan Turns Out for the Troops Biggest Parade in N.Y. History Celebrates Gulf War Victory," *San Francisco Chronicle*, 11 June 1991.
28. Jonathan Schacter, "IDF Invited to Gulf War Parade in NY," *Jerusalem Post*, 7 April 1991.

29. "International: Syrians Pull Out of Gulf Parade," *Daily Telegraph* (London), 30 May 1991.
30. Michael Specter and Laurie Goodstein, "Millions Honor Gulf Vets at Parade in New York," *Washington Post*, 11 June 1991.
31. Kristin Huckshorn, "Parade May Cost Taxpayers $7 Million Capital Homecoming to Feature Hardware, Troops from Gulf War," *Orange County Register* (Anaheim), 7 June 1991.
32. Mary Jordan, "DC Parade Plans Roar into Focus; Logistics 'Enormous' For Gulf Celebration: [Final Edition]," *Washington Post*, 16 May 1991.
33. "200,000 View War Victory Parade," *Pittsburgh Press*, 9 June 1991.
34. Fred Kaplan, "Air Force Opens Up to Save Its Stealth Capitol Hill Pitch Plays on Gulf War Parades," *Boston Globe*, 11 June 1991.
35. Michael D. Antonovich, "Letter to Linda DeHart,"8 May 1991, Document no. 208848, WHORM files, ME002 Messages (Sent to Groups/Organizations), GBPL.
36. Associated Press, "Hollywood Welcome-Home Parade Draws 1 Million," *Las Vegas Review—Journal*, 20 May 1991.
37. Scott Harris and Josh Meyer, "Gulf Troops Welcomed with Hollywood Flair Parade: Hundreds of Thousands Watch Them March in Festive Display. Veterans of All Conflicts Are Honored," *Los Angeles Times*, 20 May 1991.
38. Ibid.
39. Josh Meyer, "Raining on Their Gulf War Parade Hollywood: The City and Chamber of Commerce Awarded Broadcast Rights for the Event to One Station, KTLA-TV, Whose Vice President Is Also Honorary Mayor. At Least One Rival Station Is Crying Foul," *Los Angeles Times*, 4 April 1991.
40. Scott Harris, "Hollywood Salute to Gulf War Vets Draws Some Fire Parade: Massive Displays of Weaponry Will Be Featured. Critics Fear It's a Glorification of Warfare," *Los Angeles Times*, 22 April 1991.
41. Scott Harris, "Gulf Parade Rejects Bid by Anti-War Activist Desert Storm: The Hollywood Event's Producer Says Participation by a Peace Group Would Offend the Veterans Who Are to Be Honored," *Los Angeles Times*, 27 April 1991.
42. Lynne Junkins Cole, *Goodbye Desert Storm, Hello Bangor, Maine: Experience Welcoming the Troops through the Eyes of the Greeters* (Hampden, ME: L. Cole, 1991); Brian Swartz, *An American Homecoming* (Bangor, ME: Bangor, 1996).
43. Nok-Noi Ricker, "As Military Flights through Bangor Dwindle, Maine Troop Greeters Work to Preserve Their History," *Bangor Daily News*, accessed 6 March 2017, http://bangordailynews.com/2014/01/24/news/bangor/maine-troop-greeters-working-to-preserve-their-history-as-military-flights-through-bangor-airport-dwindle; Sephone Interactive Media, "Maine Troop Greeters: The Official Home," *Bangor International Airport*, http://www.flybangor.com/troop-greeters, accessed 6 March 2017.
44. Kenneth T. MacLeish, *Making War at Fort Hood: Life and Uncertainty in a Military Community* (Princeton, NJ: Princeton University Press, 2013), 134–35.
45. "Welcome Home Blog," Welcome Home Blog, accessed 6 March 2017, http://welcome-homeblog.com.
46. Lisa Silvestri, "Surprise Homecomings and Vicarious Sacrifices," *Media, War & Conflict* 6, no. 2 (2013): 101–15.
47. Ibid., 108.
48. Budweiser, Welcome Home Troops. Advertisement, https://www.youtube.com/watch?v=9AGay3mZHeE, accessed 6 March 2017.
49. This Budweiser commercial was the first in a wave of advertising that used soldier homecomings as plot devices. See Ford, "Welcome Home." Advertisement, 2007, https://www.youtube.com/watch?v=t44yWwkQrzI, accessed 16 December 2018; Jeep, Military Coming Home—Super Bowl Commercial. Advertisement, 2014, https://www.

wsj.com/video/jeep-coming-home/E3CAB02A-1958-44A8-BB8E-127278843FE2.html, accessed 16 December 2018; Zillow, Long Distance Returning Soldier Commercial. Advertisement, 2014, https://www.youtube.com/watch?v=HHLoWctz8q4, accessed 16 December 2018.

50. Rebecca Kheel, "McCain, Flake Slam 'Paid Patriotism' at Sporting Events," *The Hill* (Washington, DC), 4 November 2015, http://thehill.com/policy/defense/259120-mccain-flake-slam-so-called-paid-patriotism-at-sporting-events, accessed 16 December 2018.

51. John S. McCain and Jeff Flake, "Tackling Paid Patriotism: A Joint Oversight Report by US Sens. John McCain and Jeff Flake," November 2015, http://www.mccain.senate.gov/public/_cache/files/12de6dcb-d8d8-4a58-8795-562297f948c1/tackling-paid-patriotism-oversight-report.pdf, accessed 16 December 2018.

52. Beth Bailey, "The Army in the Marketplace: Recruiting an All-Volunteer Force," *Journal of American History* 94, no. 1 (2007): 47–74.

53. Budweiser, Hero's Welcome. Advertisement, 2014, https://www.youtube.com/watch?v=mVh4cwDzCgs, accessed 16 December 2018; Associated Press, "Fort Drum Soldier Lt. Chuck Nadd Gets a 'Hero's Welcome' in Budweiser Super Bowl Ad," 2 February 2014, http://www.syracuse.com/news/index.ssf/2014/02/fort_drum_soldier_chuck_nadd_budweiser_super_bowl_ad.html, accessed 16 December 2018.

54. Dan Lamothe, "Exclusive: Army Squared Off with Budweiser over Controversial Super Bowl Ad," *Foreign Policy*, 20 March 2014, https://foreignpolicy.com/2014/03/20/exclusive-army-squared-off-with-budweiser-over-controversial-super-bowl-ad, accessed 16 December 2018.

55. Michael G. Penney, "FW: Budweiser Documents," 15 November 2013, https://www.scribd.com/document/213568580/Budweiser-Commercial-Flap-featuring-disagreement-between-Anheuser-Busch-and-the-U-S-Army, accessed 16 December 2018.

56. Alexis Soto, "Documentary Featuring Lt Chuck Nadd," 16 December 2013, https://www.scribd.com/document/213568580/Budweiser-Commercial-Flap-featuring-disagreement-between-Anheuser-Busch-and-the-U-S-Army, accessed 16 December 2018.

57. Ben Fountain, *Billy Lynn's Long Halftime Walk: A Novel*, reprint ed. (New York: Ecco, 2016); Ang Lee, *Billy Lynn's Long Halftime Walk* (2016).

58. David Finkel, *Thank You for Your Service* (New York: Sarah Crichton Books, 2013).

59. Matt Richtel, "Please Don't Thank Me for My Service," *New York Times*, 21 February 2015, section Sunday Review, https://www.nytimes.com/2015/02/22/sunday-review/please-dont-thank-me-for-my-service.html; "Don't Say 'Thank You For Your Service' This Monday," NPR.org, accessed 19 August 2017, http://www.npr.org/2017/05/28/530504781/words-youll-hear-memorial-day-dos-and-donts accessed 16 December 2018; Stanton S. Coerr, "3 Reasons to Stop Thanking Me for My Military Service," *The Federalist*, 16 July 2015, http://thefederalist.com/2015/07/16/3-reasons-to-stop-thanking-me-for-my-military-service, accessed 16 December 2018.

60. Thom Shanker, "Admiral Mullen Urges West Point Graduates to Bridge Gap with Public," *New York Times*, 21 May 2011, http://www.nytimes.com/2011/05/22/us/22mullen.html, accessed 16 December 2018.

61. Ben Nuckols and Samantha Gross, "No Parade Planned for Iraq War Troops," NBC New York, accessed 6 March 2017, http://www.nbcnewyork.com/news/local/Iraq-War-Troops-Parade-NYC-DC-Soldiers-Come-Home-136272073.html, accessed 16 December 2018.

62. Joseph Straw, Erin Durkin, and Ginger Adams Otis, "Sen. Schumer Talks with Pentagon Brass about Parade for War Vets," *New York Daily News*, 14 April 2014, http://www.nydailynews.com/news/politics/sen-schumer-nyc-host-parade-war-vets-article-1.1756063, accessed 16 December 2018.

63. Lawrence Kaplan, "Where Is the Ticker-Tape Parade?" *New Republic*, 30 May 2011, https://newrepublic.com/article/89139/iraq-war-soldiers-memorial-day-military-parade, accessed 16 December 2018.

Select Bibliography

Bailey, Beth, "The Army in the Marketplace: Recruiting an All-Volunteer Force," *Journal of American History* 94, no. 1 (2007).
Camacho, Paul, "The Future of the Veterans' Lobby and Its Potential Impact for Social Policy," in *The American War in Vietnam*, ed. Jayne Susan Werner and David Hunt (Ithaca, NY: Cornell University Press, 1993).
Caputo, Philip, *A Rumor of War* (New York: Holt Paperbacks, 1996).
Carruthers, Susan L., *The Good Occupation: American Soldiers and the Hazards of Peace* (Cambridge, MA: Harvard University Press, 2016).
Cole, Lynne Junkins, *Goodbye Desert Storm, Hello Bangor, Maine: Experience Welcoming the Troops through the Eyes of the Greeters* (Hampden: L. Cole, 1991).
Courtwright, David T., "Opiate Addiction as a Consequence of the Civil War," *Civil War History* 24, no. 2 (2012).
Fountain, Ben, *Billy Lynn's Long Halftime Walk: A Novel*, reprint ed. (New York: Ecco, 2016).
Hagopian, Patrick, *The Vietnam War in American Memory: Veterans, Memorials, and the Politics of Healing* (Amherst: University of Massachusetts Press, 2011).
Huebner, Andrew J., *Warrior Image: Soldiers in American Culture from the Second World War to the Vietnam Era* (Chapel Hill: University of North Carolina Press, 2008).
Kieran, David, *Forever Vietnam: How a Divisive War Changed American Public Memory* (Amherst: University of Massachusetts Press, 2014).
Lembcke, Jerry, *The Spitting Image: Myth, Memory, and the Legacy of Vietnam* (New York: New York University Press, 2000).
MacLeish, Kenneth T., *Making War at Fort Hood: Life and Uncertainty in a Military Community* (Princeton: Princeton University Press, 2013).
Mason, Robert, *Chickenhawk*, reissue ed. (New York: Penguin Books, 2005).
O'Brien, Tim, *The Things They Carried*, 2nd ed. (New York: Broadway Books, 1998).
Ryan, David, "Collective Memory and US Identity since Vietnam," in Rüdiger Kunow, Wilfried Raussert, ed. *Cultural Memory and Multiple Identities* (Berlin and London: LIT-Verlag, 2008).
Santino, Jack, "Yellow Ribbons and Seasonal Flags: The Folk Assemblage of War," *Journal of American Folklore* 105, no. 415 (1992).
Silvestri, Lisa, "Surprise Homecomings and Vicarious Sacrifices," *Media, War & Conflict* 6, no. 2 (2013).
Sturken, Marita, *Tangled Memories: The Vietnam War, the AIDS Epidemic, and the Politics of Remembering* (Oakland: University of California Press, 1997).
Swartz, Brian, *An American Homecoming* (Bangor, ME: Bangor, 1996).

Chapter 12

How the United States Ends Wars

Marilyn B. Young

I am tempted to write a very short chapter indeed. How does the United States end wars? It does not.

It continues them, in another form, another place: permanent war; eternal war, as Andrew Bacevich put it. The transition from one war to the next is not always easy. Unconditional surrender was a one-off—or a two-off: Germany and Japan. Thereafter, America's chosen wars ended in stalemate or defeat, unless you count the indubitable victory of Operation Urgent Fury—Reagan's triumph over the massed armies of Grenada. Anything short of victory must be obscured, denied, transformed. You may have thought Korea ended in a draw rather than an American triumph and you would be wrong: the Chinese, it was claimed at the time and thereafter, were forced to accept a ceasefire on US terms in the face of Eisenhower's threat to use nuclear weapons. Or, in Reagan's version of the Vietnam War, who does not admire the country that engages in a noble fight for a just cause even if it loses? Defeat becomes incidental— replaced by the importance of carrying on the struggle elsewhere.

More recently, armed with drones and Special Forces, an American president can fight wars more or less on his own, in countries of his own choosing. American wars do not end but continue—quietly, behind the back of the public that funds them. All it takes is professional soldiers deployed in small numbers as advisers; the exuberant use of air power; the development of weapons that kill without endangering the lives of those who launch them. Reagan's sacralization of the Vietnam War was only the beginning of the transmogrification of defeat, and I'd like to talk a little more about how this was achieved.

If I asked you how the Vietnam War ended, you would probably say, in an American defeat, and in one way you would be right. The most basic US war aim, to sustain a separate anticommunist country in the south of Vietnam, could not be fulfilled despite ten years of war, billions of dollars spent, millions of lives lost, the unsuccessful pursuit of the enemy in Laos and Cambodia as well as Vietnam, and the devastation of all three countries.

Toward the end, the goal—however rationally expressed to the public—sometimes seemed to consist of something much simpler: a desire to punish the Vietnamese for not bending to America's will. For example, choosing from a rich store, there's this exchange between Nixon and Kissinger in November 1971, as reported in Tim Weiner's book on Nixon:

"We will bomb the bejeezus out of them. To hell with history. ... Just knock the shit out of them."

"That's the best—I had not thought of that," Kissinger said.

"Do they realize that they have to deal with, here, a man who if he wins the election will kick the shit out of them, and if he loses the election will do it even more?" Nixon went on, his voice becoming more and more forceful: "Did that ever occur to you?"

"I-I have to say, honestly, it did not," Kissinger replied in a tone more admiring than aghast.

"I'd finish off the goddamn place," Nixon said, "Knock the shit out of them—and then, everybody would say, 'Oh horrible, horrible, horrible.'" And he laughed with pleasure at the thought.[1]

And he did bomb the shit out of them, of course, although it made no difference to the outcome.

Henry Steele Commager, a senior historian of twentieth-century America, could not have known about this conversation but at around the same time, in October of 1972, he wrote a long essay for the *New York Review of Books* titled "The Defeat of America." It was ostensibly a review of Richard Barnet's book *The Roots of War*, but in fact it was an expression of Commager's rather desperate hope for an American defeat in Vietnam. Nixon, he wrote, was determined not to "go down in history as the man who presided over the first American 'defeat.'" But, Commager insisted, it was too late for that, "for nothing can alter the fact that we have already been defeated, not, to be sure, on the field of battle, but in the eyes of history." In a tone that few Americans have had the courage to echo he continued: "This is not only a war we cannot win, it is a war we must lose if we are to survive morally." He went on to ask: "Why do we find it so hard to accept this elementary lesson of history, that some wars are so deeply immoral that they must be lost, that the war in Vietnam is one of these wars, and that those who resist it are its truest patriots."[2] The war *was* lost but its contribution, long term, to the country's moral survival is doubtful.

For a brief period, Congress and the general public acknowledged defeat, if not entirely in Commager's spirit. Congress passed the War Powers Act in an attempt to constrain the war-making propensity and power of the executive, and it began to seem that no administration would or could commit the country to war except for reasons of self-defense, and even then only after a congressional declaration of war. The general repudiation of the use of armed force abroad was so fierce it was given a name: the Vietnam syndrome. It was as if the country had become allergic to war in *all* its forms. In the imagination of many, perhaps most, Americans what mattered about the war was the division and self-doubt it had caused at home.

America, Loren Baritz wrote in his massive account *Backfire*, subtitled *How American Culture Led Us into Vietnam and Made Us Fight the Way We Did*, insisted that America was not itself in Vietnam, although he is silent on what country it might have been.[3] The terrible thing about the war was not its immorality but its divisiveness, the worst since the Civil War. The movie made by one veteran, Oliver Stone, summed it up: "We did not fight the enemy, we fought ourselves, and the enemy was in us."[4] The figure of the veteran became central to all accounts of the war. If we fought ourselves, then the only victims of the war were—and are—American.[5]

I've written in the past about the transformation of the military and military doctrine that took place post-Vietnam as well as about revisionist historians who insist that the United States had won the war in 1968 or 1973 only to be betrayed by cowards in Congress, the liberal media, and a treasonous antiwar movement.[6] But in this chapter I want to focus on how Vietnam was memorialized in public ceremonies such that US defeat was effectively denied. The dedication of the Vietnam Memorial in Washington, DC in November 1982 was the first national event devoted to the public rewriting of the meaning of Vietnam. The night before it was unveiled, President Reagan had stopped by the National Cathedral as the names of the Vietnam War dead were read out loud. "The tragedy was that they were asked to fight and die for a cause that their country was unwilling to win," he said as he left. "We are beginning to appreciate that they were fighting for a just cause."[7] Perhaps because of the intense controversy over Maya Lin's antiheroic design, it took another six months before Reagan visited the Wall itself, stopping by for seven minutes and claiming, through a spokesman, this was his first opportunity, though he "had wanted to go for a long time."[8]

Then, on Memorial Day, 1984, after the addition of an American flag and Frederic Hart's life-size statue of three soldiers, Reagan "formally accepted" the Wall on behalf of the country. His speech that day, spoken in so low a tone that many in the crowd of 150,000 could not hear him, no longer referred to the war as a noble cause but only to the possibility of a healing, however, imperfect, from the domestic division caused by the conflict. He referred to those who opposed the war as people "unable to distinguish between their native dislike for war and the stainless patriotism of those who suffered its scars. But there has been a rethinking there, too. Now we can say to you, and say as a nation, thank you for your courage."[9]

By 1985, on the tenth anniversary of the reunification of Vietnam, the narrative was firmly in place. Those who had fought in Vietnam were courageous patriots unjustly victimized by a divided society. And yet defeat could not be denied entirely. On 25 April 1985, in a *New York Times* preview of a TV show to be aired that evening, John Corry wrote, "Television pronounces a benediction on Vietnam tonight."[10] The show, titled "Honor, Duty and a War Called Vietnam," was narrated by Walter Cronkite, whose voice ("solemn in tone and judicious in purpose," as Corry described it) had led the country through the war, night after night for CBS. Cronkite had traveled to Vietnam for the occasion (years before normalization) "not so much to report as to muse." The show had a tone of "detached mourning," and what Cronkite mused about was defeat—the "nation's only military defeat" and what, if anything, had been learned.

The last time any television network reported from Vietnam was in April 1975; Cronkite's presence in Hanoi meant, according to Corry, that "the war is now officially over." How then, did CBS believe the public should think about the war: "Solemnly, the program suggests, with a vague distrust for policy makers who got us into the war, but without assigning them much blame." The policy makers are only briefly discussed; the focus of the show is on the "live heroes" and the dead ones. Among the living heroes was John McCain, and together Cronkite and McCain visited the prison in Hanoi where McCain had been held. The Vietnamese barely put in an appearance. As in so much of American reporting, films, novels, memoirs, the Vietnamese were bit players. Cronkite concluded the program on a note of cautious optimism. While it was true that a number of conflicts around the world might become another Vietnam, there remained one element of conditional hope: "If, in the future, there is a greater reluctance to send soldiers off to some uncertain war with obscure objectives; if no war can be considered without the consensus of the American people and government."[11]

A few days later, on 30 April 1985, Charles Mohr, who had reported on the war from 1962 to 1970, wrote about the month-long "flood of retrospection and introspection" in which the public had been immersed. "The outpouring," Mohr noted, "indicates that many people are at least as interested in revising history as understanding it."[12] Then, on 7 May 1985 the revised history was embodied in a huge march and rally in New York. "Tens of Thousands of Vietnam War veterans today formed the biggest parade in the city's history," the *Los Angeles Times* reported. General Westmoreland led the parade, alongside Mayor Koch, pushing the wheelchair of John Beehon, who had lost both legs in the war and won a Medal of Honor.[13]

The following day's account carried more detail. The full line of the march had taken some three hours as twenty-five thousand veterans marched before more than a million cheering New Yorkers who lined the sidewalks shouting "USA, USA" and "Welcome home." "It was a lousy war, but a helluva parade," one veteran observed ironically. Another insisted on the justice of the war and the righteousness of his service and said he felt he had finally come home. There was only one discordant note. "I think it was a hateful war," Grace Boyer, a Gold Star mother declared. "We should never have been there."[14]

The *New York Times* reporting of the event had a slower, more dramatic buildup, beginning with a letter written by Sergeant Jack Calamia to his mother in Queens, telling her of the pleasures of swimming and sunning along a river in Vietnam. One knows from the reporter's tone that the story will not end happily, and indeed the young man died eight months later.[15] Having brought readers back to the heart of the Vietnam War—the loss of American lives—the reporter went on to describe the two-day event that had been organized by an agency Mayor Koch had created in 1982, the New York Veterans Memorial Commission. The events were "designed to honor veterans who came home a decade ago with no hero's welcome." It began with the dedication of the New York Vietnam Veterans Memorial and concluded with the massive ticker tape parade that so impressed the *Los Angeles Times*.

Koch, speaking before an invitation-only crowd of two thousand people, announced that New York had "heard the voices of a lost generation. We have opened the eyes of a new generation to the lessons of the past." And that was? One veteran summarized it for the reporter: "We answered the call of our country, and when we came back we were kicked back into society almost like criminals." Another exclaimed as he rose in his wheelchair to embrace Koch, "To see a city take it upon itself to do this!" Asked what he had said to the man, the mayor replied, "Thank you. It's as simple as that."[16] More to the point was the remark of an older veteran, Bill Campbell, then the vice-president of the Chemical Bank of New York. For him the parade symbolized an awareness that these veterans "are no different than any other veterans who ever went to any other war. We just happened to go to an unpopular war at an unpopular time."[17]

Ten years after the war ended, the main lesson learned by the American public was to forget the war and embrace the veteran. The very form of the New York Memorial and the book that accompanied its dedication — a book of letters sent by soldiers from Vietnam — compressed the war into the experience of young men, far from home, writing longingly to loved ones. They had been sent far away; many would never return; all longed for America. In the person of the veteran, America was the victim of the war — collectively and individually — as President Jimmy Carter had made clear two years after the end of the war. The United States owed Vietnam nothing, for the destruction had been mutual. "You know, we went to Vietnam without any desire to capture territory or to impose American will on other people. We went there to defend the freedom of the South Vietnamese. And I don't feel we ought to apologize or to castigate ourselves or to assume the status of culpability."[18] Carter's comfortable conclusion remained the main message offered by Reagan in 1985, by Clinton in 1995, by Bush in 2005, and by Obama in 2015.

The twentieth anniversary of the end of the war was considerably quieter. In the *New York Times*, a single paragraph on page 5 of the B section reported that General William Westmoreland would be the guest of honor at a Nassau County commemorative parade that would start from the parking lot of Nassau Community College. In Washington, it was gray and raining and, James Risen, the *Los Angeles Times* reporter wrote, "The politicians seemed to have no interest in coming out to observe the twentieth anniversary of America's greatest military defeat." "After all," he added, himself forgetting New York's great rally ten years earlier, "nations tend to celebrate victories not defeats." A small group of veterans and tourists gathered at the Wall, "drawn by the need to somehow mark the day that brought the longest war in US history to a bitter end." Many spoke angrily about Robert McNamara's recently published apologia pro vita sua, *In Retrospect*. "Why didn't he stand up and speak at the time if he knew it was a mistake and a waste," one veteran asked.[19] The American veterans were joined by five hundred Vietnamese refugees, for whom the war would not end, they said, until the fall of the communist regime.[20]

Meanwhile, at Kent State, a very different sort of remembering took place, not a twentieth but a twenty-fifth anniversary of the 4 May 1970 death of four students and the wounding of nine others at the hands of the Ohio National Guard during a peaceful protest against the invasion of Cambodia. Yet here too the Vietnam War was fading. The head of the student senate, Zach Brandon, told the reporter that, while the school should not forget 4 May, "I was the first student body president to say it's time to move on." The day was:

> losing its significance to today's students, who are more concerned with tuition increases and financial aid cutbacks and who have little appetite for the protest tactics of their parents' generation. ... We need to get past the hurt and pain. I can't feel it, I don't understand what you're trying to ram down my throat. I don't have a point of reference to even begin to understand what you as a generation went through.[21]

Most of the American action on the twentieth anniversary seems to have been in Vietnam. A small army of American reporters descended on both Hanoi and Saigon, many of whom had reported on the war twenty years earlier. The *New York Times* sent Philip Shenon to Hanoi and Saigon, where he reported at length on how the Vietnamese were marking two decades of peace. Beyond naming the day (the twentieth anniversary of the Complete Victory in the War [of] Resistance against US Aggression [and] for National Salvation), Shenon found Hanoi uncertain about how to observe it, not wishing to offend the United States in the midst of negotiations for normalization.[22]

Indeed, Vo Van Kiet, the prime minister, sent a personal appeal to Washington, saying that he "shared the pain of the families of United States servicemen killed during the Vietnam War" and hoped the United States would understand that Hanoi's celebrations "are not being held to recall hatred, but to urge American and Vietnamese people to look forward."[23] As if in answer to the prime minister's request, Jeffrey Fredrick, who had lost a leg in the war, was in Hanoi as a representative of the Vietnam Veterans of America, who had contributed more than $300,000 to open a clinic to supply prosthetic devices for Vietnamese children. "When the Army sent me to Vietnam," he told Shenon, "They told me I was fighting for the people of Vietnam. Now, at last, it's true."[24] Saigon, Shenon reported, was a boomtown whose residents on the whole deflected his questions about the past: the war, one woman told him, "is over—we do not want to talk about it anymore." A few, who had fought with the Americans, expressed their bitterness at the regime and their hopes of leaving Vietnam for the United States.[25]

From the paucity of events in the United States, one might conclude that with two major victories in succession—America's victory over the Soviet Union in the Cold War (or so the public was encouraged to understand) and the first Gulf War—George H. W. Bush's fervent hope had been fulfilled: the country had finally succeeded in kicking the Vietnam syndrome once and for all. And yet five years later, on the twenty-fifth anniversary of the end of the war, Vietnam swept back into public view. Yen Le Espiritu counted a total of 112 news stories commemorating the anniversary, 30 percent of them featuring veterans but 40 percent devoted to a new take on the war: the flood of Vietnamese refugees to the United States.[26] Espiritu suggested that veterans and refugees together comprised a new Vietnam scenario: the veterans as victims absolved the country of any responsibility for the conduct of the war; the influx of Vietnamese refugees demonstrated that America's commitment to the rescue of the oppressed remained intact. Together they cleansed the war of the discomfort of defeat as well as of responsibility for the way it was fought. To paraphrase the title of Espiritu's essay: "we-win-even-when-we-lose."

Many of the stories the *Times* carried on the twenty-fifth anniversary were filed from Vietnam and dealt with the tremendous changes the country had undergone, including Vietnam's increasingly close relationship with the United States There was a note of discovery in some of the stories. Seth Mydans, for example, spent some time with Vietnamese war photographers: "Twenty-five years after the fighting ended," he wrote, "something surprising is emerging: a new visual record of the war whose images had once seemed so familiar." So firmly was the war fixed by its iconic images from the American side that Mydans was surprised to learn there was another visual record—one made by the Vietnamese themselves. He seemed equally surprised when he asked a Vietnamese photographer how he had responded to the news that the South Vietnamese regime had at last capitulated. "We were so thrilled," the photographer remembered. "It was such a happy day. Everybody was on the streets laughing and singing." Mydans describes the man, a Mr Phong, driving toward Saigon, stopping now and then to photograph the milling troops around him. What most impressed him were the "hundreds of pairs of military boots, discarded by South Vietnamese soldiers who ripped off their uniforms to try to mingle with civilians." Phong said, "that he had also taken pictures of the fleeing soldiers in their underwear but that he had thought it too embarrassing to print." He had driven into Saigon bumping his way over the discarded boots "like a boat going over waves. I was just happy. Happy. It was fun driving over the boots, bumping up and down."[27]

All through the last week in April 2000, the *New York Times* ran stories about Vietnam—as a country, as an old war, as a learning experience for the military, as a tourist destination. But there was a sense that Vietnam was slipping away, that its war dead and living—now all welcomed home and memorialized—might at last rest. Ward Just, who had reported on the war, put it best:

> Twenty-five years after the fall of Saigon, the Vietnam of the war years seems a vanished and discredited civilization animated by obsessions worthy of Melville. The circumstance that begat the struggle—the Cold War—has vanished. The personalities that drove it—Ho, Kennedy, Johnson, Nixon, and their advisers—have vanished, mostly. All the soldiers are middle-aged or older, and many are dead. The memoirs have slowed. Of the Americans, only McNamara and Kissinger continue, self-consciously, to brood out loud.

"Yet," he warned, "the ghosts remain at the table, rising whenever Washington contemplates a military adventure. Nicaragua, Grenada, Panama, Somalia, Haiti, Bosnia, Serbia, and Kosovo were all seen through the shadow of Vietnam. For American statecraft, the legacy is as profound as that of World War Two."[28] Had he written three years later he could have added Iraq and Afghanistan to the list.

At the Wall on the twenty-fifth anniversary, a quieter ritual took place. Beginning in 1997, the Silver Springs, Maryland chapter of Vietnam Veterans of America gathered on the first Saturday of every month to wash the Wall. When it rained, one veteran said, "You see the water streaming down like tears, and you're looking at the names when you realize you're seeing yourself reflected on the wet wall. It's like the wall is crying for you. It's crying for me." Few paid much attention to the anniversary of the end of the war. "It's just another date in a lot of dates," another veteran told the reporter. "The war didn't end 25 years ago for people who were there."[29]

The *New York Times* celebrated the thirtieth anniversary in Da Nang, the *Los Angeles Times* in Hanoi. Meanwhile, the anniversary of the Vietnam Wall had begun to be marked by regular ceremonies. On the twentieth anniversary in 2002, several hundred people gathered as volunteers read the names of the dead, as they had also been read out loud in 1992 on the tenth anniversary. On the twenty-fifth anniversary in 2007 the gathering was even larger and the Wall's connection to current wars inevitable.[30] "At a time when the nation is divided over the war in Iraq," the reporter observed, "the gathering was, to many in attendance here, a momentary break from the politics of war." Colin Powell, who, the reporter reminded his readers, as secretary of state had urged the UN to threaten Iraq with war if it failed to allow weapons inspections, called for an abstention from politics or policy disagreements.

Through the early years and wars of this twenty-first century, Vietnam remained a ghost at the table, its vocabulary of quagmire, collateral damage, hearts and minds available for instant newspaper copy. Some lessons *had* been learned: a volunteer army was well tolerated by the public. Appropriately, in the year that marks the fortieth anniversary of the end of the war, there was a new, much praised documentary that I think summarizes the current state of Vietnam memorialization and perhaps its final transformation—from the immoral war Commager described to what comes close to looking like a humanitarian intervention.

Last Days in Vietnam opens with an ordinary Saigon street scene—bicycles, pedicabs, pedestrians, men, women, kids—ordinary except for the ominous music in the background, the sort of music horror movies use to let the audience know that beneath this everyday surface something dreadful is on the move. The words "Saigon, April 1975" appear on the screen and as the music, ever more ominous, continues, the credits roll. An unidentified male voice, somber, heavy with memory, intones: "As we began to contemplate evacuation, the question, the burning question was, who goes, who stays."

For the next hour and a half we follow the efforts of a small group of heroic Americans—embassy personnel, army, marine, and naval officers—to do the right thing in the face of a formidable range of difficulties among which perhaps the most difficult was the reluctance of Ambassador Graham Martin to admit the war was over. Instead of an orderly and timely evacuation of Vietnamese most endangered by their association with the American war effort there was mass panic, chaos, the storming of the embassy gates, and mobs of Vietnamese desperate to leave the country any way they could. In defiance of Martin's orders, more sensible Americans began secretly to get the Vietnamese with whom they'd worked to safety. In the end, even the most caring of them, the man whose voice opens the movie, Stuart Herrington, sneaked out of the embassy leaving 420 Vietnamese behind, falsely promising them that a helicopter would come for them soon.[31]

Although it is never stated, one has the sense that fighting is about to consume the city itself, that enemy tanks, guns blazing, will sweep all before them. It would have been easy enough to inform the audience that Hanoi had no intention of carrying the fight inside the city; nor was that even remotely necessary given the speed with which Saigon troops were abandoning their posts, their uniforms, even their army boots. But to do so would have changed the story line from a horror movie—the advancing red flood of communism (there's even a map stained with a flowing red tide) to something more complicated: the welcome end of a long civil war, a victory for Hanoi hopefully, if tentatively, embraced by many in Saigon. (That those hopes were later dashed is a separate story.)

There are occasional historical flashbacks, as for example to Nixon announcing that peace with honor had been achieved. Most disturbing is the appearance of Henry Kissinger as the voice of reason, explaining that the United States had hoped Vietnam would evolve into something like North and South Korea, sympathetically recalling President Ford's anger when Congress would not vote for additional funding for South Vietnam to continue the war, and his unhappiness at his inability to salvage the honor of America and not abandon an ally. We have left the world of Henry Steel Commager.

Yet Vietnam remains a reference point, if not for the majority of Americans then for that 1 percent that fights its wars. A 2015 headline in the *New York Times* about the fighting in Kunduz City, Afghanistan read, "US Base Seen as Monument to Futility as Afghans Watch Kunduz Fall." The story, by James Dao, ended with a quotation from a veteran who had written to Dao on Facebook: "It's difficult not to feel a sense of meaninglessness. ... I always hated the GWOT [Global War on Terrorism]/Vietnam comparison in the past. But, now I can't help but draw parallels. I wonder if this is the same feelings Vietnam vets felt watching as the South collapsed."[32] Veterans of the Iraq War felt the same way as city after city they had cleared (though of whom exactly was not always clear) have now fallen to ISIS. Dozens of stories ran with headlines like *USA Today*'s: "Veterans Feel Sting of Ramadi and Fallujah Losses."[33]

There are other parallels to be drawn: On 3 October 2015, the *New York Times* reported that US Special Forces conducting airstrikes in support of an Afghan effort to retake the city of Kunduz had bombed the only hospital in that part of Afghanistan, one run by Doctors without Borders—despite having been given the hospital's coordinates three days earlier. The attack continued for half an hour *after* hospital workers informed American officials in both Kabul and Washington, DC.[34] The laconic response of the military will be familiar to anyone who lived through Vietnam: Colonel Brian Tribus told reporters the strike had been in response to "individuals threating the force." It "may have resulted in collateral damage to a nearby medical facility" and that the "incident" was under investigation.[35]

The veteran who wrote to Dao did not question the mission on which he'd been sent, only that having once cleared Kunduz of Taliban, the

Taliban were back. Afghanistan is still a war zone in which American soldiers die and kill; Iraq has reverted to the sectarian bloodletting the US troops surge was supposed to have resolved years ago; Libya, while free of its longtime single dictator, is now subject to the rule of numerous paramilitaries, some of whom try to steal and sell Libyan oil only to be thwarted by US Navy SEALs (Sea, Air, and Land Teams). According to Patrick Cockburn, "Government authority is disintegrating in all parts of the country, putting in doubt claims by American, British and French politicians that NATO's military action in Libya in 2011 was an outstanding example of a successful foreign military intervention that should be repeated in Syria."[36]

Those doubts, combined with the public's evident war weariness, have thus far prevented just such a repetition. A poll taken by *The Onion* in 2013 surely remains true today: "Majority of Americans Approve of Sending Congress to Syria."[37] However reluctant President Obama was to increase US intervention in Syria, he continued to organize invisible acts of war: an accelerating American use of cyber war, drone attacks in Pakistan, Yemen, and Somalia. His opponents in Congress urged more forceful action. James Madison wrote:

> Of all the enemies to public liberty, war is, perhaps, the most to be dreaded, because it comprises and develops the germ of every other. War is the parent of armies; from these proceed debts and taxes; and armies, and debts, and taxes are the known instruments for bringing the many under the domination of the few. In war, too, the discretionary power of the Executive is extended; its influence in dealing out offices, honors, and emoluments is multiplied: and all the means of seducing the mind, are added to those of subduing the force, of the people. ... No nation could preserve its freedom in the midst of continual warfare.[38]

In 2012 Obama announced the beginning of a thirteen-year project of Vietnam commemoration, leading up to the fiftieth anniversary of the end of South Vietnam. Obama proclaimed:

> From Ia Drang to Khe Sanh, from Hue to Saigon and countless villages in between, they pushed through jungles and rice paddies, heat and monsoon, fighting heroically to protect the ideals we hold dear as Americans. Through more than a decade of combat, over air, land, and sea, these proud Americans upheld the highest traditions of our Armed Forces.[39]

Commemorated, enshrined as a rescue mission, a great—though not the greatest—generation can rest. The task of historic erasure complete, the health of the state guaranteed, the future is safe for eternal war.

Marilyn B. Young taught history at New York University from 1980 to 2016. She received her PhD from Harvard University in US-East Asian Relations, which was also the subject of her first book, *The Rhetoric of Empire: American China Policy, 1985–1901* (Harvard University Press, 1968). The Vietnam War absorbed her energies for all of its ten years, and she wrote about it in *The Vietnam Wars, 1945–1990* (Harper Collins, 1991). She spent much of her career following the course of America's wars and how they are fought, publishing a number of essays on Iraq and Afghanistan and coediting collections of essays on these wars, including *Bombing Civilians: A Twentieth-Century History* (with Y. Tanaka, The New Press, 2009); *Making Sense of the Vietnam War* (with Mark Bradley, Oxford University Press, 2008); *Iraq and the Lessons of Vietnam* (with Lloyd Gardner, The New Press, 2007); *The New American Empire* (with Lloyd Gardner, The New Press, 2005); *The Vietnam War: A History in Documents* (with Tom Grunfeld and John Fitzgerald, Oxford University Press, 2003); and *Companion to the Vietnam War* (with Robert Buzzanco, Blackwell, 2002). She passed away in February 2017.

Notes

1. Tim Weiner, *One Man against the World: The Tragedy of Richard Nixon*, reprint ed. (New York: St. Martin's Griffin, 2016), 141. The "madman theory" may not have been so theoretical after all.
2. Henry Steele Commager, "The Defeat of America," *New York Review of Books*, 5 October 1972, http://www.nybooks.com/articles/1972/10/05/the-defeat-of-america, accessed 16 December 2018.
3. Loren Baritz, *Backfire: A History of How American Culture Led Us into Vietnam and Made Us Fight the Way We Did* (Baltimore: Johns Hopkins University Press, 1998).
4. IMDb, Quotes from "Platoon," accessed 30 October 2017, http://www.imdb.com/title/tt0091763/quotes.
5. Viet Thanh Nguyen has critiqued this tendency at length. See Viet Thanh Nguyen, *Nothing Ever Dies: Vietnam and the Memory of War* (Cambridge, MA: Harvard University Press, 2016), 283.
6. Marilyn B. Young, "Two, Three, Many Vietnams," *Cold War History* 6, no. 4 (2006): 413, https://doi.org/10.1080/14682740600979238; Marilyn B. Young and Lloyd C. Gardner (eds.), *Iraq and the Lessons of Vietnam: Or How Not to Learn from the Past* (New York: New Press, 2007); Marilyn B. Young, "The Vietnam Laugh Track," in *Vietnam in Iraq: Tactics, Lessons, Legacies and Ghosts*, eds. David Ryan and John Dumbrell (London: Routledge, 2006), 31–47, https://nyuscholars.nyu.edu/en/publications/the-vietnam-laugh-track.
7. Francis X. Cline, "Tribute to Vietnam Dead: Words, A Wall," *New York Times*, 11 November 1982.
8. "Reagan Makes His First Visit to Memorial on Mall," *New York Times*, 2 May 1983.
9. Ben A. Franklin, "President Accepts Vietnam Memorial," *New York Times*, 12 November 1984. These days the sentence runs: "Thank you for your service."

10. John Corry, "'Honor, Duty and a War Called Vietnam' on CBS," *New York Times*, 25 April 1985, accessed 24 February 2014, http://www.nytimes.com/1985/04/25/arts/honor-duty-and-a-war-called-vietnam-on-cbs.html?pagewanted=print.
11. Corry parted company with Cronkite here, believing he did not reflect "the center of public opinion. After all, he wrote, all wars are uncertain with objectives that, at the start might seem obscure. But the Constitution delegates the authority to pursue a war, much less consider one, to the commander in chief. Consensus is to be desired, but how could it ever be defined? Even a so-called just war could never be waged." Corry seemed to have altogether forgotten that the Constitution delegated the authority to declare war to Congress, not the executive. NBC also marked the anniversary with Marvin Kalb narrating "Vietnam: Lessons of a Lost War," which, apparently for the first time on national TV, revealed that the events in the Tonkin Gulf that had enabled Johnson to begin his escalation of the war had not really happened.
12. Charles Mohr, "History and Hindsight: Lessons from Vietnam," *New York Times*, 30 April 1985, accessed 24 February 2014, http://www.nytimes.com/1985/04/30/world/history-and-hindsight-lessons-from-vietnam.html. Mohr reported for *Time Magazine* from 1962 to 1963, but when the journal refused to run his pessimistic assessment of the war, he quit. A year later, he joined the staff of *New York Times*.
13. UPI, "New York's Biggest March—10 Years Late: Vietnam Veterans Get Their Parade at Last," *Los Angeles Times*, 7 May 1985, http://articles.latimes.com/1985-05-07/news/mn-11129_1_vietnam-veterans, accessed 16 December 2018 .
14. John J. Goldman and Elizabeth Mehren, "A Homecoming 10 Years Later. Viet Veterans Bask in N.Y. Parade," *Los Angeles Times*, 8 May 1985, http://articles.latimes.com/1985-05-08/news/mn-6364_1_vietnam-veterans, accessed 16 December 2018. Michael Clark analyzed the state of Vietnam remembrance a year later for *Cultural Critique* ("Remembering Vietnam," no. 3, spring, 1986). Of the march, he observed: "The curiously perverse occasion of a decade-old defeat lent the festivities an air of historical surrealism, however, that was compounded by the oblique focus of many events," e.g., Walter Cronkite's trip to Vietnam (47). For Clark, the march was "an ideal of historical continuity that turns Vietnam into just one more chapter in the epic narrative of the American dream" (77).
15. Jane Gross, "New York Pays Homage to Vietnam Veterans," *New York Times*, 7 May 1985, http://www.nytimes.com/1985/05/07/nyregion/new-york-pays-homage-to-vietnam-veterans.html, accessed 16 December 2018.
16. Jane Gross, "New York Pays Homage to Vietnam Veterans," *New York Times*, section N.Y./Region, 7 May 1985, http://www.nytimes.com/1985/05/07/nyregion/new-york-pays-homage-to-vietnam-veterans.html, accessed 16 December 2018.
17. Goldman and Mehren, "A Homecoming." On a contemporary note, Donald Trump funded 50 percent of the memorial. At the ceremony, he said he had opposed the war but recognized that those who went to fight it were "great Americans."
18. Jimmy Carter, "The President's News Conference," 24 March 1977, online by Gerhard Peters and John T. Woolley, The American Presidency Project, https://www.presidency.ucsb.edu/documents/the-presidents-news-conference-116, accessed 16 December 2018.
19. James Risen, "A Day of Reflection for Those Remembering Vietnam: Memorial: No Official Ceremony Marked the 20th Anniversary of the War's End. But Many Veterans, Others Quietly Honor the Dead by Visiting 'the Wall,'" *Los Angeles Times*, 1 May 1995, http://articles.latimes.com/1995-05-01/news/mn-61036_1_vietnam-veterans-memorial, accessed 16 December 2018.
20. Brian Mooar, "Reflections on the War Without End," *Washington Post*, 1 May 1995, B3.
21. Edward Walsh, "At Kent State, Remembering 13 Seconds after 25 Years," *Washington Post*, 5 May 1995, A3.

22. Philip Shenon, "20 Years after Victory, Vietnamese Communists Ponder How to Celebrate," *New York Times*, 23 April 1995. In Westminster, California, former ARVN soldiers gathered to plan a mutual aid fund to help the poorest among them. "I survived the war," one said. "I survived prison. Now I must survive my freedom, and it is very hard." Seth Mydans, "Preparing to Commemorate the Fall of Saigon," *New York Times*, 1 May 1995.
23. "Hanoi Appeals to Washington," Reuters, *New York Times*, 29 April 1995, 14.
24. Philip Shenon, "20 Years after War, 3 in Hanoi on Healing Mission," *New York Times*, 28 April 1995, A3.
25. Philip Shenon, "On Saigon's Day of Defeat, a Glitter of Rebirth," *New York Times*, 30 April 1995, 1. See also his report on 1 May 1995, "Unity is Missing as Vietnam Remembers War's End," A3. David Halberstam wrote a long essay reflecting on the war for the *Washington Post*, which was published on 14 May 1995 but it was a response less to the anniversary than to the publication of McNamara's memoir, *In Retrospect*. Both McNamara and the deputy managing editor of the *Washington Post* had charged Halberstam and his generation of Vietnam journalists with supporting Johnson's escalation of the war.
26. Yen Le Espiritu, "'The We-Win-Even-When-We Lost' Syndrome: US Press Coverage of the Twenty-Fifth Anniversary of the 'Fall of Saigon,'" *American Quarterly* 58, no. 2 (2006), 333. Espiritu does not stress the veteran's victimization so much as his innocence, his loss, and his position as an individual in the "family nation" (335).
27. Seth Mydans, "A Resurrected Picture of the Vietnam War, from the Other Side," *New York Times*, section World, 19 April 2000, https://www.nytimes.com/2000/04/19/world/a-resurrected-picture-of-the-vietnam-war-from-the-other-side.html, accessed 16 December 2018.
28. Ward Just, "Why I Was in Vietnam," *New York Times*, section Magazine, 19 March 2000, https://www.nytimes.com/2000/03/19/magazine/why-i-was-in-vietnam.html, accessed 16 December 2018.
29. Carol Morello, "Clean Memorial Honors Fallen, Comforts Vets; Ritual Awash in Symbolism," *Washington Post*, 20 April 2000.
30. Editorial, "A Memorial's 20th Year" *New York Times*, 8 November 2002; Raymond Hernandez, "A Stark Reminder of War, 25 Years On," *New York Times*, 12 November 2007.
31. Rory Kennedy, *Last Days in Vietnam*, http://www.imdb.com/title/tt3279124.
32. James Dao, "US Base Seen as Monument to Futility as Afghans Watch Kunduz Fall," *New York Times*, section Asia Pacific, 30 September 2015, https://www.nytimes.com/2015/10/01/world/asia/us-base-seen-as-monument-to-futility-as-afghans-watch-kunduz-fall.html, accessed 16 December 2018.
33. Jim Michaels and Zoroya, "Veterans Feel Sting of Ramadi and Fallujah Losses," *USA Today*, 6 January 2014, https://www.usatoday.com/story/news/world/2014/01/06/fallujah-ramadi/4344011, accessed 16 December 2018; Associated Press, "Iraq War Veterans Feel Sting of Reversals in Hard-Won Fallujah," 8 January 2014, http://www.foxnews.com/us/2014/01/08/iraq-war-veterans-feel-sting-reversals-in-hard-won-fallujah.html, accessed 16 December 2018; Jeanette Steele, "Vets Outraged over Loss of Fallujah," *San Diego Union-Tribune*, 6 January 2014, http://www.sandiegouniontribune.com/military/sdut-fallujah-marines-veterans-reaction-2014jan06-story.html , accessed 16 December 2018.
34. Alissa J. Rubin, "Airstrike Hits Doctors without Borders Hospital in Afghanistan," *New York Times*, section Asia Pacific, 3 October 2015, https://www.nytimes.com/2015/10/04/world/asia/afghanistan-bombing-hospital-doctors-without-borders-kunduz.html, accessed 16 December 2018.

35. Thomas Gibbons-Neff, "From 'Collateral Damage' to 'Deeply Regrets': How the Pentagon Has Shifted on the Afghan Hospital Attack," *Washington Post*, section Checkpoint, 6 October 2015, https://www.washingtonpost.com/news/checkpoint/wp/2015/10/06/how-the-pentagon-shifted-from-collateral-damage-to-deepest-regrets-on-afghan-hospital-attack, accessed 16 December 2018.
36. Patrick Cockburn, "Special Report: We All Thought Libya Had Moved On—It Has, but into Lawlessness and Ruin," *The Independent* (London), 3 September 2013, http://www.independent.co.uk/news/world/africa/special-report-we-all-thought-libya-had-moved-on-it-has-but-into-lawlessness-and-ruin-8797041.html, accessed 16 December 2018.
37. *The Onion*, "Poll: Majority of Americans Approve of Sending Congress to Syria," accessed 30 October 2017, https://www.theonion.com/poll-majority-of-americans-approve-of-sending-congress-1819575532, accessed 16 December 2018.
38. Scott Horton, "Madison on the Dangers of War," *The Stream—Harper's Magazine Blog*, 7 July 2007, https://harpers.org/blog/2007/07/madison-on-the-dangers-of-war, accessed 16 December 2018.
39. Barack Obama, "Presidential Proclamation—Commemoration of the 50th Anniversary of the Vietnam War," whitehouse.gov, 25 May 2012, https://obamawhitehouse.archives.gov/the-press-office/2012/05/25/presidential-proclamation-commemoration-50th-anniversary-vietnam-war, accessed 16 December 2018.

Select Bibliography

Baritz, Loren, *Backfire: A History of How American Culture Led Us into Vietnam and Made Us Fight the Way We Did* (Baltimore, MD: Johns Hopkins University Press, 1998).
Clark, Michael, "Remembering Vietnam," *Cultural Critique* no. 3 (spring, 1986).
McNamara, Robert S. with Brian VanDeMark, *In Retrospect: The Tragedy and Lessons of Vietnam* (New York: Crown, 1995).
Nguyen, Viet Thanh, *Nothing Ever Dies: Vietnam and the Memory of War* (Cambridge, MA: Harvard University Press, 2016), 283.
Weiner, Tim, *One Man against the World: The Tragedy of Richard Nixon* (New York: St. Martin's Griffin, 2016).
Yen Le, Espiritu, "'The We-Win-Even-When-We Lost' Syndrome: US Press Coverage of the Twenty-Fifth Anniversary of the 'Fall of Saigon,'" *American Quarterly* 58, no. 2 (2006).
Young, Marilyn B., "The Vietnam Laugh Track," in *Vietnam in Iraq: Tactics, Lessons, Legacies and Ghosts*, ed. David Ryan and John Dumbrell (London: Routledge, 2006).
———, "Two, Three, Many Vietnams," *Cold War History* 6, no. 4 (2006).
Young, Marilyn B. and Lloyd C. Gardner, eds., *Iraq and the Lessons of Vietnam: Or How Not to Learn from the Past* (New York: New Press, 2007).

Index

9/11 terrorist attacks, 6, 101, 163, 199, 201, 204–5

A
Aaron, Grace, 239
Abrams, Creighton, 77, 98
Acheson, Dean, 2
Afghanistan, 2–4, 6–7, 9, 11, 64, 72, 76, 79, 81–83, 91–93, 101, 103, 107, 109, 143, 145, 148, 151, 162–76, 180–91, 195, 201, 205–6, 211, 213, 215–16, 219, 222, 230, 240, 243–46, 260, 262–64
Afghanization, 180–91, 190
Afghan surge, 164
Africa, 71, 90, 94, 109, 217
Agent Orange, 18, 46, 56–63, 232
air power, 100, 206, 252
air strikes, 3, 144, 153,
al-Assad, Bashar, 103, 142, 217–21, 223–26
al-Dayni, Mohamed, 148
Algeria, 216
al-Hakim, Ayatollah Mohammad Baqir, 214
al-Haq, Asaib Ahl, 141–42
al-Jolani, Abu Mohammad, 220
al-Khazali, Qais, 141
Alliance for Progress, 213
All-Volunteer Force, 197, 230–32, 235, 243, 246–47

Al-Maliki, Nouri, 102, 108–9, 146–50, 152–54
Al-Qaeda, 145–46, 152, 162–64, 167, 169–170, 174, 188, 190, 215
Al-Taie, Ahmed, 141–42
A Luoi, 58–59, 61–62
American Legion, 237
Americans for Winning the Peace (AWP), 27–28
Angola, 90, 94
anti-war movement, 22, 24–25, 29, 36, 38, 231, 233, 254
Arab League, 218
Arab Spring, 151, 213, 222
Army of the Republic of Vietnam (ARVN), 58
Asian Development Bank, 51
Astana process, 223
Attlee, Clement, 1
Autry, Gene, 238
Ayres, Drummond, 99
Aziz, Tariq, 120–22, 128

B
Bacevich, Andrew, 5, 145–46, 155, 196, 252
Baghdad, 3, 98–99, 102–3, 113, 116, 118, 122, 124–26, 133–34, 141–42, 144, 146–47, 149–53, 214, 245
Baker, James, 114, 117, 119–21, 126, 132–33
Balkans, 99–100, 217

Baradar, Mullah, 183, 186
Baritz, Loren, 254
Barnet, Richard, 253
Barno, David, 184
Barr, Roseanne, 238
Bay of Pigs, 145
Beehon, John, 256
Ben Ali, Zine El Abidine, 216
Benghazi, 218
Biden, Joe, 147, 149–50
Bien Hoa, 58
Bilmes, Linda, 143
bin Laden, Osama, 166, 169, 215
Bosnia, 99–100, 133, 260
Bouazizi, Mohammad, 216
Boyer, Grace, 256
Bradley, Gene, 27–28
Bradley, Mark, 53
Brady, Christopher, 55
Brandon, Zach, 258
Bretton Woods, 51
Brigham, Robert K., 7, 17, 19, 116, 123, 195
Bryant, Kobe, 222
Brzezinski, Zbigniew, 6, 113, 121–22
Buchwald, Art, 75
Bundy, McGeorge, 90
Burson-Marsteller, 235
Bush, George H. W., 2–3, 5, 7, 53, 56, 60, 98–99, 101, 107–8, 111–18, 122–35, 150, 204, 212, 234–37, 259
Bush, George W., 6, 8, 61, 71–80, 82, 101–3, 108, 116, 143–48, 151, 155, 163, 174, 184, 190, 211–15, 217, 257

C
Calamia, Jack, 256
Cambodia, 22, 27, 47–48, 54–56, 63, 90, 92–93, 253, 258
Campbell, Bill, 257
Carter Doctrine, 91
Carter, Jimmy, 6, 51–53, 55, 70, 91–96, 113, 257
casualties, 8, 120–24, 129, 131, 143, 148, 154, 184, 234
CBS, 255
Cedar Revolution, 217
Central America, 93–94, 96, 145

Central Intelligence Agency (CIA), 9, 90, 95–96, 127, 145, 190, 220
chemical warfare, 47, 220
chemical weapons, 103, 122, 220, 226
Cheney, Richard, 77, 121, 126, 129, 133–34
China, 49, 51, 54–55, 91–93, 181
Chollet, Derek, 142–43, 226
Citizens Committee for Peace with Freedom in Vietnam, 25
civil war, 10, 79, 77, 90, 92–93, 117, 128, 134, 152, 212–13, 215, 224, 230–31, 254, 262
civil–military relationship, 5, 114, 196, 199–201, 207–8
Clancy, Tom, 234
Clausewitz, Carl von, 97, 124
Clinton, Bill, 60, 99–101, 133, 204, 257
Clinton, Hillary, 208, 218, 220
coalition, 55, 72, 102, 107–8, 113–14, 116, 118, 120–21, 124, 126, 129, 132, 149, 154, 206, 212, 214, 237
Cockburn, Patrick, 263
Cohen, Warren, 114
Cold war, 2, 7–9, 54, 56, 69, 74, 89, 91–92, 94, 97, 108, 112, 116, 131, 151, 200, 203, 205, 217, 238, 259–60
Color revolution, 217
Colson, Charles W., 27–28, 30, 35
Commager, Henry Steel, 253–54, 261–62
Congo, 203
Congress, 4–5, 21, 24, 26–27, 29, 31, 35, 37–38, 49, 51–53, 55, 61, 88–93, 95, 97–98, 111, 114, 116, 132, 191, 200, 202, 233–34, 236, 238, 254, 262–63
Connerton, Paul, 7
Constable, John, 59
containment, 2–3, 7, 91–92, 216
Contras, 96, 145
Corry, John, 255
costs of war, 9–11, 144–45, 245
Counterinsurgency (COIN), 72, 77, 102, 152, 155, 168, 184, 206, 213
counterterrorism, 155, 165–67, 170
Crawford, Neta, 143
Credibility, 4, 24, 31–33, 35, 78, 109, 113, 115, 120, 127, 131, 134, 175, 187, 196
Crisp, John M., 80–81, 83

Cronkite, Walter, 255
Cuba, 49, 74, 203
Curtis, Tony, 238

D
Da Nang, 58–59, 61–62, 89, 260
Dallek, Robert, 70
Dao, James, 262
Davis, Nathaniel, 90–91
D-Day, 8
De Niro, Robert, 232
de-baathification, 144
Democratic Republic of Vietnam, 50
Democrats, 28, 32, 94
Dempsey, Martin E., 167
Desert Storm, 114, 120–21, 130, 134, 231, 235, 237
Desert Storm Homecoming Foundation, 237
Diddley, Bo, 237
Diem, Ngo Dinh, 11
Dinkins, David, 236
dioxin contamination, 46, 59, 62
Disabled American Veterans, 237
Divine, Robert, 1, 117–18
Doctors without Borders, 262
Dodge, Toby, 147–8, 150, 152
Doi moi, 56
Dowd, Maureen, 130–31
drone(s), 3, 206, 215, 252, 263
Dudziak, Mary, 10
Dunford Jr., Joseph F., 166

E
Ebert, Roger, 75
Egypt, 91, 132, 207, 216–18
Eisenhower, Dwight, 145, 252
El Salvador, 96
Engel, Jeffrey, 111, 133
Environmental Conference on Cambodia, Laos, and Vietnam, 47
Espiritu, Yen Le, 259
Ethiopia, 94
Europe, 1–2, 8, 11, 89, 91, 97, 102, 205, 213, 218
Exit strategy, 3, 5, 19, 99, 102, 107, 109, 111, 113–14, 116, 123, 126, 153, 164, 173

Evans, Mark, 10–11

F
Fabre, Cécile, 225
Fallujah, 142, 151–52, 222, 262
Final report of the Select Committee on Missing Persons in Southeast Asia, 51
First Blood, 232
Fitzgerald, David, 10, 108, 197
Fitzgerald, F. Scott, 1, 7
Flake, Jeff, 243
Ford, Gerald, 4, 17, 37, 39, 48, 50, 69, 88, 90–91, 94, 151, 173, 262
Fort Hood, 241
Fountain, Ben, 244
France, 53, 127, 207
Franklin, H. Bruce, 71–72
Fredrick, Jeffrey, 258
Free Syrian Army, 219
Freedman, Lawrence, 6
Freeman, Charles, 117
Future of Iraq Project, 215

G
Gaddafi, Muammar, 216, 218–20
Gaddis, John Lewis, 8
Gates, Robert, 79, 118, 122–23, 143, 151, 168
Germany, 2, 46, 49, 127, 131, 213, 241, 252
Gingrich, Newt, 234
Gitlin, Todd, 234
Giustozzi, Antonio, 6, 109
Global War on Terror (GWOT), 54, 145, 199, 201, 204–5, 207, 212, 215, 262
globalization, 100, 214, 216, 225
Golan Heights, 223
Graham, Bradley, 78
Grand Strategy, 145, 211
Grant, Johnny, 239
Green Zone, 141
Grenada, 204, 233–34, 252, 260
Gulf Cooperation Council (GCC), 118
Gulf of Thailand, 54
Gulf States, 223

Gulf War, 2, 5–6, 98, 107, 111, 113–15, 118, 120, 122, 127, 129, 132–33, 144, 150, 197, 205, 212, 214, 230, 233, 235–36, 240, 259

H
Haass, Richard, 122, 125–26, 131, 134
Hahn, Peter, 143
Haiti, 260
Haldeman, H.R. 'Bob', 35–36
Hanoi, 23, 26, 31, 33, 50, 52–54, 58, 60, 88, 93, 255, 258, 260–61
Hart, Fredric, 255
Hartley, Livingston, 1
Hearns, Thomas, 237
Hedges, Chris, 9
Henry, Amanda, 75
Herbicides, 18, 46, 57–59
Heritage Foundation, 124
Herrington, Stuart, 261
Hezbollah, 150, 221
Hien, Phan, 52
Hitler, Adolph, 28, 112, 115, 129, 131
Ho Chi Min, 37, 103
Honduras, 96
Honor, Duty and a War Called Vietnam, 255
Hope, Bob, 238, 240
hostage crisis, 92, 232
How Wars End, 115, 211, 213, 225
human rights, 91, 99–100, 149, 213, 217
humanitarian aid, 46, 48–49, 60
humanitarian crisis, 18, 56
humanitarian intervention, 218, 222, 261
Hussein, Saddam, 3, 5, 11, 72, 77, 98–99, 102, 107–8, 111–34, 145, 149, 205–6, 211–12, 214

I
Ia Drang, 263
Ignizio, Vincent, 245
improvised explosive devices (IEDs), 185
In Retrospect, 257
Indochina, 22, 45, 53–56, 63, 70, 203, 232
International Financial Institutions (IFIs), 51–53

International Monetary Fund, 51
International Security Assistance Force (ISAF), 168, 181, 183
Iran, 3, 81, 92, 112–13, 116–19, 121–22, 125, 127, 141, 148–51, 184, 189, 204, 221, 232–34
Iraq, 3–5, 7, 9, 11, 54, 64, 70–79, 82, 98–99, 101–3, 107–9, 112–34, 141–55, 162–63, 166, 172, 174–75, 182, 195, 201, 204–6, 211–17, 220–23, 225, 230, 233–34, 237–38, 240, 244–46, 260–63
Iraq and Afghanistan Veterans of America (IAVA), 245
Iraq War, 70–72, 75–78, 82, 108, 116, 143, 146, 150, 163, 211, 214, 225, 245, 262
ISIS/ Islamic State of Iraq and the Levant ISIL, 103, 142–43, 146, 151–54, 162, 166, 188, 206–7, 220–23, 226, 262
Islamism, 127, 145
Israel, 124, 126, 223, 225, 237
Israeli Defense Forces, 237

J
Jabhat al-Nusra, 220–21
Jackson, Henry "Scoop", 94
Japan, 1–2, 46, 53, 213, 252
Johnson, Lyndon B., 2, 22–23, 25–26, 28, 30, 38, 70, 73, 90, 97–98, 200, 260
Joint Chiefs of Staff (JCS), 98, 114, 167, 200, 245
Jordan, 134, 216
Jus ad bellum, 10
Jus in bello, 10
Jus post bellum, 10–11, 148, 225
Just, Ward, 260

K
Kaiser, Robert, 73
Kaldor, Mary, 212–14, 216–18, 223–26
Kamholz, Doug, 232
Kaplan, Lawrence, 101, 245–46
Karadžić, Radovan, 99
Karzai, Hamid, 11, 153
Kelly, Tom, 111
Kennan, George F., 92, 103
Kennedy, Edward, 45

Index 273

Kennedy, John F., 23, 70, 80, 90, 260
Kent State University, 258
Kenya, 91
Kerry, John, 220
Khmer People's National Liberation Front (KPNLF), 55
Khmer Rouge, 54–56, 63, 92–93
Kieran, David, 7, 19, 195
Kimmitt, Robert, 132
Kissinger, Henry, 7, 21–24, 26–27, 29–35, 37–38, 51, 70, 83, 88–91, 253, 260, 262
Koch, Ed, 256–57
Korea, 2, 49–50, 114, 230–1, 252, 262
Korean War, 17, 200, 212, 230, 237
Krauthammer, Charles, 212
Kristol, William, 101
Kunduz, 162, 182, 187, 262
Kurds, 11, 108, 113, 119, 122–3, 129, 133, 150, 206, 221
Kuwait, 98–99, 112–13, 115–16, 119–20, 123, 125–27, 129–130, 132–34, 234, 237
Kuwait Task Force/US Army Civil Affairs Reconstruction Group, 134

L
Lamothe, Dan, 243–44
Landis, Joshua, 226
Lebanon, 95, 117, 120, 122, 125, 134, 204, 217
Lee, Ang, 244
Lessons of Munich, 112
Lessons of Vietnam, 3, 19, 103, 195, 202, 232
Libya, 3, 145, 204–5, 207, 211, 213, 216, 218–222, 263
Lieberman, Joe, 77
Lin, Maya, 255
Long, Breckinridge, 1
Long War, 9, 215, 241
Lucas, Scott, 10, 196

M
MacLeish, Kenneth, 241
Madison, James, 263
Mansur, Akhtar, 186–89

Maoists, 92
Marine, Michael, 60
Marshall Plan, 2, 148, 213
Martin, Graham, 261
Martini, Ed, 11, 18
Marxist, 184
Mauldin, Bill, 230
McCain, John, 77, 146, 149, 243, 255
McNamara, Robert, 19, 70–83, 97, 195, 200, 257, 260
Memorial Day, 236, 255
Michaels, Jeffrey H., 7, 109
Michelet, Jules, 245
Middle East, 54, 64, 102, 118, 122, 127, 205, 209, 217
Miller, Robert, 49
Milošević, Slobodan, 133
Mitchell, George J., 128
Mohr, Charles, 256
Morris, Errol, 19, 70, 72, 74, 82
Moynihan, Daniel Patrick, 50
Mozambique, 94
Mubarak, Hosni, 216–17
Mueller, John, 92
Mujahedin, 6, 148
Mullen, Mike, 245
Murphy, Jeremiah, 232
Mydans, Seth, 259

N
Nadd, Chuck, 243–44
Nasr, Vali, 150
Nasser, Gamal, 124
National Academy of Sciences (NAS), 58–59
National Liberation Front (Viet Cong), 57
National security, 2, 6, 8, 21, 23, 49, 79, 90, 93, 95, 99–100, 102, 112, 150–51, 200, 202–3, 207–8, 218
National Security Advisor, 6, 21, 23, 98, 113, 115, 150
National Security Directive (NSD), 112, 118
National Transitional Council (NTC), 218–19
NATO, 103, 183–84, 218–19, 263

NATO Training Mission (NTM), 183
Neoconservative movement, 94
New Deal, 202
New York Memorial, 257
New York Times, 22, 69–70, 72–75, 77, 80, 99, 130, 149, 151, 255–58, 260, 262
New York Veterans Memorial Commission, 256
New York Vietnam Veterans Memorial, 256
Nguyen, Viet Thanh, 19, 64
Nicaragua, 96, 260
Nixon doctrine, 94
Nixon, Richard, 4, 9, 17–18, 21–39, 69, 90, 161, 173, 253, 260, 262
no-fly zones, 220, 223
Nol, Lon, 92
Nongovernmental organizations (NGOs), 217
Noriega, Manuel, 116, 120, 132
North Vietnamese, 17, 22–39, 201
NSC 68, 200
Nye, Joseph, 216

O
O'Brien, Tim, 46
Oddo, James, 245
Odierno, Ray, 153
Oil for Food Program, 144
Oman, 91
Operation Desert Storm, 114, 120–21, 130, 134, 231, 235, 237
Operation Domestic Prosperity, 235
Operation Homecoming, 232
Operation Ranch Hand, 58
Operation Urgent Fury, 252

P
Pakistan, 91–92, 148, 164, 181, 183–89, 215, 263
Panama, 114, 116, 120, 132, 204, 234, 260
Paris Peace Accords, 11, 18, 21, 39
Pentagon, 74, 77, 93, 114, 123, 142, 167, 188, 190, 200–1, 206, 235–38, 240, 242–43, 245
People's Army of Vietnam (PAVN), 88–89, 96

People's Liberation Armed Forces of South Vietnam (PLAF), 88, 96
Persian Gulf, 91, 107–8, 112, 114, 118, 121, 130, 134, 204, 207
Persian Gulf War, 118, 144, 233
Peshawar Shura, 186
Petraeus, David, 78, 145, 153, 220, 225
Phu Cat, 58, 62
Phuoc Long, 89
Popular Movement for the Liberation of Angola (MPLA), 90–91
Portugal, 90
POW/MIA (Prisoners of war/soldiers missing in action), 93
Powell Doctrine, 5, 97, 107, 113–14, 118, 123, 127–28
Powell, Colin, 96–99, 107, 114, 116–17, 121–27, 134, 235, 237, 260
Power, Samantha, 74–75, 99–100, 218
public opinion, 5, 22–24, 26–27, 29–30, 32–33, 35–36, 38, 93, 116, 200
PYD (Partiya Yekîtiya Demokrat, Syria's Democratic Union Party), 221

Q
Qatar, 186, 220
Quadrennial Diplomacy and Development (QDDR), 216
quagmire, 3–4, 6, 71–73, 75–76, 81–82, 93, 99, 115–16, 123, 161, 204, 261
Queen Elizabeth II, 216
Quetta Shura, 186–87

R
Rasool, Mullah, 187
Reagan Doctrine, 55
Reagan, Ronald, 5–7, 55, 69, 94–96, 101, 197, 203–4, 232–33, 252, 254, 257
refugees, 54, 56, 92, 223, 257, 259
Regional Peacekeeping Mission, 95
Remnick, David, 222
Republic of Vietnam (RVN), 50
Republican Guard, 117, 126–27, 132
Republicans, 146, 166
Responsibility to Protect, 217–18, 225
Rhee, Syngman, 11
Rice, Condoleezza, 217

Rice, Susan, 218
Rich, Frank, 73
Rieckhoff, Paul, 245
Riedel, Bruce, 164
Roosevelt, Franklin D., 1, 131, 212
Rose, Gideon, 8, 115, 130, 133–34, 211–14, 219, 221, 225–56
Rosen, Ruth, 74–75
Rumsfeld, Donald, 71–75, 77–78, 81, 122, 129, 195, 201
Russert, Tim, 73
Russia, 103, 220–21, 223–24
Ryan, David, 5, 107–8

S
Safer, Morley, 75
Safire, William, 2, 111
Saigon, 2, 5, 17, 19, 33, 37, 39, 45, 47, 50, 88–90, 92, 94, 103, 204, 258–63
Saleh, Ali Abdallah, 218
sanctions, 3, 5, 48, 60, 63, 108, 113, 131, 144, 215, 223
Sandinistas, 96
Sane/Freeze anti-war group, 239
sarin attack, 223
Saudi Arabia, 117, 119, 184, 217, 220, 233
Schlesinger, James, 90, 98
Shultz, George, 5, 95
Schumer, Charles, 245
Schwarzkopf, H. Norman, 118, 129, 235, 237
Scowcroft, Brent, 98, 114–16, 118, 125–27, 129–32, 134
Serbia, 260
Shenon, Phillip, 258
Shia (Shiites), 11, 54, 108, 113, 119, 122–24, 127, 129, 133–34, 142, 148–50, 153–54, 206
Shinseki, Eric, 201
Sidi Bouzid (town), 216
Silvestri, Laura, 241–42
Sky, Emma, 153
Smith, Julianne, 150
Socialist Republic of Vietnam, 50–51, 56
Somalia, 91, 100, 205, 215, 260, 263
Sons of Iraq, 152

South Vietnam, 9, 22–23, 27, 29, 31, 33–37, 39, 48–51, 56–57, 77, 88–90, 96, 161, 173, 257, 259, 262–63
Southeast Asia, 45, 47, 50, 54–56, 89, 96, 201
Soviet Union, 49, 51, 89, 111–12, 143, 212, 259
Special Inspector General for Afghanistan Reconstruction (SIGAR), 182
Stalin, Joseph, 1
Stallone, Sylvester, 232
Status of Forces Agreement (SoFA), 146, 148–50
Stellman, Jeanne and Steven, 58
Stiglitz, Joseph, 143
Stone, Oliver, 254
Strategic Defense Initiative (SDI), 96
Summers, Harry, 90
Sunni, 54, 102, 134, 148, 150, 152–54, 206, 222
Supreme Council for Islamic Revolution in Iraq, 214
Surge, 72, 77–79, 143, 148–49, 164, 166, 168–69, 174, 180, 183–85, 187–88, 190, 213, 215, 222, 245, 263
Syrian Democratic Forces (SDF), 221

T
Taliban, 4, 6, 103, 109, 148, 163–64, 166–69, 171, 173–75, 181–90, 206, 215, 222, 262
Tanzania, 91
Tell It to Hanoi Committee, 25, 28
Tet Offensive, 90, 232
Thailand, 54–55
The Fog of War: Eleven Lessons from the Life of Robert S. McNamara, 19, 70, 72–73, 82
Thelen, Sarah, 4, 17
Thieu, Nguyen Van, 17, 33–35, 37, 39
Tho, Le Duc, 35
Thompson, Sir Robert, 9
Tillerson, Rex, 155
Tribus, Brian, 262
Triet, Nguyen Minh, 61
Truman, Harry, 1–2, 114, 200

Trump, Donald, 6, 145, 154–55, 175, 182, 190, 208, 223
Truth Commissions, 148
Tunisia, 216
Turkey, 220–21, 224
Turkish Kurdish insurgency (PKK), 221
Tzu, Sun, 97

U
Ukraine, 103
United Kingdom, 216
United Nations, 2, 49–51, 53, 55, 61–62, 93–94, 98–99, 102, 112, 116, 118, 120–21, 218, 260
United Nations General Assembly, 51
United Nations High Commissioner for Refugees (UNCHR), 144
United Nations International Children's Emergency Fund (UNICEF), 144
United Nations Security Council (UNSC), 49–50, 112, 114, 120–21, 125, 128, 130–31, 172, 218
UNSC Resolution 660, 113–15, 123, 125
US Congress, House Foreign Affairs Committee, 117
US Defense Intelligence Agency, 134
US Department of Commerce, 48
US Department of Defense, 141, 235, 243
US Department of State, 1, 48, 90, 132, 142, 155, 188, 190, 215
US Department of Veterans Affairs (VA), 57–58, 239
US Navy SEALS, 263
US Senate Judiciary Committee, 45

V
Van Kiet, Vo, 258
Veterans of Foreign Wars, 237, 243–44
veterans, 25, 30, 46, 57–58, 60, 182, 190, 230–41, 243–46, 256–60, 262
victory parade, 108, 230–31, 234
Vieira de Mello, Sérgio, 214

Vietnam Memorial, 254
Vietnam syndrome, 5, 7, 19, 88–90, 92, 94–95, 98, 100–101, 103, 204, 235, 254, 259
Vietnam Veterans Memorial, 233, 256
Vietnam Wars, 2, 4–5, 11, 17, 19, 21–25, 30–31, 36, 38, 47, 59, 64, 70–73, 76–77, 82–83, 88, 90, 97–98, 100, 102, 107–9, 111–12, 115, 123, 131, 195, 197, 202, 204, 216, 231, 234, 252–54, 256, 258
Vietnamese Association of Victims of Agent Orange/Dioxin (VAVA), 63

W
War Powers Act, 254
Weapons of mass destruction (WMD), 73, 77, 118–19, 126 211, 214
Weinberger, Caspar, 5, 95–97, 202
Weinberger Doctrine/principles, 3, 95, 111, 114, 123–24, 128, 202, 219
Weiner, Tim, 253
Westmoreland, William, 90, 233, 238, 256
Wilson, Woodrow, 1–2, 133, 212
Wolfowitz, Paul, 134, 146
World War One, 1–2, 128, 211–12
World War Two, 1, 8, 10, 46, 53, 74, 107, 112, 121, 126, 127–28, 197, 202, 212–14, 230–31, 260

Y
Yakinthou, Christalla, 224
Yemen, 215–16, 218–19, 222, 263
Young Americans for Freedom, 28
Young, Marilyn, 10, 197
YPG (Yekîneyên Parastina Gel, People's Protection Units), 221

Z
Zinni, Anthony, 73

www.ingramcontent.com/pod-product-compliance
Lightning Source LLC
Chambersburg PA
CBHW072147100526
44589CB00015B/2124